JÖRG BECKER

COMMUNICATION AND CONFLICT

Studies in International Relations

For Ulli and Jones

About the Author

Prof. Dr. Jorg Becker (*b.* 1946) teaches at the Institute for Political Sciences at the Technical University of Darmstadt, Federal Republic of Germany. He is also Chairman and Director of Kom Tech GmbH, Centre for Communication and Technology Research, based in Frankfurt and Solingen. Founded in 1987, Kom Tech research and consultancy activities cover three fields: mass media, technology assessment and international studies. A special field of competence is in the area of paper technology and its relevance to developing countries. Professor Jorg Becker and his colleagues deserve great praise for their work on paper technology and its importance to the Third World. In many ways this work updates and complements the conclusions of the UNESCO Commission on Communication Problems over which presided.

Jörg Becker

COMMUNICATION AND CONFLICT

Studies in International Relations

Foreword by
JOHAN GALTUNG

Published for
KomTech GmbH
Solingen, Germany

by
CONCEPT PUBLISHING COMPANY PVT. LTD.
NEW DELHI-110059

ISBN-13: 978-81-8069-172-0

Edition 2017

Published and Printed by

Concept
Since 1974

Concept Publishing Company Pvt. Ltd.
A/15-16, Commercial Block, Mohan Garden
New Delhi-110059 (India)
T: 25351460, 25351794, *F*: 091-11-25357109
E: publishing@conceptpub.com, W: www.conceptpub.com
Editorial Office: H-13, Bali Nagar, New Delhi-110 015, India.

Cataloging in Publication Data--Courtesy: D.K. Agencies (P) Ltd. <docinfo@dkagencies.com>

Becker, Jörg.
Communication and conflict: studies in international relations / Jörg Becker ; forweword by Johan Galtung
p. cm.
Includes bibliographical references
Includes index.
ISBN 9788180691720

1. Communication. 2. Information technology. 3. Communication in international relations I. Title

DDC 302.2 21

Contents

Johan Galtung

Dr.h.c.mult., Professor of Peace Studies and
Director of Transcend: A Peace and Development Network

Foreword

Jörg Becker has produced one of the most insightful books on the general subject of communication; seen in a context of conflict. What kind of conflict? Basically class (economics), between and within countries, and conflict across the many cultural divides in our world. His basic message: by and large, what passes for "communication" does not solve or even soften these conflicts but aggravates them. Worse still: the very act, and structure, of communication as we know them are themselves parts of the conflicts, replete with direct, verbal violence, extremely hurtful across these in its lack of sensivity (sometimes intended).

Moreover, the structure of communication, the network from production to consumption of messages, are in and by themselves violent. They are top-heavy, based on technologies only the rich can afford, probably to the point that they are even undermining themselves. The reader will find not only hypotheses and theories to this effect but a wealth of data and examples, collected from all corners of the world.

But what perhaps impresses me most is his broad concept of "communication". Of course the media are there. But the essays so nicely stringed together also focus on children's books, information and communication technologies, video cassette recorders, scientific communication, and on receivers/consumers like Third World rural areas, and on all kinds of producers. The reader will be exposed to a very comprehensive bundle of the total communication network in our world. Most, or much, of it is clearly imperialist, as quoted by Jörg Becker from the former French minister of culture, Jack Lang:

> Culture and economics - one and the same fight. I ask myself, why should one accept this homogenization? Is this really mankind's destiny? The same films, the same music, the same clothes? We wish to proclaim a real cultural revolt, and embark on a crusade against - let us call it by its name - this financial and cultural imperialism.

The reader will find many reasons to agree with both Jack Lang and Jörg Becker. But it is also our task to devise new types of communication, more symmetric, more empowering. Jörg Becker opens the door for this giant enterprise. I am sure many of the readers will accept the invitation to add to this excellent exercise in empiricism and criticism a dimension of constructivism.

Jörg Becker

Introduction

The book "Communication and Conflict: Studies in International Relations" is appearing at a time when many theorists and practitioners claim that with the globally networked structure of the Internet the world-wide age of media imperialism, domination and dependencies is over. And since the following 21 essays say as good as nothing about the issue of the Web, I would like to fill the gap preemptively in this introduction.

I. Internet, Democracy and the Development of International Relations

Asked during a panel discussion some time ago who would win with the Internet and who would lose out, a German professor of sociology answered: "Well, you know that is the wrong question in the virtual era. The Internet offers everything. And because that is the case, anyone can use the net to get what he or she needs. And precisely for that reason there can be no winners and no losers any longer."

This nonchalant treatment of the issues surrounding the Internet is symptomatic of the current utter malaise in the social sciences in Germany, specifically in sociology. And in order to understand the context of this assessment somewhat better, it bears stating that during the 1970s the colleague quoted above associated himself with the dogmatic German Communist Party, the DKP. And precisely that party really caught the eye in debates on the relationship between society and technology by putting forward any number of obtuse suggestions, attributable to theoretical errors to be found in the writings of Lenin. There are neither good (East German) nuclear power stations, nor bad ones (West Germany), there is neither an automatically beneficial relationship between technical-industrial advances and social progress (Lenin), nor is technology some neutral range of offerings where you can simply help yourself (without any danger of contamination).

Internet sociology, the Internet and democracy, the Internet and dictatorships, electronic elections, development and the Internet, now these have become such customary topics addressed in many books, countless essays and a constant array of conferences that hardly anyone notices the nonsense innate in these vapid terms. After all, the focus of concern in the social sciences and specifically in sociology should really be an appreciation of social systems, groups, and living people, the simple and/or complex sets of opposing interests shaping them, and the dynamism of such relations. By contrast, the polarized fear-inculcating fascinating debate relating on the Internet is nothing other than pure technological determinism. And precisely that has eaten its way deep into the core of sociology.

Technology has become a fetish, a variable of social change that explains all and actually encourages the repression of sociologists' own specialist knowledge. Sociology has surely given itself up if it allows discussions on virtuality, simulation, simulacra, cybersociety, data super highways and electronic interactivity replace an analysis of labor, dependence, exploitation, alienation, class/stratum/social strata, socialization, social roles, interests, violence, conflict/war, liberty and justice. In such a case, it would be better if it said goodbye to the groves of the academe and renamed itself mechanical engineering or electronics, or at best social technology.

Yet there are plenty of social theories, and critical ones at that, dealing with the relationship between technology and information, on the one hand, and society, on the other. There are keen insights on the fetishizing and alienating character of technology to be found in the writings of Karl Marx (1818-1883). German philosopher Theodor W. Adorno (1903-1969) claimed that within the capitalist logic of surplus value information could not have an enlightening thrust. He simply termed it mass deception. A conservative idealist and one of German social science's leading lights in the 1950s, Arnold Gehlen (1904-1976), maintained that the soul was lost in the technological age.

In 1959, English author Charles Percy Snow (1905-1980) described the opposition between the literary intelligentsia and the natural scientists and tried to build bridges between them. Jürgen Habermas, the most important living German philosopher (born 1929), elaborated in 1962 on the decline of the bourgeois public sphere in which information could no longer function as the basis for a controversial dialogue informed by rational argument. In 1956, Günther Anders (1902-1992), the German philosopher and writer who was co-founder of the international anti-nuclear movement, compared the points of tension in the respective evolutionary dynamics of social and technological change. His friend German philosopher Herbert Marcuse (1898-1979) believed that an element of bureaucratic domination was seared into all forms of technology. Indeed, Otto Ullrich, one of Germany's current sociologists of technology, has written on the reified bloc-structure of industrial production.

It is thus evident that there are sufficient socio-scientific theorems and theories which could be assessed to see whether they can be applied in analyzing current developments in technology. Yet most Internet adepts simply babble on inanely, pragmatically and affirmatively, and even, as at the University of Giessen, accept public advance financing for an institute for the "Internet and Democracy", assuring us that this institute will pay its own way in the future. (One could argue with good grounds that precisely this neo-liberal market focus in the domain of information and communication is damaging to democracy and that for this very reason the institute *cannot* arrive at findings that foster democracy in the first place.) Electronic information and communication networks have nothing to do with democracy for the following reasons.

1. Incompatibility with political dialogue: At present, the Internet runs on narrow-band networks. Very soon this form of network access will probably be replaced by broadband Internet, and this will not be hypertext-based, but image-based, with video, film and multimedia. According to the "law" of increasing expectations, the supply of technically ever more elaborate, i.e., more expensive products will then increase. Even if everyone can then talk in the Web, this by no means implies that everyone will be heard. If the history of the mass media has taught us one thing, then that it is not he who has the best arguments who is listened to, but he who presents them best, with the most elaborate, the greatest PR. In order to generate attention in the flood of competing information, you need entertainment, shows, lotteries, coupons, and games. This will lead to an ever faster electronic race to deploy the most powerful political platitudes.

2. Fragmentation: Democracy rests historically speaking on a community being together and acting together in a shared territory. As a non-geographical medium, the Internet creates new communities, namely virtual communities, while at the same time abolishing the old, geographically specific spaces for acting and talking with each other, or at least relativizes these. Whereas geographically specific communication assumes that all inhabitants are able to engage in political conflict in all domains of politics, virtual communities are one-issue groups. Given their organizational structure and unlike real communities, virtual communities are fragmented and narrow-minded, i.e., they are essentially a-political, quite apart from the fact that such virtual communities in the broadband Web of the future will (have to) belong to "someone".

3. Control: Needless to say, mass e-mail petitions can put governments under pressure, and it is likewise obvious that it is easier for political oppositional groups to gain the limelight world-wide by using the Internet than by direct mailings. However, this does not mean that governments a) are not able to also use the Internet for their own propaganda purposes and b) are not able to control Internet communication. This is precisely the context in which we should see the ECHELON project launched by the US secret services. Since automatic voice recognition has for many decades now been stagnating and no technological breakthrough is to be expected in control of voice telephony in the foreseeable future, Internet offers an elegant way out of the problem: Nothing is technologically simpler than controlling text messages. While the virtual balance between the state and the opposition initially shifted in favor of the flexible early adaptors (the underground, the rebellious, the political opposition etc.), the state's resources are so great that after only a short time it will have moved the imbalance back in its favor.

4. Press-button democracy: Electronic voting means more than simply no longer having to wait for a polling booth to be free. In a democracy, the act of casting a vote is linked to prior political commitment. If voting is merely a matter of a mouse click, then elections will be degraded to the status of opinion polls – there then being no difference between the two. And where polls are identical to elections, a) of necessity an "election" market will arise and b) participation by the electorate will dwindle because election results will become known more swiftly than with traditional election methods. And all these arguments should likewise be seen in the context of the fact that in the Western industrialized countries there is already a great deal of ennui with elections, political parties and politics per se.

5. *Strengthening:* All demographic Internet user studies to date show uniformly that this medium by no means politicizes new social groups and instead reinforces the existing politicized groups in their behavior as regards political information. To put it in a nutshell: information rich becomes richer, and information poor becomes even poorer. And only non-social scientists will be surprised by this.

Given that, as indicated above, the sociological basics of a debate on the Internet are quite awry, and in the national context of a German discussion there is much post-modern and constructivist enthusiasm but little serious analysis, it is hardly surprising that the international perspective on the Web is even more awry. An exemplary instance: the manifesto on the opportunities and risks of the Internet for the South published in the *Frankfurter Rundschau* daily in January 1999 and compiled by Holger Baum, Klaus Boldt and Kambiz Ghawami. By way of example, we read there:

> With about 50 million Internet users at present, targeted investment in education and access to the new media is of overriding importance. This access will decide who in future is a member of the knowledge society and who is not.[1]

What is bad about such texts, and you can come across them everywhere, is that they do not contain a perception of what is really bad. For this reason, let us ask some paradigmatic questions of the above excerpt: Is it possible to "invest" in education or does not the very fact that we are borrowing vocabulary from the economic domain already point to a purely instrumental understanding of education? What are the reasons for the "targeted" didactic efforts beyond the quantitative indication that 50 million people already pursue a specific activity?

Must one affirmatively copy what most people are already doing? What is the logic of this permanent parallelism and intertwining of the concepts of Internet/education/new media/knowledge? Why is access to the Internet more important (and important for what?) than political awareness, musical abilities, mathematic abstraction capacity, social and intercultural competence or loving your neighbors or your enemies? Could it be that there are people who actually voluntarily eschew the "knowledge society" on offer here because they have a quite different vision of the future? And what about the role and function of the Internet in the international context and specifically for the developing countries?

I wish to shed some light on this initially with some thoughts and remarks on Africa and the Internet. Of the total of 800 million inhabitants of Africa, only about 4 million have access to the Internet, or about 0.54 percent of the population. Put differently: Tokyo notoriously has more phone lines than all of Africa. (Incidentally, this oft-cited figure stems from the 1984 Maitland Report to the ITU.) And in terms of the content transmitted by Internet Africa is again an essentially passive recipient of modern technology rather than an active player. Even before the Internet era, outside Africa there was often more known about Africa than in Africa itself, for example in the shape of the specialist Africa library at the University of Evanston in Illinois in the United States. And nothing has changed in this regard since the introduction of the Internet.

Anyone seeking information on Africa today will tend to land in Illinois far more frequently than in Africa. And: Africa's Web site with the most hits is a portal taking visitors straight to South Africa's national parks and game reserves (www.africam.co.za). In March 2000, it recorded some 38 million hits from all corners of the globe. To put it over-succinctly: If you wish to communicate with Africa, but land in Illinois, and if Africa continues to primarily be seen in terms of exoticism, elephants and giraffes, then such features are part of what we must still term information and media imperialism. In this context, Wolfgang Fischer and Niels Lepperhoff from the Jülich Research Institute in Germany recently published a very exciting study.[2] They systematically investigated the location of the WWW-servers of all the African government homepages. They took as their starting point the fact that in November 2001 the USA successfully pressurized the United Arab Emirates to simply turn off and discontinue Somalia's only access provider.

Now, almost 50 percent of the African government homepages are located on servers in the countries in question, but the telecoms infrastructures continue to be neo-colonial in organization. The routes for the international backbones that they pinpoint demonstrate that Africa is connected vertically and radially to a few hub cities in the North, and that there are hardly any horizontal, i.e. inner-African cable connections, in other words Africa has a very poorly developed network. It was precisely these distorted information and communication structures that prompted the call a good three decades ago for an New International Information Order (NIIO).

Additional empirical studies on the impact of the Internet or ICTs in general on other developing countries create a skeptical note. Such investigations have been compiled, among others, by Francisco Rodriguez and Ernest J. Wilson III (2000), David Canning (1999) in Belfast and Richard Heeks (1999) in Manchester, not to mention the European Commission's General Directorate for External Relations (2001)[3]. To summarize, they all state:

- The influence of ICTs is to be discerned more at the micro- rather than the macro-level.
- In the short term, the introduction of ICTs leads to a greater imbalance between countries and within countries. This also applies, for example, to India.
- The key conditions for a favorable assessment of Internet usage are: improvement in networks, an increase in literacy, the spread of computer literacy, the provision of meaningful content in the respective mother tongue or national language.
- The introduction of ICTs tends primarily to strengthen urban regions in the developing countries and has little impact on rural areas. To date, investments in ICT have only led in the OECD countries to economic growth and a simultaneous increase in internal imbalances. In developing countries, thus far investments in ICTs have not been shown to prime economic growth. This could, among other things, be related to the fact that investments in this area can flow northwards as profits, as soft- and hardware are supplied from the North.

In 2000, Richard Heeks studied the success rate of ICT initiatives in developing countries[4]. He found that at least 80 percent of the projects had in some way failed and thus led to a massive waste of invested resources. Incidentally, such initiatives have also not been overly successful in the industrialized nations, as can be seen from the following table.

Success/Failure of ICT Initiatives in Industrialized Nations

Total failure	20 - 25 %
Partial failure	33 - 60 %
Successful initiatives	15 - 47 %

Heeks sees no reason why such failure rates should be lower in developing countries. On the contrary: given the lack of technological infrastructure and human resources, the failure rate can be assumed to be even higher. Heeks suggests there are no figures on ICT project failures in developing countries because the financial backers have an interest in justifying their outlays and for them "good news" can be better promoted than "bad news". Frequently, the projects failed owing to their "ambitious and complex" objectives. "More modest" projects involving less change would have greater prospects of success.

Another reason for the failure of ICT in developing countries is, he proposes, the fact that many projects are defined by the "North" and do not sufficiently consider the needs of those "gifted". Then there is the widespread belief in the South that solutions imported from the North are better. Moreover, one must not forget that ICT costs in the developing countries are usually higher than in the industrialized nations - despite the lower cost of wages. Should a solution be transposed from the North to the South, then not only machines and knowledge get transferred, but entire collections of attitudes, values, social, political and cultural structures.

Given the European crimes in Africa, back in 1961 in his revolutionary book "Wretched of the Earth" Frantz Fanon (1925-1961) called on his fellow Africans to make a radical break with Europe. Could it be that seen against this colonial background ICTs and in particular the Internet could entail a kind of anti-colonial revenge by the Third World against the industrialized nations, with a time lag of some 40 years? The Spanish conquistadors exterminated the Indios in Latin America with cold *viruses* - today the "Loveletter"-*virus* came from the Philippines and exclusively targeted Microsoft products marketed by Bill Gates, an US-American. The German press (unintentionally) accurately spoke of a *virus* attack in this context. Now an attack is a military concept, and software can be made by anyone. Could Internet software become a kind of atom bomb for the "wretched of the earth", cheap, manufactured anywhere, and not stopped by any non-proliferation treaty?

The opportunities and risks of media, telecommunication and information technologies were discussed at the end of the 1970s and in the early 1980s at UNESCO - in terms of the political notion of a New International Information Order. At that time there was agreement that North-South communication was undermined by the following structures:

1. Information runs unilaterally and hierarchically/vertically from North to South.
2. Each center in the North communicates horizontally and direct with each other center in the North.

3. Information exchange between related peripheries only functions indirectly, and has to detour via the respective center. This principle certainly applies if the peripheries of different subsystems wish to communicate with each other.
4. There is no horizontal communication between the peripheries. For all the talk of new freedoms among meanwhile apolitical Internet apologists, these structural characteristics of globally distorted North-South communication definitely apply to the Internet, too. And precisely for this reason it is meaningful in the present book 20 years on to reprint essays on different mass media and ICTs that were first written in the 1980s.

II. The New International Information Order: Dignity and Respect

During the debates on a New International Information Order (NIIO) - i.e., between the 4th Conference of the Heads of Government of the Non-Aligned Nations in Algiers in 1973 and the United States quitting UNESCO in 1985 - the most powerful voices were raised in the Third World, putting the case for a de-colonialization of the mass media, in Latin America (one needs think here only of Columbian writer Gabriel Garcia Marquez and his fierce criticism of the MacBride Report)[5].

At that time, the Asian voices of the day tended to be boring, conformist and moderate. Today, the tables have turned completely. While Latin America has largely become a boring neo-liberal antechamber for the United States, the "Asian Age" has spawned a new cultural outlook. While in the 1970s Asian media scientist were still busy defending the "free flow of information", today Thailand feels that the US Radio Free Asia station is interfering in its internal affairs, Philippine colleagues are penning essays on TV as a "culture of idiots", and in Indonesia radical and independent journalist associations are springing up.

As can be read at the end of my book, the articles presented here were mainly written in the 1980s, in other words at the same time as the debates on a NIIO, and many of the essays were first presented in the framework of the biannual conferences of the International Association for Mass Communication Research (IAMCR). From the scholarly viewpoint, it was after all mainly the IAMCR which for years provided beneficial support for the de-colonialization process in the mass media in the interest of developing countries, before this association itself slipped into the scientific mainstream in the 1990s and thus become politically insignificant.

The 21 essays collected here were first presented or published in the following venues: Leicester, Nairobi, New Delhi, Prague, Berlin, Seoul, London, Stuttgart, Beirut, Oslo, Frankfurt, San Gimignano, Brussels, Dresden, Barcelona, Stockholm, Helsinki, Columbus/Ohio, Madrid and Corvallis/Oregon. In other words, back then I was not only interested in scholarly consideration of the role of the mass media and the ICTs in international relations, but primarily sought a direct and personal exchange of opinions with people from foreign cultures and countries.

In retrospect, I can only state with true gratitude that my key learning process stems not only from reading books by Western philosophers and scholars, but from a lively dialogue with many people, in particular from developing countries. I have them to thank for vastly enriching my angle and perspective, for kindling my curiosity and awakening new interests in me, for my positive re-discovery of poetry, spirituality, music, literature, art and culture. Without this active dialogue with people outside the European domain, and it remains so important to me to this very day, my academic career in Germany would have been impoverished, and I would have landed in the mainstream mindset of so many German professors, who only work *on* the Third World, but hardly ever work *with* people in the developing countries in a spirit of cooperation among equals.

When, at the IAMCR Conference in 1984 I ardently championed holding the next IAMCR Conference in New Delhi and not in Latin America, and when I was then voted by a great majority in Prague to be the German representative on the IAMCR's International Council and by this vote replaced the previous German representative, namely conservative communications scientist Professor Elisabeth Noelle-Neumann, it was to have severe consequences for my career. By virtue of the vote I became a "borderline scholar" in Germany, and I was often greeted with skepticism.

My campaigning for the "wretched of the earth", for the weak and poor, for developing countries and migrants and for all those rendered voiceless, my theoretical roots in the writings of Karl Marx, the Frankfurt School and Sigmund Freud, my references to liberation theology in Latin America, to Paulo Freire, Mahatma Gandhi, Julius Nyerere, Frantz Fanon, Léopold Sédar Senghor, Angela Davis, Eldridge Cleaver, James Baldwin, Amilcar Cabral, Ho Chi Minh, José Carlos Mariátegui or Edward Said and my (ongoing) insistence advocacy of the humanitarian potentiai of Islam led in Germany to my research work being regarded dubiously and caused various obstacles to be placed in my professional path by the establishment.

The following quotes from various German experts are paradigmatic for the way my work was rejected. Prof. Siegfried Magiera claimed that Becker's arguments "contradict the German Constitution"; Barthold C. Witte was of the opinion that I "denounced the Western industrialized nations"; while Dieter Weirich suggested that my report on TV broadcasts by Deutsche Welle in Asia "is a concoction of dubious and in part erroneous statements on international media politics". Professor Jürgen Wilke suggested that in the 1980s Becker "fought against recognition of the principle of free information flow and thus indirectly supported the aspirations of the Soviet Union", while Professor Michael Kunczik stated I conducted "slapstick research". Professor Hans-Dieter Kübler, for his part, wrote that "one would have expected something with more empirical substance, something more up-to-date from Jörg Becker". I gladly cite the most famous philosopher of Medieval Europe in my cause here, namely Thomas Aquinas (1225-1274), who wrote: "Should someone wish to write against me. Pray do so! Iron is sharpened by iron."

For the criticism I have quoted above was not intended to communicate anything, it was meant to stigmatize, and was and is purely polemical, not argumentative and instead condescending and conceited. Enough of this nasty and petty-minded game.

By contrast, my research work met with approval when I talked with Melina Mercouri, Greek Minster of Culture, with Ernesto Cardenal, the Nicaraguan Cultural Minister, with Valentin Falin, former Soviet Ambassador to Germany, or Vietnamese Revolutionary General Vo Nguyen Giap. I am happy to say that four important African intellectuals are represented in essay collections I have published or I have contributed to collections they have brought out, namely Léopold Sédar Senghor from Senegal, Ngugi wa Thiong'o from Kenya, Amadou Hampâté Bâ from Mali and Joseph Ki-Zerbo from Burkina Faso. And I am incredibly proud that two Nobel Peace Prize winners have provided prefaces for various of my books, namely Willy Brandt, Nobel Peace Prize winner in 1971, and Seán MacBride, who won the same in 1974. I have so much to thank for their recognition of my work! And with this book I would again like to thank them for their support and solidarity.

After recently reading two seminal works, namely "The Decent Society" by Avishai Margalit[6] and "Respect in a World of Inequality" by

Richard Sennett[7] it became clear to me what the central concept was that brackets all the 21 essays collected here. The concept is dignity, even if the concept is not reflected on in any of the articles reprinted here.

What Karl Marx called "walking upright" and Sigmund Freud (1856-1939) considered a "mature personality", is to be found in the German Constitution (1949) as the concept of the "dignity of man" in the very first sentence of Art. 1. And with this clear emphasis, political philosophy in Germany is substantively different from that in the United States: The key defining political concept in the US "Declaration of Independence" (1776) is "liberty" and not "dignity" as it is in Continental Europe. The dignity of man signifies personal autonomy and integrity, is inviolable, and guarantees free self-expression. Obstacles to free self-expression, the denial of recognition, respect, approval and support by others lead to a person admittedly existing in his dignity, but only in an alienated, depraved form.

Human dignity cannot unfold under conditions of poverty, and poverty certainly means more than the absence of material misery. Algerian doctor and revolutionary theorist Frantz Fanon even went so far as to say that hunger under conditions of human dignity was to be preferred to bread in bondage. "Conditions of human dignity" means two things. First, it signifies not only the material but also the spiritual dimension to human existence; second, it hinges on the individual's social relations to other people. Human dignity requires affirmation by others; and this also applies to the domain of human rights. A right to your mother tongue cannot be asserted by one person along, but only within a linguistic collective. This collective who speaks the mother tongue, be it a family, a village or a primary school can also be termed a culture. To put it differently: there is no distinguishing between the positive experience of human dignity and the positive experience of your own culture.

From 1930 to 1960, many different theories focused on this interaction between dignity, personal development, autonomy, liberation and culture. As a psychology of the individual and as social psychology such theories formed a necessary complement to an economically ossified Marxism that concentrated more on overcoming economic rather than psychological alienation. For Existentialists like Albert Camus (1913-1960), Jean Paul Sartre (1905-1980) or Pierre Teilhard de Chardin (1881-1955) the focus was on a life in good faith - beyond all psychological exploitation, crises, despair, death, nausea, fragility and failure.

Debates on the interaction between dignity and culture culminated in a sense in the anti-colonial manifestations of self-expression and liberation, be it in the United States in the poetry of the Harlem Renaissance, in Peru with José Carlos Mariátegui (1895-1930), in Italy with Antonio Gramsci (1891-1937), in Senegal with Léopold Sédar Senghor (1906-2001), in the Caribbean with Aimé Césaire (born 1913), in Vietnam with Ho Chi Minh (1890-1969), in Algeria with Frantz Fanon (1925-1961) or in Iran with Ali Shariati (1933-1977). At present, the concept of dignity forms the core of the theoretical writings of Subcommandante Marcos in Chiapas/Mexico.

While the political Left defined its concept of dignity using the Marxist concept of alienation, the term actually was a fighting slogan of the labor movement in the 19th century and mutated from there to become a central concept in the anti-colonial struggle for liberation. The political Right anchored its concept of dignity not only in natural law, but linked it to international law with the right to self-expression and to a home - in post-War Germany this was particularly true of the associations of displaced persons expelled from formerly German territories in East Europe.

In other words, it is very interesting to see that there is no noteworthy disagreement between Left and Right on this central concept in the German Constitution, and when the latter was being compiled, there was no controversy on the term in the Parliamentary Council which authored it.

"The dignity of man is inviolable". So the statement is not "the dignity of German people" or the "dignity of adults" or the "dignity of men". The concept of dignity in the German Constitution is universalistic, it covers the dignity of all people equally, and that includes children, women, the physically or mentally challenged, gay/lesbians, Christians or Muslims. It bears stating precisely as regards interaction with the Turks who live in Germany that the originally feudal term dignity cannot simply be rejected as out of date and surpassed, just as the two Turkish concepts of "çeref" and "namus" are not simply a matter of the past. And just as the semantics of the German concept of dignity are difficult, so too are that of the two Turkish concepts. The latter designate honor, a feeling of honor, sincerity, blamelessness, a good reputation, a good name, and thus also respect, dignity, credit, fame and pride, çeref and namus: are they perhaps one of many bridges between Turks and Germans?

Just how important a political theory of dignity is specifically for migrants and neo-colonialized developing countries can be illustrated by one example among many, namely the oeuvre of Iranian literary scholar Ali Shariati. In particular in his lecture given in the 1960s and entitled "Exploitation and Refinement of Cultural Sources", Shariati reflects on dignity and identity, alienation and a substitute culture. Colonialism, he suggests, has stripped people in non-European cultures of their dignity. Only someone who has been robbed of his personality can be enslaved, as he has been made a non-person in his own eyes. For Shariati, the immense destruction and distortion of all things non-European, this cultural elimination has a clear economic function for the Western industrialized nations. The machine-based nature of the West compels it to engage in excess production, saturating markets, and to exports worldwide.

Since there is often no use for Western goods in other cultures, local customs, tastes and habits have to be broken and replaced by the European versions. In this way, so Shariati, the locals are transformed into second class and second-hand Europeans. The colonized person becomes a doll, bereft of any personal dignity, alienated from himself, on whom anything can be imposed from without, who has lost the ability to make a choice in keeping with his own culture and tradition. Shariati concludes that only if the colonized person returns to himself, only if he knows his own history and culture does he have dignity; and only then does he have the power to choose, only then can he interact with the Other, the foreign, as an equal.

Dignity can thus be experienced quite substantially and in particular (not only) in one's own culture, in the symbolic world of one's own peer group. And such a form of dignity must also be able to develop freely in polyethnic societies. If dignity cannot develop there, because one's own language, mass media, political symbols, religion and traditions (clothing, food, gender roles, notions of upbringing) are not accepted by the dominant society, or are actually discriminated against or even in part despised by members of one's own group, then the consequence are aggressions (toward the Others) and auto-aggression (toward oneself). Against the backdrop of a mixture of despising-oneself and encountering contempt and rejection by the Other, the migrant in Germany is rendered unwilling to integrate and indeed incapable of integration.

Back in 1961 Frantz Fanon wrote of the "Wretched of the Earth" that colonialization psychologically cripples its victims, that colonial cultural conflicts drive their de-humanized objects into schizoid neuroses and those objects can then no longer say what their identity is. Today, the above-average incidence of psychosomatic illnesses among migrants in Germany is well proven by medical statistics.

In particular, the skin complaints encountered to an above-average extent among migrants can be seen as a quite literal expression of their cultural conflicts: "Frightened out of your skin" means losing yourself; "mit Haut und Haaren" or "down to the roots of your hair" indicates that the link between migrant and dominant society is too close; if something gets "under your skin" then the process is again too intense and close so that identities may be destroyed. If you "deine Haut zu Markte trägst" (bear your skin to market) the skin expresses when things get too much, when you are being suffocated and squeezed, crushed, robbed of your self-determination and liberty.

Many third-generation Turkish migrants have learned from the conflicts described here to the extent that they are dynamically and independently going their own way. And this way is not that of the Turkish father and also does not entail conformity with the dominant German society. Instead, they follow the insight described above that you can only communicate with the Other if you are clear about your own status. Being able to let go is therefore simply lived as the precondition for holding on. Well-meaning social workers and harmonistic-integrationist intellectuals, universalist socialists and German extreme right-wingers nurturing a projective xenophobia are having ever greater problems with the reality of the migrants in Germany who are taking their fate into their own hands. The former Minervas call such trends "ghettoization" and a "parallel society". They are more or less unable to realize that a form of integration that is socially and culturally compatible for all sides is not to be had without the self-determined possibility of cultural self-definition by the migrant groups.

If all this cognitive processes are grasped and are possibly also actively translated into political action, then, and only then, can and must we relativize them somewhat. However, this qualification can only come at the end of the deliberative process, it cannot constrain the latter at the outset. In polyethnic societies the path of dynamic, active and intensive cultural self-definition must submit to the following four conditions: *peaceful*, *voluntary*, *flexible* and *selective*.

Perhaps a loving form of com-munication is then possible between "letting go" and "holding on", as in the Qur'an in sura 49, verse 13:

> O mankind! We have created you from a male and a female, and made you into nations and tribes, that you may know one another.

III. My Thanks to India and Friends from Other Countries

In that last 30 years I visited India about 15 times - as a scientist, a researcher, a journalist and a tourist. I have a very great deal to thank this country, its people, its researchers and its philosophers for! And since two of the articles reprinted here were originally presented for the first time as lectures in India, I would like to give back to India something of what I have received and learned from it, namely many a new idea and inspiration. And recently I have found great and exciting intellectuai stimulation when reading the works of Indian thinkers as different as political activist Arundhati Roy or Amartya Sen, the Indian who won the Nobel Prize for Economics in 1998.

When compiling this book I have often had in mind my countless Indian friends, colleagues and partners as well as all those with whom I have debated in India, and all of them have contributed in the one or other way to the success of this book. In particular, I would like to mention Gita Bhalla, Subhash Chandra, Eapen K. Eapen, Dipak Guha, Tirath Gupta, Sudhir Kakar, A. K. Jallaluddin, Meheero Jussawalla, Rajan Malaviya, Ashok Kumar Mittal, Jyoti Motihar, Nandkumar K. Naik, Shashikala Paranjpe, Rohit J. Patel, Manjunath Pendakur, Sam Pitroda, Usha V. Reddi, Arbind K. Sinha, Navina Sundaram, Pradip Thomas and Stephen Thottathil.

And above all I would like to thank my friend Binod C. Agrawal, with whom I have enjoyed such a long and cordial friendship, with whom I have together pursued this or that joint project, and with whom I hope to continue collaborating in the future, too. Moreover, I would like to thank my colleague, friend and peace researcher Johan Galtung for his kind and warm preface, Jeremy Gaines from Frankfurt for the arduous task of preparing the translations, and not least one of my first students and now my friend Eckhard Schmidt from the village of Wetter-Amönau in Hessen and not far from my university town of Marburg, who undertook the difficult task of compiling the texts and handling the layout for the book.

Precisely because at present I observe with great concern how the three pillars of the Indian nation, namely its socialist, secular und democratic nature, are wobbling dangerously and because I have often been inspired by Mahatma Gandhi, the father of that selfsame Indian nation, I would like to close this introduction with a quote from Gandhi. And as a communications scientist I cite him with great pleasure for hardly any other philosopher so admirably captured that communications dialectic between inside and outside, between prison and freedom, or between "breathing in and breathing out", to use the expression for this dialectic coined by that great German poet Johann Wolfgang von Goethe (1749-1832) in his poetry cycle "West-East Divan" published in 1814. So here is Gandhi in a text written in 1927:

> I do not want my house to be walled in on all sides and my windows to be stuffed. I want the cultures of all lands to be blown about my house as freely as possible. But I refuse to be blown off my feet by any. I refuse to live in other people's houses as an interloper, a beggar or a slave. I refuse to put the unnecessary strain of learning English upon my sisters for the sake of false pride or questionable social advantage. I would have our young men and young women with literary tastes learn as much of English and other world languages as they like, and then expect them to give the benefits of their learning to India and to the world like Bose, a Roy or the Poet himself. But I would not have a single Indian forget, neglect or be ashamed of his mother-tongue, or feel that he or she cannot think or express the best thoughts in his or her vernacular. Mine is not a religion of the prison-house. It has room for the least among God's creation.[8]

Notes and References

1. Baum, Holger; Boldt, Klaus and Ghawami, Kambiz: "Der Handel mit Informationen wird zum Wettbewerbsfaktor. Welche Chancen bringt das Internet dem Süden?", in: *Frankfurter Rundschau*, January 23, 1999, p. 9.
2. Cf. Fischer, Wolfgang and Lepperhoff, Niels: *Wo stehen die WWW-Server der afrikanischen Regierungsseiten?* Gedanken zu einer "Geopolitik" des Internet, Jülich: Forschungszentrum Jülich 2002.
3. I would like to take the opportunity to thank my friend Uwe Afemann at the University of Osnabrück for bringing the following empirical studies to my attention: Rodriguez, Francisco and Wilson III, Ernest J.: *Are Poor Countries Losing the Information Revolution?*, Washington DC: The World Bank 2000; online: http://www.infodev.org/library/wilsonrodriguez.doc (access: August 29, 2001); Canning, David: *Information Technology and Economic Development*. Session Transcript, Havard Institute for International Development, Sept. 30 - Oct. 1, 1999; online: http://www.hiid.harvard.edu/groups/macro/da21/transcrp/brk2_tr.html (access: December 14, 2000); Heeks, Richard: *Information and Communication Technologies, Poverty and Development*, Manchester: University of Manchester, Institute for Development Policy and Management 1999 (= Development Informatics Working Paper Series, Paper No. 5); General Directory for External Relations of the European Commission: *The Information Society and Development: A Review of the EC's experience in Asia, Latin America and the Mediterranean*, Brussels 2001; online: http://www.europa.eu.int/comm/external_relations/info_soc_dev/index.htm (access: October 15, 2003).
4. Cf. Heeks, Richard: *Lessons for Development from the "New Economy"*, Manchester: University of Manchester, Institute for Development Policy and Management 2000; online: http://www.man.ac.uk/idpm/dislesson.htm (access: February 19, 2001).
5. Cf. Garcia Marquez, Gabriel and Somavia, Juan: "General comments", in: *Many Voices, One World*. Communication and Society, Today and Tomorrow, ed. by Séan MacBride, Paris: UNESCO 1980, p. 281.
6. Cf. Margalit, Avishai: *The Decent Society*, Cambridge, Mass.: Harvard University Press 1996.
7. Cf. Sennett, Richard: *Respect in a World of Unequality*, New York: W. W. Norton 2002.
8. Gandhi, Mahatma: "English Learning", in: *Young India*, June 1, 1921, pp. 170-171.

1
Third World Images in West German Children's Books

1. Critical Approach to Research on Children's Books in Germany

In Germany, the scholarly analysis of children's and young people's literature tends to lag several decades behind other disciplines, and is largely left in the hands of elementary schoolteachers and teacher training colleges as the direct successors of the kindergarten supervisors and elementary schoolteachers who introduced such investigations following the educational reform policy of the 1920s. This explains the failure as yet to adopt an interdisciplinary approach to the study of children's literature by including knowledge drawn from the social sciences, psychology, pedagogic theory, literary scholarship, linguistics, mass communication research and other relevant sources. The terms *children's* and *young people's literature* are used interchangeably below for lack of a clear differentiation between the two terms. Most West German studies of children's literature overlook the sociopolitical factors that determine form and content, and exhibit a naively idealistic belief in the innocuous political character and influence of such literature. It is in precisely this idealistic spirit that R. Bamberger compiled his extensive standard work on the function of children's literature:

> Fiction instills faith in mankind and provides building blocks for our sense of humanity. It nurtures our imagination, courage, thoughts

> and desires. Fiction imbues us with the capacity for joy and sorrow, kindles our awareness, sheds light upon our inner selves. It enhances the ethical, traditional and religious elements of life as well as our individual tastes and capacity for critical judgment.[1]

Bamberger's language clearly betrays - not merely in passing - the ideological orientation of his work, which is by no means unique in studies of young people's literature. Such literature is expected to reflect "an intact world". Media, such as movies, TV films and comics are spurned for being in R. Bamberger's "inferior literature", while escapist romantic novels about archetypal heroes calculated to appeal to children all over the world are in high favor. All this is supposed to instill an appreciation of literature in children. The durability of this romantic model for children's literature is revealed by the following passage from a Workshop Resolution passed at a 1972 meeting of the International Board on Books for Young People (IBBY) in Nice, France:

> The major purpose of children's books is to instill a vision of hope, trust and affirmation. Childhood is the time of innocence in the life of every human being and to foster this innocence one of the functions of children's literature. Most children's books are too realistic and consequently tend to arouse in children feelings of insecurity.[2]

It should not be overlooked that the above nonacademic and conservative approach to the study of young people's literature still exerts a major influence upon teachers, publishers and international organizations such as UNESCO and IBBY. All advances in the study of young people's literature over the past decade have been principally due to the efforts of Malte Dahrendorf and Dieter Richter. In his book *Das Mädchenbuch und seine Leserin* (The Book for Girls and Its Girl Readers) published in 1970, Dahrendorf took direct issue with the idealistic educational theories of his predecessors. Pointing out their conservative bias, he demonstrated the presence of counter-progressive trends in the books he analyzed, exposing their rôle stereotypes, sexist values and social bias. His studies led him to the following conclusion:

> Books for girls abjure the historical development of female emancipation from male domination, confine their female characters to constricting social roles, and favor authoritarian educational methods conceived to stultify liberal tendencies. Neither the chosen

> role models nor the literary style correspond in any way to present-day educational needs. A psychological analysis shows that to a great extent these books satisfy the current interests of many girls, especially young girls and those who belong to the lower working-class or lower middle class. The books are thus in close accord with the psychological expectations of the majority of their readers.[3]

Dieter Richter helped move the analysis of young people's literature forward by focusing attention on the interaction between such literature and the prevailing political system. His analysis of socialist children's books written in the 1920s and of their hitherto neglected historical perspective have been particularly helpful. In the introduction to *Das Politische Kinderbuch* (The Political Children's Book) he writes :

> As a title The Political Children's Book does not imply that there are both political and apolitical children's books. On the contrary, it implies that children's books are political, for the experience they impart is invariably that of actual social reality. Their child readers are always presented with attitudes and behavioral responses that have much in common with their own lives in a given society governed by specific principles, rules and regulations.[4]

Richter's standpoint concerning the analytical impossibility of differentiating between the categories "political" and "unpolitical" became almost commonplace with the rise of Critical Theory in the 1920s and '30s. Any reference thereto still provokes head-shaking disbelief and even harsh comments from the analysts of children's literature - a further manifestation of the naivety and ideology of current workers in this field. Children's literature is produced under the control of a powerful interest group - publishers - for consumption by socially impotent juveniles. This situation applies to published studies of children's books. My own historical synopsis of the unsatisfactory state of research in children's literature and the ideological content of children's books is, unfortunately, too short and fails to come to grips with the social conditioning of media production, distribution and consumption. Research in children's literature should start off by focusing upon the following issues:

- The way in which the form and content of children's books are chosen to secure the psychological and sociopolitical impotence and oppression of children.

- The way in which the social status of children is directly or indirectly reflected in children's books, with or without a time-lag.
- The way in which the publishers of children's books communicate with children.
- The ease with which ideological bias is introduced into children's books along with the special interests serving their publishers.
- The way in which children's books may be influenced due to their authors being lower royalties than the authors of books for adults.
- The influence the respective authors' individual socialization processes have on the children's books.
- The extent to which the content of children's books is influenced by the keen competition between publishers.

The majority of these issues remain open to question due to the general lack of empirical data and a viable general theory of children's literature. If we return to the problem of explaining the unsatisfactory situation regarding children's books, then it bears emphasizing that neither their sometimes crude subject-matter nor their inadequate analysis can properly explain the ideologies inherent in the books themselves or in their analyses. Instead, the generally recognized fact that young people have no political power is the root cause of the mediocre quality of the children's books that are perpetually churned out and the inadequacy of subsequent analysis. Those who would argue that such criticism is too radically utopian should consider a telling observation by Bertolt Brecht in his book on *Broadcasting Theory* (1932): "Those who think these ideas are too utopian should ask themselves why they are utopian."[5]

2. Images of Third World Countries

Introduction

As numerous studies have already revealed, the German public's general knowledge of the Third World is sparse to say the least, for it is a) derived from unreliable sources, b) distorted by a variety of prejudices, and c) eurocentric. Knowledge of the Third World consequently fails to do any justice to the international significance of Third World countries and, in particular, their bearing on German foreign policy. Our attitude towards the Third World and our relations with Third World countries are, moreover, primarily determined by self-centered national interests that are decidedly of an economic nature, not to mention by sociopolitical interests (inherited prejudices, group behavior, national consciousness) that exclusively take their cue from our own system.

The schoolbook analysis presented by Fohrbeck, Wiesand and Zahar[6] comes to the conclusion that, at best, the people of the Third World are seen as "also-humans" inhabiting a "residual world". This attitude is based on the common differentiation between "our world" and "Eastern bloc countries" ("First" and "Second" World), with everything else on earth labeled "Third World".

In this view, the capitalist Western world is characterized by advanced technology and the Third World by its economic and technological deficits. Factors such as poverty, illiteracy, hunger, high infant mortality and an underdeveloped industrial and technological complex are regarded as the starting point for efforts at development ultimately intended to imitate our own way of life. Numerous sociological studies hinging on the Latin American Dependencia Theory have arrived at the conclusion that this model is wrong. A more adequate global model featuring a predominantly capitalist mode of production would see the Third World as an essential part of the capitalist system. The Third World is not an as yet underdeveloped world; instead, it is part of a global capitalist system in which the central political systems exploit and dominate those on the periphery. This exploitation is primarily achieved by the "regulation" of world market prices. In this way the gap between poverty and prosperity, between the peoples of the Third World and West Europeans increases rather than decreases by the year.

Whereas assessments of the Third World and its peoples have so far mainly been based upon premises that could be characterized as exotic and adventurous, moralizing and patronizingly benevolent, ethnically Darwinist or person-oriented, the foregoing model composed of central and peripheral political systems strongly suggests that only sociopolitical analysis will yield an accurate representation of the Third World. This similarly applies to the sociopolitical analysis of children's literature as a socializing leisure-time instrument. Advanced capitalist social systems such as that in Germany are characteristically marked by a pronounced division of labor, workplace alienation, and an expanding services industry. This leads to increasing mental impoverishment and greater opportunities for media producers to play upon the emotions of media consumers by the way in which they report on public events.

The more global and intensive the character of a given capitalist system, the more global and intensive the coverage its media news services provide of events in geographically remote parts of the earth in which its media consumers have absolutely no personal interest. The objective distance between German media consumers and the public events reported by the media does not, however, preclude individual Germans from identifying themselves subjectively with specific heroic figures or specific events in the Third World presented by the media.

The dialectical process of identification and emotional dissociation involved in media coverage may be seen as a form of media socialization the sociopolitical importance of which grows with the increasing globalization of the former numerous unstructured individual political systems. Whereas, for example, the Crimean War (1853-56) was never more than an exotic event for the citizens of the Duchy of Baden as existed at the time in south-west Germany, media coverage of the war in Vietnam influenced German media consumers far more directly.

The figure of the woolly-headed blackamoor in Heinrich Hoffmann's *Struwwelpeter* (1844) is nowadays of political significance more because of the social struggle for school desegregation in the USA and the opposition to apartheid in South Africa than because it is the first time most children today are confronted with a person with a non-white skin.

Within the context of the present global system, the media presentation of the Third World offers not only opportunities for ideological manipulation (which are widely exploited) but also opportunities for the dissemination of counter-information reflecting specific national or economic interests or attempting to foster solidarity between the underdogs within the global system. Child socialization as regards the Third World is essentially media-dependent. Children's and young people's books and other media instill define the children's first affective, cognitive and behavioral responses to the historical and sociopolitical background of the Third World and its peoples. Children are neither able to verify empirically the value of this media-related teaching process within their own environment, nor to resist the process. If one considers the importance of the early socialization phase as a basic step towards later political awareness, then the need to investigate how Third World subject matter is presented in children's books becomes self-evident.

A political inquiry into children's books dealing with Third World problems would usefully contribute to the ongoing debate between various schools of educational thought concerning the relevance of Third World problems for the political situation in Germany and for German students. As a literary medium, children's books may contain elements of fantasy, adventure, humor and excitement that can be used to provide their readers with a practical approach to Third World problems. If Third World subject matter in children's books and other media is to be of any real educational value, however, what Bertolt Brecht wrote in 1948 in his *Kleines Organon für das Theater* should necessarily apply:

> The business of the theater, like all other arts, has always been to entertain. This business endows it with its inherent dignity: it need promise nothing more than amusement - if without reservation. Since its status cannot be elevated by transforming it into, say, a market of morals, it must take care not to become degraded - as would immediately occur if it failed to render whatever is moral amusing, i.e., amusing to the senses, through which the moral, of course, only stands to gain.[7]

In order to analyze children's and young people's literature as a medium of socialization, we need to answer the following questions:

A. Criteria for the Appraisal of Content:

1. How is the economic, sociopolitical, historical and cultural situation of the Third World presented?
2. How are the associated problems handled?
3. What are the values and moral attitudes underlying children's books and designed to be passed onto the young readers?
4. How are the themes of colonialism, imperialism and Christian missionary activities presented?
5. How is the relationship between industrial nations and the nation states of the Third World defined?
6. In what way are the social movements in Third World countries defined?
7. What kind of image of man is presented in children's books?
8. What strategies do children's books advocate for the solution of individual sociopolitical and socioeconomic problems?

B. The above list should be supplemented by the following pedagogical queries:

1. What pedagogical function do these books perform through their specific method of presentation and analysis? What are young

readers expected to learn from these books and, specifically, what should they preferably not learn?

2. How and in whose interests do these books influence the way young readers' opinions are shaped with regard to sociopolitical problems relating to the Third World?
3. How are class and gender-specific factors treated in children's literature?

C. Analyses should relate the economic, political, and social problems of the Third World specifically to those of the First and Second Worlds in such a way as to contribute to the meaningful political education of German children. A worthwhile subject would be the "The Third World in Our Own Country" (foreign workers, ethnic and religious minorities).

D. The analyses should extend from children's and young people's literature to the widely and avidly read children's comics and paperbacks, etc., especially those that, in passing, touch upon the Third World and its problems.

Typical Content Structures and Patterns of Argumentation

A critical survey of existing secondary literature allows the following classification of German children's books published since 1945:

a) Stereotype topographies about the Third World in German children's books:

Africa: Dark continent, vast jungles, wild beasts, animal parks, primitive natives, native rites and dances, safaris, naked blacks, modern big cities, academically trained Africans.

Arabia: Islam, veiled women, harems, blood feuds, fast horses, secret wine-drinking, freedom-loving nomads, sons of the desert, Mecca.
India: Silk-clad maharajas, jewels, the goddess Kali, temples, religious fanaticism, pilgrims, fakirs, the city of Benares, the caste system, tiger-hunting, enormous wealth amid dire poverty.

East Asia (mainly China): Yellow-skinned slit-eyed people, large families, high culture, Tong members (secret societies).

African Americans: Famous athletes, sports champions, jazz artists, vocalists, submissive slaves, good-natured blacks, Uncle Toms (blacks that pander to whites), deep religiosity (black Southern Baptists), acceptance of white world as model.

Latin America: Incas, Mayas, Cortez, Pizarro, Columbus, natives with poisoned arrows (curare), German explorers, the Amazon river, rain forests, lamas, bandits, big modern cities, poverty.

Native Americans (American Indians): Prairies, horses, buffaloes, tepees, war paint, medicine men, cowboys, partial extinction by whites.

The stereotypes in these topographies suggest that all are readily interchangeable and may be used as stock items to form images in which the mention of a single piece is sufficient to recall the entire picture to the minds of readers.

b) The following stereotypical patterns of argumentation on social conflicts are to be encountered in German children's books concerning Third World countries:

The Avoidance Syndrome: All mention of social conflict is avoided; personal and small-group conflicts usually go unmentioned. Books marked by this syndrome assume conflicts have no legitimate place within the children's world.

The Adventure Syndrome: Conflicts are presented in a manner similar to that encountered in adventure and detective stories and other forms of trivial literature. Conflicts arise at random, or due to a misunderstanding between persons, or as the result of a crime, or the occurrence of a natural catastrophe. The conflict is usually solved by a European; the Third World serves merely as the backdrop.

The Harmonizing Syndrome: Conflicts due to the dependence of a peripheral upon a central power are described but kept strictly within the apolitical antipodes of prosperity vs. poverty, progress vs. regression, religion vs. the supernatural, knowledge vs. ignorance, education vs. jungle life, urban vs. tribal culture, modern administration vs. tribal authority, civilization vs. the primitive. In such depictions, the maturation from the negative to the positive is usually triggered by an individual rather than a collective. Depending on the prevailing ideology, the conflict will be resolved by the intervention of a dominant personality who restores the colonial or semi-colonial status quo ante, a kind of patri-arch who forces Europeans to accept the inhabitants of the Third World as equals.

The Syndrome of the "White Man's Burden": This syndrome appears in endogenous conflicts common to the Third World such as inter- and intra-tribal feuding, religious feuding, personal quarrels, usually attributable to ethnological and/or bio-ethnical factors. Such conflicts are characteristically resolved by European intervention. The European ruler assumes the burdensome and unrewarding duty of liberating the oppressed. The perspective of the conflict-resolving narrator is generally that of a European farm owner, merchant, scientist, traveler, or son of a diplomat. Conflict resolution is possible in the same way as with the harmonizing syndrome, or through the intervention of:

- Christian missionaries,
- Members of foreign development aid services or the peace corps,
- European "pioneers" such as Cecil Rhodes, Paul von Lettow-Vorbeck, Albert Schweitzer.

The Oasis Syndrome: In this syndrome, an individual inhabitant of the Third World appears as it were as the foil to the majority of Europeans, like an oasis in a completely differently structured world. If the perspective of the narrator is that of a European, the problematical situation of the Third World and its inhabitants will be depicted as nothing more than a backdrop. The inhabitants will fulfill subservient roles such as servants, farmhands, errand boys, shoeshine boys, etc. Conflicts within the Third World are overlooked. If, however, the narrator is a Third World inhabitant, the recommended methods of conflict resolution will be:

- integration into the European capitalist life style,
- individual striving for more (usually formal) education,
- individual striving for accumulation of wealth (savings),
- change of domicile (from kraal to big modern city.

The foregoing classification of syndromes is, of course, purely analytical, whereas in practice the stereotypes are combined to form a "Third World in which everything is all right". The following brief analysis of a few recently published children's books is intended to characterize their stereotype topographies and patterns of argumentation.

Exemplary Brief Analyses

In the second volume of the series entitled *Elefanten-Boy* (Elephant Boy) sold in 1973 mainly in department and stationery stores we come across the narrative:

> At the Indian animal station Namanpur, all is in a state of uproar. Suddenly turning wild, the normally peaceful elephant Kala Nag is tugging at its chains and has almost killed one of its keepers. But the two Indian brothers Toomai and Ranjit, discover the reason for the erratic behavior of their elephant. One of the keepers has intentionally neglected to feed Kala Nag to make him wild so that his own elephant can take Kala Naag's place in the great elephant parade.

The mechanism and intention of this conflict presentation are clear enough. By playing up structural or personal conflicts within Third World countries, the global conflict between the latter and industrial countries is played down. It is also telling that the supervisor of the Indian animal station is a blue-eyed fair-haired moody European who, with insightful paternalism, settles all major or minor personal conflicts arising between Indians. In contrast to literature for adults, children's books rarely note sociopolitical changes, and then only with an immense time lag.

When a leading West German politician visited the People's Republic of China in 1975, children in West Germany were shown books about China such as *Die grünen Bergdrachen* (The Green Mountain Dragons), *Pong Tschuli - du Strolch* (Pong Chu-li - You Rascal), *Herz im Koffer* (Heart in a Suitcase), *Felix und die Bande der Roten Laterne* (Felix and the Red Lantern Gang) and *Der Drache mit der Silberkralle* (The Silver-Clawed Dragon). These titles, which are typical of trivial literature in general, were followed by others in which the exotic Third World served as a backdrop for German children's adventure stories at their worst.

The exoticism of the Third World is projected into juvenile dreams and fantasies that are far removed from the real-life conflicts encountered at school or in the home. Nevertheless we may in the near future expect the publication of new children's books about China containing stories that no longer take place in the feudal China described by authors such as Pearl S. Buck, but at last reflect life in present-day China. Children's books about Africa typically reflect western perspectives of the Third World as may be seen from the following example.

In September 1971 the West German branch of the Exxon Corporation brought out a series of three picture-books which included one by Hans-Otto Meissner entitled *Expedition ins Abenteuer. Männer erobern die Welt* (Expeditions as Adventures. Men Who Conquer the World). This book (retail price DM 3.95) was distributed free of charge at gas stations to customers buying more than five gallons of gas. This three books in the series achieved a circulation of 2.5 million copies (children's books are normally published in editions of ten thousand). A list of chapter headings in Meissner's book characterizes its ideological leanings:

- Leif Erikson. The First Discovery of America
- Christopher Columbus Discovers a New World
- Vasco da Gama. The First Voyage to India
- Hernando Cortez Conquers Mexico
- Francis Drake. The Terror of the Seven Seas
- Captain Cook Discovers a Thousand Islands
- Alexander Mackenzie. The First Crossing of North America
- David Livingstone. A Life for Africa
- Henry Stanley. The Rockbreaker

In this book the historical origins of the dependence of peripheral territories upon central powers is credited to the energy and courage of individual personages. Third World countries are presented as objects to be discovered, whereas the geopolitical and economic interests that prompt such discoveries are entirely neglected. The chapter on Stanley as "The Rockbreaker" (i.e. a trailblazer in the rocky territory of creeks) contains the following:

> Stanley was underway for a thousand days - almost three years - before reaching the Atlantic coast on August 12th 1877. The river Lualaba turned out to be nothing less than one of the two sources of the vast Congo river. Stanley had crossed equatorial Africa from East to West. For the outside world this was a great sensation and Henry Morton Stanley went down in history as one of the major explorers of his age, for which he was awarded honors and praise in abundance. Stanley entered the service of King Leopold II of Belgium in 1879 and significantly contributed to the fact that the entire Congo basin gradually came under Belgian administrative control.

> From 1887 to 1889 he embarked on a second expedition, this time following the Congo upstream to the sources of the Nile. Stanley married in England in 1890. Awarded a knighthood by the Queen, he became Sir Henry Morton Stanley. In the same country from which, as a penurious 15-year-old lad, he had escaped from a reform institute for juvenile delinquents, he was to end his days as an estate-owner and Member of Parliament. The great adventurer, journalist, explorer - the man known in Africa as "The Rockbreaker" - died on May 10th 1904.

The events and facts in the history of Third World countries that are invariably ignored in German children's literature are highly revealing. The above reference to the entire Congo basin "gradually coming under Belgian administrative control" is significant not only for its pro-colonialist bias, but also because it completely neglects to mention the atrocious sociopolitical conditions prevalent in the Congo basin under Belgian administration. This brief phrase is typical of the way colonialism is passed off in children's literature.

Nowhere is it stated, for instance, that the Congo was virtually King Leopold II's private colony, that between 1891 and 1905 1.5 million "natives" were massacred and that King Msiri was assassinated by order of the Congo Society. Holding women hostages, forcing native dignitaries to perform demeaning tasks for colonial officials, and brutally whipping natives were part of daily life. Nor should we overlook the enormous wealth accumulated by Leopold II from the sale of copper, high-quality timber and rubber exported from the Congo.

References to colonial rule in children's literature are always phrased to justify past and present exploitative relationships. The allegation that pure distortion of fact is usually only to be found in the low-priced children's books sold in department stores or distributed as free handouts at gas stations is simply not true. On the contrary, in 1968, prestigious German publishers J. G. Cotta brought out a book by the same Hans-Otto Meissner entitled *Stanley 1871. Der Kongo gibt sein Geheimnis preis* (Stanley 1871. The Congo Reveals Its Secret). In this coffee-table book Meissner propagates his colonialist ideology with still greater fervor without the slightest criticism of the atrocious behavior of Leopold II or the notorious ruthlessness of Henry Morton Stanley.

Most children's literature dealing with the Third World takes its cue from a notion of development based upon capital and economic growth, which has come under scathing criticism from the exponents of the

Dependencia Theory. Undaunted by such criticism or actual conditions on the ground in Third World countries, so-called modernization is recommended and the industrialized city is envisaged as the desirable objective of all structural transformations in the Third World. This modernization theory, which does not perceive history as a change from national to international forms of dependence, but as issuing from step-by-step autochthonous developments in individual regions, is brilliantly illustrated in a children's book by Karen Olsen entitled Aus Njagwe wird Peter (Njagwe Becomes Peter). In her foreword she writes:

> Dear Reader, Have you ever tried to imagine how a person from the Iron Age would react if suddenly thrust into the 20th century? We do not know what he would think or feel, but are rather certain he would experience great anxiety and wonderment, and make many mistakes. In reality, however, many people living on this earth today are comparable with the people of the Iron Age. Thousands of people were still living as primitive tribes in remote areas before they suddenly came into contact with modern civilization. How do they react to the world we know so well? What do they think and feel?

Set in Liberia, Olsen's story describes in a favorable light the development of a Liberian youth from a jungle village who got a job as a boy by a married Danish couple engaged in African research. Attending school in Monrovia turns him into a "civilized" human. The story concludes:

> Ultimately it became clear to Peter that the jungle world was lost to him forever. No choice was left open to him other than to return to the new world. He would doubtless have to fight hard to achieve full recognition, but was resolved to do so. Thus Peter entered civilization and became one of the tens of thousands who are helping to bring the new era to Africa.

Earlier on he had explained: *"Now I can read, my name is no longer Njagwe, but Peter."* To adopt European names is perfectly normal! In Germany, the demand for children's literature capable of awakening the consciousness of readers to the development problems for peripheral Third World peoples will not be met until the sociopolitical importance of children's literature is duly recognized. Children's and young people's books that go beyond the traditional concepts of underdevelopment and the associated patterns of argumentation are few and far between.

When children's literature dealing with Third World development problems is used in schools or for educational purposes outside the normal school system, the primary objective must always be to teach readers how to read between the lines.

A notable exception among children's books is Sven Wernström's *Der Schatz im Dorf der Armen* (The Treasure in the Village of the Poor) published in 1972 in Berlin. The jury of the West German section of the International Board for Books for Young People nominated this book for the German Young People's Book Award for 1973.

The author portrays a 16-year-old Swedish youth Mike who accompanies a film team to Guate-mala, where they plan to make a realistic film about that country. Struck by the stark difference between the spurious film scenes and daily reality in the Guatemalan village in question, the youth swiftly realizes how phony the film is not to mention the Guatemalan political system existing in this village.

The learning process Mike undergoes during the production of the film is readily understandable to young readers. Wernström's book, which employs sociopolitical categories to explain underdevelopment and dependence, is, moreover, written in an exciting style and effectively satisfies the principal requirements for familiarizing German children with the situation in Third World Countries.

Notes and References

1. Bamberger, Richard: *Jugendlektüre,* Vienna: Jugend & Volk 1965, p. 19.
2. Actes du 13e Congres de l'U.I.L.J.: *Le rôle de la lecture dans le développement des enfants et des adolescents de nos sociétés en transformation*, Paris: U.I.J.L. 1972, p. 100.
3. Dahrendorf, Malte: *Das Mädchenbuch und seine Leserin*, Hamburg: Verlag für Buchmarktforschung 1970, pp. 234.
4. Richter, Dieter: "Vorwort", in: *Das politische Kinderbuch.* Eine aktuelle historische Dokumentation, ed. by Dieter Richter, Darmstadt and Neuwied: Luchterhand Verlag 1973, p. 23.
5. Brecht, Bertolt: "Der Rundfunk als Kommunikationsapparat", in: Brecht, Bertolt: *Gesammelte Werke in 20 Bänden.* Vol. 18, Frankfurt: Suhrkamp Verlag 1967, p. 132
6. Cf. Fohrbeck, Karla; Wiesand, Andreas J. and Zahar, Renate: *Heile Welt und Dritte Welt.* Medien und politischer Unterricht I. Schulbuchanalyse, Opladen: Leske Verlag 1971.
7. Brecht, Bertolt: "Kleines Organon für das Theater", in: Brecht, Bertolt: *Gesammelte Werke in 20 Bänden.* Vol. 16, Frankfurt: Suhrkamp Verlag 1967, p. 665.

2
Disarmament in the Press

1. By Way of an Introduction: Five Scenarios

First Scenario

On May 21, 1935 the Chancellor of a European government made a speech before his Parliament in which, towards the end, he stated:

> When present-day Germany espouses the cause of peace, it does not do so from a position of weakness or pusillanimity. It espouses peace on the grounds of National Socialism's different concept of nation and state. This ideology sees no desirable political aim in forcing one nation to integrate with another one alien to it, but sees any such event as a threat to internal unity and hence to national security for a long time to come. [...] Every war starts by consuming the flower of the nation. Since, however, Europe has no more unoccupied living space, any conquest can only lead to a rise in population that would in no way mitigate Europe's root problem.
>
> [...] I started the Nazi revolution by creating the movement I have since led to victory. I realize that we will all only experience the first stirrings of this great revolutionary development. So what else should I desire but peace and tranquility? If the objection is raised that only the leadership desires this, then my response would be: Only the leader and the government need to desire peace - nations never desire war! Germany needs peace and wants peace.[1]

The speaker in question had already presented this call for peace at length in an interview given to the Polish journal *Gazeta Polska* (January 26, 1935) which was then taken up and discussed in his own national press. The London *Times* also came out in praise of this appeal for peace in its issue of May 23, 1935. It is not too difficult to recognize that this official government statement formed part of a speech by Adolf Hitler to the German Reichstag. Hitler's appeal and the ensuing press comments are typical of the frequently repeated declarations of peace by the Nazi leadership from 1933 to 1935. Such declarations sought to distract attention away from the rearmament plans of the Nazis backed by the German armaments industry from 1935 onwards. This was followed in 1936 by the military occupation of the Rhineland and German military support for Franco in the Spanish Civil War, the annexation of Austria in 1938, and the occupation of Czechoslovakia and invasion of Poland in 1939.

First Inference: *Even though the press may be full of talk about peace, rearmament and war preparations, war may - in certain political circumstances - nevertheless be underway.*

Second Scenario

As clearly shown in the 1980 IAMCR (International Association for Mass Communication Research) study on the images of foreign countries presented in the press of some 30 countries, almost every country's press concentrates mainly on reporting events occurring in its own region.

In Latin America, one third of the reported news items are regional. Mexico looks towards the United States for news items, whereas Argentina and Brazil look more towards Western Europe because of former colonial links and, to a certain extent, also towards the Middle East. In Africa, the demand for regional news currently runs high because of the elections in Rhodesia and the downfall of Idi Amin in Uganda. Six of the seven African countries covered by the study are interested first in regional news, then in news about the Middle East as their territorial gateway to Europe and Asia, and only third in news about Western Europe due to earlier colonial ties with France and England. In the press of the Middle East almost 50 percent of all news items are regional, the rest being divided between West Europe, Africa and the USA, with only the Lebanon focusing considerable interest upon East Europe. Regional reportage in the Asian press is about 40 percent. Australia and India exhibit an Anglophonic preference, while

Indonesia and Thailand look more towards West Europe and the Middle East. The press in East Europe exhibits the least interest in regional news.[2] Studies show that the press in developing countries reports very little on the nuclear arms race, disarmament negotiations and the activities of the peace movements in the USA and West Europe.

Second Inference: *If a national press reports little about the arms race, this does not necessarily imply that the respective country is not interested in peace. The press of some countries may consider factors such as hunger, famine, disease and foreign pressure to be of greater interest to readers than reports on the nuclear arms race between the major powers.*

Third Scenario

In his study on the Iranian press, Amir Taheri notes:

> The Persian daily newspaper *Kayhan* took the first step. On October 10, 1978 it appeared with a huge photograph of Khomeini on its front page, capped by a giant headline announcing the possibility of the Ayatollah's imminent return. Within a few hours, some 700,000 copies of the paper were sold in Tehran alone. Thus began a circulation war among Iranian newspapers in which Khomeini's pictures and statements provided the pièces de résistance.[3]

Similar reactions are reported in A. Wadi's analysis of the Iranian press during the last days of the Shah's regime.[4] It is of interest to note here that some Iranian journalists circumvented the Shah's strict censorship by writing critically about conditions in foreign countries in such a way as to imply criticism of the political repression in their own. Readers were readily capable of recognizing this indirect criticism of the Shah's regime. There is apparently a delicate balance between a censored press and reader credibility. Once the discrepancy between the ideology imposed upon the press from above and the daily experience of its readers becomes too great, journalists and readers alike enter a secret alliance in coding and decoding press reports contrary to official intentions.

Third Inference: *When a national press writes far more about peace and disarmament than about the social problems experienced daily by its readers, then the readers will not take that press very seriously.*

Fourth Scenario

In his 1982 study, German political scientist Lothar Kalka, analyzed the discussion of the neutron bomb in the West German press.[5] In his quantitative and qualitative analysis he examined in depth the press reports appearing in the national dailies *Die Welt*, *Süddeutsche Zeitung* and *Frankfurter Rundschau* during the period June 6, 1977 to April 9, 1978.

In accord with earlier studies Kalka determined a considerable increase in West German press reporting on military policy. The neutron bomb was discussed during the period analyzed in 107 articles in *Die Welt*, 106 in the *Süddeutsche Zeitung* and 70 in the *Frankfurter Rundschau*. Analyzing the substance of these articles Kalka discovers that the conservative *Die Welt* approves the deployment of the neutron bomb within the strategic framework of flexible response, the *Süddeutsche Zeitung* maintains a balance between the pros and cons, while the social-democratic *Frankfurter Rundschau* generally rejects the neutron bomb. All three newspapers made above-average use of commentaries, background information and interviews. Kalka concludes:

> The neutron bomb discussion was scarcely conducted critically, i.e. from the aspect of political strategy. [...] Coverage was of greater quantitative than qualitative force. The question as to what the neutron bomb means within the context of the security of the Federal Republic and whether its political price is justified was barely touched upon. The frequency of press items that fall under the category of "further information" shows the reporting to incline towards personalization and dramatization, and to concentrate upon isolated topical or sensational events. [...] No significant differences of a general nature appear to exist between the individual newspapers, although disparities may be noted in the handling of details. On the whole the quality of discussion remains on an even level.[6]

Fourth Inference: *In West European industrialized nations, the intensive reporting on the nuclear arms race tallies more readily with the mass media's tendency to indulge in dramatization, sensationalism, personalization, etc. rather than to provide explanations based upon rational analyses, background reports, discussions, etc.*

Fifth Scenario

In the West German *Handbuch der Weltpresse* (Handbook of the World's Press), the reference to the press of the USSR concludes:

> The position of the press and all other mass communication media can only be understood within the context of the Soviet society in general, which is not primarily influenced and directed by divergent interests but solely by those of a single political party.[7]

This characterization of the Soviet press can be rejected outright as rigid anti-communism without seriously jeopardizing the author's academic qualifications as an analyst. Although almost no quantitative or qualitative analyses are available concerning the treatment of certain topics - such as Third World countries - in the press of Eastern bloc countries, a 1979 analysis by Egbert Jahn und Jutta Tiedke of the presentation of Soviet détente policy in Soviet magazines[8] could well provide a useful starting point for a discriminating discussion. In their qualitative analysis the two authors examine the treatment of the problems of security and cooperation policies in the 1969 issues of the following magazines: *Mezhdunarodanya zhizn* (International Life), *Kommunist* (Communist), *Mirovaya ekonomika i mezhdunarodnye otnoseniya* (World Economy and International Relations) and *Kommunist vooruzhennykh sil* (Communist of the Armed Forces).

Before dealing with the specific interest and function of each magazine, the authors make it clear that none of the magazines reflect anti-détente tendencies. Since, however, the subject of military threats is not treated uniformly, the authors conclude that some magazines are more reserved with regard to détente policy than others. In its 1969 issues the armed forces mouthpiece *Kommunist voorukzhennykh sil*, for example, does not refer to détente with the West in a single article and reduces the security-through-policy option to "security through arms"; the magazines *Mezhdunarodnaya zhizn* and *Mirovaya ekonomika i mezhudunarodnye otnoseniya* are far more positive in their editorial policy.

This situation poses a multitude of theoretical problems. Although in the countries of Eastern Europe one cannot speak of a class society in the sociological sense due to the state control of the means of production, it is nevertheless possible to determine the influence of diverse interest groups.

Fifth Inference: *Even though no anti-détente press media are operative in the socialist states, a close content analysis will nevertheless reveal which print and other media are used by interest groups to voice their views on the arms race and détente, and which of these groups are able in this way to influence public opinion.*

These five scenarios, to which various others could be added, are presented to show that an international cultural comparison by way of content analysis of the treatment of the arms race and détente by the press and other media will bear scholarly fruit only as long as it is appropriately embedded in an historical and social structure analysis of the national system in question.

2. Peace and Media Analysis

Within the framework of its past history, constitution, accomplishments and present program, UNESCO has always been dedicated to the concept of peace. This is true not only in a moral and political sense, but also as regards international law. Although the various UNESCO resolutions passed with regard to peace are not binding in international law as far as treaties are concerned, they can nevertheless be considered legally binding in character. Long before the controversial mass media debate concerning UNESCO and the peace-promoting role of the press, another mass medium - the school textbook - was assigned a peace-promoting function. It is of interest at this point to recapitulate briefly on the long-term work performed by UNESCO and other institutions in the field of peace-promotion through school textbooks. The international revision of school textbooks was attempted in the United States as long ago as the beginning of this century through, for example, studies initiated by the Carnegie Endowment for International Peace.

These studies became increasingly important after World War I under the auspices of the League of Nations. In 1926, the League of Nations' Casares Resolution attempted with small success to persuade league members to agree to the mutual revision of school textbooks. Somewhat more successful was an agreement on 40 controversial points in Franco-German relations concluded in 1935 through the private initiative of teachers' organizations in both countries. In Northern Europe, *Foreningen*

Norden, founded in 1919, succeeded in getting the subject of peace dealt with in numerous Scandinavian school textbooks. The 1928 Historians' Congress in Oslo was also influential in this connection. Walter Mertineit in a 1937 declaration demonstrated just how controversial questions of school textbook revision are:

> It was a characteristic feature of the League of Nations era that only 15 small to medium-sized states signed the Declaration on the Teaching of History drafted in 1937. All the larger powers rejected the Declaration, albeit for different reasons. The British opposed all outside interference in educational matters. The USA refused to sign because education does not come under federal control. France insisted on upholding the independence of teachers and historians. Nazi Germany rejected the principles of the Declaration as a whole. The Declaration had been the outcome of the League's long-term continuous endeavor to formulate a constructive plan of operation.
>
> In the period between the wars there had been widespread agreement on the role of teachers, historians textbook authors, school authorities, etc., in putting an end to the "drum and fife" approach to teaching history, in stamping out chauvinism and prejudice and teaching in its place reconciliation and international understanding. Since nation states will not readily accept a purely international approach to the teaching of history, strategies had to be developed for at least bilateral or, where feasible, multilateral revision. The interested parties accordingly formulated rules of conduct and even considered the right to appeal to the International Institute of Intellectual Cooperation for arbitration whenever any two countries failed to reach an understanding.[9]

It was not until after many decades of effort following World War II that the Peace Mission of the mass medium school textbook found general acceptance. The International Textbook Research Institute was founded in Braunschweig, West Germany in 1951 with the support of UNESCO. Under its aegis, numerous congresses and symposia were organized, resolutions passed and treaties concluded. Promising talks are currently in progress on the revision of history and geography in German and Polish school textbooks. The cultural agreement of June 13, 1976 between the Federal Republic of Germany and the People's Republic of Poland pays tribute to the work of their bilateral Textbook Commission.

Parallel to the new peace movements in the United States, West Europe and Japan, the topic of "Peace and Textbook" is again under discussion in academic circles as well as among the general public. In Japan, public criticism of the inadequate information provided in school textbooks on the nuclear devastation of Hiroshima and Nagasaki is on the increase.[10] In West Europe, a recently published analysis comparing the Federal Republic of Germany, the German Democratic Republic, France, Switzerland, the UK and Poland notes that war is treated in the textbooks as a constant quantity, but not peace.[11] Before the theoretical and methodological results of 50 years of research in international textbook revision are applied to the subjects of the arms race and the détente under discussion in the press, I shall first examine the trend to date briefly.

Contrary to the peace mission of the textbook, the mission of the press has never as yet been clearly defined, but only sporadically explored by the League of Nations and UNESCO. Analyses of the presentation of war and peace in the press have been yielded by individual research activities.[12] An institutional start was made with the 1978 UNESCO Mass Media Declaration (Article III):

> The mass media have an important contribution to make in the promotion of peace and international understanding by opposing racism, apartheid, human rights violations and incitements to war, and thereby helping to overcome ignorance and misunderstandings between nations.

The contribution of the press is already intimated in the title of this declaration. The expression "the promotion of peace" does not imply a passive role for the press, which should indeed actively engage itself for peace and not merely abstain from warmongering. As already shown elsewhere,[13] a multitude of links of various kinds exists between the connotations peace/arms race/détente on one hand and press/mass media/ communication on the other.

As shown in detail in the present study, the category "Content" - from the practical as well the theoretical viewpoint - must be understood as a function of the interplay between the categories production, effects and history (or vice versa). The theory of the American communication scholar, Phillips Davison, according to which "Any communication must be about something; one cannot escape ultimately dealing with content"[14] simply implies that whoever is concerned with the content of mass media cannot avoid having to analyze its historical and social embodiment in the conditions of production and consumption. This idea can also be grasped technologically, for it is the inherent laws governing a specific communication or information technology that reinforce, admit or prohibit the communication of a certain content.

When certain Western nations participating in the UNESCO debate on communication policy demand that UNESCO abjure all interest in the content of the media, then they are demanding nothing less than the exclusion of the theoretical and methodological treatment of communication problems.* It is in this context that UNESCO activities in the field of textbook revision assume importance in the press debate. After all, it has been generally accepted that the revision of the contents of the mass medium textbooks should represent one more small step in the direction of peace.

The textbook debates of the past fifty years could also provide a methodological basis for enriching the debate on content with reference to the press. Since the textbook debate has traditionally been conducted by members of the teaching profession, its methodology for content analysis was of a therapeutic nature and qualitative rather than quantitative. The methodology traditionally used for analyzing the press was always very different. As it was most often performed by political scientists, its methodology was oriented towards empirical social research. It is thus hardly a coincidence that the first systematic and quantitative content analyses were conducted on political propaganda material by the US War Department in World War II.

It is largely due to progress in structural approaches to empirical communication research over the past 15 years that the isolated analysis of the mass media contents must be seen as scientific regression. To plan a content analysis of the presentation of the arms race and détente in the press in concrete terms would mean that the conditions of production and consumption, be they the promotion of peace or warmongering, should be taken into account in the research methodology employed. It may be said in conclusion that content analysis is only practical if it is at the same time medium analysis, i.e., if it further takes into account the conditions of production and consumption. In this context the need for research discussed by James Halloran in 1974 still applies.[15]

---

* In the 115th Session, September 17-28, 1982, of UNESCO Executive Board, the USA, FRG, Denmark i.a. demanded that communication should not be used as a tool for achieving any such goal as peace and development. Moreover the USA emphasized that UNESCO should not permit itself to become involved in studies which touched upon communication.

3. Disarmament in the West German Press

As Jürgen Habermas forcefully argued in his *Strukturwandel der Öffentlichkeit*[16] (Structural Transformation of the Public Sphere), the middle-class public in an absolutist state forms a reasoning audience that reacts to governmental measures as a critical and controlling factor. In such a model critics are admittedly excluded from political power. The raison d'être of present-day Western democracies corresponds to an even more far-reaching model of critical public opinion: citizens have not only to be critics of governmental decisions, but the bourgeois public should itself constitute the system and form the basis of and condition for social organization and power.[17]

Any real structural transformation in West European industrial societies will, however, prevent the critical public from effectively assuming its role. Any tendency towards structural transformation will force the (social and welfare) state to interfere increasingly in the private sphere of the individual, thereby reducing the latter's autonomous sphere of responsibility in the face of an increasing number of power centers.Military publications likewise fall in line with this procedure. On the one hand, they have to remain critical and fulfill the dual function of correctly reproducing and editing military, strategic, technological and détente material as dealt with in journals dedicated to science and technology.

> The political press in Germany should examine the results of the strategy discussions in so far as these bear upon social and political matters.[18]

On the other hand they must judge the extent to which organizational power in the military sphere can be influenced by public opinion. In military matters public opinion is confronted with a basic contradiction between bourgeois thinking and military ethos. Gerhard Brandt and Ludwig von Friedeburg have observed:

> Irrespective of the class background of the military leadership caste, its members ultimately aim at the collective use of power and are in this respect diametrically opposed to the domain of productive work and peaceful commerce. The relationship between the military apparatus and bourgeois society always remains antagonistic and communication between the two remains problematic.[19]

Due to the nuclear overkill capacity of both friend and foe during the nuclear age, the militarily novel possibility of mutually assured destruction is shared by both aggressor and victim. This makes it more difficult than in the past to distinguish between aggressive and defensive action, or between a just and an unjust war. In this situation national security is not feasible without détente, which is only achievable through communication and public discussion. For détente to be negotiable, reliable information on the weaponry of the potential foe has to be accessible. The mutual exchange of information on armaments between rival nations is, however, insufficient: the nuclear age demands nothing less than "public inspection".[20]

It is difficult to define the actual relationship between public opinion and détente in the Federal Republic of Germany because this has hardly ever been seriously analyzed. The social sciences have been crassly negligent in this respect. Two recent news items demonstrate, however, that this relationship is relatively insubstantial.

1. In 1960 a sensational article in the news magazine *Der Spiegel* raised serious doubts about the Federal German army's defense capability against a possible attack by socialist countries. As reported by the French political scientist Alfred Grosser and others[21], this gave rise to a serious constitutional crisis in Bonn, but failed to provoke any public discussion concerning the military capacity of the Federal Republic in an East-West conflict.

2. Until far into the 1970s no controversial debates ever occurred in the Bonn parliament concerning the annual defense budget. During the annual budget debates the Opposition invariably voted against all items in the government's budget except for defense items.

The limited number of content analyses of the treatment of détente and security by the West German press yielded the following conclusions, the value of which is questionable because they are rarely based upon the methodology and criteria of critical theory described below in Section 4.

Gerhard Brandt and Ludwig von Friedeburg (1966) conducted a qualitative analysis (using the methodology of critical theory) of West German press coverage in the 1960s of the proposed purchase of Swiss Mirage fighter planes, the alleged missile gap in the USA and the creation of a multilateral nuclear force (MLF). The national dailies and weeklies addressed themselves to three major themes: deterrence, defense, détente.

Fundamental political decisions governing the security policy of West Germany were not questioned and no alternatives were discussed.[22]

In 1969 von Bredow conducted a qualitative analysis of media reports on the ombudsman's 1963 annual report on the Federal German army in 35 dailies, weeklies and monthlies as well as in all relevant radio and TV commentaries. The army ombudsman of the day, ex-Vice-Admiral Hellmuth Heye, former MP for the conservative CDU (Christian Democratic Union), had his annual report published in a popularized form in the magazine *Quick* in the summer of 1964. Heye dramatically warned against restorative and antidemocratic tendencies in the Federal German army. Von Bredow focused attention upon the subsequent press coverage, concluding that the press had not exercised its critical public function and had even succumbed to the obstructive influence of government-controlled public relations.[23]

In two theoretical studies (1975, 1979) Christian Potyka examined the relationship between the Federal German army and the public, concluding that the mass media play no significant role in the discussion of security policy. In general the West German mass media merely inform the public of the prevailing views of the political elite; they have never been particularly critical of the Federal German army and even media that used to voice criticism in earlier years have since acquiesced to the prevailing doctrine of deterrence.[24]

In a theoretical text in 1980 Anton-Andreas Guha analyzed press coverage of the NATO decision of December 12, 1979, concluding that the press had concocted a Manichean view of the world, manipulated statistics when comparing armaments and ignored expert studies that question the doctrine of deterrence. Guha finally concludes:

> Federal German press reporting on the complex problem of shadow trading in weapons must be regarded as a flop.[25]

In 1982 Matthias Wegener arrived at similar conclusions in his quantitative content analysis (sometimes a little weak in methodology and theory) of the treatment of the NATO rearmament resolution in two West German regional newspapers.[26] As stated earlier, Lothar Kalka demonstrated (in 1982) in a quantitative-cum-qualitative content analysis that West German press reporting on the neutron bomb had been grossly superficial.[27] The most recent qualitative analysis is by Kurt Kister (1983), who studied West German press coverage of the first-strike capability discussion after 1977.

He reveals that the conservative national dailies *Die Welt* and *Frankfurter Allgemeine Zeitung* were the only ones to treat the discussion seriously. The other dailies supported the first-strike idea, but failed to back it up with a rational argument.

All the major dailies came out in favor of the NATO doctrine of flexible response without discussing the alternative defense concept.[28] It is of interest at this point to note that political figures representing all shades of opinion complained of the inadequate reporting on military policy by the West German press. The conservative politician, Lothar Rühl, observed:

> For many years only two West German dailies with a nationwide circulation, *Frankfurter Allgemeine Zeitung* and *Die Welt*, have published articles and reports on defense and security issues. Even today systematic reports and comments on these topics only appear regularly in these two dailies, while others, such as Munich's *Süddeutsche Zeitung* and the *Frankfurter Rundschau*, tend to satisfy their readers' interest with a limited amount of copy covering security, arms control and defense.[29]

Günther Gaus, a Social Democratic intellectual, criticized press reports on the Geneva disarmament talks in the following terms:

> With few exceptions the coverage of the missile debate by the press as well as radio and TV commentators has become totally lukewarm in terms of ideas and language. Analyses and commentaries by columnists and ordinary journalists alike are composed of stock arguments couched in empty phraseology.[30]

In conclusion it may be said - always with the necessary reserve concerning the use of methodology - that West German press reporting on the arms race and détente is incapable of aiding readers to form a personal critical assessment of the value of military and strategic decisions. This seems to be especially true with regard to biochemical warfare, although, according to the Stockholm Peace Research Institute (SIPRI), the requisite expert information is readily accessible to the readers of science and technology journals. These tentative conclusions need, however, to be empirically reinforced by further studies.[31]

4. Content Analysis and Critical Theory

A critical confrontation with the methodology of content analysis automatically implies confrontation with positivist epistemology in the social sciences. Although this positivist epistemology is deeply rooted in the North American scientific tradition, such confrontation will not be limited to the social sciences in the USA alone. Since North American social research based on science and technology and education and culture transfer attained global importance after 1945, a critique of positivism will likewise imply a critique of the current global concept of empirical social research. Although Marxist communication research has, on the theoretical plane, always disavowed positivism, it nevertheless falls back upon positivism in numerous concrete content analysis studies.

This is not surprising. Although Marxist epistemology is historically rooted in the Enlightenment and in German idealism, whereas its theoretical relevance evolved empirically from the workers' movement, its historical link with French positivism is evident in the works of Karl Marx. The positivist contribution to Marxism is manifest in its understanding of technique and technology, but is further determinable from content analysis. For abrogating reification in Marxist epistemology, theoretical contradiction cannot be excluded when quantitative, i.e., highly reified, methods are employed to this end. This primacy of quantitative methodology is reflected by a bureaucratized world characterized by the mediatization, finalization and formalization of human communication.

Although the phenomena of quantified and bureaucratized capitalist and socialist worlds stem from different sources, all produce reification. The primacy of quantitative methodology in content analysis reveals "one-dimensional thinking" (Herbert Marcuse) and, being only an expression of "instrumental reason" (Max Horkheimer), have either very limited validity or are simply a scientific reflection of reification instead of placing it critically in question.

Once we start to criticize the methodology of content analysis within the limited frame of positivist thinking, we are forced to consider the obviously negligent treatment of semantic aspects, the frequency-counting orientation upon which all methodological analyses are based, and the essentially unresolved problems of reliability and validity. Even if the foregoing demands were met, content analysis would still not come up to the critical standards of sociology based on critical theory.

Positivist methodology in content analysis is marked by a tendency to quantify all social data for the purpose of assessment. Epistemologically it is oriented towards the primacy of quantification in the physical sciences. As explained by John C. McKinney: "We wanted to start measuring social phenomena immediately with all the precision of the physical sciences."[32] Suffering from an inferiority complex for not having as yet attained in the field of the social sciences the objectivity of the physical sciences, content analysis based on critical theory must sooner or later encounter difficulties due to the fact that it overlooks phenomena that should be of interest in all social-scientific epistemology. Or, according to Dallas W. Smythe, content analysis oriented towards the primacy of quantification reveals an "immaturity of science in which objectivity is confused with quantification."[33]

The pursuit of objectivity in empirical social studies is a wild goose chase. Its modified form - the pursuit of "near-objectivity" and reliability - is marked by the same fanciful characteristics. What is needed is an objectivity that yields precise and plausible socio-scientific results, not an objectivity which, due to subjective factors, is already problematic in terms of choosing what to study. Proceeding beyond semantics, a critique of quantitative content analysis is desired because its methodology involves the fragmentation of textual content. As noted by Max Horkheimer:

> The subsumption of similar results in abstract categories causes their primary aspects to be presented in a false light, or even totally obfuscated. Instead of the conditions under which people exist, or the objective function they perform in society, subjective reflections often come to the fore. Without critical reflections about whether the behavior and convictions of individuals have been subsumed or induced by society, empirical social science research [along with quantitative content analysis, J.B.] falls victim to its own results.[34]

Quantitative content analysis thus describes an existing situation instead of placing it in question.[35] Ideology-critical qualitative content analysis based on critical theory takes account of the ambiguity, irrationality and ideological conformity of the studied text.[36] It will apply to the text on the one hand a critical theory capable of identifying a form of society that should be rejected, and on the other existing political and socioeconomic power structures and relationships. Critical analysis methodology also continuously probes initial qualitative data such as purpose, objectives, hypotheses, evidence collection and general theoretical content, and, as has been shown, excludes quantitative analysis due to the inflexibility of category formation and its concept of reliability.

The ideology-critical method stands in contrast to quantitative content analysis. Relying on the integrity of the studied text structure, it seeks the contextual significance of the notions, symbols and arguments used in the text. Ideology critique comprehends text structures as specific expressions of collective social interest, whereby ideology is defined as "historically transparent knowledge unconscious of its dependence".[37] The methodologically constituent comparison between the theoretical knowledge of an object and its concrete presentation should be expressed by comparing the results of peace and disarmament research in the press.

The following qualitative methodologies are available as concrete forms of analysis.[38]

1. *Analysis of social conditions:* Such an analysis should take into account the operating conditions of the mass medium under study, e.g., the press (production and consumption) as well as the subject under study, e.g., détente.
2. *Analysis of the historical context of the subject under study:* Most content analyses, whether quantitative or qualitative, operate without an historical context and disregard the fact that ideas, concepts, opinions, topics and ideologies always have a historico-ideological context that leaves a decisive mark on the present at a pre-communicative level.
3. *Analysis of verbal provocations:* Verbal provocations are pre-communicatively imparted notions whose mere mention in a text will initiate associative communication and a teaching process between the readers and the medium without the affectivity of the notion being immanently clear within the text.
4. *Analysis of the latent content:* Every text explicitly contains only part of what it seeks to express. What the author ideologically considers to be self-evident is omitted.
5. *Deficit analysis:* a) Arguments and conclusions that have been suppressed by the media as well as their causes and functions should be examined as they appear in the connotation of the text structure. b) Information on a specific topic that the media have suppressed should be studied to establish the social relevance of omissions for promoting a given ideology.
6. *Analysis of involuntarily revealed content:* Every text consciously or unconsciously reveals motives that the author would like to suppress. Such mechanisms can be raised to the state of awareness

by psychoanalysis and social psychology (analysis of anxiety, repression, projection, errors, etc.), these being of particular value in the analysis of ideologies.

7. *Analysis of extreme connotation:* According to Theodor W. Adorno it is acceptable that the momentum of recurrence of the eccentric and unusual and things having a certain relevance to the theory should have a key function in the decoding of an entire text.[39]
8. *Analysis of microstructure:* Again according to Adorno it is acceptable that the microanalysis of text structures should reveal things which elude the imprint of generality. Ideologies that are otherwise concealed by conformity with official consciousness become especially apparent in the details of a text.[40]
9. *Analysis of the political in the apolitical:* It must be accepted that the political attitudes of a consumer are formed or reinforced less by manifest political reporting on the part of a print medium than by political stances in entertainment reporting that are imparted in passing or more or less spontaneously. A good example for this phenomenon is a press photograph in the Swedish morning newspaper *Dagens Nyheter* of August 14, 1982. Two beaming Swedish army officers are shown welcoming a French Exocet missile with open arms; the large missile occupies the whole of the foreground of the picture. The bold headline to the photograph reads: "My happiest day!" In this way the picture and the headline cover a completely different event in everyday life, namely a newly fledged father taking his newborn baby from the arms of his wife and proclaiming radiantly: "My happiest day!"[41]

Finally, the following should be noted in the context of a qualitative content analysis, which should, for instance, employ the foregoing nine methodologies. Quantitative analyses here have a different value from that of positivist scientism. Aware of the basically restricted validity of quantitative content analyses, the reduction of textual reality to mathematical connections between numbers there practiced is suitable as a structuring aid for qualitative ideology-critical analysis. Quantitative results cannot present the empirical proof of assertions contained in the text (as positivism would require), but can, however, enhance the precision and plausibility of qualitative analyses.

5. Recommendations

The MacBride report Many Voices, One World presented an impressive conceptual global minimum consensus regarding the future forms and contents of a new international information order. Due to its principal instructions, the report had to leave many questions unanswered and could not develop an all-round concept for democratizing information and communication. Every national press system is subject to exogenous as well as endogenous influences. In numerous developing countries especially, the exogenous influences on the national press system are greater than the endogenous influences, and it is this particular difference that comes out very clearly in the MacBride Report.

To support the 1978 UNESCO Mass Media Declaration, i.e., to work actively for disarmament, endogenous changes are required in all national presses. It is interesting to note in this context that relatively harsh criticism of the press has grown in intensity in the politically most divergent regions of the earth. The three following remarks have been chosen because they do not derive from opposition politicians or regime critics. Representative of the developing countries is the self-criticism of the press in Sudan leveled by Mahjoud Mohammed Salih, a journalist who played an important role in the nationalization of the Sudanese press in 1970:

> Although there are many statements from the government, including the President, about the freedom of the press, as a reader I don't sense this freedom in press criticism. There is a complete lack of initiative. They wait, for instance, until the President attacks the civil service before they become inundated with articles and letters on the subject.[42]

Representative of the socialist countries is the following excerpt from a declaration of May 7, 1979 by the Central Committee of the Communist Party of the Soviet Union:

> Serious negative factors which often substantially degrade the effectivity of educational efforts to influence people's consciousness and feelings are literary formalism, empty phraseology, stock arguments and the mechanical repetition of truisms instead of creative presentation and lively formulation. In place of competent theoretical treatment backed by in-depth analyses and cogent

> reasoning that would enlighten readers, one encounters bombastic language, superficial erudition and pedantry. All these negative factors in our daily work need to be eradicated.[43]

Finally, representative of the capitalist nations, we are able to quote a critical assessment of the press system in the Federal Republic of Germany by Paul Sethe, a West German conservative journalist:

> Freedom of the press is the freedom of two hundred wealthy people to disseminate their opinion. [...] But do people who are of a different opinion have the right to express it? The Constitution grants them this right; economic reality nullifies it. Whoever is wealthy is free. [...] Journalists, not being wealthy, are not free.[44]

If the validity of the foregoing self-critical insights that the press rarely, if at all, comes up to its self-imposed standards is accepted, practical countermeasures should be undertaken. What applies to press coverage of general news applies to an even greater extent to its treatment of the subject of disarmament. In our nuclear era inadequate press reporting on the threat of a nuclear holocaust could have fatal results. As to the problem of how the press should treat news concerning disarmament and the arms race, four scientifically-based conclusions are to be drawn:

1. Research must be intensified, amplified, systematized and coordinated.
2. Content analysis is only scientifically useful when embedded in an analysis of the exogenous and endogenous influences within the existing society.
3. Content analysis is only scientifically useful when embedded in an analysis of the conditions of the media (history, production, consumption) within the existing society.
4. Content analysis is only scientifically useful if the primacy of quantification is abandoned in favor of synthesized quantitative and qualitative methodologies.

Notes and References

1. Hitler, Adolf: "Rede des Führers im Deutschen Reichstag über die deutsche Friedenspolitik am 21. Mai 1935", in: *Deutschlands Weg zur Freiheit*, 1935. 4th edition, ed. by Axel Friedrichs, Berlin 1939 (= Dokumente der Deutschen Politik. Vol. 3). pp. 73-74.
2. Cf. Sreberny-Mohammadi, Annabelle; Nordenstreng, Kaarle; Stevenson, Robert and Ugboajah, Frank: *The World of the News: The News of the World.* A Draft report of the Foreign Images Project undertaken by IAMCR for UNESCO prep. for presentation at the 12th General Assembly and Scientific Conference of the IAMCR in Caracas, August 1980 (mimeo), p. 32.
3. Taheri, Amir: *Noose-Pepper*. A Study of the Persian Press in a Period of Turmoil, London: The International Press Institute 1980, p. 7.
4. Cf. Wadi, A.: "Dorost az mijane-e-goud" (From the Center of the Arena), in: *Iranshahr* (London), Mehr 28, 1357 (= 1978/79), p. 2.
5. Cf. Kalka, Lothar: *Sicherheitspolitik und Öffentlichkeit.* Darstellung und Analyse der Diskussion über die Neutronenbombe in der Tagespresse der Bundesrepublik Deutschland, Tübingen: Institute of Political Science at the University of Tübingen 1982 (mimeo).
6. Ibid., p.82.
7. *Handbuch der Weltpresse*. Vol. 1: Die Pressesysteme der Welt, ed. by Institut für Publizistik der Universität Münster, Cologne and Opladen: Westdeutscher Verlag 1970, p. 501.
8. Cf. Jahn, Egbert and Tiedtke, Jutta: "Politische Strömungen in der sowjetischen Entspannungspolitik", in: *Friedensanalysen* (Frankfurt), No. 9/1979, pp. 50-80.
9. Mertineit, Walter: "Strategies, Concepts and Methods of International History Textbook Revision: A German Share in Education for International Understanding", in: *International Journal of Political Education* (Amsterdam), No. 2/1979, p. 102.
10. Cf. Crome, Peter W.: "Viele japanische Schüler wissen nichts mehr vom Krieg. In Schulbüchern wird der Abwurf der Atombombe auf einer Seite abgehandelt", in: *Frankfurter Rundschau* (Frankfurt), November 19, 1981.
11. Cf. Kuhlmann, Caspar: *Frieden - kein Thema europäischer Schulgeschichtsbücher?*, Frankfurt and Berne: Peter Lang Verlag 1982.
12. Tapio Varis reviews such individual studies in: "Peace and Communication. An Approach by Flow Studies", in: *Journal of Peace Research* (Oslo), Vol. XIX, No. 3/1982, pp. 241-50. A systematic evaluation of the last five years' issues of the following communication science journals by Jörg Becker showed that not a single content analysis of the presentation of war and peace was published in the mass media: *COMBROAD; Communication*

Socialis; Communication Research; Intermedia; Journal of Broadcasting; Journal of Communication; Media, Culture & Society; Media Perspektiven; Medien + Erziehung; Public Opinion Quarterly; Rundfunk und Fernsehen.

13. Cf. Becker, Jörg: "Communication and Peace. The Empirical and Theoretical Relation Between Two Categories in the Social Sciences", in: *Journal of Peace Research* (Oslo), Vol. XIX, No. 3/1983, pp. 227-240.

14. Davison, Phillips: *Mass Communication and Conflict Resolution*, New York 1974, p. 39.

15. Cf. Halloran, James: *Mass media in society*. The need of research, Paris: UNESCO 1974 (= Reports and Papers on Mass Communication), p. 59.

16. Cf. Habermas, Jürgen: *Strukturwandel der Öffentlichkeit*. Untersuchungen zu einer Kategorie der bürgerlichen Gesellschaft, Neuwied & Berlin: Luchterhand Verlag 1962.

17. Cf. in general: Brandt, Gerhard and Friedeburg, Ludwig von: *Aufgaben der Militärpublizistik in der modernen Gesellschaft*, Frankfurt 1966; Bredow, Wilfried von: *Der Primat militärischen Denkens*. Die Bundeswehr und das Problem der okkupierten Öffentlichkeit, Cologne 1969; Mutz, Reinhard: *Sicherheitspolitik und demokratische Öffentlichkeit in der BRD*. Probleme der Analyse, Kritik und Kontrolle militärischer Macht, Munich 1978.

18. Brandt, Gerhard and Friedeburg, Ludwig von: *Aufgaben der Militärpublizistik*, op. cit., p. 136.

19. Ibid., p. 8.

20. Cf. *Inspection for Disarmament*, ed. by S. Melman, New York 1956, pp. 38-43.

21. Cf. Grosser, Alfred et al.: *Die Spiegel-Äffäre*. 2 vols., Olten 1966.

22. Cf. Brandt, Gerhard and Friedeburg, Ludwig von: *Aufgaben der Militärpublizistik*, op. cit.

23. Cf. Bredow, Wilfried von: *Der Primat militärischen Denkens*, op. cit.

24. Cf. Potyka, Christian. "Bundeswehr und Öffentlichkeit. Zur Diskussion gesellschaftspolitisch orientierter Militärfragen in der Presse", in: *Sicherheitspolitik heute*, No. 1/1975, pp. 19-34; Potyka, Christian: "Dimensionen der Sicherheitspolitik in der Öffentlichkeit", in: *Sicherheitspolitik vor neuen Aufgaben*, ed. by Karl Kaiser and Karl Markus Kreis, Bonn 1979 (= Rüstungsbeschränkung und Sicherheit), pp. 353-373.

25. Cf. Guha, Anton-Andreas: "Beispiel 'Grauzone'. Anmerkungen zur Presseberichterstattung über militär- und verteidigungspolitische Fragen", in: *Aufrüsten, um abzurüsten?* Informationen zur Lage, ed. by the Studiengruppe Militärpolitik, Reinbek: Rowohlt Verlag 1980, pp. 94-106.

26. Cf. Wegener, Matthias: *Berichterstattung der "Westdeutschen Allgemeinen Zeitung" (WAZ) und der "Westfalischen Rundschau" (WR) über den "Nachrüstungsbeschluss" der NATO vom 12. Dezember 1979 in Brüssel*

und dessen Folgen. Eine vergleichende Analyse, Dortmund: Institute of Journalism of the University of Dortmund 1982 (mimeo).

27. Cf. Kalka, Lothar: *Sicherheitspolitik und Öffentlichkeit*, op.cit.
28. Cf. Kister, Kurt: *Journalismus und Sicherheitspolitik*, Munich: Institute of Journalism at the University of Munich 1983 (mimeo).
29. Rühl, Lothar: *The Media and the Image of Defence Policy - Europe*. Paper presented at the 24th Annual Conference of the International Institute for Strategic Studies, The Hague, Netherlands, Sept. 9-12, 1982 (mimeo), pp. 6-7.
30. Gaus, Günther: "Wahlkampfrückblick", in: *Konkret* (Hamburg), No. 3/1983, p. 64.
31. Cf. *Technical Aspects of Early Warning and Verification*, ed. by Carl-Göran Heden, Stockholm: Stockholm International Peace Research Institute 1975 (= The Problem of Chemical and Biological Warfare. Vol. VI), p. 25.
32. McKinney, John C.: "Methodology, Procedure and Techniques in Sociology", in: *Modern Sociological Theory in Continuity and Change*, ed. by H. Becker and A. Boskoff, New York 1957, p. 202.
33. Cf. Smythe, Dallas W.: "Some observations on communication theory", in: *Audio-Visual Communication Review*, Vol. 2, No. 1/1954, pp. 248-60.
34. Horkheimer, Max: "Soziologie und empirische Sozialforschung. Auseinandersetzung mit quantitativen Methoden in den USA", in: *Soziologische Exkurse*, ed. by Theodor W. Adorno and Max Horkheimer, Frankfurt 1967, p. 109.
35. Adorno, Theodor W.: "Soziologie und empirische Sozialforschung", in: *Logik der Sozialwissenschaften,* ed. by Ernst Topitsch, Cologne/Berlin 1970, p. 516.
36. Cf. Pollock, Friedrich: *Gruppenexperimente*, Frankfurt 1965, p. 57.
37. Horkheimer, Max: "Ideologie und Handeln", in: *Sociologica II*, ed. by Max Horkheimer and Theodor W. Adorno, Frankfurt 1962, p. 47.
38. Cf. Ritsert, Jürgen: *Inhaltsanalyse und Ideologiekritik.* Ein Versuch über kritische Sozialforschung, Frankfurt 1972; Lissman, Hans-Joachim; Nicklas, Hans and Osterman, Änne: "Empirische Ideologiekritik als Beitrag zur Gesellschaftsanalyse", in: *Friedensanalysen* (Frankfurt), No. 3/1976, pp. 186-96.
39. Cf. Adorno, Theodor W.: *Probleme der qualitativen Analyse*, Frankfurt: Institute for Social Research 1961 (mimeo), p. 13.
40. Cf. ibid., p. 14.
41. Cf. Hasselgren, Kristina: "Språketen fråga om liv eller död", in: *Nya lakttagelser från Journalisthögskolan i Stockholm*, Stockholm, No. 3/1982, pp. 3-5.
42. Quoted in Sir Sidahmed: "The Press: Looking at the Structure", in: *Sudanow* (Khartoum), February 1979, p. 21.
43. Quoted in *Osteuropa-Archiv* (Cologne), November 1979, p. A689.
44. Quoted in *Die Zeitung*, ed. by Hans Schuster and Leo Sillner, Munich and Vienna 1968, p. 52.

3
Publishing for Rural Areas in the Third World

1. Introduction

In her analysis of the image of India in West German children's books, one of the conclusions Indian librarian Shashikala Paranjpe comes to is that such books distort Indian reality. Clichés about Indian myths, sacred cows, golden temples, beggars, fakirs and snakes predominate in such books, which are of great importance in imparting to children a knowledge of foreign countries.[1]

Another ethnological analysis on the same topic shows the majority of West German children's books about India to be latently racist, exhibiting European contempt for the heroes in Indian novels. A close look at the occupations of the persons depicted in these books reveals a pronounced Eurocentric bias. In these novels only Europeans hold status positions - they are development-aid specialists, engineers and teachers - while the Asians are assigned the lowly roles of shoeshine boys and servants.[2]

The findings of such analyses are by no means restricted to the medium of children's books or even to West Germany. Numerous sociological, literary and communication analyses conducted in the United States and various West European countries show that European and North American TV, as well as the print media, normally present a distorted image of the Third World. The treatment of the subject of the Third World is characterized by omissions, misgivings and projections. Reports on natural disasters predominate; conflicts are personalized; the

East-West conflict is transferred to the Third World; cultural arrogance and the total subordination of Third World countries to the "security" (economic interests) of Europe and the USA abound.

Table 3.1:
White Heroes and their Indigenous Companions in West German Children's Books About Asia

Fathers of white heroes		Indigenous companions	
Architect		Farmer (hotel secretary)	
Zoo director		Game warden	
Chemist's assistant		Colleague	
Plantation manager		Plantation hand	
Police commissioner		Tracker	
Veterinarian		Plantation hand	
Engineer		Hotel bellboy	
Female biologist		Farmer (market seller)	
Function of hero's father		**Function of indigenous companion**	
Development-aid specialist	12	Subordinate	10
Tourist	2	Leader	4
Missionary	4	Non-indigenous companion	2
Number of books	18	Number of books	18

Source: Spielmann, Hansjürgen: "Großer weißer Bruder als Geburtshelfer für den armen braunen Helden? Neue Tendenzen im Kinder- und Jugendbuch über Asien", in: *Die Dritte Welt im Kinderbuch 1967-1977*, ed. by Jörg Becker and Rosmarie Rauter, Wiesbaden 1978, p. 124.

It was precisely this cultural distortion which, in the early 1970s, spurred Third World countries to their first efforts to establish a New International Information Order (NIIO) and kindled a discussion that continued through a great many conferences, particularly in the Nonalignment Movement and UNESCO. Parallel to these political conferences, communications research also devoted particular attention to the role of mass media in the North-South conflict. While transborder border data flow and satellite technologies were still in the initial phase of development in the sphere of new IT, including microelectronics, the numerous findings of research relating to the earlier media such as the press, news agencies, TV and radio broadcasting are sufficiently consistent as to allow valid generalized conclusions to be drawn from these sources.

First, since international information systems run parallel to North-South economic dependences, the problem of the cultural and information sovereignty of Third World countries is very closely linked with their economic sovereignty. The two problems can only be solved jointly.

Second, the US-American media are definitely dominant in international information systems with respect to both hardware and software. The more modern the media the greater the US-American dominance.

Third, the analysis of international information systems in particular reveals that their participants are more frequently transnational media corporations than sovereign states. These transnational media corporations neutralize practically all UNESCO agreements because the latter were concluded by sovereign states incapable of influencing the scope of activity of transnational corporations. It is clear from the problem presented by these corporations that the questionable nature of present international information systems is by no means confined to the North-South context. As is revealed not only by the Canadian parliamentary debates, government reports and administrative regulations safeguarding the Canadian market from penetration by US-American commercial TV, but also by the French Nor/Minc report on the computerization of society and the consequently growing dependence of Western Europe upon IBM computer technology,[3] alongside the North-South conflict, a global conflict exists between capital-intensive metropolises and under-capitalized peripheral territories.

Fourth, the media penetration of the Third World is proceeding through a system of media linkage through press agencies as well as radio and TV broadcasting corporations.

Fifth, West European-oriented media fail to satisfy the needs of the peoples of the Third World. The Third World's mass media have often developed as economic byproducts of the industrial nations, not in a more or less natural and spontaneous process as part of their self-guided development. Neither in form nor in content do the products of the Western mass media satisfy the needs of Third World peoples. Western notions of what a leading article, feature film or TV program should be like are far removed from what is expected by the peoples of the Third World.

This situation resulted in the 20th General Conference of UNESCO in Paris in November 1978 issuing what came to be known as the Paris Mass Media Declaration of November 1978. Comparison of the text of this declaration with the expectations of the Third World countries set forth in the 1973 conference documents of the Nonalignment Movement in Algiers shows the Third World countries to have failed to induce the

UNESCO to back their principal demands. This is likewise particularly evident from a comparison of the final draft of the declaration with the earlier draft by UNESCO Director-General Amadou-Mahtar M'Bow. The M'Bow draft contained the following points:

In *Article I* the original demand for the "free flow of information", which obscures the actual one-sided situation, is reformulated to read "free, reciprocal and balanced flow of accurate, complete and objective information".
Article II demands "public participation in the evaluation of information".
Article VI demands a "new balance and greater reciprocity in the exchange of information" and the need "to correct quantitative and qualitative imbalance in the flow of information to and from developing countries".
Article XI makes member states responsible for enforcing the implementation of this declaration.

In the final declaration, however, the responsibility for Third World mass media called for by all major theorists and Third World leaders for over thirty years (Mahatma Gandhi, Jawaharlal Nehru, Ahmed Sukarno, Kwame Nkrumah, Julius Nyrere or Salvador Allende) was annulled along with the demand for the "free, reciprocal and balanced exchange of information" and "public participation in the evaluation of information".

In *Article VI* the demand for association with the New International Economic Order (NIEO) and the New International Information Order (NIIO) was likewise annulled. Efforts to modify the structure of international information systems are reduced in par. 16 to "aspirations of the developing countries for establishing a new, more just and more effective world information and communication order"; the earlier reference to the factual existence of global imbalances was deleted.

In this context it is hardly a coincidence that the peasant population is "overlooked", for the majority of government officials and theoreticians attending international conferences are urbanites. In the industrial nations as well as the Third World countries the urban elites, having all too frequently lost touch with the rural population, tend to approach problems bureaucratically from on high and devote too little attention to the communication needs of the majority of the world's people.

According to United Nations statistics, the rural population of industrial nations (370 million) is 32.6 percent, while that of Third World countries (2,070 million) is 72.5 percent. Altogether 61.3 percent of the world's population live in rural areas.

New development theory has shown in numerous analyses that the development policy advocated hitherto, namely a forced pace of industrialization for Third World countries, will not help them in their struggle to satisfy their basic needs. Whereas "technological progress" in the urban areas of the Third World was at one time expected to gradually trickle down to the agricultural villages, it is now known that this does not occur. On the contrary, urbanization increases the disparity between urban and rural populations, leading to the uprooting and subsequent marginalization of villagers. The course of development in Third World countries is inconsistent with both dogmatic Marxist and capitalist development theories, each of which follows a one-dimensional evolutionary and technology oriented concept:

Third World agricultural produce is often exported to earn foreign currency for importing Western consumer goods and technology for the urban population in the Third World. In many countries where this is practiced agriculture has tended to decline even to the point where it is no longer capable of feeding the native population. Tied in this way to the contingencies of the world market as a result of abandoning the economic laws of the Third World, such countries soon find themselves in grievous situations - like Iran after the "Green Revolution" - of having to import grain from industrial nations although they had hitherto been well able to feed themselves. It follows from this that agriculture must always be accorded top priority in future development efforts in Third World countries. Only by assigning agriculture a higher place in the macro-economic structure of a Third World country and orienting it towards autonomy, which in some cases could even render it independent of the world market, can conditions be realized that will open the way to genuine autonomy and sovereignty in the Third World.

2. The Book as A Mass Medium and the NIIO

There were various reasons why books were overlooked as a mass medium in UNESCO debates on a New International Information Order (NIIO). One was that books, as one of the oldest mass media, are, compared to electronic media, more dependent upon the private economic sector.

Since the public is less aware of the social, pedagogical and political functions of this medium, no-one in publishing is interested in participating in a global discussion of this particular medium. Another reason is that, on the one hand, public fascination with new information technologies is undoubtedly greater and, on the other, the national sovereignty and cultural identity of Third World countries is less threatened by print media than by communication satellites and transborder data flow.

Last but not least, a broadly overlooked reason is that, since various branches of UNESCO are responsible for both mass media and print media, a coordinated political policy for integrating books into UNESCO's overall media policy has never been developed. This lack of integration is clearly apparent in the approx. 300-page MacBride Report, where only a few scattered pages are devoted to the print medium. The problems arising from the print medium are essentially similar to those encountered with other mass media in the North-South conflict. For a start, a glance at the worldwide regional differences in book production reveals the same imbalances as in other mass media.

The impediments to the free flow of books described by O.P. Ghai in his paper[4] presented at the Seminar on Educational Publishing in Developing Countries in New Delhi in February 1978 correspond in principle to those that impede a really free flow of TV news :

1. Taxes,
2. Tariffs,
3. Exchange control, licensing, scarcity of foreign currency, export restrictions,
4. Internal transportation charges,
5. Air freight charges,
6. The very high prices of books in industrial nations,
7. The restrictive trade practices of multinational book companies,
8. Copyright difficulties,
9. Double taxation of royalties,
10. Last but not least, readers are restricted in their freedom of choice of reading material.

Thus there are cogent reasons for including the book medium in NIIO debates. As reported by the Belgian communication researcher Armand Mattelart, North American electronics and telephone corporations are buying up the software branch of book publishing on an ever greater scale.

The media-multi Radio Corporation of America (RCA), for instance, has taken over Random House, Alfred Knopf, Pantheon Books, Vintage Books, Ballantine Books, Grove Press and Wildwood House; the International Telephone and Telegraph Corporation (ITT) has taken over Bobbs-Merrill and Howard Sams and other publishing houses.[5] In the future it will be increasingly difficult to distinguish between the traditional book medium and other mass media because the international regulations governing the various media are steadily becoming more and more alike.

While O. P. Ghai's list of impediments to a really free exchange of books is perhaps somewhat too technocratic, from a pragmatic viewpoint it nevertheless makes sense to enumerate the everyday problems of publishers in the Third World. From a more structural viewpoint it is possible to characterize the situation of the international book trade as follows:

1. The flow of books between the northern and southern hemispheres is marked by an extreme imbalance. While, for example, in 1979, the Federal Republic of Germany exported to Africa (mainly Algeria and South Africa) books to the value of approx. DM 8 million, in return, it imported from Africa books to the value of only approx. DM 200,000, the majority of these imported books presumably being products of the "Africanized" offsprings of publishing multis. There is a 40:1 imbalance between the books exported by a single European country to approx. 40 African states and the books imported in return from those states. Translation statistics likewise manifest this imbalance. While the African book market is always virtually swamped with European books, throughout 1979 the German book market had not a single book to offer that had been translated from an African language.

   According to the annual statistical analysis Buch und Buchhandel in Zahlen (Books and the Book Trade in Figures) published by the Börsenverein des Deutschen Buchhandels (Association of the German Book Trade) books in only five African languages - Old Ethiopian, Amharic, Ndonga (Angola), Coptic and Afrikaans - had been translated. Of these, the majority were religious tractates in Old Ethiopian. Coptic and Amharic, while Afrikaans has almost nothing to do with Black African literature. No books written in any of the black African languages in current use (Swahili, Kikuyu, Hausa, Duala, Wolof, Yoruba) have been translated, nor has any of the rich oral literature in black languages.

2. The Third World book market is marked by typical metropolis/ periphery distribution patterns. Spain still dominates most of the Latin American book market. In 1973 the former Italian colony of Ethiopia still imported approx. 20 percent of its books from Italy. Liberia, originally founded by African Americans, still imports over half of its books from the USA The former British colony of Kenya imports 80 percent of its books from England. Francophone Black Africa is virtually a book colony of the Hachette publishing empire. Needless to say, no direct commercial relations exist between the book trade of the former French colony of Cameroon and its counterpart in neighboring Nigeria, a former British colony. Indirect relationships between peripheral markets only exist at metropolitan trading centers such as the annual Frankfurt Book Fair.

3. Extremely imbalanced access to capital, technology, know-how, education and resources forces the book trade of developing countries into political and economic dependence upon the industrial nations as is demonstrated by the following example: Whereas a Scandinavian household receives gratis more than 200 pages of unsolicited advertising material in four-color print every two weeks, Africa failed in 1980 to produce 120 pages per household per annum. Black Africa's few paper mills, low in efficiency because technologically outdated, are ill-equipped to meet existing needs. Africa has become the cat's-paw of a small group of North American and Scandinavian papermaking and pulp multis.

4. Book multis possess great advantages over indigenous publishers in the Third World that the latter have no chance of competing with them with any hope of success. The advantages of these multis are:
   - access to more capital,
   - outsourcing of printing work to low-wage countries,
   - editions in the same language for more than one country,
   - access to the latest and lowest-priced print technology,
   - higher royalties for authors,
   - highly lucrative exploitation of subsidiary rights in the media of industrial nations (e.g., in bestseller business in the USA),
   - subsidiary rights are more profitable than original rights.

5. Existing copyright laws serve the same function in the international book market as patents, licenses and standards in the international

information industry. They have legal force and are instrumental in perpetuating the structural imbalance between the Northern and Southern hemispheres. The existing copyright system in particular prevents the specialized textbooks of industrial nations from being adapted to Third World requirements flexibly, rapidly and at a low-cost. Manuel Valdehuesa, Director of the Philippine Book Fair, sees existing copyright laws as an instrument employed by Western industrial nations to control the book markets of the Third World.[6] His Philippine colleague Louie O. Reyes recently demonstrated in a statement addressed to the World Intellectual Property Organization in Geneva in March 1983 that the Western copyright system possesses a basic advantage over that of the Third World:

> During the London Conference on Books, the question of piracy was also discussed. Unfortunately emphasis was again placed on authors' rights rather than users' needs. One of the most serious impediments to the wide dissemination of good books is the exorbitant price tag the western world places on intellectual property - its overemphasis upon authors' rights over and above users' needs and interests. [...] I would appeal to one and all to have the courage to open the way to the sharing of intellectual property. In conclusion, let me pose a single question: Would you charge a starving man US$10,000 for a loaf of bread if you well knew he could only afford US$ 1,000? Is the difference of US$ 9,000 sufficiently important to withhold from that man a source of knowledge?[7]

3. Some Conclusions for "Publishing for Rural Areas"

In the limited research on the book medium presented in the NIIO debates,[8] political and economic dependences were discussed on an international level without any reference to books for Third World rural areas. The numerous research studies and project evaluations of "rural communication in Third World countries" undertaken over the past 20 years only occasionally consider the book medium. It must be concluded that most media projects for rural areas, as evaluated in terms of their objectives, failed. Factors contributing to these failures were the urban background of project managers, which led them to inflict upon farmers procedures evolved for an urban public; they were also ignorant of the sociopolitical and religious conditions in villages. Such projects were bound to fail not only because the modernization ideology mentioned earlier did not appeal to farmers, but in particular because the projects were steered from outside with farmers being assigned the roles of passive consumers and not active participants in the communication process.

The majority of farmers were hostile to such media projects, which were only acceptable to people already partially alienated from their rural culture. In other words, the already knowledgeable became more knowledgeable, while the ignorant remained ignorant. In their extensive study on the "Diffusion of Innovations in Brazil, Nigeria and India" Everett M. Rogers et al. found that the farmers most receptive to "modernization" are those who are in close contact with an agricultural adviser, have access to the mass media, often go to town and can afford a higher standard of living than other villagers.[9] Whereas Rogers et al. conclude from this that future media projects should be especially directed at these sophisticated types, the reverse appears to be the case if one desires to preserve the unity of rural culture rather than treat it merely as an appendix to urban civilization. This requires a redefinition of the concept of development such as that suggested, for example, by Julius Nyerere:

> Man can only liberate himself. He cannot be liberated or developed by another. For Man makes himself. It is his ability to act deliberately, for a self-determined purpose, which distinguishes him from animals. The expansion of his own consciousness, and therefore of his power over himself, his environment, and his society, must therefore ultimately be what we mean by development. So development is for Man, by Man and of Man.[10]

Therefor the mass media can only function successfully in the Third World's villages if accepted by the farmers, who must be actively involved in decision-making concerning the introduction of the mass media, must participate in production and distribution, and all share access to the mass media. This in turn requires that villages should be conceded a certain political autonomy such as once demanded by Mahatma Gandhi:

> My idea of village Swaraj is that it is a complete republic independent of its neighbors for its vital wants and yet interdependent for many things in which dependence is necessary. Thus every village's first concern will be to grow its own food and produce its own cloth. [...]

> The village will maintain its theatre, school and public hall. It will have its own waterworks. [...] As far as possible every activity will be conducted on a cooperative basis.[11]

This self-reliance concept, which is also based on mother-tongue education, cultural identity and decentralization, makes the interests of farmers and their active participation the focal point of all considerations concerning rural communication with the media. On this basis the following points should be taken into account.

Traditional Media

H. K. Ranganath[12] emphasizes that traditional media such as dancing, drama, music, puppetry and so forth are far more readily accepted by farmers than mass media imported from the West such as TV films, the press and books. Hence it appears that rural communication is meaningful only in so far as traditional media remain tolerated and are even promoted. How effective and appropriate such an approach can be may be judged from the case of the Kenyan author Ngugi wa Thiong'o. When he staged the play "Ngaahika Nideenda" together with Ngugi wa Mirii it represented for him a definite rupture with his past. Whereas he had hitherto used English, he now wrote in his Kikuyu mother tongue. Formerly he had used the novel as his favorite literary vehicle, but now he switched to the theater, which comes closer to the Kikuyu tradition. One-way communication between author and reader is here replaced by active theater audience participation as introduced by Bertolt Brecht. It may be the combination of these three factors which on the one hand contributed to Ngugi wa Thiong'o's popularity with his fellow countrymen and on the other caused him serious political difficulties with the leadership of his country.

Illiteracy

The campaign against illiteracy initiated after World War II has remained relatively ineffective. The success of later campaigns in Nicaragua, Ethiopia and Guinea-Bissau is still dubious. Only in the USSR, Cuba and in parts of Tanzania have literacy campaigns met with success. It was the objective of UNESCO's Experimental World Literacy Programs to teach a million people to read and write. Yet only 120,000 persons completed a literacy program and a great many of these sank back into illiteracy after only three years. Research seems to have come to the conclusion that the effectiveness of conventional literacy programs is limited. It is interesting to note that a few governments have seriously attempted to launch literacy programs, possibly because they fear that literacy might open the way to politicization and thereby disrupt their power basis. Rather than promoting literacy as a basis for education, the teaching of social skills would seem to be more practical for improving the social system. Mahatma Gandhi clearly defined the problem of literacy versus illiteracy as follows:

> Indian villagers were, perhaps, illiterate, but they are not ignorant regarding the problems of life, whether social, medical, economic or moral, and they possessed much useful knowledge concerning them. Though they might not know how to express this knowledge through a written symbol, they were not ignorant or uncultured. [...] During the past century, education became more widespread. But it was unrelated to life, given as it was through the medium of either the spoken or written word. It made the student diffident and ignorant about the actual problems of life.[13]

The failure of literacy programs is largely due to the fact that they were not oriented towards the social situation of their participants. Further factors of their failure were the urban cultural background of the project supervisors, whose condescending attitudes alienated the villagers; the urban orientation of the texts used, the project supervisors' ignorance of the sociopolitical and religious conditions in villages; and, worst of all, the misuse of literacy campaigns to propound the ideal of modernization. Peasants in developing countries tend to shun literacy programs because they are imposed upon their communities from above and assign them a purely passive role in the learning process. The success of literacy campaigns is dubious. On the one hand literacy and literature are internalized as symbols of progress, while on the other literacy remains without any significant function within the peasant environment. This lack of function was clearly demonstrated by a team of psychologists in their study of the psychosocial conflicts of the Dogons in West Africa. According to this study, Dogon males who remain in their village make no use of the school knowledge they have acquired and do not even read newspapers.

> Schooling is used only for lack of an alternative and especially when there is a need to prove one's self-respect. The few women who have

been to school tend to completely play down their acquired knowledge. A knowledge of French undermines their identity as women. If they speak French they feel themselves isolated from their female peers.[14]

The uselessness of literacy for many Dogons is evident from the following observation. When villagers seek to entice a fellow villager to their home "their intention will often be to enhance his social status, offer him a wife (yabiru) or build him a house. Europeans would invite him by letter. To write a letter of invitation would never occur even to literate Dogons".[15] Most peasants have no use for literacy - and this is true of some 80 percent of the entire population of Africa - and the failure of literacy campaigns has little to do with backsliders, i.e., former program participants who have fallen back into illiteracy. In rural areas of the Third World, where oral communication is still the norm, print literature and books are rarely in evidence. The emancipation potential inherent in literacy programs is not of the kind that could be exploited to develop political power. The ability to read legal texts is no guarantee that the reader will understand them. No direct link exists between literacy and liberation. The ability to write is no guarantee for freedom of expression.

Development policy for rural areas should therefore not rely too much on books and the press. In Tanzania, for instance, there are many projects for broadcasting orature - oral literature - over the radio. Any concept for "basic education" will nevertheless require the use of books, magazines, newspapers, posters and other printed matter that will serve the immediate needs of the peasants. Non-formal education could be organized in line with Paulo Freire's concept of *conscientizaçao*. The idea of social teaching is also growing in importance in West Germany. Since cognitive teaching, i.e., formal literacy promotion in the broadest sense, is unrelated to the everyday life and interests of pupils, it fails to equip them to play an active role in society and may consequently be thrown overboard as a source of "political illiteracy".

Decentralization

Concepts for decentralization are in themselves no guarantee or warrant for participative democracy. The democratization of society depends upon a flexible compatibility between centralization and decentralization. As book publishing in developing countries is still largely centralized, however, efforts in the direction of decentralization are greatly needed. A minor example of decentralization is the organization of the Philippine Book Fair. In contrast to Book Fairs in Mexico City or Cairo, the Philippine Book Fair is not confined to the nation's capital. After opening in Manila, the Book Fair moves on to Cebu City and from there to the island of Mindanao. As a traveling exhibition, the Philippine Book Fair is able, by motivating authors, publishers, printers and booksellers, to spread its public relations work throughout the land.

Appropriate Technology

Since the dissemination of ideology by the media cannot bring about any real advance in social development but only a change in human attitudes, it is essential to give villagers the chance to participate in media projects. The media that immediately come to mind in this context are print media and the tape recorder. Both technologies are nowadays relatively cheap, easy to operate, useful in many ways and decentralized. For this reason appropriate attention should be devoted to printing and publishing in Third World rural areas.

Hardware and Software

A survey of media projects that have been in progress for many years in Third World countries shows that considerably more interest is devoted to the technology used, their organization and formal aspects than to the content of their programs. This is due in part to the empirically unattested belief that teaching with electronic media is more effective than with print media or by personal instruction. The priority of technology over content is also due to the former's political clout being far greater than that of publishers, authors, journalists and teachers. One may be skeptical for a number of reasons of the various satellite TV projects planned for Third World rural areas, but it is realistically foreseeable that a great many experiments of this type are to be expected in the coming decade which will open up an important new field of operation for rural publishing. Satellite TV appears pedagogically meaningful only in a media-mix in which TV is combined with various print media. Only in this way can satellite TV be successfully used for villages that differ greatly from one another.

4. Conclusion

It is impossible to generalize on the potential role of the book as a medium in Third World rural areas because given conditions are too complex and varied. The role of the book in literacy programs was earlier overrated in the blind pursuit of modernization. As a medium for teaching in a social environment, however, print media produced in decentralized printing plants have a major social function. Publishing for rural areas would appear to be meaningful only if it happens in rural areas and together with a peasant population. If an NIIO policy were realized in purely formal terms, i.e., if nothing more were demanded than for all people to share equal access to the mass media both now and in the future, this would enable the currently dominant Western mass media to penetrate the remotest parts of the globe. It is, however, feasible to redefine the policy of an NIIO to secure the active involvement of all the people in media production in the sense of a participatory democracy.

Notes and References

1. Voegeli-Paranjpe, Shashikala: "Das Indienbild in westdeutschen Kinder- und Jugendbüchern", in: *Die Menschen sind arm, weil sie arm sind.* Die Dritte Welt im Spiegel von Kinder- und Jugendbüchern, ed. by Jörg Becker and Charlotte Oberfeld, Frankfurt: Haag & Herchen 1977 (= Studien zur Kinder- und Jugendmedien-Forschung. Vol. 1), pp. 197-237.
2. Spielmann, Hansjürgen: "Großer weißer Bruder als Geburtshelfer für den armen braunen Helden? Neue Tendenzen im Kinder- und Jugendbuch über Asien", in: *Die Dritte Welt im Kinderbuch*, ed. by Jörg Becker and Rosmarie Rauter, Wiesbaden: Akademische Verlagsgesellschaft 1978, pp. 110-136.
3. Cf. Nora, Simon and Minc, Alain: *L'Informatisation de la Société*, Paris: Edition Seuil 1978.
4. Ghai, O. P.: *Imports & Exports Including Free and Balanced Flow of Educational Material.* Paper presented at the Seminar on Educational Publishing in Developing Countries by the National Book Trust, India, Feb. 12-15, 1978, p. 6.
5. Mattelart, Armand: *Multinational Corporations and the Control of Culture.* The Ideological Apparatuses of Imperialism, Brighton, Sussex: Harvester Press and Atlantic Highlands: Humanities Press 1979, pp. 128.

6. Valdehuesa, Manuel E.: "Copyright and Piracy at the 21st IPA Congress", in: *Asian Book Development Newsletter*, No. 2/1980, p. 9-12.
7. Reyes, Louie O.: *Statement at the Worldwide Forum on the Piracy of Broadcasts and of the Printed Word by the World Intellectual Property Organization*, Geneva, Switzerland, March 16-18, 1983 (PF/II/S/12), pp. 2 and 6.
8. Cf. especially Altbach, Philip G.: "Publishing in developing countries", in: *International Social Science Journal*, No. 3/1974, pp. 458-73; *Perspectives on Publishing*, ed. by Philip G. Altbach and Sheila McVey, Toronto and London: Lexington Books 1976; Smith, Keith: *The Impact of Transnational Book Publishing on Intellectual Knowledge in Less Developed Countries*, Paris: UNESCO, Division for the Study of Development 1977 (= Studies TNC. 3); *Publishing in the Third World*, ed. by Philip G. Altbach and Keith Smith, in: *Library Trends*, Spring 1978, pp. 449-599.
9. Cf. Rogers, Everett M.; Ascroft, Joseph R. and Rölling, Niels G.: *Diffusion of Innovations in Brazil, Nigeria and India*, East Lansing, Michigan: Michigan State University, Department of Communication 1970 (= Diffusion of Innovations Research Report 24).
10. Nyerere, Julius: "Liberated Man - The Purpose of Development", in: *Convergence*, 9:4, p.10.
11. Quoted from Kripalani, J. B.: "Was Gandhi a Traditionalist?", in: *Harijan*, September 9, 1950, p. 234.
12. Ranganath, H. K.: *Not a thing of the past: Functional and Cultural Status of Traditional Media in India*, Paris: UNESCO (= International Commission for the Study of Communication Problems. Document No. 92) n.d.
13. Quoted fromy Solanki, A. B.: *The Technique of Correlation in Basic Education*, Ahmedabad 1958, p. 48.
14. Parin, Paul; Morgenthaler, Fritz and Parin-Mattèy, Goldy: *Die Weißen denken zuviel*. Psychoanalytische Untersuchungen in Westafrika, Munich: Kindler n.d., p. 450.
15. Ibid., pp. 451.

4
Cultural Paper and the Third World

The saying that fish cannot swim without water may be taken as a parallel to the situation of the print media, which cannot produce books, newspapers, magazines, comics, etc. without paper as its principal raw material. While fish can swim as long as there is water, the mere existence of water does not reveal how many fish it can accommodate, the direction in which they can swim or for how long they can be expected to survive. The general lack of interest by Western media analysts in paper as a raw material for the print media reveals an intellectual bias which causes them to take a far greater interest in the content of information disseminated by the print media than in the economic, technological and political conditions under which this content is printed and distributed to consumers.[1]

If the mass media are categorized according to the basic production techniques employed by the print media on the one hand and by the electronic media on the other, then paper, as raw material for the print media, may be equated with the radio frequencies that similarly serve as raw material for the electronic media.

Paper, a product of fossil energy resources, shares the common characteristic of radio frequencies that neither the fossil energy resources nor the number of usable radio frequencies can be increased beyond what is given by nature. One result of the worldwide energy crisis that set in during the early 1970s was that the supply of paper used as raw material by the print media became as sparse as the other raw materials of limited resources required by other branches of industry. It is suggested below that discussion of the political aspects of the international print media book medium (political bias, literacy campaigns, free exchange of information) should take account of international competition for the acquisition of paper for the print media, which has come to be defined as cultural paper.

All discussion concerning international competition for the acquisition of raw materials is nowadays conducted within a multifactorial frame. The problem of the distribution of cultural paper among various nations and groups needs to be considered. Since economic, political, technological, ecological and social causes and effects must likewise be considered, monocausal diagnosis and treatment will lead nowhere. Unlike debates on minerals and other raw materials, any debate on the distribution of cultural paper has additionally to take account of both economic and ideological factors as the crucial points around which the entire debate revolves. As far as print media are concerned, the democratic right to disseminate and receive socially relevant information is directly related to the type and quantity of cultural paper distributed to chosen nations and social groups.

The Third World, and black Africa in particular, is greatly handicapped with regard to the supply of cultural paper. Statistics covering the supply of cultural paper to Third World countries show the latter to suffer from more serious drawbacks than industrial nations. This situation is only understandable within the context of a broader international analysis, for it can only be basically improved through the instrumentality of the NIEO (New International Economic Order) or the NIIO (New International Information Order). To assure the equal and just distribution of cultural paper among all nations and groups, certain fringe "democratic" requirements must be met.

1. Global Aspects: The Triangle of Economics, Politics and Ecology

In his 1979 essay "Teaching about the Third World and its Development Problems", Upper Volta's distinguished social scientist Joseph Ki-Zerbo recorded the following observation:

> What can be in the interest of the masses? Surely the gratifying of basic needs. This is fundamental to all development concepts. One should take care, however, not to reduce basic needs to the absolute

> minimum necessary to stay alive. That basic human rights like freedom of opinion are among these needs does not, however, mean that basic human rights should necessarily be defined according to western concepts of law and morality. [...] This leads me to a further principal characteristic of development: cultural identity.[2]

If one concurs with such conclusions it is clear that the search for identity and the establishment of communication must be included as essential elements of a "basic needs" strategy. To avoid all possibilities of misunderstandings, it must be stressed that there can be no abstract "basic need" for books, TV sets, microchips, but only for what can properly gratify the now relatively long-established need for communication. In this qualified sense, cultural paper constitutes a basic need for numerous Third World countries and certain regions thereof. The current paper shortage in the Third World opens the way for its domestic markets to be flooded with foreign books, engenders conflicts of identity, degrades the educational system, reduces the plurality of standpoints in press opinion, encourages political censorship and imposes a strain upon the foreign trade balance. The grounds for the paper shortage in the Third World are manifold. In essence they are the result of global influences upon the paper market. The following five principal factors will be outlined below.

Trend in Energy Costs

From 1973 to 1980 the world pulp and paper industries were burdened by the upward trend in energy costs, especially for oil and related products. The production of pulp, and especially of paper, consumes an enormous quantity of energy. To produce 6.8 million tons of paper and cardboard in West Germany in 1978 approx. 400,000 tons of black coal, 300,000 tons of brown coal and 1.6 million tons of fuel oil were required. The same quantity of fuel oil could have heated 2,000 private apartments for a whole year.

According to a World Bank study, pulp and paper production are among the most intensive energy-consuming branches of industry[3]; their energy costs ranging between 15 and 50 percent of the total cost per production unit. Although the paper sector is actually less energy-intensive than, for example, the metal-producing and working industries, an average of between 1 and 2 tons of black coal or 0.7 to 1.4 tons of natural gas are nevertheless still required to produce one ton of paper.

The Third World needs above all to drastically reduce its consumption of energy. A further Third World study undertaken by the World Bank predicts that smaller paper mills would save up to 11 percent and larger ones between 12 and 15 percent in energy costs.[4] Smaller mills could save energy through better insulation and heat exploitation. Larger plants could make more efficient use of their waste heat, introduce minor modifications in their production process, and use more energy-efficient mills.

Trend in Paper Prices

The price trend for paper as the final product is closely but not exclusively influenced by the trend in energy costs, which is still more important for pulp as the intermediate product. In 1972-73 all forms of pulp experienced a considerable price increase, while the rise between 1973 and 1975 was almost 70 percent. According to the German Federal Bureau of Statistics the price for wood pulp showed the highest increase among all kindred products such as sulfite pulp, sulfate pulp, kraft pulp and newsprint.

Even the lowest price in 1980 was at least 25 percent above the level of 1970. World market price increases give only a very rough idea of the effective costs for buyers and consumers in a Third World country because they fail to include factors such as freight costs, national customs-and-excise rates, national regulations governing distribution and finally the traditional black market prices for products in short supply. Whereas in the late 1960s one ton of newsprint cost US$ 200 in New York, in South-East Asia it cost US$ 300, while spot prices ranged between US$ 500 and 600. Or, to take another example: whereas in 1981 the Paper Industry Corporation of the Philippines bought newsprint at US$ 550 per ton, it retailed it to newspaper publishers at about US$ 900 per ton.

A further study of the price trend in Third World export goods and that of paper or pulp imported from Western industrial nations shows that any drop in the prices of copper, jute, iron ore, raw rubber and tea reduced the amount of foreign currency that many Third World countries were able to spend on importing paper. Third World countries that want to continue importing pulp from Western industrial nations are forced to pay higher and higher prices. Whereas in India the need for foreign currency for importing paper quadrupled between 1972 and 1976, in Costa Rica it rose during 1979 from US$ 55 million to US$ 66 million.

Concentration in the Paper Industry

The pulp and paper products market is controlled for the most part by Western industrial nations. First and foremost among these is the dual economic system of North America (USA and Canada), Finland, Sweden and, to a certain extent, Japan, which controls more than 80 to 85 percent of the world market for end products in the pulp and paper industry. Diverse antitrust court proceedings against the paper industry are among the many indications of the extraordinarily high degree of concentration in this branch of industry.

Due to a regional concentration in Scandinavia and the USA, the turnover of the hundred largest paper producers in the non-socialist world doubled over the period from 1975 to 1980, pulp production increasing by 50 percent and paper and cardboard by 40 percent. Whereas in 1975 these hundred multis controlled about 46 percent of the world production of paper and cardboard, by 1980 their share had increased to approximately 51 percent, representing about 70 percent of the pulp market. The degree of concentration of pulp production, which exceeds that of paper and cardboard, increased many times over. A few select corporations have a worldwide monopoly on producing and marketing certain end products.

Although Third World countries have never at any time produced more than six percent of all chemical pulp, the Philippines, the People's Republic of China, South Korea, India and Brazil have succeeded in increasing their production considerably in recent years. Whether such economic growth actually benefited the Third World and its populations in general is doubtful. The principal beneficiaries were North American and Scandinavian pulp producers, who had provided chosen Third World countries with capital, technology, know-how and advisors for building up and operating a paper industry.

The recently built CELLUC AM paper mill in Edea, Cameroon, represents, for instance, a model case of technology transfer that Ignacy Sachs defines as pseudo-transfer.[5] Although more than 50 percent of CELLUC AM shares are owned by the Cameroon state, a Swedish paper producer only minimally involved financially in CELLUC AM controls the export rights on all the paper produced.. In this way transnational paper corporations exercise considerable influence over the marketing and worldwide distribution of pulp produced in the Third World. Although individual cases of economic growth are on record, it is hardly possible to claim the existence of Third World paper or pulp production.

Wood Resources in Industrial Nations

Expenditure for wood forms the largest single cost item in the production of paper and pulp. Wood accounts for about 33.3 percent of overall production costs, which range from 50 percent in Sweden to 25 percent in Brazil. Global afforestation efforts naturally have an aftereffect upon the price calculations of paper products.

Since approx. 80 percent of the world's pulp is currently produced in Western industrial nations, the ongoing deforestation in the Third World has only subsidiary effects upon world paper prices, particularly as the paper industry's share in the destruction of tropical rain forests should not be overestimated. It is therefore of greater interest to take a glance at the ecological stability of Northern hemisphere forest areas. It is notable that nearly all the major global models proposed in recent years - from the Club of Rome to Global 2000 - take the stability of these forests for granted.

This assumption, however, is quite unjustified in view of the enormous damage caused to forests in North America and Europe by acid rain. Despite the difficulty of determining all the deleterious effects of acid rain, the following approximations are nevertheless significant. OECD estimates that approx. 3 to 5 percent of the gross national product are required for the "repair" of dying forests. In the USA from 6 to 35 billion US$ are needed to redress the damage caused by acid rain, while an additional 2 to 12 billion US$ are needed to enable power stations to convert their existing plants. The influence of deforestation due to acid rain on global paper prices is currently difficult to determine because a variety of factors have to be taken into account. The trade journal *Das Papier Magazin* notes the following effects of acid rain :

> For technological reasons only green wood is used in the production of wood pulp. We obtain this as what is known as inferior wood when forests have to be thinned out to encourage the healthy growth of valuable hard timber. If young trees become diseased, our supply of green wood is endangered, for we are unable to use trees that are diseased beyond a certain extent.[6]

This situation has the following consequences for the Third World. Damage caused to forests by acid rain as well as increased expenditure for prophylactic measures will cause a worldwide rise in paper prices with serious economic consequences for the Third World. Only recently West

Germany's largest forest owner, Johannes von Thurn und Taxis, predicted that the rising price of wood from Northern hemisphere forests will lead to the increasing destruction of tropical rain forests in the Third World.

Future Market Trends in Industrial Nations

The global consumption of cultural paper reveals the gap between the Third World and industrial nations that also exists in other spheres. While Western industrial nations have a superabundance of cultural paper, Third World and various East European countries suffer from a shortage of this product. The difference between a scarcity and a surplus economy is forcefully illustrated by the following example. Whereas in 1980 Black Africa set as its goal an annual book production of 120 pages per person (which it fell short of achieving), a Scandinavian household receives gratis every two weeks more than 200 pages of advertising material in four-color print. Although the theoretical and empirical relations between scarcity and surplus economies are multicausal and the disparity between them cannot be resolved simply by surplus societies passing on a little of their surplus to scarcity societies, it should nevertheless be considered whether a cutback in paper consumption by industrial nations might not result in lower wholesale paper prices for the Third World. According to all available predictions, the demand for cultural paper for books, newspapers and magazines in the industrial nations will continue to grow, albeit at a slower rate than in the 1960s and 1970s. The following forecast for the 1980s published by the Arthur D. Little consulting agency is typical:

> Printing and writing paper in general will continue to be the fastest growing products in the pulp and paper side of the forest products industry. We expect the demand for coated groundwood paper to continue to increase at about 5 percent/year through the 1980s. Demand for this product is rising because of shifts in advertising expenditures from television towards the print media. Not only has the amount of prime-time television available for advertising decreased, but also the spread in the cost of advertising between broadcast media and print media is steadily widening. We expect some continued cyclicality in the demand for coated groundwood paper as a function of advertising linage demand swings during business cycles, but we expect the magazine expenditure revival of the past four years to continue into the 1980s.[7]

If predictions concerning the future trend of the cultural paper market in Western industrial nations take account of technological advances, the following situation is to be expected. While magnetic data carriers are cheaper and absorb far more data than paper, they cannot offer the same advantages as conventional print media. Photocopying and computer printouts will increase the demand for paper. In 1970 1.5 billion normal photocopies and 1.2 billion photocopies on coated paper were produced in West Germany. By 1977 these figures had increased to 10 billion normal photocopies and 1.5 billion on coated paper, representing an annual increase of approx. 23 percent. A further factor that is bound to increase paper consumption is the more widespread use of word processors and electronic printers.

Expressions such as "the paperless office" and "a paperless society" have turned out to be empty slogans introduced in the interest of the suppliers of electronic services and have little in common with empirically verifiable reality, especially since the global depression has reduced the rate of office automation, which is feared by some and welcomed by others. Most forecasts predict an annual increase in the consumption of cultural paper of 2 to 3 percent in Western industrial nations up to the year 2000. This saturation of Northern hemisphere markets can hardly be expected to profit the Third World. From the development aspect in the Third World the five principal factors governing the world paper market are as follows:

1. Only paper production plants with the most modest demand for imported technology, energy and raw materials truly benefit Third World countries, for they do not upset the latter's foreign trade balance.
2. Of the three cost factors - technology, energy, raw materials - only the primary energy required for paper production allows for possible savings.
3. For many Third World countries the terms of trade governing paper imports have rapidly deteriorated in recent years, especially for countries exporting tea, raw rubber and iron ore. Yet more favorable terms of trade would not necessarily enable the majority of consumers in a Third World country to import paper at a lower price than at present.
4. The steady global trend towards the concentration and oligopolization of the pulp and paper-making industry in North America, Scandinavia and the Common Market [now E.U.] countries does not promise the

possibility of trickledown effects for boosting the domestic paper industries of Third World countries.

5. The economic consequences of pollution in the forests of Northern hemisphere countries, the rising cost of antipollution measures and the gradually growing demand for cultural paper (for photocopies and PC printouts) in industrial nations will lead to a further rise in the world market prices for paper to the detriment of the Third World.

The above five factors allow two distinct conclusions to be drawn:

1. No improvement of the paper situation in the Third World will be possible without structural transformations having to be made in international technology and raw material policies, i.e., in line with NIEO and NIIO as referred to in the Introduction.
2. Although many theoretical and political factors support our first conclusion, a considerable element of doubt remains. Thus an alternative conclusion should be drawn from the analysis of global conditions. Since no structural transformations are essentially possible in international technology and raw materials policies, or at least none are foreseeable in the near future, it would appear advisable for Third World countries to entertain second thoughts far more than at present concerning their own potentialities and their own raw materials for the production of pulp and paper.

2. Technological Alternatives for the Third World

Large transnational paper production corporations do not invest in paper mills for Third World countries because their own natural resources and social conditions disallow large-scale development. It is more profitable and less risky to export to such countries. Some large machine-building concerns, supported by general contractors and international consultants, are prepared to supply paper and pulp mills to Third World countries on credit against financial guarantees, and also boast sizable fiber resources of their own.

However, only a few oil-rich countries qualify in this respect and the results have not so far been wholly encouraging. The intrinsic costs of such plants are higher than normal on account of the need for imports and the associated freight costs, with the result that the financial burden is too high for viability. The efficiency of such mills seldom reaches the level of those in the industrial nations because of the inadequate human resources, for efficient plant operation requires the know-how of high-salaried foreign experts as well as imported materials, with the result that production costs are abnormally high. In consequence the paper produced cannot be marketed at an attractively low price.

Large-scale development is impracticable in Third World countries for more reasons than the high cost level. Wood, the most concentrated source of fiber and a determining factor for the possible scale of development, is seldom available in the Third World in suitable forms and sufficient quantities, or, if available, requires the provision of an enormous infrastructure that would greatly exceed the financial resources of even a government-backed sponsor. Although pulp and paper mills need wood, it is not economically viable to fell trees for paper alone. To run a mill economically nowadays it needs to be coupled with timber production, thereby involving greater capital investment.

Besides the natural resources of wood, which most Third World countries lack, non-wood fiber resources - mainly in the form of agricultural waste - are highly promising but seldom available in sufficient quantities to support scale. The most readily available fiber resources are straw, bagasse and bamboo, while in some regions there are reeds and other suitable resources. Large to medium scale can be obtained from these matérials, but there are restricting factors that make scale impossible or unsuitable. Non-wood fibers like bagasse, straw and reeds are, however, less than ideal for paper production because of their inherent weakness since they are shorter than the fibers from coniferous wood. Long-fiber reinforcement ranging from 15 to 40 percent of the total fiber is needed depending on the given paper substance and quality, but is unlikely to be available in the quantity required to support scale at an acceptable price.

Even for a small mill it might have to be collected from sources scattered over a vast area or imported. Bamboo alone among non-wood fibers possesses sufficient strength, but all readily available resources have been exhausted almost everywhere. The market situation may also limit the use of scale. Even where the overall market is sufficient to support large scale, the cost of the infrastructure required for its distribution may result in prohibitive prices.

Small strategically located mills are liable to prove more viable. Natural resources other than fiber also have a bearing on scale. Paper production may require up to 80 tons of water per ton of paper produced, resulting in a correspondingly large effluent disposal problem. Sites where water is available in sufficient quantity are very hard to find in most Third World countries.

Fuel for producing processed steam is required for treating the fiber and desiccating the finished paper. A fully integrated mill uses about 1.5 tons of fuel oil or its equivalent in coal for every ton of paper produced. Fuel oil in sufficient quantities to operate a large mill is unlikely to be available in Third World countries that are not rich in oil and it is even less probable that the sources of fiber, water and fuel will all be available in an area from which they can be collected and transported at reasonable cost.

There is also a requirement for a reliable power source that can supply, depending on the fiber source and paper quality, upwards of one megawatt per hour per ton of paper produced. This is unlikely to be available in Third World countries in a quantity sufficient for large-scale. For additional capital investment and higher fuel consumption a mill can be made self-sufficient in power, large mills usually being equipped for partial or total self-sufficiency in this respect.

By current general standards a wood-based mill has natural advantages in terms of fuel and, consequently, power. Wood waste and bark are usually available as supplementary fuel sources, especially for mills also involved in lumber operations. Efficient chemical recovery for producing high-pressure steam is also practical and can satisfy the thermal requirements of pulp production with a margin for paper. It can further provide steam with a power-generating potential exceeding the given requirements.These advantages are considered natural because they are already exploited for wood. This was not always the case, pulp and paper production having originally been based on sulfite pulping without chemical recovery, a practice which continued up to World War II. The consequent pollution of lakes and rivers is still ongoing in Canada and Scandinavia, where mountainous heaps of bark still exist as a memorial to the wastefulness of an industry based upon the expectation that cheap fossil fuels would forever be available.

New developments in chemical recovery and fuel conservation since applied to the wood-based pulp and paper industry involved considerable research and development costs, but could well be afforded by this expanding and profitable industry whose survival they assured. The non-wood pulp and paper industry offers similar intrinsic advantages which, for lack of funds, have not so far been exploited to the same extent.

In a broad sense wood cannot be expected to satisfy the needs of Third World countries to any significant extent except in climatically favorable parts of Africa and South America. Even in these regions, where positive long-term prospects are seen in reforestation with suitable species, short-term prospects are poor unless they can be realized economically on a small scale. The costs for large scale are too great to be affordable and the market is too small to absorb the output. Export, as has already been recognized, offers no solution. The world market is already saturated with high-quality pulp that is sold below production cost. The immediate future of the Third World therefore lies mainly in the use of non-wood materials such are straw, wheat, rice, maize, bagasse and bamboo.

Bamboo, being economically viable, is already fully exploited. It is a self-sufficient source of fiber, highly versatile and it does not require long-fiber reinforcement. The paper industry in India is largely based on bamboo. Bamboo is not planted but grows naturally in tropical forests and can be collected by low-cost labor. Its widespread use, however, requires the penetration of inaccessible forest areas, which inevitably involves enormous infrastructure costs. Bamboo planting has been considered, but the cost of growing anything solely as raw material for the production of paper would be prohibitive. Moreover, the choice of fiber is narrowed by its having to be available as a byproduct from other industries.

Straw, the most commonly available fiber, is an agricultural by-product. The total quantity available could largely meet the requirements of the paper mills in Third World countries, but is normally put to other uses, varying from feeding cattle to providing fuel for boilers. Ironically, in some industrial nations with limited fiber resources for paper-making, vast quantities of straw are wastefully burnt annually. Where collection is efficiently organized, straw-based mills can produce up to 100,000 TPA as paper, while mills of much smaller capacity can, under suitable circumstances, be run economically to the mutual benefit of mill and peasants.

Bagasse, an agricultural byproduct obtainable wherever sugar is extracted from crushed sugarcane, is an excellent source of fiber. If a paper mill can be installed adjacent to a sugar mill, the cost of fiber will compare favorably with that of almost all other materials. Bagasse also serves as the traditional fuel for the sugarcane industry. Efficiently incinerated bagasse - moisture content about 50 percent - can yield a bagasse surplus at all sugar mills ranging from about 20 percent at fully refined sugar mills to more than 50 percent at unrefined sugar mills. Efficient bagasse incineration requires efficient boilers, which are not always present; and arrangements have to be made for the storage and handling of the surplus, which involves additional cost. Many sugar mills use their boilers to provide whatever steam is needed and for incinerating the residual bagasse.

Properly organized, the paper mill can also be used for collection and storage. If the bagasse can be wholly or partially desiccated prior to incineration and the sugar mill or paper mill is equipped to incinerate the pith that has to be removed, thermal efficiency will be greatly improved. Under these conditions it is not unreasonable to visualize a combined plant in which the sugar mill requires no supplementary fuel and the paper mill operates with reduced fuel requirements. Although such a plant is entirely feasible, considerable research and development would be required for its realization. Where replacement fuel (possibly provided by new boilers) is available, some bagasse mills will attain a paper production volume of 100,000 tons TPA. Such mills have become more frequent in recent years since the development of newsprint production from bagasse. Being essential for the press, high-priced newsprint has to be imported by even the poorest Third World countries.

Non-wood fibers already satisfy about 60 percent of the paper consumption in Asia and China, and this figure is expected to increase. Although paper consumption in these regions is low, it cannot be covered by domestic production. Technical limitations to the efficient production of quality paper from non-wood fibers tend, however, to discourage potential investors and sponsors. It should be added that very similar limitations used to apply to the international wood-based paper industry in its formative years, but have since been overcome through the introduction of new technologies. The first was efficient chemical recovery. For wood-based mills this is a highly efficient and economic process, conserving about 95 percent of the boiling chemicals with a consequent reduction not only of production costs but also of the cost of realizing acceptable effluent disposal standards. The process additionally provides steam at pressures allowing power generation, thereby greatly reducing energy costs. Non-wood fiber pulping produces boiling liquors containing silica, the presence of which increases the viscosity of the liquor when evaporated. Consequently, such liquor cannot be concentrated to the same degree as that from wood, and this reduces its combustion efficiency.

Moreover silica may produce scale which, being almost impossible to remove, limits operating temperatures. There is a great need for an efficient economic process for removing silica from boiling liquors. One such process has been developed and is used in the Rakhta mill in Egypt. It is said to be very efficient, but is naturally a prototype requiring further refinement. A reliable process would not only increase evaporation and combustion efficiencies, but also permit recausticized lime recovery, thereby reducing the cost of production and effluent disposal.

Bagasse has advantages over straw but requires long-fiber reinforcement. If imported kraft is affordable, a straw- or bagasse-operated mill can produce a broad range of different sorts of paper competitive in quality with the best, but this is only feasible in oil-rich Third World countries. For the vast majority, low-priced local substitute materials must be found. Cotton waste is excellent but in very short supply and limited to cotton-growing areas. Other suitable textile fiber wastes are jute, sabai grass and sisal, but here again supplies are limited. The most promising source of long fiber for Third World countries is kenaf, one of the few materials that can be grown in suitable areas exclusively for use in paper. A comprehensive study on the potential uses of kenaf conducted in recent years in the USA suggests that it could be grown there in a given area for newsprint production and would provide a greater yield at lower cost than wood. In Third World countries its growth for cattle fodder and long-fiber pulp is seriously under consideration and seems to be a most promising project.

The poor chemical recovery that has long handicapped small non-wood based mills can nowadays be overcome by installing a modern recovery boiler, a highly efficient sophisticated unit capable of recovering the liquors from pulp with a capacity of up to 1,000 TPD as unbleached pulp. It is less efficient at below 400 TPD and almost impossible to realize in a similar form for levels below 150 TPD. Taking into account additives and moisture content, this implies that a paper mill must produce upwards of 60,000 TPA in order to reach a chemical recovery level that will produce steam in excess of its own and its pulp mill needs.

A more reasonable level that would take into account the market and other limitations in Third World countries would be around 10,000 TPA, which is also the level specified by the Indian government in its plan to encourage paper mills to use indigenous fibers. Chemical recovery boilers are economic in terms of chemical costs at levels down to 15 TPD as pulp, but are consumers and not producers of steam and the efficiency of chemical recovery is only between 15 and 25 percent. There have been encouraging developments such as the Babcock Krauss Maffei approach and the French Sulzer separate combustion approach, but the latter has since been abandoned for lack of funds. Limited funds are undoubtedly impeding progress in what is probably the most promising field.

Non-wood papermaking offers advantages that to a certain extent offset its drawbacks. Fiber preparation is simpler, less capital-intensive, boiling is faster and chemical consumption, except for recovery, is normally lower. Adequate bleaching is achieved by a simple three-stage process, whereas wood requires five stages, thereby involving higher capital investment for chemical preparation and consumption. That the refining power required for non-wood fibers is also considerably less than that for wood is a significant factor in overall energy requirements.

Contrary to popular belief, there are practically no economies of scale in Third World countries except as regards chemical recovery. It is technologically unsuitable, socioeconomically less rewarding, capital expenditure is higher and the total financial burden exceeds the resources of most private enterprises and the funding acceptable to governments. Scale is very attractive in industrial nations with high wage levels because it requires less manpower, but in Third World countries it would require highly trained native personnel in all departments and high-salaried foreign experts would have to be engaged for running the plant.

Third World countries need efficient paper mills based on indigenous fibers that assure viability for investors right from the start, which is something modern multinational corporations will not find even in industrial nations. Capital costs per unit of production may be lower for scale at around 10,000 TPA because less high-priced construction materials are required than for large mills. High quality and production efficiency are obtained without the need for highly trained native personnel and high-salaried foreign experts. The enormous potential market for paper mills in Third World countries offers prospects for design standardization that will further reduce capital expenditure and the need for highly trained personnel. This opportunity is not open for large scale.

The paper consumption rate in Europe around 1900 would be a reasonable present target for Third World countries. The paper mills of that era usually had a standard width of 2 to 3 meters and operated at a rate of 100 meters per minute. Low-priced and easy to run, they became the standard units upon which the present industry is still based. The Third World needs a similar basis for its present paper industry and could have this in an improved form due to the significant technological advances since achieved. Indigenous fibers should be used. Initially at least non-wood fiber sources should be chosen for the majority of mills.

The two major impediments to progress are the need for efficient chemical recovery and reliable long-fiber reinforcement. Although there is evidence that chemical recovery can be be improved and the need for long-fiber reinforcement reduced by appropriate plant design modification and the use of a more economic operating rate, the overall situation will still need substantial improvement. Kenaf might provide a solution and, along with other alternatives, needs to be thoroughly investigated on an industrial basis.

The paper problem of developing countries cannot be expected to solve itself, but will persist for as long as communication and education are top priorities. The decline of plastics as oil supplies become exhausted will increase the demand for paper for the media, commerce and industry. No Third World countries can hope to increase their print media output without an increased supply of paper, which is only possible by exploiting their natural resources to produce their own paper. There are signs that small-scale paper mills using indigenous fibers could prove viable in Third World countries, albeit the production efficiency level would be lower than that expected by Western standards. There is no intrinsic reason why production standards should be inferior, but more effort than native industry is currently capable of providing would be needed to accomplish the improvements that are actually within reach.

Notes and References

1. Cf. Hellmann, Heikki; Nordenstreng, Kaarle and Varis, Tapio: *Idealism, Aggression, Apology, and Criticism: The Four Traditions of Research on 'International Communication'*. Paper presented at the 12th Congress of IAMCR; Caracas, Venezuela, August 26-29, 1980.
2. Ki-Zerbo, Joseph: "Unterricht über die Dritte Welt und die Probleme ihrer Entwicklung", in: *Die Dritte Welt in Schule und Jugendarbeit*, ed. by Jörg Becker, Frankfurt: Haag & Herchen 1980, p. 20.
3. Cf. Beak Consultants Ltd.: *Environmental Considerations in the Pulp and Paper Industry*, Washington, D.C.: The World Bank 1980.
4. Cf. *The Energy Transition in Developing Countries*, Washington, D.C.: The World Bank 1983.
5. Quoted in Contreras, Carlos: *The Transfer of Technology to Developing Countries*, Caracas: Instituto Latinoamericano de Investigaciones Sociales 1978, pp. 28.
6. Jäger, Hans Wolfgang: "Die saure Quittung", in: *Das Papier Magazin*, No. 7/1983.
7. Iannazzi, Fred D. and Firth, Louise M.: *Outlook for the Forest Products Industry 1978-88*, Cambridge, Mass.: Arthur D. Little, Inc. 1979 (mimeo), p. 11.

5
Information and Communication Technologies (ICT) and Cultural Change

In 1851, the first-ever World Exhibition took place in London, a splendid event on the back of a euphoric wave of industrialization. In 1851, the world's first underwater cable was laid between Dover and Calais, and in the same year the first telegraph line - linking Calcutta with Diamond Harbor - went into service in India.

It was against this background that the nationalistically-minded German satirical magazine *Kladderadatsch* published a caricature of the London World Exhibition entitled "The Civilizing Steam Engine" with the caption: "The wild tribes are poured down the funnel of this engine and, a couple of minutes later, reappear completely civilized as educated Europeans."

In his book The Machine in Caricature, which appeared in 1917, i.e., amid the blazing inferno of the barbaric war in Europe, Hans Wettich, a German engineer, made the following caustic comment on this 1851 caricature:

> This civilizing machine strikes a telling blow at the superficiality of European civilization, which can still only produce 'colored Englishmen' even though, way back in the 1850s, *Kladderadatsch* naively assumed the English civilizing machine would ultimately be capable of turning colored Englishmen into white ones. And why not? What would be the difference?[1]

The ambivalent symbolism of this caricature prevails to this day. In a text by Joseph Weizenbaum or Neil Postman criticizing technology, for instance, it might prompt viewers to think exactly the opposite of what was intended in 1851. Whereas it had originally implied that European industrialization was contributing to civilizing and modernizing colonial territories and their colored inhabitants, it could now be read as a scornful indictment of cultural imperialism as innate in technology transfer.

These two contrary interpretations are in no way new, but as old as the industrialization of the productive forces and the advance of technology itself; indeed, we encounter them with regard to the fields of telephony and telegraphy. Werner von Siemens, an army lieutenant, inventor, scientist and company founder, was an exemplary exponent of boundless optimism in progress through technology. In a memorable lecture in Berlin in 1886 he posed the question:

> Who is nowadays surprised by these obvious things. [...] When the telegraph as a world uniter can no longer cope with our communication needs it will be forced to give way to telephony for the transmission of the living word. We believe that progress in the realm of the sciences will, when applied to technology and transportation, facilitate the exchange of goods between countries and climes, rendering men's lives more pleasurable and overcoming local constraints. [...] We must remain steadfast in our belief that research and innovative activities raise the cultural level of humanity, empowering men to pursue high ideals.[2]

Then as now, critical voices claimed the exact opposite. John Rushkin, for example, in his letter of 1896 addressed to the workmen and laborers of England, posed a very basic question concerning the function of intercontinental telegraphy:

> Telegraphic signalling was a discovery; and conceivably, some day, may be a useful one. And there was some excuse for your being a little proud when you knotted a copper wire all the way to Bombay, and flashed a message along it, and back. But what was the message and what the answer? Is India the better for what you said to her? Are you the better for what she replied?[3]

Social reformer Ruskin suspected that the telegraph link between India and England really only served a spurious intercultural communication effort. Johann Wolfgang von Goethe's criticism of "all the possible communication facilities" seems moderate by comparison. In a letter written in 1825 Goethe anticipated that these facilities would bring about a "medium-quality culture",[4] something we would now term a "homogenized culture". The Königsberg historian Johann Karl Friedrich Rosenkranz was far more pointed than Goethe in his 1872 essay "Progress in the Uniformity of our Civilization":

> Just a hundred years on, and the poetic contrast in the colorful multiplicity of primitive peoples will be destroyed by the uniformity of civilization on our planet, just as the virgin forest was destroyed by the plough and the wild beasts by the rifle. There will be only cultivated plants, cultivated animals and cultivated peoples. Just as the primitive peoples disappeared and their place was taken by civilized peoples, so, too, national costumes will be replaced by a uniform fashion which changes periodically. [...] Similarly the languages of the primitive peoples will yield to those of the dominant cultivated peoples. Even within a cultivated people the same process will take place in the relationship between dialects and the written language. [...] The most powerful vehicles for the acceleration of progress in our uniform civilization are the railways and steamships. But stranger still is the effect of telegraphy in reducing spatial distance to zero.[5]

At this point, it bears offering a preliminary summary.

1. Both the warning against cultural homogenization as well as the participation of all peoples in progress, modernization and wealth through technology transfer are part of the standard repertoire of scholarly thought in Europe.
2. Both arguments are revived with the advent of technological innovation.
3. The similarity of these arguments reveals, however, little about their applicability to new technical constellations. A vaguely prophetic pessimistic comment of the 19th century can - as presently in the case of Joseph Weizenbaum - assume the quality of comprehensive analytical criticism and, due to the cumulative effects of current large-scale technology, even become a reasonably realistic argument.

The negative symbol of the funnel in the *Kladderadatsch* caricature into which whatever is poured reappears transformed culturally and socially into something other offers no escape from the dilemma between "belief in progress and fear of the future", between a positive evaluation of global village civilization and a negative evaluation of cultural homogenization. This funnel model remains valid up to the present day, although varying in theoretical scientific garb. It reappears, for instance, in the traditional empirical communication research of Winfried Schulz:

> Of all research models only [...] the experimental process is in a position to give causal relations a functional thrust so as to take accurate account of the logical structure of effects hypotheses. This process is therefore the only method that yields acceptable evidence of causal relations.[6]

The same funnel model also stands godfather to many social scientists concerned with studying the social impact of information technologies on cultural change in the Third World. One of these, Cees Hamelink, writes in this context:

> Information processes that reflect existing power relations usually follow a synchronic mode. In this mode a great distance separates sender and receiver; the receiver is supposed to synchronize with the input from the sender. The sender becomes the specialist who alone can select, process and distribute the messages. Messages are 'prescribed' to the passive receiver, who is expected to register and store them in his 'archives'.[7]

The common theoretical weakness of funnel models is that they look for causal relations to explain socio-cultural dynamics. Also, being bound to a "content"-based social science, they falsely infer that the consciousness of the individual is essentially determined by the content of circumambient images. It is not the content of these images that imparts meaning, but rather their social context and treatment. This social context can be complex, contradictory, varied, tortuous and thorny. Canadian social scientist René Jean Ravault has pointed out yet a further weakness in such an approach.[8] There is a certain correspondence between these funnel models and the "bullet" or "boomerang" theories in which Third World cultures are regarded as the passive victims of the Western industrialized nations. In line with such notions, the culture of a developing country has only two options: either to perish after being fatally wounded by an imperialist cultural bullet, or to intercept the bullet and return it to the aggressor in the form of a resistance movement, which may likewise prove lethal. These bullet and boomerang theories are somewhat questionable because:

a) they construe the cultures of the Third World as passive essentially defenseless victims of Western influences and
b) the concept of culture used is a relatively arbitrary surplus variable that is liable to become the manipulated victim of economics and technology.

Such assumptions are both morally and analytically questionable, for they sidestep any real confrontation with the given culture and with the concept of progress. For traditional Marxists the term progress presents few difficulties. On this subject they can refer inter alia to Marx's newspaper article on British rule in India (which also contains some very pointed remarks on the military and economic function of telegraphy in the interest of British colonial rule). On Indian village communities Marx writes:

> Now, sickening as it must be to human feelings to witness those myriads of industrious, patriarchical and inoffensive social organizations disorganized and dissolved into their units, thrown into a sea of woes, and their individual members losing at the same time their ancient form of civilization and hereditary means of subsistence, we must not forget that these idyllic village communities, inoffensive though they may appear, had always been the solid foundation of Oriental despotism, that they restricted the human mind within the smallest possible compass, making it the unresisting tool of superstition, enslaving it beneath traditional rules, depriving it of all grandeur and historical energies.[9]

In other words, in traditional Marxism undifferentiated social organizations and a low level of technological development in the forces of production - above all in Africa and Asia - are seen as obstacles to social progress in general. If such obstacles are overcome and the private ownership of the means of production is abolished by a revolutionary liberation movement, harmony may then exist between technological and human progress.

From this basic reasoning it was possible to derive the notion of the purely instrumental character of technology. Its social acceptability was thus essentially related to its tool character. From this utilitarian aspect the social use of technology becomes the focal point of scientific interest. As technology itself is neutral, the social organization of its implementation determines its normative designation as good or bad. With regard to new information technologies such as artificial intelligence, expert systems and electronic data processors, postmodern Marxism sees the productive forces as being neutral in character and even introduces the term "mental tools" as a parallel to "work tools".[10]

This conceptual insistence on the social organization of newly implemented technologies is still a strong argument for social movements such as communism, social democracy, trade unions, churches, all of which favor the welfare state and the socialization of economics and politics. For two reasons, however, this reasoning is not entirely in order.

a) The cumulative chain effect of industrialization as it matured in history has long since taken on a social quality through which individual technologies, while still having a certain tool character, have combined to form a single large-scale technology that influences the whole of society.

b) Marx's analysis of alienation and identity has inadvertently come to represent a construct of German idealism. At the German Sociologists Conference in 1968 Theodor W. Adorno already observed:

> More than ever before the forces of production are mediated by production relations, perhaps so completely that the latter seem to be the essence and have become second nature. They are responsible for the fact that, in insane contradiction of what is possible, people all over the world have to suffer. Even where goods are in abundance, they exist somehow under a curse. [...] The unfettering of the productive forces resulted in new shackles in the form of production relations: production became an end in itself and blocked the realization of freedom as a goal. In both systems [capitalism and real existing socialism, J.B.] the bourgeois notion of socially useful labor is parodied in a satanic manner. On the market this notion reveals itself as profit, never as a transparent utility for mankind, nor even for its well-being.[11]

Moreover, under conditions of socialized production the forces of production are not, as Marx had hoped, unleashed such as to prevent the alienation of the individual, something to which Jürgen Kuczynski, a leading German Marxist theorist, tirelessly refers, sometimes with resignation, at others with bold theoretical audacity. The most recent example of this is to be found in his book Dialogue with my Great-Grandson.[12]

Even though it is still possible to use the term progress in a utopian social sense, it is no longer theoretically feasible to assign to it any concrete meaning. And however irrationally a technologically mediated reality may develop, it still cannot be adequately defined, let alone politically analyzed, through the use of the antirational theories of a Fritjof Capra or any other exponent of the New Age. It is no coincidence that the traditional Leftist conception of progress breaks down in the face of the alienation and identity problem of not only the individual but also, in particular, of non-European cultures.

In his essay "Civilization and Modernism" Iranian sociologist Ali Shariati presents a broad definition of the term culture. To his mind, and his view is shared by many other scholars in the Third World, culture is "the sum of all the spiritual, artistic, historical, literary, religious and emotional manifestations" of a people, and explains its "sufferings, needs, spiritual quality and disposition, social features and relations, material life and economic structure".[13] Culture is here seen as a factor determining the relations of production, whereas Dieter Senghaas assumes in the classical Western tradition that culture has an inherent "relative plasticity" that varies according to the given constellation of political, social and economic forces.[14] Comparing Shariati with Senghaas we note on the one hand various conceptual differences and on the other a common failure to define the specific level of culture they have in mind. Johan Galtung, for his part, is mainly concerned with "social cosmology".[15]

While traditional Marxism assumes culture to be determined by socioeconomic structures and Idealism envisages culture as being primary, Galtung's "social cosmology" takes a median path. The chicken-and-egg problem being insoluble, social cosmology points to a lower-lying system embracing both socioeconomic structure and culture as a manifestation of one and the same phenomenon. However much it may vary between one culture and another, a social cosmology will include the human reference systems of time, space, knowledge, nature, society and the divinity. Viewed as deep-level mental systems, social cosmologies are obviously so old and deeply internalized in the collective unconscious of a people as to be almost totally resistant to change.

Whereas culture in the restricted sense of a commodity with an exchange value (TV film, PC software) or an ideological symbol (Hollywood, the free West, do-it-yourself happiness) is industrialized and marketable (with regard to the North-South conflict we are here confronted with cultural, media and information imperialism), social cosmologies seem to escape all such instrumentalization. In this context, the concept of identity assumes a leading role. While European colonialism sought to impose its social cosmology upon the Third World, it was really only successful in Latin America, where it consciously risked the almost total extermination of the indigenous population.

Anti-colonial movements in present-day Latin America actually can only take their cue from European social cosmology, i.e., either Christianity in the form of Liberation theology or Marxism. In Africa and Asia, by contrast, which had different and less genocidal colonial pasts, the cultural identity crises analyzed by Al Shariarti were nevertheless serious and far-reaching. The "social cosmologies" of these continents were able to survive relatively untouched by colonialism. If, therefore, developing countries are viewed less from the perspective of progress and closer attention is devoted to their social cosmologies, it will be perceived that progress is most in evidence wherever a strong common cultural identity prevails.

This right of individuals and groups to self-determination with regard to their own culture without having to bother with notions of progress related to the development of the forces of production as rooted in the European tradition is fundamentally humanist. Yet the universalist right to culture is equally humanist: with its renunciation of all conceivable forms of oppression, it is unable to forego the notions of either reason or progress, or yet of the social differentiation and further development of the productive forces. Both these notions have a long ideological tradition. In Third World countries the universalist position often came to nothing more than cultural imperialism, the relativist position serving to legitimate the atrocious treatment of the members of some other indigenous culture in the Third World.

As the development of information and communication technologies will reinforce the familiar behavior patterns of the United States and West Europe towards the Third World, cultural conflicts between compliance and resistance will become more pronounced and bitter than ever before. Europe's social cosmology with its constraints regarding activity, energy, achievement, development, change and progress could provide practical behavior patterns with regard to foreign relations for all political tendencies from Left to Right. A social cosmology can be evaluated as "good" for the Third World if it accepts the humanist goal of progress, although this term is barely definable in an abstract form. Europe, however, has contributed little to the realization of that other equally humanist objective, viz., the cultural self-determination of all peoples, a goal that sometimes stands in opposition to progress.

While the inconsistency between a universalist goal of freedom and progress and its relativization through notions of continuity and identity is barely acceptable to Europeans, Africans and Asians do not seem to have the same scruples. Since European nations seem incapable of dialogue in the culturally relativist sense, they continue to foster and intensify their links with universalist forces in the Third World irrespective of whether these are currently in power or have been ousted.

Changes in the Islamic world since the Iranian Revolution in 1979 illustrate how "reconciliation" can be achieved between cultural and technological policies, and how progress and cultural identity can be married. The Iranian Revolution was on the one hand a typical culturally relativist reaction to Iran's subjection to the constraints of the capitalist world market, although directly after the revolution technology-transfer from the West to Iran was not significantly reduced. The significance of such external influence upon the internal cultural situation in present-day Iran must however be judged differently than the situation preceding the revolution.

Long before 1979 it was clear that the strongly developing cultural identity of Iran's elite went hand in glove with an increasing disaffection with European culture. This elite looked to Europe only in the single area of high technology, which was judged to be purely instrumental and neutral, and it was only when a point was reached where the foreign influence mediated by technology could no longer be effectively integrated into Iranian culture that the revolution broke out.

The present situation, however, is entirely different. Adopting a relativist strategy in foreign affairs, Iran is pursuing an autocentric development policy, lending special support to small and medium-sized enterprises, stabilizing agriculture and promoting the vertical and horizontal integration of the various branches of the indigenous economy. That some Islamic countries demonstrate the feasibility of a "reconciliation" between culture and technology is attributable to the "social cosmology" of Islam having always allowed a positive evaluation of natural science and engineering. Although a relativist strategy in the cultural sphere is impossible under the despotic regime of the Ayatollah

Khomeni, it would be feasible in an Islamic system as visualized by Asgher Ali Engineer, an Indian Muslim Liberation theologian, who asserts that the decentralization of power, the just distribution of wealth and the principle of equality are basic tenets of the Koran.[16]

The informatization of society strains the relations between culture and technology as well as identity and progress not only in the Third World but also in Europe to increasingly existential degree, for it is our experience that every technologically induced advance is always more than offset by social and cultural setbacks. We are no longer in a position, as was the English philosopher William Whewell at the London World Exhibition in 1851, euphorically to declare art and culture to be the daughters of natural science, or, like Werner von Siemens in 1886, to claim that the era of natural science represents a "higher cultural level".

In such 19th century statements it is of interest to note that engineers and entrepreneurs were all interested in culture, which they perceived as an important link between technology and society, and were not merely concerned with the social acceptability of user appliances like so many present-day informatics specialists and representatives of the major industries.

In Europe informatics must therefore be used to stimulate European culture and identity by means of a Europeanizing strategy for which Thomas Mann in 1953 provided a significant guideline when he condemned "Europe's weak-kneed self-surrender and servitude to America" and stressed the need for Europe to abandon its "unseemly dedication to money and power as evident in the outstretched begging palm and excessive admiration for the impressive success story of American history". And Thomas Mann concluded: "In freedom alone can Europe regain its self-esteem and decorum."[17]

Notes and References

1. Wettich, Hans: *Die Maschine in der Karikatur*. Ein Buch zum Siege der Technik, Berlin: Verlag der "Lustigen Blätter" 1917, p. 40.

2. Siemens, Werner von: "Das naturwissenschaftliche Zeitalter", in: Siemens, Werner von: *Wissenschaftliche und Technische Arbeiten*. 2nd Vol.: Technische Arbeiten. 2nd ed., Berlin: Julius Springer Verlag 1891, pp. 493, 495 and 499.

3. Ruskin, John: *Fors Clavigera*. Letters to the Workmen and Labourers of Great Britain. New Edition. Vol. I, London: George Allen 1896, pp. 90.

4. Goethe, Johann Wolfgang von: "Brief an Zelter vom 6. Juni 1825", in: *Goethes Briefe*. Hamburger Ausgabe. Vol. IV, pp. 146.

5. Rosenkranz, Johann Karl Friedrich: *Neue Studien*. Vol. I, Leipzig: Koschny Verlag 1875, p. 545.

6. Schulz, Winfried: „Ausblick am Ende des Holzweges. Eine Übersicht über die Ansätze der neuen Wirkungsforschung", in: *Publizistik*, No. 1-2/1982, p. 66.

7 Hamelink, Cees: *Cultural Autonomy in Global Communications*, New York: Longman 1983, p. 114.

8 Ravault, René Jean: "International Information: Bullet or Boomerang?", in: *Political Communication Research*, ed. by David Paletz, Norwood, NJ: Ablex 1987, pp. 245-265.

9. MEW. Vol. 9, p. 132 [Facsimile of the article "British Rule in India" in the *New York Daily Tribune*, June 25, 1853].

10. Hörz, Herbert: *Zur Bedeutung der Information für Individuum und Gesellschaft*, Berlin 1983.

11. Adorno, Theodor W.: "Einleitungsvortrag zum 16. Deutschen Soziologentag", in: *Spätkapitalismus oder Industriegesellschaft?*, ed. by Theodor W. Adorno, Stuttgart 1969, pp. 22.

12. Kuczynski, Jürgen: *Dialog mit meinem Urenkel*. Neunzehn Briefe und ein Tagebuch. 6th edition, Berlin: Aufbau Verlag 1983.

13. Schariati, Ali: *Zivilisation und Modernismus*, Bonn: Botschaft der Islamischen Republik Iran 1980, p. 18.

14. Senghaas, Dieter: "Kultur und Entwicklung. Überlegungen zur aktuellen entwicklungspolitischen Diskussion", in: *Zeitschrift für Kulturaustausch*, No. 4/1984, p. 419.

15. Galtung, Johan and Nishimura, Fumiko: „Struktur, Kultur und Sprachen: Indo-europäische, chinesische und japanische Sprachen im Vergleich", in: *Leviathan*, No. 4/1984, p. 478.

16. Engineer, Ashgar Ali: "On Developing Liberation Theology in Islam", in: *Islam in the Modern Age*, No. 2/1982, pp. 101-125.

17. Mann, Thomas: „Comprendre", in: Mann, Thomas: *Deutsche Hörer! Europäische Hörer!* Radiosendungen nach Deutschland 1940-1945, Darmstadt: Verlag Darmstädter Blätter 1986, pp. 166.

6

Information and Communication Technologies (ICT) and Transnational Culture

1. Media and Cultural Imperialism

Klaus Pütter, the President of the Euro-African division of Coca Cola, presented a paper on his company's market strategy on the future development of the so-called "new media" (Pütter 1985) to the international "Inter Media Congress" in Hamburg in November 1985. I will briefly describe the main hypotheses he voiced because, however uncritically, they cover in a plausible manner all of the important dimensions of this theme.

At the very beginning of his paper, the author admits that Coca Cola's success is, to a large degree, also the result of the advertising media. He also congratulated the "quickly expanding media" which are to be found all over Europe because they have eliminated "some of the consequences of national borders. Through this process Coca Cola aims at establishing a globally common identity through the creation of identical products, trade marks, designs and target groups."

This market strategy, which stresses "the similarities rather than the differences in the international Coca Coal operation" was developed with help from one of the corporation's internal databases which stored global market, customer and consumer data. Coca Cola regards TV worldwide as its primary advertising medium. In the United States, TV swallows 83 percent of its advertising budget.

In Europe, however, TV commercials account for a substantially smaller portion of the related overall budget. In the Netherlands, for example, it comes to only 23 percent while in Germany it amounts to 44 percent. The author cites two reasons to explain the lower European figures: 1. TV programming lacks due care and 2. sub-optimal broadcasting times for TV. In order to overcome this unfavorable situation, the Coca Cola corporation gears its advertising first at "target group" oriented "special interest magazines" and second at the swiftly expanding satellite and cable TV market. Pütter concluded his paper with the following statement:

> We look optimistically to the future, a future which will see Coca Cola being one of the most intensive users of the expanded medium of TV in Europe. Our investment in advertising will increase as television ratings, or to bemore precise, advertising television ratings themselves, increase, providing that the ICTs' fee/performance ratio is fair. This would act as an enormous boost for the advance of the refreshment beverages market in Europe which could be of advantage not only to us, but also to our many partners, such as, our industry itself, the suppliers, the customers, the agents and, last but not least, the media themselves. We will no longer be restricted by national boundaries in the promotion of our audio-visual message (Pütter 1985, 14).

If one were to translate the ideas presented in this paper into the analytical language of the social sciences, then its central message could be expressed as follows: advertising is a necessary component driving the West European, as well as, the world market forward. In order to develop an optimal dynamic, national and cultural peculiarities have to be homogenized. This market homogenization can be achieved through cross-border satellite technology. This depends on the privatization of television which is considered a pre-requisite for attaining the necessary combination of mass audience entertainment with advertising during "prime time" viewing hours. The mass communication component of ICTs (in satellite and cable TV) is used as a form of rationalization, i.e., homogenization of the external environment of media and advertising concerns; ICT's specialist internal communications component (databases), however, fulfills the function of corporate control and rationalization.

It is no accident that such a paper was presented to the "Inter Media Congress" in Hamburg. As a means of escaping the worst consequences of the transition to the second Industrial Revolution, the city's social-democratic government intends to create an international "telecommunications port." The "Inter Media Congress" is but one of many PR exercises in the pursuit of this goal. The social democratic government in the competing province of Bremen has initiated a "Hig-Tech-Zentrum Nord" project to counteract the effects of the demise of the shipping industry there.

Greater Liverpool, after the Republic of Ireland, Northern Ireland, Sicily and Calabria, the fifth poorest area in the European Union, having lost out in economic stature owing to the development of the forces of production, is now consigned to the backwaters of history. It serves as an example to the two major political trends in Europe, the Christian democrats and the social democrats, who agree that only through High Tech can an adequate industrially-based solution be found to the current structural crisis. However, the positions of the two camps in relation to how far they are prepared to accept the social consequences associated with such growth strategies differ. This is also the case when it comes to the question of how quickly or how slowly ICT should be implemented on the societal level.

Inasmuch as these growth strategies require cross-border and cultural homogenized components, it is possible that from the very beginning they rest on sand. It is also possible that they are too rash in their estimation of culture as a variable which can be instrumentalized at any given time. Therefore, we must consider fundamental aspects of the link between ICT and culture, and analyze them using recent concepts developed by research into media and cultural imperialism as a starting point; research into mass communications (Prokop 1985, 530) has produced high quality and varied analyses showing the existence of interaction between the economic and ideological penetration of the Third World by oligopolistic media corporations from Western industrialized nations with their inherent pressure for the mass and worldwide production of inherently deceptive products.

The resulting cultural imperialism could be the most widespread and flexible attempt at cultural genocide in the name of Western progress and civilization in the history of mankind. As relevant on a moral and scientific level as this analyses is, it is necessary to refine it on the basis of the following basic observations. The affirmative communications research of the 1950s and 1960s and the critical media and cultural imperialism research which has been current since the 1970s have the following unintentional similarities. While the one cites empirical evidence to suggest that the media play an effective role in the conquering of "backwardness "and "primitiveness", critical research shows that the introduction of metropolitan media in the Third World has led to the destruction of the latter's cultural identity. What both approaches have in common is their mechanistic agreement that an endogenous culture is static and can be controlled from externally at a variety of levels. Both methods must be contrasted with the following arguments :

a) Tran van Dinh (1983) has stated that every person, thing and interaction exists in a state of permanent contradiction. This applies, particularly, to intercultural communication. It hides not only the possibility of dialogue between equals, but also the seed of resistance and self-discovery. Whenever the United States has brought particularly strong military, economic or technological pressure on Latin America, it has been met by a decisive cultural counter offensive such as the "Indigenismo" of the 1920s and 1930s which included Ruben Dario, José Mariategui, Jacques Roumain, Nicolas Guillen or contemporary movements such as Liberation theology, the Sandinistas or the Latin-American socialism of Gabriel Garcia Marquez. It is specifically these cultural counter-offensives in the countries of the Third World which have played a decisive role in the process of decolonization.

b) Amilcar Cabral (1983, 298) has vehemently rejected the proposition that the African was robbed of his cultural identity by colonialism. He maintains that such a loss of identity has occurred only among the relatively small Western orientated African elite. The peasant - representing more than 80 percent of the African population - did not have to heed any "back to the roots" slogan because he was never very far removed from them in the first place. The same applies to the term "Re-Islamization" which infers that Islam had, at least for a time, lost its cultural relevance for its followers.

However, the Iranian Revolution has shown that the continuity of the Islamic world view is much stronger than the signs of externally-induced discontinuity perceived by observers from outside this culture. The ultra leftist speculation that Coca Cola's entry into the Chinese market in 1978 heralded the end of authentic Chinese culture should be seen, for precisely the reasons mentioned above, as the product of historical and ill-founded projections by European intellectuals. The idea that the mass distribution of a can filled with a brown sweet liquid can change a two-and-a-half-thousand year old traditional Confucian culture can only be described as an arrogant and completely narrow perspective. The idea that the process of change within the endogenous cultures of the Third World is not an automatic side effect of economic external dependency is grounded in the specific patterns of domination in colonialism.

In his analysis of the master-slave relationship in Hegel (1980), Frantz Fanon (1980 pp. 137) elaborated on the difference between colonial and non-colonial forms of domination in great detail. In Hegel's writing, the master, originally an independent being, is in fact dependent because he can only satisfy his needs through the slave's work. In this way the slave can secure his own self-reliance, i.e., his identity. In as far as his work creates substance it is a possible source of his liberation. The colonial master-slave relationship is different in that the slave cannot even be seen as a human object. Qua inter-changeable nonentity, within colonial structures of domination, the slave has no opportunity to enter into a "dialogue" (even as an unequal partner) with his European master.

This form of master-slave relationship can only acknowledge the latter's existence by non-communication. It is precisely this colonial relationship which is still in place today and it shows that the rejection of the possible effects of cultural imperialism in the Third World is just as important as its acceptance. The question must be asked as to why this form of imperialism, with all its attendant destruction, was not particularly successful, given the massive level of investment which the Euro-American media and the culture industry have pumped into the Third World. It is not just bad market strategies which have caused many western European breweries, after long ad campaigns, to withdraw in frustration from the Greek market.

The simple fact is that they did not change the Greek public's preference for wine. The same can be said for the use by ESSO of the slogan "Put a tiger in your tank" in Malaysia which was received with anything but enthusiasm (Killough 1983, 65). Such unsuccessful ad campaigns are in fact the result of a deep-seated refusal to engage in dialogue with the colonizer. Besides being counterproductive and thus against the intentions of its creators, this form of cultural imperialism has also created a trans-cultural, psycho-social constant in every Third World country, namely, the image of the "Ugly American" (Lederer and Burdick 1966). This image can be found in overt or covert form in every shade of political opinion in the Third World

c) In the tradition of abstract critical communications research, Nordenstreng/Schiller (1979, 6) have written that "it is precisely the international socio-politico-economic system that decisively determines the course of development within the sphere of each nation." Even accepting the correctness of the weight attributed here to the influence of exogenous factors on the endogenous societal development within the Third World, it also must be said that the determinism expressed herein is not pertinent to the subject matter, particularly as regards processes of communications. French and Italian structuralists and semiotic scholars, in particular, have demonstrated that the political and economic control of the sources of communication (e.g. private media corporations) and the communications channels (e.g. satellite technology) cannot be equated with control over the recipient's ability to decode what is to be communicated.

   Umberto Eco, amongst others, has correctly commented that: "The recipient has one remaining freedom left to him, namely, the ability to interpret the message differently" (Eco 1985, 149). The scope and quality of this remnant of freedom is determined by the specific historical, cultural and individual situation of the recipient.

   It covers such phenomena as the faithful reproduction of the European "Negro image" on the cinematic screen by the black Antillian (Fanon 1980, 107), the approval expressed by an Algerian Muslim patriarch of the Ewings in "Dallas" because he himself lives in a large family-clan (Stolz 1983, 84) as well as the fact that a censored edition of an Iranian newspaper was completely sold out during the detested Shah's rule because it contained a picture of the esteemed Ayatollah Khomeini even though the text severely attacked Khomeini himself (Taheri 1980, 7).

Imitation, reinterpretation and outright falsification of the communicator's intentions are just three of the possibilities which the recipients can employ when decoding a message. There is a certain irony to the fact that US communications research is rarely able to identify such processes of communication in the Third World. The worldwide expansion of behaviorism and neo-positivism is in itself an expression of cultural imperialism. This instrumental approach undermines the possibility of understanding the processes of qualitative change because of the scope of its influence, its territorial size and its many sectoral aspects. Indeed, if maintained only by instrumental means, it can also be said that such dominance is particularly fragile and vulnerable.

In the form of Hollywood, the US social system has achieved perfection within the realm of instrumental media impact research where in TV tests viewers' increased pulse rates are monitored, as a re hormone changes or adrenaline rushes. Yet, at the same time US diplomats and experts are unable to identify the religious nature of the opposition's communication channels during the reign of the Shah in Iran. They were also unable to overcome their inability to recognize the religious opposition within Washington's governmental communications apparatus. The stronger this domination tries to consolidate itself in line with the logic of a capitalist information society at the instrumental and technical levels, the more a culture creates a means of avoiding such attacks.

Since Karl Marx, at the latest, the idea that culture is a reflection of concrete historical production relationships, must be seen as banal. It is just as banal to assert that culture is also the expression of particular class relationships and that within every national culture there is a ruling culture in opposition to oppressed cultures. Beyond this apt conceptualization, culture should be seen, outside of the dialectics of base and superstructure as a kind of "super-phenomenon" which, comparable to language (Stalin 1964), has influenced the relationship between the two. Even if the socio-linguistic definitions of the domination and class character of language have to be considered, the Russian feudal lord addresses his kulak not in Kisuaheli, but in Russian. Put differently: In capitalism, the productive sector is necessarily reflected in a competitive and aggressive culture. At the same time this cultural combativeness is a prerequisite for the evolution of capitalism It is precisely because of this that capitalism itself originated in Europe and not with the Hopi Indian in the USA.

Johan Galtung (1985, 122) has christened this comprehensive and class transcendent view of culture as "social cosmology." This concept deals with people's different systems of reference. It encompasses space, time, nature, man and work and is pertinent to many areas of culture. Such social cosmologies are over long periods of time integrated so deeply into the collective unconscious of a people through their specific cultural outlook that they are, more or less, resistant to change. While culture can, of course, be marketed and industrialized, such social cosmologies seem to the able to withstand industrialization. Even though television has created something which can be called the "electronic church," this does not mean that religious spirituality in itself has been domesticated.

In summarizing the above it can be stated that cultural transfer via the mass media contains not only the potential to dominate another culture but also innately offers the basis for resistance. In the recipient's country the transfer does not take place within a cultural vacuum and it does not really undermine his reduced ability to decode messages to his own liking. If culture is industrialized, then the cultural cosmology, which can be seen as the collective correlation to the individual in psycho-analysis, will be able to withstand external instrumental control.

2. ICT and European Cultural Change

Long before the capitalist era, Europe's social cosmology was decisively influenced by characteristics which first fully emerged with the growth of capitalism: examples are the external expansion of space and time, the domination of nature, self-realization and the creation of surplus value through labor. The evolving integration of ICT is one of the most logical developments of this social cosmology. Computer "real time" satisfies the need to extend time in itself. The flexibility of future transnational ISDN networks will make the concepts of time and space obsolete (and with it excellent political slogans such as "think globally, act locally"). The wish to dominate nature has achieved new dimensions through manned space flights, the moon landing, bio-chips and cloned plants.

Fully in the tradition of the labor movement Maxim Gorky once said that "a new culture begins with respect for the working people." Yet this component of European cosmology is less and less in evidence. With the implementation of ICT actual human labor is becoming increasingly unimportant in production itself and in shaping working people's identities. Labor is thus being reduced in scope, plunging Europeans into an increasingly strong cultural identity crisis. This is particularly true for Protestant-dominated Northern European with its corresponding work ethic. This cultural crisis is also fueled by internal repercussions brought on by the increasing external domination of time, space and nature. Europe was and remains the center of the globe in the imperialist worldview.

Yet the center itself is increasingly undermined by destructive mechanisms which were originally created as a tool in the domination of the peoples in the periphery. It can be said that this is the belated revenge of the colonized, whereby the perpetrators become the victims of their own actions. This revenge is best understood through the increasingly technological medium of culture. There are four general trends which can be described in the relationship of ICT to culture.

a) The first and most obvious trend is the commercialization and privatization of culture. Culture was for decades a small social niche into which the principle of capitalist value made only superficial inroads. Yet culture has now become a kind of "free lunch" for the advertising sector where it is used as a vehicle for, as well as a by-product of commercially marketed services. Culture can become industrialized through the storage and transmission potential of computers and network technologies and it is through these media that the prediction which critical social scientists made in the last fifty years is becoming reality.

The advance in this industrialization of culture is not without highly particular ideological contortions on the part of its political protagonists. The Canadian government with its "third-option policy" used the notion of Canada's cultural identity as a lever in order to gain an edge in its dealing with its own ICT industry - to disastrous effect. By contrast, Diana Lady Dougan, the U.S. coordinator for inter-national communications policy at the State Department argued vehemently against the concept of culture as economics in the following manner:

We must be particularly cautious of the growing view of 'information' as an economic commodity, taxation, tariff, and even economic embargo. This 'commodity' approach has particular appeal to governments which are inclined to view information services as a source of tax revenue. This approach could sanction increased government control of the free flow of information (Dougan 1983, 3).

What is stated above would appear on a superficial level to run against the policies and judgments of the European Commission and the European Court of Justice. Both these institutions, through the green paper entitled "Television without Borders" (Kommission 1984) and the relevant legal rulings have already agreed that culture is indeed a service. This has eliminated the national element from cultural policy and has created a legal precedent by resolving that national and regional quotas for the cross-border exchange of television programs are not permissible. In reality, there is only a superficial and tactical difference between the position of the State Department and that of the European Commission. The Commission has abandoned the concept of an independent cultural policy as it considers this as a potential spanner in the works of its own technology policy. Given that the Commission is trying to define away the concept of culture using different technical premises than those envisaged by the Treaty of Rome in 1957, it can be said that the State Department with its totally different form of argumentation is intent on achieving the same goal - simply ignoring the economic character of cross-border communication and culture, and thus de facto removing a major obstacle to the US global service sector.

b) The trend towards commercialization is closely associated with the tendency to break taboos. The mass media's capitalist production conditions of necessity compel an ever faster creation of new and novel phenomena and engender both enlightening and repressive elements. Because the bourgeois liberal arts thrive on the fact that they unmask the dominant moral ambiguity of officialdom and that openly breaks social taboos, the private mass media must market this form of undermining.

If a play, for example, challenges the ambiguity surrounding homosexuality, then the mass media, after a certain period of time, first of all will dull the original critical edge of this statement and secondly, will, in the followers of time, give the former taboo a new media reality. While homosexuality can be transformed into mass media "normality" it can then lead to the denial of discrimination of homosexuals in the real world. The competition between the necessary undermining of taboos and the marketing of this process has led to the situation where pigs have been slaughtered live and a poet has mutilated himself with a kitchen knife during a competition while the TV cameras ran live. The numerous additions to each household's capability to receive TV programming will certainly accelerate this spiral. Art has been left very little space to undermine social taboos. If the media's seeming undermining of the totality of social taboos is fully realized, then art itself has no longer a progressive function because real ambiguity no longer has a public object.

c) Marginalization represents a third trend within the relationship between ICT and culture. The "revenge of colonialism" (immigration, centralism and resistance to it in the form of regionalism) has been evident in the unequal development in the former leading colonial countries such as England, France, Spain and Portugal. ICT have greatly contributed to the strengthening of these trends. As in every other field of technological expansion, ICT have led to a distinct differentiation between the center and the periphery, between the consolidation of power and impotency, between the domination of the many by the few.

This development can be seen within the relationship between the technologically advanced and the techno-logically backward areas. It can also be seen within individual countries and, last but not least, as an expression of social difference and political and economic domination. Even if given the increasing knowledge gap, research is still in need of much more empirical evidence in order to validate and refine its assertions, the specialist media's and task-specific ICT data on end users, for example, give a very clear idea of what is being discussed here.

The following are excellent examples of this phenomenon: A survey shows that active users of the online catalogues in 15 scientific libraries in the US were already heavy users of the libraries facilities; over 60 percent of the users were men and approx. 70 percent were graduate students (Jones 1983). In other words such end user data shows all too clearly that what is involved is the pattern of an existing small, established information elite. Further data confirms this: ICT contributes to the development of a politically and socially explosive division of "information rich" and "information poor."

If one includes future development within the mass media sector in this consideration then the realization of the following becomes all the more probable: It is likely that the entertainment requirements of the "information poor" sector of the population will be satisfied to an increasing degree by new, cheap electronic mass media such as video, cable television and pay TV, while the information rich section will acquire expensive, high-quality and detailed information through specialized print and electronic text storage media.

d) Finally, segmentation can be said to constitute a fourth trend in the relationship between ICT and culture. In this area, we have seen the strengthening of previously perceptible developments. The "two cultures" concept (Zwei Kulturen? 1978) has been deployed to describe and analyze such processes of segmentation. Within West European industrial societies there is an unacceptable discrepancy between individual self-realization and state regulated planning, between the fulfillment of desires and labor, between the same individual's various and contradictory role expectations, and between internal and external processes of learning.

> This has led to a situation where the social cosmology (which regardless of class structure acts as a social cohesive) has either disappeared or has re-emerged in a loosely segmented form. West Berlin can be cited as an extreme example of this process of decay. On a purely quantitative level, the Berlin suburb of Kreuzberg is already, after Istanbul and Ankara, the third largest Turkish city on earth. The ghettoization of this suburb - in partly a consequence of the advance of ICT and their attendant work rationalization policies - has also given birth to a highly developed punk culture. While both the Turkish and punk phenomena in Berlin can be considered rich sources of cultural identity in themselves, there is no communication between the veiled Muslim housewife and the unemployed tattooed punk. There is no level of commonly held and interactive existential perceptions.

ICT persuade the lower middle classes to identify with Dallas, the feminist with her woman program, the manager with his financial magazine, and adherents of alternative cultures to identify with local radio stations. Similar processes exist in the productive sector. Flexible working hours, the extreme increase in the division of labor, and the distribution of work through electronically equipped private homes leads to the individual isolation and the undermining of the principle of collective solidarity as a necessary prerequisite of societal existence.

The four trends towards cultural change, commercialization and segmentation, of course, contain contradictions in their relationship to ICT. As a consequence, there is scope to utilize remnants of free choice. This is true as regards communication of our remaining abilities to decode content and image in specific user situations, and it holds true for the technology from producer to end user. External conditions, even formal user technical instruction manuals, i.e., those formal aspects of the users' implementation of technology may have a stronger effect on the process of homogenization than the content of the mass media. They narrow even further what remains of freedom of choice.

While it is difficult in relation to the processes of segmentation and the undermining of taboos to perceive counter trends which increase what residues of free choice still exist, the opposite is the case within the other two trends and they are clearly visible. The commercialization of culture also necessitates the "culturalization" of commerce. Such tendencies were already to be discerned in the 1960s, in the writings of international management institutes where the need for cultural sensibility as a component of US multinational market success was mentioned. Two examples will suffice to demonstrate this form of the "culturalization" of commerce.

In the period after Franco, Spanish media capital among others brutally smashed the government's television monopoly by setting up the private TV 3 station. Yet this channel is Catalonian. It promotes a culture which had been suppressed for decades and allows for its exposure as well as the discovery of its own identity (Darnton 1984). This is comparable to the totally different situation of post-revolutionary Iran. Iran, and particularly its oil sector, still maintains extremely close ties with the western banking sector. This situation - it also exists in other Islamic countries - has necessitated the introduction of new legal concepts within the banking sector itself. In attempting to create their own Islamic economy as a third way between capitalism and socialism (Dia 1975), a phenomenon which is to be found throughout the Islamic world, a means had to be found to comply with Koranic law on usury and interest. It is now possible for Europeans with Islamic partners to charge interest provided it is called by another name such as payment-commission or fee. One of the surahs in the Koran lays down ground rules on how to act in relation to contracts between Muslims and non-Muslims where Islamic law alone can be applied and where the rule of all other systems of law is excluded.

Such phenomena as US TV series dubbed into Catalan and electronic banking according to Islamic law demonstrate the commercialization of culture, as well, the "culturization" of commerce. The successful battle of a periphery to preserve and extend its own world of cultural symbols can, to some degree, create a force which at some later period, could minimize or even abolish the commercialization of culture. This possibility has raised a number of fears on the part of a German industrial consultant:

> The fact that Islamic and international law operate side by side is responsible for an increasing amount of German industrialists' headaches. This is particularly so when Saudi Arabia and Iran are among Germany's most important export markets outside Europe (Höppner 1984, 50).

Cultural resistance and rejection, as has already been stated, are always inherent in the marginalization of cultural itself. The development and integration of the telecoms infrastructures between Spain, Portugal and the core countries of the EU will naturally lend to dependency on the part of the Iberian partners. This also raises the hope that through extending the south, the Northern European Protestant culture, traditionally oriented towards the United States, will in the final instance encounter a necessary counter-weight in the form of exuberance, sensuality and the joy of life or even in Spanish cultural resistance (Flamenco, Federico Goya, Francisco Garcia Lorca, Pablo Picasso). Historical experience suggests that the dominant pattern of exchange will for once proceed in exactly the opposite direction. It is probable that with the growth of authentic Spanish film the latter will at least initially be popularized in much the same way as the Spanish tomatoes. Before Spain's membership of the EU it was possible, at particular times of the year, to find wrinkled and marked Spanish tomatoes of differing sizes which tasted extremely good in German supermarkets. Since January 1, 1986 however, this is no longer possible.

The Spanish farmer has been hit by an avalanche of EU food laws which decree that the Spanish tomato shall have exactly the same dry insipid taste as its counterpart grown in the plastic greenhouses of the Netherlands. Yet when one examines the history of West Europe over the last 20 years it soon becomes clear that political resistance which is always hidden in an atmosphere of symbolic cultural resistance against the "core societies" of central Europe can only grow out of the periphery. Finland in the far north and Malta in the deep South are active members of the non-aligned movement. Norway and Greenland have opted out of the EU and Greece, Spain and Portugal have demonstrated a potential for social consciousness which is barely conceivable in the main EU member states.

It is indeed no accident that it was Melina Mercouri, a culture minister from a country at the community's periphery, and Jack Lang, a culture minister solidly in the Roman-European tradition, who vehemently argued for the promotion of cultural identity at the UNESCO's World Conference on culture in Mexico in 1982. As if to confirm Jack Lang's hypothesis on cultural imperialism, Charleston Heston, a symbol of Hollywood's commercial cinema and the US delegate at the conference attacked Melina Mercouri in such a inflamed manner that this sensitive, self-assured Greek with impeccable democratic credentials had to abandon her speech in tears. Because of this it is all the more important to seriously consider Jack Lang's speech at the MONDIACULT Conference:

> Culture and Economic - one and the same battle. [...] I ask myself: [...] why should we accept this homogenization? Is this really mankind's destiny? The same films, the same music, the same clothes?

> [...] We wish to proclaim a real cultural revolt, to embark on a crusade against - let us call it by its name - against this financial and intellectual imperialism (Lang 1983).

3. ICT and Europe's External Cultural Relations

Given that ICT's technical potential to increasingly dominate time, space and nature is a reflection of what typically constitutes European social cosmology and its contemporary manifestation as a capitalist information society, then all signs point to the fact that West Europe's external relations will continue in their present form. Cultural conflict and its attendant momentum towards resistance will continue to increase within Europe's external cultural relations.

When one considers that the single market has grown only to an insignificant degree since its foundation in 1957 if one excludes the new members then this phenomenon can be seen not just as a techno-economic strategy to realize quicker and easier profits in external markets. Behind this stratagey lies also the traditional collective external orientation of societies which seem to be unablė to build and sustain their own internal consciousness. West Europe's answer to the demands of ICT can only be social and participative if, to a much greater level than has been the case up until now, it concentrates on its own situation implementing the economic and socio-psychological elements of the theories of auto-centric development.

There are two reasons why West Europe will find it very difficult to change its cultural relationship to the USA. First, it shares the same social cosmology as the USA and, second, the non-colonial relationship between the two unequal partners works against West Europe's much needed process of emancipation. In other words: Liberation from a dominant father is more difficult than from a cruel slave owner. In this way, West Europe also is the object of a belated colonial revenge. How can it, when it still acts out its role of the colonist in the Third World, free itself from a partner? Once more to formulate it differently: Is it not more difficult for Western Europe to demythologize the friend image than the enemy image?

Table 6.1:
Cultural Development Strategies in the Third World

Domination		Oppressor	Oppressed
Culturally Relativist Strategy		I	II
	Actors	– Iran, Ayatollah Khomeini – Libya, Muammar al-Qaddan – Burma, U Ne Win	– Rastafarians in Jamaica – Aborigines in Australia – Native Americans in the US – Opposition in Afghanistan – Miscitos in Nicaragua
	Theorists	– Mainly anthropologists, psychologists and linguists	– Frantz Fanon, Ali Shariati Bob Marley, Jack D. Forbes, Russel Means
	Social Change	– Continuity versus stagnation	– Continuity and Identity
Culturally Global Strategy		III	IV
	Actors	– Singapore, Lee Kuan Yew – Kenya, Daniel Arap Moi – Afghanistan, Babrak Karmal	– Oppositional trade unions in Latin America – Opposition in the Philippines under Corazon Aquino
	Theorists	– Mainly economists and social scientists; socialist and conservative versions	– Leftist intellectuals, unionists, women's groups
	Social Change	– Discontinuity; modernism versus social up-rooting	– Socialism and social justice

Given that the development of ICT can strengthen West Europe's relationship to the Third World within the context of the above-cited models, the cultural conflict that it has created between acceptance and rejection is now more critical and pronounced than ever before. Europe's obsession with activity, energy, achievement, development, change and progress which are used as role models by all shades of political opinion can be of positive value when it is bound to the deepest humanitarian goal of freedom.

Over a long period of time, Europe has not contributed to the realization of another deeply rooted humanitarian objective, namely the cultural self-determination of a people which at times stands in opposition to the concept of freedom. The relationship model between the Third World and Western Europe as shown in Table 6.1 is a clear preference for dealing with sections III and IV. By the year 2000 the earth will be predominantly Muslim with Islam claiming the adherence of over half of its entire population. It is this group which among others constitutes sections I and II. Both Islam and Jamaican Rastafarianism have embraced cultural relativist strategies that totally avoid identification with European notions of right or left, that allow little external cultural penetration and that display a high level of cultural autonomy in their communication and mass media.

Interestingly enough, this high level of autonomy is valid not only for traditional and pre-industrial communication such as the religious communications network of Bazares, Mosques, Pulpits and Sermons in Iran (Borthwick 1973; Fathi 1977; Fathi 199). The highly effective use of audio cassettes and video film during the Iranian Revolution and the Rastafarian's conceptual control of reggae (Campbell 1980; Cuthbert 1984) shows that cultural autonomy and resistance to cultural imperialism is also possible through the use of modern mass media.

4. Conclusion

Europe bought its own social security, an almost complete satisfaction of its basic material needs and the fragile absence of war, with a loss of its cultural identity. This cultural decay is much more strongly evident in the protestant North than in the catholic South. The ICT of the Second Industrial Revolution will stimulate both the process of decay and its opposite, in an even more active manner. Whenever the instrumental and technical domination which lies behind this revolution becomes more integrated into the social cosmology which is in complete opposition to it, then cultural imperialism becomes all the more hollow and empty.

I would like to end this paper keeping the Chinese New Year's celebration on February 9, 1986 of the Year of the Tiger in mind by conducting an excursion into the realm of zoology. In coining the phrase "I don't think that a tiger has to go around proclaiming his tigritude", Nigerian author Wole Soyinka meant that African poetry contains so much beauty and is so deeply rooted in itself that it is no longer necessary for it to separate itself from European literature by using the term "Negritude". To this image should be attached another by Mao Ze-Dong:

> In the long term and from a strategic point of view, imperialism itself and all reactionary forces must, essentially, be seen as paper tigers. Our strategic thinking must be anchored to this procession. On the other hand, however, tigers of iron can really devour people, thus, our operative and tactical thinking must be based on this point (Mao Tse-tung 1969, 47).

When this is applied to the European situation it can be said that the louder the European tiger growls, the more process of change, another real tiger, that of Africa, Asian and Latin American culture is awaken.

References

Borthwick, Bruce M.: "The Islamic Sermon as a channel of political communication", in: *Intercommunication Among Nations and Peoples*, ed. by Michael H. Prosser, New York: Harper & Row 1973, pp. 369-82.

Campbell, Horace: "Rastafari: culture of resistance", in: *Race & Class*, No. 1/ 1980, pp. 1-22.

Cabral, Amilcar: *Die Theorie als Waffe*. Schriften zur Befreiung in Afrika, Bremen: Edition Con 1983.

Cuthbert, Marlene: *Young People and the Music Industry in Jamaica*. Paper at the Wingspread Conference on Youth and the International Music Industry, Racine, Wisconsin, August 17-19, 1983 (mimeo).

Darnton, John: "Private Catalan TV Station Ends Spain's Government Monopoly", in: *International Herald Tribune*, January 1, 1984.

Dia, Mamadou: *Islam, Sociétés Africaines et Culture Industrielle*, Dakar: Nouvelles Editions Africaines 1975.

Dougan, Diana Lady: *Remarks to senate panel U.S. Information, Communication Policies Outlined*, October 31, 1983 (mimeo).

Eco, Umberto: *Über Gott und die Welt*. Essays und Glossen, Munich: Hanser 1985.

Fanon, Frantz: *Schwarze Haut, weiße.Masken*, Frankfurt: Syndikat 1980.

Fathi, Asgar: „The 'Minbar' as Medium of Public Communication in Islam", in: *Communications and Development* (Tehran), No. 1/1977, pp. 11-12.

Fathi, Asgar: "The Role of the Islamic Pulpit", in: *Journal of Communication*, Nol. 3/1979, pp. 102-06.

Galtung, Johan: "Social Communication and Global Problems", in: *Communication for All*. The Church and the New World Information and Communication Order, ed. by Philip Lee, Indore: Satprakashan Sanchar Kendra 1985, pp. 118-31.

Hegel, Georg Wilhelm Friedrich: *Phänomenologie des Geistes*, Frankfurt: Suhrkamp 1980.

Höppner, Rolf-Roger: "Islamisierung. Allah ist groß", in: *Industriemagazin*, No. 3/1983, pp. 44-50.

Killough, James: „Grenzüberschreitende Werbung: Barrieren und Chancen", in: *Harvard Manager*, No. 1/1983, pp. 60-67.

Kommission der Europäischen Gemeinschaft: *Fernsehen ohne Grenzen*. Grünbuch über die Errichtung des gemeinsamen Marktes für den Rundfunk, insbesondere über Satellit und Kabel, Brüssel 1984 (= KOM 84, 300 endg.).

Lang, Jack: „Aufruf zum kulturellen Widerstand", in: *epd-Entwicklungspolitik*, No. 3-4/1983, pp. a-c.

Lederer, William J. and Burdick, Eugene: *Der häßliche Amerikaner*. Im Zwielicht der Diplomatie, Reinbek: Rowohlt 1966.

Lee, Jones C.: *Die Auswirkungen der Technologie auf die Benutzer wissenschaftlicher Bibliotheken*. Paper at the IFLA Conference, Munich (mimeo) 1983, p. 20.

Mao Tse-tung: *Das Rote Buch*, Frankfurt: Fischer 1969.

Nordenstreng, Kaarle and Schiller, Herbert I.: "Communication and National Development: Changing Perspectives", in: *National Sovereignty and International Communication*, ed. by Kaarle Nordenstreng and Herbert I. Schiller, Norwood, NJ: Ablex 1979, pp. 3-8.

Prokop, Dieter: "Die Bewusstseinsfixierung", in: *Medienforschung*. Vol. 1: Konzerne, Macher, Kontrolleure, ed. by Dieter Prokop, Frankfurt: Fischer 1985, pp. 504-39.

Pütter, Klaus: *Wie entwickelt sich die Konkurrenz der allgemeinen und Special-Interest-Zeitschriften und elektronischen Medien?* Paper presented at the Inter Media Congress, Hamburg, November 27-30, 1985 (mimeo).

Stalin, Josef W.: "Über den Marxismus in der Sprachwissenschaft", in: *Marxismus and Literatur*. Vol. III, ed. by Fritz J. Raddatz, Reinbek: Rowohlt 1969, pp. 7-27.

Stolz, Joelle: „Algerien sieht 'Dallas'", in: *Palaver* (Munich), No. 1/1983, pp. 83-85.

Taheri, Amir: *"Noose-Pepper"*. A Study of the Persian Press in a Period of Turmoil, London: The International Press Institute 1980.

Tran Van Dinh: *Blue Dragon, White Tiger*. A Tet Story, Philadelphia: TriAm Press 1983.

Zwei Kulturen? Tunix, Mescalero und die Folgen, ed. by Dieter Hoffmann-Axthelm et al., Berlin: Ästhetik und Kommunikation 1978.

7
Acculturation Clusters in Telecommunication Over Time and Space

In a detailed status report on research in the field of the origin of technology in Germany by Werner Rammert published in 1991 the author sums up:

> The prevailing view, not only among the wider public but also among academics, of the all-powerful rôle of economics and the military is giving way - if only very slowly - to more differentiated concept in which *cultural* aspects are being attributed a leading role. [...] wherever, due to indeterminatedness, economic calculations cannot be brought to bear, *cultural* models and values come into play as orientation points.[1]

However necessary it may be to react along with Werner Rammert against the monocausal deduction of all phenomena from the areas of economics and the military, and however welcome the fact may be that the cultural factor is gradually coming into its own in the reciprocal relationship between society and technology, it is not really possible to now attribute a "leading rôle" to cultural features: Karl Marx and Max Weber cannot be reconciled with one another simply by exchanging priorities.

Despite this, I would still like to go into the question of which conditional cultural patterns accompany, or have accompanied, the evolution of telecommunications, in particular of the telephone. And I would like to look at this question from two points of view: on the one hand with the aid of a historically-informed comparison between France and Germany (chronological level), on the other, by means of a comparison between different developments in the early Soviet Union and in various developing countries (spacial level).

Over the past few years three larger works have appeared in Germany on the subject of the telephone, the history of its technological development and its diffusion, all of them availing of comparisons of several countries. Firstly, there is Werner Rammert's own work of 1990,[2] then another published in the same year by Jörg Becker,[3] and a third work by Wolfgang König[4]. Despite their varying theoretical approaches and their different points of departure, all three works are in agreement on one point, namely, that it is not possible to seriously attribute theoretical priority either to the economy or to culture - the military seems to play scarcely any rôle in the early history of the telephone! On the contrary, all three authors bring a whole multiplicity of structural factors to bear on the discussion, factors such as population composition, size of the market, the relationship between rural and urban societies, substitution by other technologies, property relationships, etc. Of course, the emphasis on cultural factors in research work on the origins of technology still retains its importance, if only as a necessary counterbalance to the somewhat blinkered economic perspective which has been prevalent within the gamut of the social sciences over the past few decades.

1. Comparison of Germany and France

Intercultural comparisons are particularly difficult for methodological reasons. If cultural patterns and initial features - Johan Galtung would say: social cosmologies - are to be established empirically in a comparison of cultures, then one method which would seem fruitful, among others, is a comparison of popular literature from the different cultures. The reason for this is that popular literature is prime transmitter of everyday consciousness, that is to say, it reflects a state of consciousness which is scarcely subject to the restraints of public consciousness. In view of the fact that in France the diffusion of the telephone proceeded so much more slowly than in Germany (in 1921 Germany had almost four times as many installed telephone connections as France) then the question which might be asked in relation to the early history of the telephone is in what context motifs related to the telephone occur in the novels of the two contemporary best-selling writers Jules Verne (1828-1905) for France, and Karl May (1842-1912) for Germany. It would go beyond the framework of this essay to try to provide systematic empirical data on this question, but some initial empirically-enriched thoughts may well suffice here[5].

As for Jules Verne, let it be pointed out from the very start that he was fascinated by modern technology, and that his technical (and in part social) imagination accurately anticipated many future technological developments. By contrast, in the works of Karl May there is an all-pervasive, Romantic and anti-capitalist skepticism towards technology. This is particularly so in his Wild West novels, where the railway crops up as a constant symbol of a power which is destroying the natural life of the Native Americans and which emanates from the East Coast of the United States: Yankees, pale faces, crooks, banks and insurance companies.

Jules Verne's novel "L'île à hélice," a novel teeming with telephone motifs, was published in 1895, 34 years after Philipp Reis presented his paper on telephony in Frankfurt, 19 years after Alexander Graham Bell received his patent, and 14 years after the foundation of the first French telephone company in 1881. In this novel, every room in the luxury hotel on the artificially created island has its own "room telephone. Not only could you call all the other rooms in the hotel from your own room, but you could also call the city, and - possibly - even other cities in the United States."[5] At another point in the novel the reader learns that the Commodore is navigating his city-ship in constant telephone contact with the Electricity Supply Company, and that in the reading room of the library there are "phonograph books" - at the push of a button "the voice of an experienced reader" reads the desired book to the library user.

In Karl May the situation is quite different. In his case it is important first of all to indicate that the telephone as a motif does not appear anywhere in his entire work. This itself is an interesting initial point. However, it has been possible to track down a total of three places in Karl May's approximately 80 novels where mention is made of telegraphy. In the first instance the passage is about coded telegrams between Ludwig II and Richard Wagner aimed at bringing about a secret meeting between those two men. Coded telegrams turn up again in another novel, and significantly, in this particular scene the text runs: "Monsieur, am I now in the telegraph or police bureau?". Finally, in a third novel a telegram to Bismarck serves to successfully convict someone of high treason.

"Here man had won a victory over nature" the narrator comments affirmatively on the artificial island in Jules Verne's "L'île à hélice", while in Karl Mays' essay, "with the Iron Horse", one reads affirmative statements such as "nature's power is subject to him", or, "Iron [...] teaches man about power, which has been given to him over all creation". In the light of the subject-object-relationship existing between man and nature which formed their common spiritual background, the respective concrete descriptions given by Verne and May of the social use of telecommunications could not be farther apart: in Verne's work there is a positive, technological utopia in which no bounds are set to human fantasy and creativity in the pleasurable use of the new telecommunications instruments and services; in May there is a pervasive gloomy, dark and secretive association of telegraphy with the police, repression, crime, coded messages and secret meetings.

At this point I would like to offer the following interpretation, yet with no claims to providing a definitive clarification or evaluation. While technologically-speaking France clearly lagged behind Germany in the third quarter of the last century, as confirmed by all the statistical indicators of the level of technological standards (the number of technical colleges and engineers, the number of high-tech patents, the number of high-tech companies, the productivity levels for high-tech products, etc.), nevertheless, in an unbroken tradition, France's cultural conception of itself was orientated towards the conception of science, and this also means of technology, as put forward by a Rene Descartes and an Auguste Comte.

A positive image of technology obviously corresponds to this tradition of "clarity of thinking". Even if at the end of the 19th century France was in fact in danger of lagging behind and falling to the level of a technologically underdeveloped country, her culturally transmitted, fictional self-image functioned in a contrafactual and anti-cyclical manner. The poor telephone system which actually existed there at that time was confronted in fiction by an optimum telephone system. Thus, popular literature had a compensatory function. In Germany, things were just the reverse. It is no coincidence that Jules Verne gave the figure of the deadly, coldly-calculating technocratic engineer in his novel "Les cinq cent millions de la Bégum" (1879) the most German of all German names, Schultze. Germany's successful technology policy was in fact of such a caliber that it possibly kindled anxiety in its French neighbor. However, real developments in Germany, with their own respective chronological shift, also clashed with traditional cultural patterns.

There was in Germany the tradition of idealism accompanied by constant Faustian doubts, thus, it was also possible for a position of doubt about technical advance to develop from this. Although in 1900, Germany had the highest telephone density in Europe (even higher than in Great Britain), and was in fact one of the leading technological powers world-wide, still in sections of its popular literature one is confronted with a fictional self-image of quite another kind, an image full of yearning for an intact, pre-industrial world. Here too, at the social level, popular literature fulfilled a compensatory function.

In comparing the current skepticism in Germany towards nuclear technology with the widespread confidence in the achievements of this same technology in France, one has to keep in mind that at the roots of these ever so different attitudes lie social and cultural cosmologies which have been determined and nurtured in historically different ways.

2. Comparison of the Early Soviet Union and Some Developing Countries

Recent reports by ethnologists illustrate the term "telephone" cropping up in Southern Sudan as a first name. Although there are no comprehensive onomatological studies available specifically on names in developing countries containing elements from technology, many Third World travelers can quickly and spontaneously provide examples or request of names which they personally have heard. In West Africa "Lufthansa" has been met with as a first name, in Southern India the family names "Engineer" and "Petrowalla" (that is, someone who has to do professionally with petroleum), in Panama someone came across the first name "Usnavi" (borrowed from the *US Navy* ships patrolling the canal), and in the coastal region of Ecuador (Namabi) "Coca Cola" has been heard as a first name.

There are more systematic onomatological studies on the early Soviet Union than on the Third World, and in them special attention has been given to names containing technical terms. These studies have listed the following proper names derived from the fields of electricity and electrical engineering, to take just one example: "Elektrifikacija" (electrification), "Amper" (ampere), "Vol't" (volt), "Elektrina" (derived from electrification), "Ates" (ATS telephone exchange) or "Kinemm" (cinematograph).

What is the significance of such names derived from the technology of the western industrial nations? How would the phenomenon be evaluated? In all cultures, proper names, of all words or terms, have an immensely important, a mythical, sometimes even divine significance. Depending on the culture, the situation and the social context, there is the belief that at the root of the proper name lies an identity between the name and the essence of the person named, that it can express the good wishes of the parents or god-parents or the promise of good luck; that it exerts a magic influence; that uttering the name can exert power over the essence of the named person or can counteract the power of evil, etc. By contrast, namelessness means the impossibility of grasping hold of a thing, mastering a magic spell. When a child is given the name "Telephone" or "Ates" (telephone exchange) the following becomes evident:

1. By means of such technical influenced names autochthonic cultures adopt the world of the industrial nations so alien to them.
2. As these cultures even give up their own proper names in favor of these strange technical names, they obviously attribute an immense, even magical significance to the technical achievements of the industrial countries.
3. Depending on the culture, the situation, and the social context, such technical names express the desire to participate in the technology, to master it, or perhaps just envy of it.

In the case of the early Soviet Union there may also have been other, ideological reasons, not to mention the fight against the use of saints names from the Christian calendar. Yet these explanatory patterns still do not go far enough. It would seem more plausible that names such as these reflect the almost religious idea, so deeply rooted in Marxism-Leninism, that "the electronic revolution" - to quote Friedrich Engels - might finally free the mass of enslaved, powerless, hungry and destitute propels from their indescribable misery. V. I. Lenin's knowledge of the natural sciences in general and of electrical engineering in particular, is well established[6], as also is his enthusiasm for radio broadcasting[7] and the telephone[8].

His popular catch-phrase of 1920, "Communism - that means, Soviet power plus electrification of the whole country," expressed not just his own political credo but also corresponded to the dominant political hope which existed at the time in almost all countries and cultures, the hope of being able in the future to overcome the drudgery of the 19th century by means of a harmonious mixture of technical and social progress.

It is in this social context that the technical names given in the 1920s in the Soviet Union are to be seen. When considering similar names given in the Third World there is another important factor involved which is more closely related to the history of colonialism. Domination via language has always found expression in the right to bestow names. Given the fact that for hundreds of years missionaries in Africa, Asia and Latin America had forced Christian names on the indigenous people being baptized, it is possible that the observed tendency to voluntarily choose a first name containing elements derived from European technical artifacts is a particularly forceful symbol of political emancipation.

In studying material culture, ethnologists have concerned themselves in various ways with artistic and functional objects from Third World countries which provide evidence how technical artifacts from Europe have become integrated. Thus, Julius Lips talks about one example on the Nicobar islands of a picture, painted on wood, of the creator god Deuse in which he is surrounded by numerous symbols of European omniscience; a chair, a hat, a wheel, a bottle, a letter, a weapon, a pocket knife, a mirror and a comb[9]. The Colon figures (i.e. sculptures representing Europeans or with accessories of the European modern era) in the Voodoo cult of the Ewe in West Africa offer a possible key to the understanding of such pictures and figures. Alongside the Voodoo deities, other associated figures have a place here, "telephones, rifles, trains and airplanes, all the gestures and instruments of the military, the mission and industry"[10]. Like the tin plates on the roof of the dwelling of a wise man in a village in the Egyptian oasis of Dakhla, a widely visible symbol of a European TV satellite dish, such objects are more than just accessories and emblems of power.

> [They are] means and signs of the debate being carried on with colonialism: they serve the task of working over the trauma of colonization. [....] Resistance through identification with the aggressor is the form in which conservative satire urges a return to traditional norms. The inclusion of modern motifs [....] is evidence, therefore, not of any preparedness for progress, nor of the decline of tradition, but rather of the latter's power to assert itself behind the facade of modernity through self-alienation.[11]

Technical motifs originating from Europe and the United States of America also crop up regularly on the highly artistically decorated roofs of trucks in Pakistan. The choice of technical motifs is restricted to the area of transport, with almost exclusive reproductions of the most modern trains, ships or airplanes (copied from postcards and magazines). That these motifs are painted in the colours of the Pakistani Flag, or that a supersonic jet - which Pakistan does not possess - is decorated with the national emblems of that country, is intended to demonstrate the high state of technical development in Pakistan, or at least the desire for such a standard. On such painted trucks "a parrot regularly depicted on the telephone is a reference to the fact that the owner of the vehicle is available by phone. The telephone number is usually integrated into the painting."[12]

One final example of the adaptation of western telephone equipment by non-European cultures comes from the Native American peoples in the United States in the 19th century. The history of the telephone in America is full of reports about Native Americans destroying the first telephone transmission wires. In this context American provincial newspapers were still complaining about such "bad men" as "Chief Geronimo and his band of renegade Indians"[13] even as late as 1930. To see in these acts merely the destruction of western technology is just one way, the exogenous way of looking at things. The other, the endogenous way, sees the re-working of copper wire into artistic ear-rings, necklaces or other personal jewelry. If the functional use of western technology is not recognized at once then the technical artifacts in question can instead undergo a sometimes decidedly creative change of function, more appropriate to the respective context, be that the use of the spare tank of an MIG 21 in paddle boats for tourists in post-war Vietnam, or sandals made out of car tires, children's toys made out of empty tin cans, or even jewelry made out of telephone wires.

It should not be assumed that actively changing the function of western technology to suit one's own cultural peculiarities is a phenomenon of the past, or something that is only found in connection with the transfer of material cultural goods. The opposite is the case; this applies particularly in the case of the extremely creative functional adaptation of numerous elements of the information and communication technologies in the different countries of the Third World. For example, the possibility of connecting computer supported working places through a network despite spacial separation is used in Saudi Arabia in order to link up jobs which are segregated by sex in accordance with Muslim morality. In Abu Dhabi theological discussions were held on the question of whether video images are in conflict with the Koran's prohibition of representational images, the conclusion reached being that they did not[14].

In trying to bring the use of western technology into harmony with Jewish belief the ingenuity of ultra-orthodox groups in Israel knows no bounds: thus in January 1993 the Israeli Telephone company Besek installed a fax machine at the Wailing Wall in Jerusalem. All written texts which arrive there per fax are immediately stuck into gaps in the wall, in accordance with the tradition, so that God can hear the prayers. The only theological requirement for this possibility of "faxing God" is that the fax machine is turned off on the Sabbath. Finally, in Mozambique a group of critical journalists made itself independent of the government's restrictive allocation of paper to printing and newspaper companies by inaugurating a fax-"newspaper" called "Media Fax".

As the 48,000 characters of Chinese script (or their reduction to 7,000 in simpler dictionaries) was an obstacle to the possibility of sending telegraphs in Chinese, a system of telegraphy was developed early on in China which got around this difficulty elegantly. A Chinese telegraphic code is based on a clear assignment of characters to natural four-digit figures so that a total of 9,999 characters can be transmitted telegraphically. If the sender and the receiver had an identical code-table then these 9,999 characters were sufficient for them to communicate.[15]

Making a virtue of necessity: in the 1970s in Japan the difficulty in electrically transmitting thousands of characters constituted the driving force behind the development of fax machines for the mass market, although the innovative telecommunications concepts at the basis of fax machine technology originated in Europe in the 1930s and 1940s. Japan, after all, provides the most conclusive evidence for the fact that a non-European culture can incorporate western technology, develop it to its individual needs, and later influence the world market considerably as an exporter.

Instead of continuing to be taken in by the superstition that Japan owes its industrial progress merely to copying Western technology, it should be noted first that imitation presupposes an existing cultural climate of curiosity and openness to what is new. Second, just as, at the beginning of the 19th century German engineers were involved in industrial espionage in England, which at that time was technically superior, so, too, in the 20th century Japan has imitated many of Europe's and American technological developments. Thus, imitation seems to be a general pattern in the process of industrialization. Third, the history of Japanese technology does not just consist of imitation but has for many centuries entailed a highly systematic build-up of a Japanese techno-structure which has also resulted in independent technical developments.

3. Summary

On reviewing the comparison between Germany and France and their strikingly different adaptations of technological policy, one is also tempted to see cultural cosmologies as invariables in the process of technological change. In particular in a comparison of two immediate neighbors and cultures, this would be a very remarkable finding.

If we call to mind the different examples of the acculturation of European telecommunications technology in non-European cultures (proper names, Voodoo cult and colon figures in Black Africa, truck art in Pakistan, jewelry among the Apache people in America, the fax machine at the Wailing Wall in Jerusalem, code table for telegraphy in China, the development of the fax machine in Japan) it becomes evident that Max Weber's assumption is less and less tenable, his assumption, namely, that for its dynamic development capitalist industrial technology needs an economic ethics comparable to Protestantism and an extreme rationalism, "right as predictable as a machine," and a culture in which "ritual, religious, and magical viewpoints have no role to play."[16] What is really interesting and fascinating about the technology transfer from North to South, contrary to Max Weber, is not whether it functions or does not function there in the sense of rational capitalism.

The cultures of the developing countries are not "black boxes" into which technical products are either just thrown mechanically as into a funnel, or which simply reject technical products returning them mechanically like a boomerang. The exciting thing is the form in which such cultures adapt strange technical products to suit their local requirements. It was to this phenomenon which the French ethnologist Andre Leroi-Gourhan referred in 1943 already, in his book "L'homme et la matiere". Universal technological trends may of course be discernible but the actual form they take is always subject to different, that is, relative cultural starting positions. Thus, the German ethnologist Bernhard Streck is quite justified in saying that:

> It is, however, the other partner in the process of cultural contact who decides on the usability, the realization, in Leroi-Gourhans' sense of the term. The Sudanese need petrol canisters (safiha) as a raw material in their everyday life, but they can only get hold of them when the inland air-transport network is maintained with the help of foreign aid.[17]

The different patterns in the utilization of technology can be summarised once again with reference to the conflict arising out of jewelry production by the Apache people using telephone wires. The Western view: illegal destruction of new telecoms infrastructure aimed at linking less developed areas with the modern metropolitan centers. The endogenous view: legitimate alteration of strange technologies to fulfill culturally-adapted and self-determined functions and needs. That in this process breaches of the law occur does not meet with any consciousness of wrong-doing on the part of the representatives of the respective endogenous cultures because they at least suspect, if not actually know, that foreign law has an instrumental character in the extension of political and economic dominance. If these two contrary patterns are borne in mind it becomes clear that firstly, we are no longer dealing here with a micro-structural view limited to a restricted numbers of examples, and secondly, that it is precisely these patterns which are still relevant in the current battle about the conditions for technology transfer and in the closely related discussion about copyrights, patent rights and licence rights in the present North-South conflict.

When the western industrial countries, at their head the United States, demand from the developing countries billions of dollars in compensation for income losses resulting from illegally copied records, tapes, films, books and, above all, computer software, put pressure on them to accede to the new copyright regulations in the future GATT framework, close their local markets to them in cases of law infringements, and call the behaviour of the developing countries "product piracy," then the developing countries, for their part, react by calling the same procedure "reverse engineering", referring to their own economic losses due to local software specialists emigrating to industrial countries, or to the fact that intellectual knowledge does not belong to any one nation alone but could be a "common heritage of mankind".

Notes and References

1. Rammert, Werner: *Entstehung und Entwicklung der Technik: Der Stand der Forschung zur Technikgenese in Deutschland*, Berlin 1991 (= Papers des Wissenschaftszentrums Berlin für Sozialforschung, FS II 91-105), p. 31.
2. Rammert, Werner: "Telefon und Kommunikationskultur. Akzeptanz und Diffusion einer Technik im Vier-Länder-Vergleich" in: *Kölner Zeitschrift für Soziologie und Sozialforschung*, Vol. 42, No. 1/1990, pp. 20-40.
3. Becker, Jörg: "Aus der Geschichte lernen? Die Zukunft des Telefons", in: *Nachrichtentechnische Zeitschrift*, No. 5/1990, pp. 360-67.
4. König, Wolfgang: "Nutzungswandel, Technikgenese und Technikdiffusion. Ein Essay zur Frühgeschichte des Telefons in den Vereinigten Staaten und Deutschland", in: *Fern-Sprechen.* Internationale Fernmeldegeschichte, -soziologie und -politik, ed. by Jörg Becker, Berlin 1994, pp. 147-63.
5. For reasons of simplification exact bibliographical references to the sources in Jules Verne and Karl May have been dispensed within the following.
6. See for example Melestschenko, J. S. and Schuchardin, S. W.: *Lenin und der wissenschaftlich-technische Fortschritt*, Leipzig 1972.
7. See for example Guback, Thomas H. and Hill, Steven P.: *The Innovation of Broadcasting in the Soviet Union and the Rôle of V. L. Lenin*, Urbana, Champaign 1972 (mimeo).
8. See for example Solnick, Steven L.: "Revolution, Reform and the Soviet Telephone System, 1917-1927", in: *Soviet Studies*, Vol. 43, No. 1/1991, p. 166.
9. Lips, Julius: *Der Weiße im Spiegel der Farbigen*, Munich 1983, p. 166 [English Original 1937; re-translation into English]
10. Kramer, Fritz: "Die Fremdheit afrikanischer Colon-Figuren", in: *Colon.* Das schwarze Bild vom weißen Mann, ed. by Jens Jahn, Munich 1983, p. 213.
11. Ibid., p. 210 and 212.
13. Cf. Devine, Betty: "Howard Theodore Vaille Retires", in: *The Mountain States Monitor*, July 1930, p. 11.
14. Cf. Rahman, S.C.K. Abdul: "Video and Photography", in: *Emirate News* (Abu Dhabi), March 23, 1990.
15. Cf. Seelemann, Claus: *Das Post- und Fernmeldewesen in China.* Post über 10.000 Meilen Lebensadern eng verknüpft, Munich 1992.
16. Weber, Max: *Wirtschaft und Gesellschaft*, Tübingen 1976, p. 812.
17. Streck, Bernhard: „Was wird aus 'unserer Entwicklungshilfe' gemacht? Kulturhistorische Gedanken zum Technologietransfer", in: *Freibeuter*, No. 13/1982, p. 67.

8
Video Cassette Recorders in Third World Countries

Tanzania, like most African countries, is football mad. But during the 1982 World Cup in Spain, this mania went a stage further. The day after each match, video recordings were circulating in the houses of the wealthy elite and on the black market in Dar-e-Salaam. This was an extraordinary development in a country whose leaders preach austerity and where there is supposed to be no TV. Video Cassette Recorders (VCR) and TV sets are now the new status symbols. The one snag was that it was illegal to import videos, unless the Governor of the Bank of Tanzania provided an exemption. This state of affairs would probably have continued happily but for the unfortunate intrusion of a government anti-corruption campaign. There were many red faces when videos were uncovered in the houses of prominent Tanzanians. The problem was resolved by the finance minister, Cleopa Msuya, who lifted the restrictions on video imports. He justified this by saying that it was very difficult to control illegal importation, and he imposed a 500 percent luxury import duty on videos, but did not explain how people could afford them. The IMF has been pressing the government to recognize the country's unofficial economy, and the lifting of controls on videos implies that it has. An irate Tanzanian student said:

> Although the government claimed to be working towards an egalitarian society, they were not following the rhetoric. Lifting the restrictions on videos was a move to placate the people. They were saying 'now that we have them, you can have them too'. The government is now working pragmatically.

1. Lack of Research

Although the popular scientific press sometimes deals with the topic of video cassettes in Third World countries, there is no scientific research project on this complex subject and even the McBride Report to UNESCO omitted it. The scholarly community's neglect of video is astonishing, hard to explain and, in addition, calamitous. Whereas, ten years ago international debate concentrated on the role of the press and news agencies in the North-South conflict, subsequently it turned to questions of high technology (transborder data flow, computers and satellites), and "forgot" the rapid development, capture and penetration of the world market by VCRs and video film cassettes.

Political solutions concerning the role of the press and news agencies using the formula of a "free and balanced flow of information" became discernible - it was "merely" a question of conditions and the quality of technology transfer, when the development of the video market made nonsense of all such projected solutions. The cross-border smugglers of small video cassettes obey no regulative principle except the purchasing power of the consumers. The so called free flow of information has been completely successful, as far as video cassettes are concerned, in the crudest commercial form possible in many Third World countries.

The video boom set in about the middle/end of the 1970s, was virtually disregarded by scientific observers. As a result of the private enterprise nature of the video market and because of the black market component, reliable data (global, regional and national) about the spread of the most important systems (VHS, Betamax and V-2000) are virtually unobtainable. Consequently, only rough data about some regions and countries hint at the extent of the video market. At the end of 1983, there were 40 million VCRs in the whole world. The way was led per capita by Kuwait (92 percent of households) followed by Great Britain (30 percent), Japan (26 percent) and Germany (15 percent).

What is true of the Western nations also seems to apply to many Third World countries, namely intensive market penetration in a very short time. In 1980, for example, 374,000 sets were sold in West Germany; in 1981 the number had more or less doubled to 750,000 sets. In Jordan, in 1980 the VCR was legally marketed; in 1982 12,000 sets were in use. Including the sets illegally smuggled into the country, 30,000 sets are conservatively estimated to be in Jordan at present. This rate of growth clearly shows an essential difference to TV, which needed/needs - varying from country to country - between 5 to 10 years to become established on a large scale.

Further data drawn from selected Third World countries should clarify the quantitative dimensions of this phenomenon. In 1979 in Malaysia 2,800 VCRs worth M$ 4.8 million were imported; in 1981 there were already 46,000 sets with a combined value of M$ 59 million. Three-quarters of the set owners are Chinese, which presents a special problem for the Malaysian government: whereas, the government attempts to develop a common cultural TV policy for all the various peoples living in Malaysia, the wealthy Chinese minority has found a way - by means of VCRs - to maintain and cultivate their own cultural identity.

In Mexico, to cite a different example, experts estimate that there are 70,000 VCRs spread across three percent of households in the capital with a combined value of US$ 35 million. In this case these are also low estimates because of the black market, and because most sets were bought at a time when the US dollar exchange rate was low.

In Jamaica, where video recorders played an important role in the 1980 election campaign, the total number of VCRs is estimated at 10,000 with a combined value of approximately J$ 30 million. With a set costing J$ 3,000 it is easy to see that such appliance can only be bought by the wealthy upper class in the capital.

A further completely different example indicates the penetration pattern of VCRs. Socialist Ethiopia has so far, for good reasons, almost no television. Approximately 45,000 TV sets (i.e., 0.15 percent penetration) can be found in the houses of the rich and expatriate community, mainly in Addis Ababa. The estimated total of home VCR machines in Ethiopia is 300 and over 90 percent of them are to be found in the capital, among the expatriate community and the well-to-do. In other words, first and foremost it is the foreign experts, foreign aid workers, diplomats and the like, who form the phalanx in the capture of the VCR market.

The role and effect of video cassettes evidently differs greatly from one country to the next. Although, for example, no data are available about the spread of VCRs and cassettes in fascist Chile, video cassettes are known to play an important role in the political underground work of democratic groups. And thus, in spite of justifiable aesthetic criticism of the soap-opera Hollywood feature film *Missing* by the Greek director Costa Gavras, it was this film which experienced widest distribution on video cassettes. For the young people in Chile, who were too young at the time of the fascist putsch in 1973 to remember it consciously, this film on video cassette has become an important political instrument in Chile's re-democratization process.

2. Video Film Content

Data on the favorite types of films is even more scarce than quantitative data about the spread of VCRs in the Third World. The assumptions that the majority of video films are European and/or US feature films is not always correct. In Asia, Asian films probably predominate. The skimpy literature assumes a preponderance of entertainment, sports, musical, adventure and pornography. Whereas, in Western industrial nations VCRs are often used to select and copy films presented on TV, in the Third World it is mainly a question of obtaining a private chance to show feature films which the national TV network (if one exists) or the national cinemas do not show or perhaps will only show at a later date. The German Video Institute assumes the changes in turnover listed in Table 8.1 in its study *The Video Market* 1983.

Table 8.1:
Sales of the Most Important Program Categories on the West German Video Market in 1982 and 1983

Type	1982 (percent)	1983 (percent)
Action/Science fiction	19	28
Adventure films	13	13
Erotic films	10	12
Thrillers	8	10
Horror films	14	10
Comedies/Light comedies	11	8
Westerns	9	7
War films	10	7
Children's and Juvenile' films	5	4
Entertainment-Musicals (Popmusic/musicals)	1	1
Classical music films (Operas/Concerts)	0	0
Leisure and hobbies	0	0
Education and Vocational Training	0	0

Source: Deutsches Video-Institut: Der Video-Markt 1983, Berlin 1983 (unpublished and mimeographed study).

What is striking in this survey is the high percentage of films of pornography and violence in various forms, which using the categories here tends to be covered up rather than revealed. In the opinion of many experts in the Third World, the prime problem is that of films regarding pornography and violence. The social and cultural effects will prove to be considerably more intensive in these countries than in the Western industrial nations. Whereas, such films rely on already brutal and commercialized sexual mores in the West, in many Third World countries, especially Islamic ones, such films offend traditional religious and cultural taboos.

On the other hand, the remarks of Japanese film director Nagisa Oshima are relevant. He reports that the East Asian video producers make the same pornographic film in three different levels of "hardness". While the hardcore version "A" is only sold on the East Asian market, European clients accept the same film only in soft version "C". However, varied the role of pornographic video films in industrialized and developing countries, the following mechanism seems to apply to all countries: pornographic video films are introduced very consciously and aggressively at the onset of a developing market. Sex films seem to be the most important instrument for expanding an underdeveloped video market, opening it up for a more diversified approach later.

Another strategy to conquer a market, used by producers but also by some naive scientists and educationalists, is to point out the educational deployment of video films in schools and teaching. However, subjectively well-meaning such ideas may be, objectively they result in conditioning the market, the viewing and use patterns, behavioral patterns and consumer habits to a Western consumer culture. Speaking more generally, even technology-happy educationalists can become "useful idiots" for commercial interests if the infrastructural conditions for general pedagogy are not more firmly based than it is the case in many Third World countries.

3. Social Background of the Users

The data on buyers and users of appliances and films is likewise a matter of conjecture. If it is true, for example, for West Germany that three-quarters of VCR buyers enjoy an above-average disposable income and an above-average degree of formal education, and that 85 percent of all buyers are men, this still says very little about the actual users.

A further question would be how the class of buyers and users change in the course of time as penetration of the market increases. There are already many indications that the proportion of actual, youthful users is much higher than their proportion in general population. VCRs are probably used most intensively during the daytime, when parents are not at home because of their occupations. As with TV at the beginning of the 1950s, video films seem to be viewed collectively at present. These rough data and assumptions about consumer behavior seem to be true for most of the Third World countries as well, with some reservations:

- Buyers and interested parties are mainly wealthy men from the capital.
- The appliances are mainly used in a circle of private friends - usually excluding women; VCRs and corresponding film material mean a high degree of social prestige for the owner - they document that he is "modern" and "western".
- Young people clashe with their parents about authority and culture to watch forbidden films in their parents' absence; dependent on market penetration, VCRs and corresponding films can already be found in remote villages in some countries (e.g., Malaysia).

In this phase of political development, during which the aims of a New International Information Order can only be secured, continued and developed via national plans for the development of mass media and information technology, video film has struck like a bombshell. Whereas press, radio and TV can principally be regulated by means of various national instruments (supply of paper, energy, distribution of air waves, imposition of taxes and import restrictions, state press and broadcast monopolies, etc.) to support the aims of national development, video films cannot be similarly manipulated.

Essentially there are two reasons for this: video cassettes are so small and can so easily be transported that their importation can never be effectively regulated; and copying facilities have put traditional copyright completely out of action; it is no longer possible to distinguish a copy from an original. If only one video cassette is successfully imported into a country, the multiplication of this one copy into any number of cassettes only depends on the existence of two VCRs; distribution is only limited by the purchasing power of the consumers.In this way video films are possibly becoming an important force in achieving McLuhan's vision of a "global village", in a quality and form, however, which can only be defined as a trend towards cultural homogeneity with the West. As with the beginning of the TV age, today some Third World countries show a decrease in cinema visits and TV ratings as a result of the video boom. However, one should be careful of offering glib explanations for such conjectures, as it is not yet clear whether, in the case of further market saturation, there is not a cumulative media effect, video films, TV and movies mutually boosting one another.

4. Production and Distribution

About 90 percent of the world market for manufacturing VCRs is controlled by the two Japanese firms of Sony and Matsushita; the V-2000 system by the European producers Philips-Grundig is not relevant for developing countries. In the production of the cassettes themselves, there is no discernible oligopoly. At the beginning of the video age there were a large number of small, innovative software producers and the well-known US and European electronic entertainment firms hesitated to enter the market as there was no clear way of calculating profit margins given the prevalence of illegal copying.

After careful observation and market analysis of the activities of the small producers, the big ones waited for a while before getting into the act. And so today we find that the leading software producers on the video scene are the following well-known US entertainment firms: MCA, Gulf and Western, Warner Communications, Coca Cola, NBC, CBS, etc.

As far as Third World countries are concerned, however, the business practice of the regional video merchants - operating in the shadow of the Western firms - is more important. Hong Kong is the hub of the whole video trade for the entire South-East Asian region. One of the leading software dealers is *Esquire International*, which, among others, has recently founded a subsidiary in India - *Esquire Video* which turns around 1,000 Indian feature films and 600 English-language titles onto the market.

Also operating from its base in Hong Kong is Soid Video Ltd., a label that has been specially founded for the Chinese market and which is a subsidiary of the China Film Export and Import Corporation of Beijing and the Sam C.L. Co. Another major dealer who also supplies the West European and American market with Asiatic violence and horror films, as well as covering the South-East Asian region is Inter Continental

Video, also based in Hong Kong. KPS Video Network, a division of Kam Production Studios in Hong Kong has useful market connections with Taiwan, South Korea, Indonesia, the Philippines and Thailand. Apart from the Asian vendors, Europeans and Americans also have their finger in the pie: World Vision, New York, has created its own label, Worldvision Home Video Inc. for the world market and the Balfino enterprise in Liechtenstein more or less covers the needs of the Near East and Latin America.

Regional distribution companies are important because producers have to respond differently and sensitively to various viewing habits - which have been formed social, culturally and religiously and by existing cinema and TV presentations. At the same time the black market, smuggling and "piracy" are also determining factors of the market. These business practices within the framework of underground economies enable video users in the Third World to partake of the Western consumerist world which, strictly speaking, is taboo to them culturally, religiously and as a result of official government policy. The economics of distribution and consumption of video films in Third World countries can only be examined from this dual perspective of "illegal" copying and smuggling.

The importance of "illegal" copying of video films, especially in South-East Asia, can only be understood in the general context of historically conditioned Western copyright, patent and license laws, labels and trademarks. Taiwan is a prime example of an economy which no longer worries in any way about such laws. A few examples will suffice to illustrate this. By late 1982, anything from 40 to 100 Taiwan outfits were believed to be producing parts for Apple Computer imitations or supplying complete look-alike systems.

Although many were sold in Taiwan itself, exports were reckoned to run at 1,500 a month. Some of the clone computer companies used similar names. Others simply supplied equipment without bothering to affix a label. If the wholesaler or retailer who bought them choose to put on a sticker that said Apple, or something like it, that was his business. One Taiwan firm that imitates American video recording equipment simply ran off exact copies of the US company's brochures as promotional literature and then imitated its products too.

The distribution of video films in the Third World can finally only be adequately understood if one sees it as part of the black market which supplies the wealthy upper classes with all the Western consumer goods known on the world market. Behind this phenomenon looms the increasing importance of underground economics in the Third World. Such sham economies are the result of complicated coincidences. On the one hand, the remains of pre-capitalist and feudal process of production manifest themselves here, which have never subjected themselves to the exchange value principle of capitalism. On the other hand, the sham economic market is created by extremely unbalanced levels of development in one and the same national economy, in which a small but wealthy class of the population effectively resists the effects of a deficient economy and an incomplete national economic cycle, by investing and consuming in the black market.

Black market economies in many Third World countries already represent 40 to 50 percent of the GNP, they elude any nation-state or international form of control, so that the IMF, for example, is anxious about a drastic reduction of its control of Third World economies. In this way the black market contains an "anarchic" component which can effectively resist external economic control. At the same time it contains a repressive element, by creating a production sector and employment market which is elitist at heart and makes social security provisions for workers preposterous.

It is significant that the whole topic of "black markets" has been left out of all theoretical developing countries research projects. Our knowledge and theories about the economic situation in the Third World are, therefore, very incomplete and distorted. All the above arguments suggest that research on the uses and social functions of video films and on the economics of the black market in Western consumer goods, including VCRs and video films, is long overdue.

References

Agrawal, Binod C.: *Communication Revolution:* A Study of Video Penetration in India, Ahmedabad: Indian Space Research Organisation 1989.

Alternative Medienarbeit. Videogruppen in der Bundesrepublik, ed. by Köhler, Margret, Opladen: Leske Verlag 1980.

Deutsches Video-Institut: *Der Video-Markt 1983*, Berlin 1983 (unpublished and mimeographed study).

Gopal, B. V.: Video Piracy and the Law, New Delhi: Deep & Deep Publications 1986.

Hoffmann, Kay: *Am Ende Video – Video am Ende?* Aspekte der Elektronisierung der Spielfilmproduktion, Berlin. Edition Sigma Bohn 1990.

The VCR Age. Home Video and Mass Communication, ed. by Levy, Mark R., Newbury Park, California: Sage 1989.

Video World-Wide. An International Study, ed. by Alvarado, Manuel, Paris: UNESCO 1988.

Videokunst in Deutschland 1963-1982, ed. by Herzogenrath, Wulf, Stuttgart: Verlag Gerd Hatje 1982.

Zielinski, Siegfried: *Zur Geschichte des Video-Recorders,* Berlin: Volker Spiess Verlag 1986.

Zimmer, Dieter E.: *Ein Medium kommt auf die Welt.* Video-Kassetten und das neue multimediale Lernen, Hamburg: Christian Wegner Verlag 1970.

9
The Gulf War, Culture and the Media

In his address to the nation at the start of the Gulf War, President George Bush declared that "Saddam Hussein was a threat to the American way of life". This justification of a war is revealing. Does it usher in a new era of "culture wars"? Similar trends are now evident in the war in former Yugoslavia and in some of the Republics of the former Soviet Union. The arguments put forward to legitimize war and conflicts by the Iraqi government and by Muslim leaders in several other countries of the Middle-East have a similar cultural and religious ring to them. The West, and the United States in particular, are seen as the "capitalist satan"; the enemy is the "infidel" or, in the case of Salman Rushdie, "the blasphemer". This leads me to formulate my first hypothesis: the war in the Persian Gulf and other conflicts with Muslim countries in the Middle East can only be understood against the background of a deep seated conflict of cultures.

1. Orientalism

Edward Said's seminal book Orientalism (1978) explains that the conflict of culture between the Islamic and Western worlds dates back almost to the origin of Islamic faith. "Orientalism" is, according to Said, a Western concept formed to legitimize the colonial and neo-colonial expansions of the west in the Middle East.

On the one hand, it glories and mystifies the "Orient", on the other, it claims that Islamic culture is incapable of development and progress. Or it leads to structural analyses such as that put forward by Bassam Tibi (1981 and 1991), which sees the current ferment in the Islamic world merely as a response to and defense against outside forces. The thought patterns underlying "Orientalism" tend to operate according to the dualism of the following scheme.

Orient	Occident
Islam	Christianity
Revenge	Forgiveness
Passion	Reason
Heart	Intellect
Old World	New World
Force	Peace

It is no coincidence that the war in the Persian Gulf took place at a time when communism in Eastern Europe had collapsed. For forty years the dominant image of the Western "enemy" was communism. Has Islam replaced the old anti-Communist image and become the new "enemy"? The mass media have built up both "enemy" images: Communism and Islam. A review of the literature on the development of foe stereotypes is revealing in this respect (Feindbilder 1975; Frei 1985; Feindbilder 1985).

"Religion is the corpse in the cellar of the average consciousness of the west European, particularly the German left," says Helmut Thielen (1991) in his essays on the philosophy of religion. This can be illustrated by an event that took place in January 1990 in the trade union building in Frankfurt, Germany, in response to the Iranian mullahs' fatwa on Salman Rushdie. Roter Stern (Red Star), a renowned and originally a communist Frankfurt Publishing House, helped the left-liberal coalition groups behind the protest to prepare for the event. It printed an invitation card showing an 18th century etching with the caption "The Saracens burn the library of Alexandria." The parallel between the burning of the famous library and Rushdie's book is obvious.

The reproduction implies that the Muslims are anti-intellectual and anti-book. And they have been portrayed like this for centuries, from the Saracens to the Mullahs in Iran. The fact of the matter, however, is that the famous Alexandrian library was not destroyed by Muslims, but in 391 AD at the instigation of the Christian patriarch Theophilos.

The legend first emerging in the 13th century, that the most famous library in western antiquity had been burned down on the order of Caliph Omar lacks any historic foundation. Sigrid Hunke (1991) devotes a full chapter to this incident in his study on anti-Muslim prejudices. The anti-Muslim stereotypes are much more resilient than the anti-communist. They are much older and also have a racial component. With the disappearance of East-West polarity, these prejudices are likely to influence the West's perception of the South in general.

2. Post-modern Fallacies

The Gulf War marks the beginning of a new era in international media policies in which CNN has played a special role. Diplomatic negotiations which used to be conducted in secrecy behind closed doors were suddenly to be seen on television with both George Bush and Saddam Hussein seeming to address each other. The concentration of the media on the Gulf war was total as was military censorship and intended disinformation. However, Michael Schmolke (1991) has shown how these phenomena have their historic precursors.

I am not sure that the relationship between war and news management contains anything qualitatively new since the war in the Gulf, as some post modern philosophers seem to imply. As long ago as 1984, Paul Virilio proposed his thesis on "War is cinema and cinema is war." This hitherto relatively unknown French philosopher became a media celebrity in Germany during and after the Gulf War.

Virilio's thesis is based on two arguments. First, that modern audio-visual mass media mix symbolic representation and reality in such a way that the two become indistinguishable. Second, he maintains that there are similarities between war and media technologies. His first argument is questionable because viewers can easily distinguish between subject and object. His second argument is merely cynical. The computerized weapons in American air-force planes are significantly different form the computerized war games for young people in entertainment arcades. Behind such post-modern thinking and squabbles is an attitude which refuses to see history for what it is and ignores culture and cultural policies.

3. Empathy as Method

For the economist, culture is merely an irritant; for the political scientist, an indefinable border; for the electro engineer, it is at best the noise in a filter. In short, culture and cultural politics are the stepchildren of western institutions, not worthy of much attention let alone support.

Norbert Ropers (1990) has pointed out that inter-cultural learning is only possible on the basis of empathy, i.e., one has to develop a capacity to think from the standpoint of the other, in our case the Muslim. Ropers refers to the theory of symbolic interaction developed by George Herbert Mead. According to Mead, communication is only possible when both partners attach the same value to the symbols used. As a result, the speaker is at the same time the hearer of his or her own utterances. Therefore, Mead says, people cannot hear their own words unless they adopt the same attitude which another person would adopt if he or she uttered those same words. Meaningful communication between people of different cultures can only take place if there is reciprocal anticipation of the expectations and perceptions of the other. Using this concept of empathy, I shall now discuss three political areas from within the context of Islamic culture: namely human rights, social justice and transfer of technology.

Human Rights

According to Islamic law, there are four sources for human rights: the Koran, the Sunna of the Prophet, the Igma - the consensus regarding legal tradition - and the Giyas (legal analogies). According to Abul A'la Mawdudi (1976), the Koran alone guarantees 13 different human rights:

- Security of life and property (Sura 4.93),
- Protection of honor (Sura 49.11-12),
- Inviolability and security of private life (Sura 49.12 and 24.27),
- Guarantee of personal freedom (Sura 4.58),
- The right to protest against tyranny (Sura 4.148),
- Freedom of expression (Sura 9.71 and 22.41),
- Freedom of assembly (Sura 3.110),
- Freedom of conscience (Sura 2.256),
- Safeguard of religious sensibilities (Sura 6.108 and 29.46),
- Protection against arbitrary detention (Sura 6.164),
- The right to basic human needs (Sura 51.19),
- Equality before the law (Sura 49.10),
- The right to participate in political affairs (Sura 42.38).

Equality among races is referred to in Sura 30.21 which reads: "And among His (Allah's) signs is the creation of the heavens and the earth, and the variety of your tongues and your colors." The sunna explicitly confirms the equality of the sexes: "All humans are equal like the teeth of a comb. There is no justification whatsoever, that an Arab is worth more than a non-Arab, that a white person is worth more than a black, and a man worth more than a woman. God favors only those who fear Him", (May 1980). In other words, Islamic law has many similarities with human rights as formulated in the Western tradition.

Social justice

The principle of social justice is one of the pillars of Islam. The economic principle behind it is distributive justice of goods and means of production, by which certain standards of living are set and social peace is achieved. All legal sources prescribe a tax in aid of the poor, charitable foundations, and governmental insurance and credit banks. Islamic law prohibits single inheritance and interest on capital (usury) in order to avoid progressive accumulation of riches in the hands of a single family (Dia 1975). Maxime Rodinson (1986) summarizes the ideal of social justice as put forward in the Koran as equality before divine law, mutual aid in Islamic communities at the cost of the rich and for the benefit of the poor.

Technology transfer

The dominant technology transfer up to the 15th century ran from East to West. Most of what Europe possessed in the way of mathematics, natural sciences and engineering depended on the theoretical and practical work and discoveries of Islamic scientists. This was particularly true of mechanical instruments, road and bridge building, military technology, ship building and navigation, textile and paper industries, mining and metallurgy (Al-Hassan and Hill, 1986).

I have chosen these three examples from a perspective of empathy. I have deliberately tried to find points of contact within Islamic culture that are meaningful to our own way of thinking. All three examples present a variety of similarities between the two cultures. Yet I am conscious of the limitations of this type of methodology. Religious and legal sources are usually normative. Therefore, there is always a difference between norms and social reality. Secondly, most of these sources are ancient. Technology transfer at the present time would be more of a problem. But despite these limitations, there are still many advantages.

They show that Islamic culture had its own indigenious traditions which were independent of western ideas of development. They further demonstrate Islamic culture's potential for individual human rights, the welfare state, and active technology transfer. They could be the backbone of development policies as well as structural social changes and a dynamic regional economic community. In this context, I question the suggestion by Dieter Senghaas (1984) that "traditional cultures are relatively flexible in the face of political, social and economic forces which aim at economic development". The changes in East Europe and the cultural conditions and effects of the Gulf War demonstrate that cultural policies are a neglected engine for development.

4. Individual and Society

Although I have stressed Islam's potential for the recognition of individual human rights, I must now put this argument into perspective. Islam, contrary to European tradition, does not know the concept of individuality. Yet the individual is the focal point of the philosophical and sociological theories of human rights as espoused in the West. This is the basis on which Westerners extol the "dignity of the individual", "freedom of the individual," and "right to self development". I deliberately stated that Islam did not know the concept of individuality rather than saying that it lacked it. This is because some might have drawn the conclusion that it was impossible to implement human rights in Islamic society lest Islam itself change, viz. "modernize".

The individual as the prototype of socialization in Europe had its own origins, arising during the revolutionary struggle of the middle class against the nobility in the 18th century. This class, however, has not existed in many countries of the South until very recently. Therefore, one should not be surprised that the Western and bourgeois concept of human rights does not exist there, either.

There has been widespread criticism in the social sciences of the concept of bourgeois autonomy (Abercrombie, Hill and Turner 1986). However, in the discussion on Islam and human rights, that criticism has conveniently been forgotten. Not only Islam, but also Confucianism in China and the political cultures of India and Japan, do not accept the principle of the autonomy of the individual. It follows, therefore, that we need a concept of collective human rights in order to supplement the concept of individual human rights. Tensions between individual and collective human rights are inevitable. In practice, however, it means that collective human rights must be taken as seriously as those formulated by the Declaration of Human Rights in 1948. Only recently have we given weight to economic, social and cultural rights in Western societies.

Amilcar Cabral (unlike Frantz Fanon) developed a cultural theory which maintained that in spite of the injuries and destructions colonialism wrought on social structures, the masses of indigenous people are still meaningfully aware of their own culture, dignity and identity (Cabral 1983). It is this cultural force which could propel a people towards change and development. Current unrest among Islamic and Arab people could be the right time to promote the indigenous cultural potential for structural change and socio-economic development.

References

Abd-al-Aziz: *Islam and the race question*, Paris 1970, p. 27.

Abercombie, N.; Hill, S. and Turner, B.S.: *Sovereign Individuals of Capitalism*, Winchester, Mass. 1986.

Al-Hassan, Ahmad Y. and Hill, Donald R.: *Islamic Technology*, London 1986.

A'la Mawdudi: *Human Rights in Islam*, Leicester 1976, pp. 25.

Carbral, Amilcar: *Die Theorie als Waffe*. Schriften zur Befreiung in Afrika, Bremen 1986.

Dia, Mamadou: *Islam: sociétés africaines et culture industrielle*, Dakar.

Feindbilder, ed. by Reiner Steinweg, Frankfurt 1975.

Feindbilder oder: Wie man Kriege vorbereitet, ed. by H. P. Bleuel et al., Göttingen 1985.

Frei, Daniel: *Feindbilder und Abrüstung*, Munich 1985.

Hunke, Sigrid: *Allah ist ganz anders*. Enthüllung von 1001 Vorurteilen über die Araber. 3rd edition, Bad König 1991, pp. 85-90.

Rodinson, Maxime: *Islam und Kapitalismus*, Frankfurt 1986, p. 54.

Ropers, Norbert: "Vom anderen her denken. Empathie als paradigmatischer Beitrag zur Völkerverständigung", in: *Die vergessene Dimension internationaler Konflikte: Subjektivität*, ed. by Reiner Steinweg and Christian Wellmann, Frankfurt 1990, pp. 114-150.

Schmolke, Michael: "Dass die ganze Welt zuhört. Kriegsberichterstattung zwischen Prohibition und Exhibition", in: *Medien-Journal*, (Salzburg, Austria), No. 1/1991, pp. 3542.

Senghaas, Dieter: "Kultur und Entwicklung. Überlegungen zur aktuellen entwicklungspolitischen Diskussion", in: *Zeitschrift für Kulturaustausch*, No. 4/1984, p. 419.

Thielen, Helmut: *Revolution des Glaubens*. Religionsphilosophische Versuche über die Befreiung, Berlin 1991, p. 3.

Virilio, Paul: *Guerre et cinéma*. Vol. 1: Logistique de la perception, Paris 1984.

10
The Image of Islam in the German Media and Among the German Public

1. Islam in the German Media

Without doubt, in Germany - and in other European countries, too - the media, intellectual and public discussion of the terrorist attacks on the World Trade Center and the Pentagon on September 11, 2001, the subsequent Afghanistan War, and the current debate on a possible attack against Iraq by the United States rests on a bedrock of anti-Islamic images of an enemy, foundations that have emerged over the course of time. They form the foil as it were against which the media's treatment of current conflicts updated individual fragments of an already firm image of Islam: "Language not only defines and condemns the enemy, it also creates him; and this product not only constitutes the enemy the way he really is, but also the way he must be in order to fulfill his function for the establishment," German social philosopher Herbert Marcuse once stated when defining the role and function of images of the enemy.

Only a few years ago, anti-Islamic images of the enemy were being busily updated during the Gulf War of 1990/1, as analyses of the press back then readily showed, and as were elaborated with great precision by Christina Ohde in her doctoral thesis with the illuminating title "Der Irre von Bagdad" (The Madman of Baghdad)[1]. The level the empirical social sciences term "content revealed involuntarily" when describing the methods they use for qualitative content analysis is exactly what was involved in the two ostensible Freudian slips made by the US President and the Italian premier in Fall 2001. The one spoke of a "Crusade against Terrorism" and the other went so far as to suggest that Western culture is superior to that of Islam. The PR consultants were admittedly able to apologize for the statements after the event and correct them accordingly, but such spontaneous utterances specifically by virtue of their spontaneity reveal the actual, namely publicly not sanctioned thoughts of the speaker.

Scholars of Islam the world over warn against the Western media presenting a distorted image of Islam; in fact they have been pointing out almost in despair how nonsensical the image of Arab irrationality, of Islamic backwardness or of a typical Islamic fundamentalism is (and also point out that the concept of fundamentalism is quite unsuitable for an analysis of Islam anyway). Yet today there are any number of social scientists who are working away at building such anti-Islamic images of an enemy.

In the German media world, it has in particular been magazines such as *Der Spiegel*, *stern*, and *Focus*, with their sensationalist covers and headlines who have been warning us all against the "World Power of Islam" or the "Mystery of Islam". In order to make a splash, these print media have relied on a mix of pictorial images and symbols, with seemingly threatening "masses", with images of angry men and veiled women. On October 8, 2001 *Der Spiegel* ran its cover story on: "Religious mania. The Return of the Middle Ages". It displayed the face of Osama Bin Laden between the burning World Trade Center, masked machine-gun-touting warriors and a crescent moon. *stern* followed suit on October 25, 2001 with a front cover portraying the narrow section left for the eyes in a woman's veil above war-like hordes of horsemen. The headline ran: "The New Series: the Roots of Hatred. Mohammed's Angry Descendants. 1,400 Years Between Pride and Humiliation".

For some time now, in particular *Der Spiegel* can no longer be regarded as the flagship of critically-minded journalism. Instead, it has become the intellectual mouthpiece for xenophobia and animosity toward Islam.[2] For example, the cover of *Der Spiegel* no. 16/1997 ran the headline "Foreigners and Germans. The Failure of the Multicultural Society" and beneath it a young woman with a Turkish flag evidently yelling. In front of the young pupils of a Koran school and a group of boys looking tough and armed with clubs, the flag-waving Turk becomes the symbol of nationalist incitement. *Der Spiegel* has since made systematic use of this approach.

Illustration 10.1:
Front cover of the magazine *Information for the Troops* (IFDT) published by the German Armed Forces, fourth quarter 2001. The main headline: "Islamic Fanatics". This German Army publication currently has a print run of about 50,000 copies per issue.

In the early 1990s, psychologist Ute Gerhard drew attention to the way *Der Spiegel* used such a cover-picture policy, in particular the xenophobic cover page for the April 6, 1992 issue. Large type framed by a red bar proclaims "Asylum - The Politicians Fail Us", mounted across a photo of a mass of people storming a gate guarded by two policemen. The visual message is obvious: "We're being stormed", and "There's no space left".[3] A comparison of front covers by the main-selling magazines on the topic of Islam with those of only marginal significance demonstrates how homogeneous the perception of this topic has become. Even magazines with small print runs like *Spektrum* or *Information für die Truppe. Zeitschrift für Innere Führung*, (see Illustr. 10.1) published by the German Army, use the same clichés and project the same fears as the megasellers do.

Media images of the enemy and bad images can in fact have very real consequences. A long time before September 11, 2001 the EMNID opinion poll experts established that Muslims in Germany face the sharpest prejudices compared with members of other religious communities. While Jews were strictly rejected by 11 percent of those polled, the proportion rose to 20 percent in the case of Muslims.[4] For the period September 11 through October 19, 2001 the EU's European Monitoring Center on Racism and Xenophobia (EUMC) in Vienna identified a clear increase in racist violence and animosity towards in all the EU member states.

In terms of its reporting on Islam in the aftermath of September 11, 2001, the conservative daily *Frankfurter Allgemeine Zeitung (FAZ)* compares favorably with *Der Spiegel*. For example, despite the compulsion shared by many of the mass media to provide a homogenized viewpoint - in its October 22, 2001 edition it printed the following reports all of which revealed a differentiated discussion of Islam: "The Search for the Moderate Taliban", "Disapproval of the US Military Strikes by the APEC Countries", as well as a decidedly positive appreciation of Muslim mosques in Hamburg, an approving analysis of Pakistan Muslim League's peace plans, religious tolerance in Morocco and a lengthy article on Iran's religious and political tightrope between the USA and the Islamic world. Or: In the *FAZ's* weekend supplement of November 10, 2001 there was a whole page devoted to Ignaz Goldziher, the German founder of Islamic scholarship and an extensive review of a new Turkish novel. Images of the enemy, and not just those of an anti-Islamic ilk, tend to obey the mirror-opposite theorem as postulated by David J. Singer in the early 1960s,[5] and peace research has known for long that the concepts of "friend" and "foe" is such a mirror opposition, dividing into the "good" and the "bad" camps. Swiss political scientist Daniel Frei once concluded in this contest:

> Mutual accusations tend to be identical: Each side accuses the other of striving for world domination, of being driven by an insatiable urge to expand, of not deserving trust, of using the means of power to political ends, of planning an atomic strike and thus distorts and slanders the respective opponent."[6]

US President George W. Bush's political rhetoric is entrenched precisely in such a dichotomic mind-set. "This is the battle for civilization" and "The civilized world flocks to America's cause" he suggested in his address to the US Congress[7], and the US Senate approved US$ 40 billion for the "war against evil in the world". German Chancellor Gerhard Schröder seconded Bush when he stated that the terrorist attack in New York was a "declaration of war on the community of civilized peoples"[8] and in Germany's *Frankfurter Allgemeine Zeitung* daily Günther Nonnenmacher even went so far as to talk of a "final struggle between good and evil".[9] Amartya Sen, the Indian winner of the Nobel Prize for Economic in 1998, has criticized this dichotomic approach for being based on a compulsion to homogenize either by the one side or by the other, meaning that the numerous intrinsic differences innate in both sides get elided.[10] Such a division into a "civilized" and an "uncivilized" world only serve to deepen the trenches between them, and is, moreover, part and parcel of the more or less fatal colonialist tradition of the North vs. the South. It is as if Osama Bin Laden had read the works of David J. Singer and Daniel Frei when he endeavors to strengthen the dichotomic outlook. In one of his videos broadcast by the Al-Jazeera TV station he declares:

> The world is sub-divided into people who rejoiced at the attacks on the unjust giant America and those who condemned these attacks.[11]

Indian authoress Arundhati Roy put her finger on the well-estab lished insights of peace research ever since the first publications of David J. Singer when she wrote in the *Frankfurter Allgemeine Zeitung (FAZ)* that "If there were no Osama Bin Laden then the Americans would have to invent him. [...] He is the US president's dark doppelgaenger."[12] What she was able to state without fear of prosecution in India, a so-called developing country, was something it was hardly possible to utter in public in an industrialized nation such as Germany in the fall of 2001, given the prevailing mood. Writing in an opinion column in a magazine in early October 2001, well-known German TV anchorman Ulrich Wickert compared Osama Bin Laden to George W. Bush and penned the sentences:

"Bush is not a murder and terrorist. But the mindset is identical." Thereupon, the German conservative party CDU called for his dismissal from the German public TV station for which he works and Wickert swiftly opted for self-critique. Freimut Duve, Germany's Freedom of the Media Representative at the Vienna-based Organization for Security and Cooperation in Europe (OSCE) even took this as the occasion to express concern about the freedom of the press in Germany.[13]

2. The German Left and Islam

I do not wish to go into a detailed discussion of labels such as "conservative", "critical", and "left" here. They can be located in the framework of West European intellectual and cultural history and can best be understood in that context. The Left in Germany has always felt indebted to the ideas of the French bourgeois revolution, that tradition of enlightenment, transparency, the reduction of prejudice, the destruction of taboos, demystification, ideology critique, tolerance, human rights, solidarity with poor and the inalienable dignity of Man. Unlike that leading light of the German Enlightenment and play-wright Gottfried Lessing (1729-1781), who in his play "Nathan the Wise" (1779) thought Islamic theology through favorably and in such a way as to suggest that the power of Reason is the innermost form of devotion to God,[14] the current German Left has a highly ambiguous, in part clearly negative attitude toward Islam.

This ambiguity was very visible in recent times during the Gulf War, when Leftist German intellectuals such as philosopher Jürgen Habermas, writer Hans-Magnus Enzensberger and musician Wolf Biermann justified this war by arguing that Germany's "Western ties" should not be called into question. While in the days of the Gulf War the main arguments demonstrated ambivalence, an explicit anti-Islamic position has since emerged among many members of the German Left, in particular in the aftermath of September 11, 2001. A few quotations perhaps illustrate this. Although the account Jürgen Habermas, currently Germany's leading philosopher, gave of his trip to Iran in June 2002 stood out for a quite astonishing and decidedly rare detailed knowledge of philosophical debates within Iran, but even the most well-inclined of readers of his report will have been brought up short by the following sentences:

> But the prejudices with which one arrives become more [...] differentiated. The notion of a society subject to centralized control by the secret services, a society that has fallen silent, simply does not fit - or not with the experiences that I gained through encounters with intellectuals, with citizens who are members of a non-intimated urban population who are spontaneous and self-confident.[15]

There is no getting around the question here as to who has what prejudices toward Iran. Is perhaps a possibly arrogant philosopher ascribing these prejudices only to the "stupid plebs" or does he perhaps have them himself? A passage from Ulla Berkéwicz, actress, author and since 1990 wife of Siegfried Unseld, the publisher of Suhrkamp Verlag, in other words the company which brings out all Jürgen Habermas' writings and in particular the German publishing corporation without whom enlightened, progressive and democratic discursive culture would have been inconceivable in Germany over the entire last half a century possibly provides an answer to this question. In May 2002, Berkéwicz wrote of Islam:

> Oppressed, suppressed, made stupid, prevented from making progress, forced into regression, the Muslim peoples of the East today enjoy a level of education far below that of the West. People who act intuitively, beasts of belief, hysterical and fanaticized, who have been compelled to rely on the laws of the herd and the rules of cattle traders, with the justified outlook that injustice has been done to them yet without the intellectual means to fight against this in the framework of Reason, which or so Occidental wisdom would have it, is the weapon of first and last resort."[16]

It is harder to imagine a more spiteful text than this of German author Ulla Berkéwicz, other perhaps than the anti-Islamic attacks launched by Italian journalist Oriana Fallaci in the *Corriere della Sera* newspaper in September 2001, soon to appear as a book entitled "The Rage and the Pride" and where one can find sentences about how Muslims "reproduce like rats" and that "they do not contribute to human progress". Like Oriana Fallaci, German writer Ralph Giordano must also be considered a member of the West European Left, and for decades he has been a champion of civil commitment and actively campaigned on behalf of oppressed minorities and has frequently as a consequence been at loggerheads with the German government. Yet his perception of Islam conforms with the angle taken by Ulla Berkéwicz and Oriana Fallaci. He explicitly refuses to make the distinction between "Islam" and "Islamism". He is convinced that Islam is the totalitarian threat of the years before us.[17] A last quote: In keeping with her book "Die Gotteskrieger und die falsche Toleranz" (God's Warriors and False Tolerance), which dripped in hatred, editor Alice Schwarzer equated "Islamic crusaders" and the "fascists", showing with this and other comparisons that she was not interested in any conceptual-theoretical approach, but only in anger, aggression and fear.[18]

What such quotations contain in the guise of a description of Islam, has also been the object of theoretical analysis by the German Left and even been presented as a theory of modernity per se. A specimen of this approach is to be found in the journal *Bahamas*, produced by persons formerly associated with the Kommunistischer Bund, the German Communist League. For example, in a leader in the journal following the September 11, 2001 attacks the editors approved of military action by the USA and called for as "consistent as possible" a response to Afghanistan and other targets. They argued:

> Eliminating Islamic rule would tear the population of these countries from the Muslim idolatry in order to subject them with all the brutal consequences to the capitalist commodity fetish.
>
> [And the same periodical also states:] The praise of the stupidity and poverty that Islam sings as the ideology of archaic societies of simple exchange is also the melody of the German mind. [...] Islam is Heidegger for the illiterate. Jihad is being for death. [...] Islamicization is in reality liberation from all possibilities of liberation.

Islam is thus seen by the authors as a "modern form of managing immiseration", the "dark and murderous obverse" to the shine of Western civilization.[19]

3. Analysis

If one seeks to establish the reasons for this anti-Islamic image of an enemy that is now so wide-spread not only in the mass media in Germany but also among Leftist intellectuals then we must analytically examine and elucidate layer after causal layer.

1. The first reason worthy of mention is the historical context and conditions. Anti-Islamic thought and anti-Islamic prejudices have a long ominous historical tradition that goes back - with interruptions - to the Crusades in the European Middle Ages. Such traditions continue to have an impact right through to the present. It is in the nature of such prejudices that they can repeatedly be re-activated in times of crisis and conflict, even if they then seem to become extinct in the interim. Because anti-Islamic prejudices run deeper and older in German culture than, for example, the images of a communist enemy, the West German anti-communism of Cold War days died out fairly quickly and likewise anti-communist journalists among the Cold Warriors such as Herbert Kremp were able to smoothly switch horses from anti-communism to anti-Islamism. His aggressive article on "Islam the World Conqueror" in December 2001[20] could, if a few words were exchanged, swiftly be transformed into an article on the danger of "Moscow's communist world conquest" in the 1960s.

2. Historically speaking, a second line of argumentation must be mentioned. With the loss of its African colonies at the end of the First World War in 1918, which were only in German hands for 40 years, and intensified by the then following 12-year phase of international isolation during German fascism from 1933 through 1945, Germany has to this day not been able to rely on a sense of openness toward the world, international know-how and experience. This becomes especially apparent if we compare the everyday discourse in Germany on the topic of migration with that in the old "established" colonial countries France, the Netherlands and Great Britain.

   Public debates in Germany are by comparison highly outmoded and provincial. Whereas one of the most aggressive attacks against French colonialism was published in France itself and precisely not in a French colony and were even strongly supported on the home front by French philosophers - I am speaking of Frantz Fanon's "The Wretched of the Earth" and the fact that Jean-Paul Sartre championed its cause in 1961 - such a phenomenon and such a subsequent public debate on colonialism never took place in Germany. A strength form of "colonial revenge", albeit with a considerable time lag.

3. It is on account of the specific form of Germany's colonial past that a specialist academic discipline such as "Oriental Studies" never gained the relevance that it has in France, for example. Although

the beginnings of an institutionalized German "Oriental Studies" were evidently linked to German foreign policy, namely the German alliance with the Ottoman Empire at the time of the First World War, but these beginnings never led to an independent discipline emerging. German "Oriental Studies" is a) primarily philological and does not have a focus on the social sciences, b) has hardly any intellectual resources with which to conduct a epistemological debate, for example, on Edward W. Said's book "Orientalism" (1978) and to draw the relevant conclusions and c) has frequently enough over the last 50 years of its history led an existence in the social sidelines - what springs to mind in particular here was the embarrassing Festschrift German "Orientalists" prepared for Shah Reza Pahlevi on the 2,500-year celebration of the Persian dynasty.

Given tight public budgets, at present (i.e., after September 11, 2001, too) many "Orientalist" institutes in Germany are facing fierce financial cut-backs. On the one hand, such reductions are more than counter-productive given the miserable state of Islamic-European dialog, yet, on the other, they encounter an academic field that has often shown that it is unable to learn for this dialog.

4. Talking about Islam requires not only an empathic approach with something alien and quite evidently requires also an understanding for religious questions. Since the modernization process in Germany has always squeezed religious, theological and church issues to the margins of public social debates, there is hardly any realization in Germany of how necessary religious thought and life is.

But how can you speak positively about an alien religion if you have lost your own? This problem of inter-religious ethics was something Albert Schweitzer (1875-1965), German theologian and 1952 Nobel Peace Prize winner, was very conscious of in distant Africa in the 1920s. Back then he asked: "Who wants to interpret the belief of others if your own has become foreign to you?"[21] It bears assuming that it is the degree of alienation from one's own Christian creed that distinguishes a cosmopolitan, liberal and republican *Der Spiegel* reader from a conservative *FAZ* reader, and explains why *Der Spiegel* is now opposed to Islam and foreigners, while the *FAZ* endeavors to present a more differentiated discussion of Islam.

Evidently, that part of the German Left which adopts explicitly anti-Islamic positions is strongly in the (conscious or unconscious) tradition of that renowned German sociologist Max Weber (1864-1920), who with his strict and dichotomic sub-division into that which is traditionalism and rationalization continues to influence thought. Anyone like Max Weber (and following him not only parts of the German Left but also obviously parts of the German Right) decrees with theoretical certainty that religion, ethnic membership, clientele policies, close bonds to family and relatives, personal rather than media-based communication, minor political participation etc. are the outdated categories of traditionalism that need to be overcome en route to progress for civilization, simply fails to discern the decisive feature of what characterizes modernity.

Just as both the historical European and the historical Islamic Enlightenment can only be understood in light of their intrinsic roots in the respective mystical movements, so, too, modernity as we know it today is not only a matter of human progress, but also of regression. As long ago as 1946 the two great German social philosophers Theodor W. Adorno and Max Horkheimer outlined the dialectic of enlightenment. To put it differently and in the form of two propositions: First, technological and civilizational progress is not possible without strongly barbaric elements, and, second, the instrumental reason of technological progress is definitely not the same thing as an advance in human reason.

Notes and References

1. Cf. Ohde, Christine: *Der Irre von Bagdad.* Zur Konstruktion von Feindbildern in überregionalen deutschen Tageszeitungen während der Golfkrise 1990/91, Frankfurt: Peter Lang Verlag 1994.
2. For an extensive study see Niehr, Thomas: "DER SPIEGEL und die Asylanten. Über eine angebliche Wende in der Wortwahl eines deutschen Nachrichtenmagazins", in: *Sprache und Literatur*, 1996/78, pp. 84-92.
3. Cf. Gerhard, Ute: "Fatale Folgen! Die Mediendebatte zum Thema Asyl", in: *Gute Absichten - fatale Folgen? Fremdenfeindlichkeit in den Medien*, ed. by the Westdeutscher Rundfunk, Cologne: WDR 1992, pp. 27-34.
4. Cf. Pötzl, Norbert F.: "Schlechtes Image", in: *Spiegel Special*, No. 1/1998.
5. Cf. Singer, David J.: "Soviet and American Foreign Policy Attitudes: Content Analysis of Elite Articulations", in: *Journal of Conflict Resolution*, 1964, pp. 424-85.

6. Frei, Daniel: *Feindbilder und Abrüstung*. Die gegenseitige Einschätzung der UdSSR und der USA, Munich: Beck 1985, pp. 107.
7. Bush, George W.: "Entweder Ihr seid für uns, oder Ihr seid für die Terroristen", in: *Frankfurter Allgemeine Zeitung*, Sept. 22, 2001, p. 8.
8. Schröder, Gerhard: "Solidarität mit den Menschen in den USA", in: *Das Parlament*, Sept. 21, 2001, p. 11.
9. Quoted from Precht, Richard David: *Die deutsche Betroffenheit*. Commentary in the "Kritisches Tagebuch"-series run by WDR 3 Radio Station, September 13, 2001.
10. Cf. Sen, Amartya: "The World Can't Be So Easily Divided", in: *International Herald Tribune*, Nov. 24-5, 2001, p. 6.
11. Quoted from, Anne-Beatrice: "Bin Laden und sein Freund-Feind-Schema", in: *Solinger Tageblatt*, Nov. 5, 2001, p. 2.
12. Roy, Arundhati: "Terror ist nur ein Symptom. Ein Kontinent brennt. Warum der Terrorismus nur ein Symptom ist", in: *Frankfurter Allgemeine Zeitung*, Sept. 28, 2001, p. 49.
13. Duve, Freimut: "Das Ende der Vielfalt. Die Anti-Terror-Allianz als Risiko für die Pressefreiheit", in: *Frankfurter Rundschau*, October 12, 2001, p. 23.
14. Cf. Niewöhner, Friedrich: "Vernunft als innigste Ergebenheit in Gott. Lessing und der Islam", in: *Neue Zürcher Zeitung*, Nov. 10-11, 2001, p. 83.
15. Habermas, Jürgen: "Der Westen interessiert sich für Köpfe nur, wenn sie rollen", in: *Frankfurter Allgemeine Zeitung*, June 13, 2002, p. 47.
16. Berkéwicz, Ulla: "Du bist getötet worden, weil du getötet hast", in: *Frankfurter Allgemeine Zeitung*, May 11, 2002, p. 47.
17. Giordano, Ralph: "Islam, Islamismus - Totalitarismus des 21. Jahrhunderts? Gedanken über eine nahe Zukunftsgefahr", in: *Mut. Forum für Kultur, Politik und Geschichte*, July 2002, pp. 48-53.
18. Cf. *Die Gotteskrieger und die falsche Toleranz*, ed. by Alice Schwarzer, Cologne: Kiepenheuer & Witsch, 2002.
19. Quoted from: Bahamas-Redaktion: "Hinter dem Ruf nach Frieden verschanzen sich die Mörder!", in: *Bahamas*, Fall 2001, p. 31.
20. Cf. Kremp, Herbert: "Welteroberer Islam. Im Anspruch eines Gottesstaates 'ohne Grenzen' erfüllt sich die Tragödie einer großen Religion, die über eine Milliarde Gläubige zählt", in: *Rheinische Post*, Dec. 28, 2001.
21. Cf. Schweitzer, Albert: *Kultur und Ethik in den Weltreligionen*, Munich: Beck 2001.

11
Peace and Communication

1. The Problem

The Constitution of the UNESCO of 1945 contains a clear and unqualified statement on the relationship between communication and peace:

> Since wars begin in the minds of men, it is in the minds of men that the defense of peace must be built; [...] For this reason, the states agree to the free exchange of ideas and knowledge and are determined to develop and to increase the means of communication between their peoples and to employ these means for the purposes of mutual understanding and a truer and more perfect knowledge of each others lives [...].

This monocausal, one-dimensional perspective that assumes an automatic favorable impact of communication on international peace finds its echo even today in a number of documents concerning international law. Thus, for example, the signatories of the Helsinki accords of August 1st, 1975, declare in the preamble to Basket II, "that increased exchange in the areas of culture and education, dissemination of information and contacts between people" would contribute to strengthening of peace and understanding between people. Similar arguments appear in the so called mass media declaration of the UNESCO (Nov. 28, 1978), notably in Art. III:

> The mass media have an important contribution to make to the strengthening of peace and international understanding and [...]

> in countering [...] incitement to war. [...] the mass media, by disseminating information on the aims, aspirations, cultures and needs of all peoples, contribute to eliminating ignorance and misunderstanding between peoples (...) thereby promoting [...] policies best able to promote the reduction of international tension and the peaceful and equitable settlement of international disputes.

The supposed peace-inducing properties ascribed to communication - and here in particular to the mass media - are generally assumed to exist not only in the realm of international relations, but also appear in the fundamental premises of many psychological, educational and sociological theories. The communicative act *per se* is frequently said to possess the function of awakening mutual understanding, of helping to reduce conflicts, of stimulating social action and even of helping to bring about a state of harmony where previously there were arch conflicts of interest at play. A consistent pursuit of this train of thought might ultimately lead to the demand (as voiced by Jürgen Habermas) that communicative competence be the primary goal of teaching, since that would be a precondition for the peaceful co-existence of individuals, groups and nations.

These ideas are not so much to be criticized because they have been proven faulty by many empirical analyses; nor do they deserve criticism because (as Theodor W. Adorno and Max Horkheimer pointed out in their *Dialectics of Enlightenment*) they more or less naively wish into being the existence of social and individual conditions that do not and cannot exist in reality. The object of critique must instead be the matter-of-fact acceptance of non-peaceful, violent and, indeed, "overpowering" communication, because of the exceptions which that permits. To paraphrase Adorno and Horkheimer, mutatis mutandis: Because such peace efforts leave the abolition of injustice to the fortuitousness of peaceful communication, they accept, in reality, the very law of a universal violence which they wish to ameliorate. Discussing universal violence and the exceptional characteristics of peaceful communication at this point would precipitate conclusions which must be arrived at through careful and systematic analysis and exemplification; and that, precisely shall be the focal point of this study. To be sure, it would go beyond the scope of this study to analyze all aspects of the inter-relationships between peace and communication, hence, the area of personal and direct communication between individuals and groups shall be omitted. Chart 11.1 on mass media and peace serves to illustrate the most important theoretical points.

Chart 11.1:

Mass Media and Peace. A Comparison of Concepts and Results of Communications Research and Peace Research

	Categories	Critical Communication Research	Critical Peace Research
Production of the Mass Media	Control and Disposition	Concentration in the centers; transnational media oligopolies	Structural violence
	Access	Inequitable, vertical, non-reciprocal for peripheries	Structural violence
	Technology	Spin-off from military technology	Military-industrial complex
Ideologies of the Mass Media	Content	Elitism, racism, materialism, sensationalism, conservatism, conformism, authoritarianism, romanticism, fatalism, sexism aggression, individualism	Enemy images, prejudices; psychically manifest/latent structural violence
	Forms	Stereotyping, dream production	
Effects of the Mass Media	Use	Increasing knowledge gap	Class structure, social stratification, marginalization
	Reception	Receptive	Personal-psychic violence
	Effect	Reinforcement, affirmation, desensitizing, everyday colonialization,	Militarization of everyday life
	Function	Individual/societal control	Legitimating the dynamics of armament
History & Future of the Mass Media	Historical change in the relevance of popular reading matter, mass media, telecommunication, ICT	Culture, media, information and informatics industry	Dynamics of armament, militarization, spiral of violence, military-industrial complex

This choice may well result in the objection that communication is being reduced here to its media aspects and that its function strengthening interpersonal and social relationships is not perceived. Such criticism, however serious, can be countered by remarking that the historical changes in capitalist societies have been assigning an ever-growing influence and importance to media communication, as is evident, for example, in the increasing relevancy of medial socialization; in the ever larger domain of the media industry; and in the present innovation and explosion of media technology.

The first point of discussion must be the ideological aspects of the messages conveyed by the mass media, for it is particularly these aspects which are alluded to in the initially cited documents. If you were to search for empirical data on the representation of peace in the mass media, you would hunt in vain: there are no such analyses, nor does the topic itself appear to be attractive to the media in the first place. As is the case with other concerns of peace research, here, too, the most promising approach to an understanding of peace is to begin with a definition of its opposite: violence. To be sure, empirical analyses of the representation of violence in the mass media, beginning in the 1940s, may well be so numerous as to fill several libraries. Hence, a careful and critical selection of the material is essential. The major body of this empirical literature focuses on representations of manifest, physical, direct and personal violence (to use Johan Galtung's terminology). That is to say, subjects under examination were military violence, homicide, capital crime, assault and battering, physical brutality and aggression.

Nearly all of the analyses agree that the representation of personal violence takes place with a frequency and an intensity that is all out of proportion not only when compared to its existence in reality, but also in comparison to the possible reality inherent in the media. This consensus applies to the empirical quantitative studies - e.g. to the well-known violence profile by George Gerbner[1] - as well as to empirical qualitative analyses such as those produced by the Frankfurt school. Although Frankfurt school analyses of the representation of structural violence in the mass media are of relatively recent origin, their conclusions correspond convincingly to what the previously mentioned studies have said about overemphasis on personal violence, since forms of structural violence are hardly ever an issue in the mass media.[2] In this context, the results of two different studies on two different subject areas shall be discussed: a) advertising for the weapons industry in trade journals and b) crime reporting in the mass media.

In his analysis of advertising for armament and weapons marketing in West German trade journals, Karsten Weihe presents the following persistent pattern: weapons ads tend to evoke associations with old traditions and experience, emphasize implementation of the latest technological know-how, lean heavily on ideologically-charged concepts like partnership and trust, and use sexual symbolism, ultimately zeroing in on superiority and a representation of the potential for destruction.[3] There is no point in playing this down by arguing that the dissemination of military trade journals is limited and that their use is restricted to professionals in the field. As a team of authors in a subsequent analysis were able to show[4], this type of advertising in Germany is the tip of an international iceberg.

Similar material is found in French and English trade journals as well as in the Arabic and Spanish editions of the German publications, and all of them are aimed at a new market: the political and military leadership of Third World countries. The question of media effectiveness is quite easily answered for the advertising in these military trade journals. As probable links between mass and professional media, these trade journals must be intended to stimulate the sale of industrial products; hence, their effectiveness has been much better researched and documented than that of ordinary mass media. Their intensive use by professionals, not to mention their subjective as well as objective importance for the user are as well understood as their actual contribution to the increase in sales.

The second subject area (crime reporting in the mass media) reveals that the representation of "civil violence" in the mass media dovetails with the representation of military violence. Two recent criminological studies of the representation of "civil violence" and crime in the mass media particularly in the pulp magazines simultaneously came to the conclusion that the image of crime disseminated by the mass media is far from realistic: crime is almost always reduced to the individual fates of criminals and victims; structural violence is ignored. Suspects are mainly seen from the perspective of the states' authorities; the criminal conforms to the widely accepted and disseminated stereotypes of criminals; the social phenomena of the so-called abnormal behavior are degraded to (secretly savored) entertainment.[5] The representation of "civil violence" was characterized as a complement to "military violence" because together they provide a fairly accurate reflection of "everyday violence" as experienced by the average television viewer. In addition, they have a political function in that they support the existing conditions of organized "non-peace". The ownership of the military means for destruction must be justified either directly by referring to tradition, to technological innovation or superiority, or

- subiminally - by using sexual symbolism. By contrast, the individual criminal is made to appear as a person who is "by nature" mean or evil.

Since both forms of representation exclude the problem of structural violence, the violence perpetrated by the state is legitimized (in contrast to the "naturally" bad guy) either in the figure of the police commissioner or within the world of weapons advertising. In scholarly discussion, the question of violence in the mass media has always also been a question about its effect on the viewer/reader. Putting aside for the moment the effect that violence in the media has on children - present research shows that under certain circumstances, the principles of learning by success and/or imitation apply here - the entire controversy on the problem can be reduced to different approaches in methodology and epistemology.

At present, there are essentially two diametrically opposed schools of thought: On the one hand, there is an approach that focuses on the message as part of campaign research; on the other hand, a user oriented approach as part of the "uses-and-gratification" model. The controversy between the two is complicated because both schools are aware of their positivistic as well as their critical variants. For example, while the positivistic content analysis rejects any statement about inference and effect, the critical schools maintains that what media producers expect when they represent violence is already the expression of an effect inherent in the existing society. In contrast, many a critical qualitative analysis claims the existence of certain medial effects without having empirical data to prove them. Similar problems exist for the proponents of the "uses-and-gratification" theory. One group considers it proof of its assumptions about the effects of mass media when a certain user group confirms its own social or psychological status by selecting specific crime and action features; the other group interprets such selections as proof of the lack of effect of the mass media, because the users merely make their choices in accordance with their own pre-existing socio-psychological situation.

To make matters worse, both the use as well the media oriented theories can serve as alibi for political domination. The user oriented theory can exculpate the media industry of its political responsibility for the production of massive representations violence; the other side is frequently reproached for neglecting the actual violence existing in society: it tends to blame mass media for causing violence that is in fact, caused by certain social conditions. Interestingly enough, Michael Kunczik, who has been the most vocal German proponent of that school of thought which maintains that violence in the mass media has no effect on the actual social behavior of the viewer/reader, Kunczik, then, has recently shown a slight change of heart.[6] But it is not possible to solve the entire problem in this manner. Like the old question of the chicken and the egg, it is useless to pose an either/or question when trying to analyze the causal relationships between representation of violence in the media and its assumed effects. Instead, an approach to that question must begin with a thorough analysis of the society structure as a fertile soil for medial violence. In other words, one will have to ask to what extent medial violence has to be seen as an integral part of media production itself. Thus, communications research as a part of peace research would have to give up its role in the area of social psychology, a role that Dieter Senghaas assigned as recent in his significant study on "Composition problems of Peace Research"[7] in 1972. Instead, one would have to demand (quoting Frieder Naschold) "that especially in communications research, the concept of power must be introduced as a variable"[8].

2. Technology

Calling to mind the history of mass media technology the direct interest of the military in these technological developments is readily apparent. Beginning with the first wireless transmission of words and later, picture, to the transistor, the first generation of computer in the fifties, to the laser beam, satellite technology, fiberglass and finally, to the micro processor - all of these technological intentions were commissioned and developed by the military and tried out and used in military actions and wars. The use of these technologies was often restricted to the military establishment which exercised political, economical and legal control over them for long time, at least long before the general public learned about their existence in one way or another or experienced them in the form of mass media.

Military interest in communications technology dates back to before the time of wireless transmission of news. An optic-mechanical telegraph line between Berlin and Koblenz, for example, was under the jurisdiction of the Prussian Ministry of War. This medium was operative between 1834 and 1852 via sixty two masts, each outfitted with six pairs of wings, a message containing 30 words could be sent form the Rhine to Berlin in an hour and a half weather conditions permitting. Licensed exclusively to a federal news service, the purpose of this telegraph line was to transmit to the Prussian military as quickly as possible any information about rebellious movements in the rebellious Rhenish provinces during the run-up to the abortive bourgeois revolution of 1848. But the real break through came during World War I, when the wireless telegraph opened up previously unheard-of opportunities for the military.

Until the turn of the century, the German empire had to depend almost exclusively on British sea-bed cables for overseas communication. This dependence became a particularly weak spot in the empire's sovereignty and its radius of action as communication between the empire and its colonies grew in importance, economically as well as military. The British cable trust had made rigorous use of its monopoly on several occasions - thus, for example, during the Boer war, when great Britain provided cable service only for pro British news. To counteract this monopoly, the German colonial administration as well as the military pressed for two countermeasures: installation of a German-made and international system of undersea cables and a world wide, German-owned wireless network. To be sure, the military had every reason to be concerned about being dependent on British cables: within a flow hours of the declaration of war on August 4th, 1914, the British had destroyed the most important German sea-bed cables in the North Sea. Winfried Lerg, a historian who researches into radio, has the following to say on the beginning of World War I:

> There can be no doubt that in August of 1914, the efficiency and performance in the three most important areas of wireless transmission were considerably below international, and especially below British standards: in the era of military telecommunication for the army and navy; in the area of world-wide continental and marine telecommunication; and in the area of communication with the colonies. In all three areas, there had been an atmosphere of experimentation until 1914. [...] This attitude changed quickly, however, as soon as World War I began. [...] Private use of radio was [...] discontinued on the first day of mobilization. All radio installations [...] were requisitioned for military use. The licensing authority for such installations was transferred from the federal post office to the Ministry of War.[9]

Although technologically possible, the ideological use of radio as a means of "psychological warfare", played only a minor role during World War I. The radio was strictly the domain of the military. The German radio industry - AEG, Siemens and Lorenz - existed almost exclusively on contracts for army and navy at that time. As Winfried Lerg explains:

> With the aid of improvements and innovations of the industry [...] which finally moved laboratory findings right up to the hard reality of the front lines, radio technology developed into a tactical and strategic weapon. Its significance was equally great for army and navy, for the latter particularly during the submarine war. The aerial war had, in fact, only become possible through the development of wireless message and navigation systems. [...] By an order of the cabinet of July 18th, 1917, the existing Telegraphentruppe [telegraph corps] was named Nachrichtentruppe [news corps, i.e. signal corps] and declared an independent army corps. At the end of the war, 4,381 officers [...] and 185,000 enlisted men of the signal corps returned.[10]

This segment from the history of communications technology is significant for several reasons. It exemplifies a number of constellations that were to repeat themselves or which became the beginnings of historically new power structures. The following points are of particular interest.

- The political, economical, military and even personal dovetailing of the electronics industry and the military during World War I actually marked the modest beginnings of the full-blown military industrial complex that was to develop in the United States after World War I.

- Innovations in communications technology are exclusively geared toward and used by the military; war provides the most favorable conditions for research and testing. World War I was the testing ground for radio technology, and likewise the Arab-Israeli War of 1967 became the testing ground for satellite technology.

- The ideological, content-oriented use of new communications technology is of secondary importance. With variable time lags, it comes into play only after military use has become fully operational.

- It is particularly enlightening to observe the history of the changing function of telecommunications from a tactical instrument of war to a public medium of entertainment - the radio. After the war, the former members of the signal corps were looking for jobs. At the same time and more significantly the electronics industry had to look for new and promising markets, if it was to survive. Similar development took place in the USA after World War I. Immediately after World War I, for example, the US government still advocated an international frequency regulations policy that would have allowed for pluralism and compatibility in the international radio appliance industry; by the end of the 1920s, however, the US government had drastically changed this direction by pursuing policies that were clearly intended to create a world-wide, exclusive market for North American radio sets. The pressure exerted by the electronics industry (which was, originally, a military one) was aimed at world-wide standardization patterned on North American radio technology with the ultimate goal of penetrating foreign markets with indigenous, that is US, appliances.

The example from World War I could easily be repeated for other communications technologies and other periods of time. Even without a world war, similar mechanisms for computer and satellite technology obtain today. These technologies, such as telecommunications, are military in nature, too; two thirds of all present day satellites are military satellites for reconnaissance and early warning systems. A few of the high frequency bands are even licensed for military use only. In contrast to this militarization of space, there is a growing demand from Third World countries for civilian use of satellites and frequencies, since satellites would render superfluous in the many extensive areas of Third World countries the much more costly construction of earthbound telecommunications infrastructures. Significantly, a request for demilitarization of the respective high frequencies made by India in 1979, at the World Administrative Radio Conference in Geneva, was rejected by the USSR as well as the USA, against the votes of the entire Third World.

In summary, communications technology must be understood as a byproduct and spin-off of military technology. The greater the significance of communications technology for the national economy, the tighter it is bound to the military industrial complex.

3. Access

As soon as communications technology becomes part of the civilian domain and this applies to hardware as well as software it is no longer enough to explain questions of access to this technology by considering military power structures alone. As the overthrow of Salvador Allende's

Government in Chile documented all too clearly[11], its success depended to a decisive degree on the direct, intentional and well coordinated cooperation between the local and the foreign military, the secret services and the electronics as well as the entertainment industry.

All in all, access to civilian communications technology, command of its resources, participation in the decision-making process as to the use of these resources and the position of the peripheries in the flow of information must be recognized as expressions of structural violence. The term structural violence is understood here as a politico-economic system in which the chances for participation in power are extremely unequal, a system in which, using the center-periphery model, the peripheries are subject to directives by the centers in the interest of the latter. Asking the question of access to communications technology and production, the model of structural violence could well be discussed within an international, national or social individual frame of reference. International relationships may serve here as an exemplary case for all with an analysis of the structure of news agencies as important gatekeepers of the press.

The present international system of news reporting is dominated by five news agencies. Only UPI, AP, Reuter's, AFP and TASS operate world-wide and have the organizational technological and economic capacities to fulfill all the functions of a news agency. While these agencies circulate approx. a million words daily, there are many Third World countries that do not even possess a single national news agency of their own. By contrast, a few of the "threshold countries" of the Third World produce only about 10,000 words per day. Heading this communication and information export are the two North American agencies. For example, approx. 40 percent of all news items in the 14 politically most important and most widely sold Latin American newspapers are bought from UPI, 31 percent from AP. Most of the remainder is divided up by Reuter's and AFP.

Similar surveys with comparable results exist for various time periods and regions. Taking into consideration all necessary individual differences, they all confirm the pattern of a one-sided flow of information, a one-way-street for news agencies leading from the metropolitan centers to the peripheries.

That means in effect, that the filters and criteria for selection of a piece of news are determined by and dependent upon the economic value of that information for the centers - dependent, who had in turn their political interests, socio-cultural distortions and selective patterns of perception. Since this one-way flow of information has been proven to exist in other media, too, the phrase "free exchange of ideas and knowledge" (as quoted initially from the UNESCO document of 1945) can no longer be seen as a statement of fact, but only as a political imperative. If the international flow of information be merely a reflection of actual international power structures, then it follows that this formula of a "free exchange" merely serves to obscure the true nature of these power structures.

A historical survey of the origin of this formula makes it ideologically suspect. As Herbert Schiller has outlined convincingly[12], this formula - this coin - was phrased jointly by US politicians and media corporations in the early forties. At that time this was done not only as part of the resistance against fascism but very soon also as an ideological basis for the massive onslaught of North American media which was to hit Western Europe after 1945. Together with the above mentioned principle of assignment of radio frequencies on a first come first served basis to the technologically most advanced applicant by the International Telecommunication Union, this principle of the free flow of information ensures the dominant position of the metropolitan centers.

In 1975, Fernando Reyes Matta further differentiated the existing studies on the one-way flow of information[13]. As a kind of case study, he carefully analyzed Latin American newspapers during the week following the independence day of the former Dutch colony Surinam. This date - so important for the process of decolonialization - was either completely ignored by the Latin American press, or mention of it (and this is the significant factor) reached the Latin American reader only via the detour of a UPI press release.

Considering this and later analyses, the justifiable conclusion is that the international flow of information not only runs in one direction, but in addition, that it also shapes the structure of the flow of information within the peripheries themselves. Summing up, then, the international structure of the news systems can be characterized as follows:

- The flow of information follows a one-way vertical course from the center to the periphery.
- The centers among themselves exchange information directly and reciprocally.
- The exchange of information between neighboring peripheries functions indirectly, by means of detours through the respective centers. If the peripheries are part of differing sub-systems, the exchange of information is even more indirect.
- A horizontal exchange of information of the peripheries among each other is minimal.

This structure of the international news system must be seen as nothing short of a "classic" expression of structural violence, for it systematically denies the periphery (and even indeed the peripheries within the periphery!) access to communications production and technology. "Classic" is indeed the proper term to apply to this structure because the unmistakable imbalance of power in favor of the centers automatically makes the peripheries even more dependent on the metropolitan centers for access to the communication media than they are, for example, for access to property ownership, work, capital and raw materials. Thus, the existing international information system and not only that of the news agencies is not merely an expression of structural violence but in addition an essential instrument for the stabilization of this system of violence.

4. The Power of Control

As numerous studies have shown, multinational mixed-media corporations which are part and parcel of the military industrial complex play the key role in the international information order. In other words: the power of control over and distribution of information is closely tied to the very existence of this societal power structure. The structural violence of multinational mixed-media corporations can tolerate sovereign autocentric and participatory development of the information systems only for very limited periods of time and in a few historical, anachronistic and relative areas of free interplay between the oligopolies; in principle, however, it can only promote a development in dependency as it were.

And we can assume that in the future, a very limited kind of development will take place, not so much in the realm of content but rather in the structural areas. Transnational mixed media corporations are now standing on the threshold of an era of technological development in which content (software) will be of secondary importance, an era in which almost every target group will be adequately supplied with (what the industry deems to be) its very own content.

"Knowledge is power", wrote the English "enlightener" Francis Bacon in his *Essays* of 1598. Such a statement had to remain idealistic and hence ideological as long as an accumulation of power was, indeed not possible through an accumulation of knowledge, but rather, through the material exploitation of labor aimed at accumulating surplus in the era of a society which produced material goods. As long as this material exploitation determined the essential character of a historical stage, it was possible to unmask and personally experience Bacon's message as a fraud. Speaking abstractly: There was still a gap between ideology and social reality. But if, in the light of present day experience, the ideological mainstays "centralism" and "modernism" were to become reality which would seem to be the logical continuation of a seemingly inexorable historical process, then Bacon's words would, indeed, hold true, if applied to the present day and reformulated to elucidate their inherent dynamics: Knowledge presupposes social power (a) and at the same time produces it (b) - power presupposes knowledge (c) and at the same time same time produces it (d). The following examples are offered as illustrations:

a) Lockheed's largest database owes its existence entirely to the power constellation of a multinational corporation (the economic basis of knowledge).
b) Technological expertise on how TV satellites functions such as was gained through the Indian SITE experiment is helping the Federal Government of India to consolidate its drive toward becoming a sub-metropolitan superpower (power through knowledge).
c) Only its monopolized lead in computer know-how and information and communication technologies (ICT) enabled IBM as a multinational corporation to blackmail Indonesia into exempting it from nationalization. (knowledge as a basis for economic power).
d) The power concentration in the metropolitan centers leads (in the centers) to an accumulation of knowledge on the peripheries (knowledge through power).

This spiral of reciprocal dependence between knowledge and power creates its own dynamics of development which seems to be a historic societal necessity. Its course and its goals frequently defy rational analysis, so that - at least on the surface - only the technological autodynamics remain visible. But actually, the process of transformations toward a global "post industrial" society is much more complex than that. The scholars of the Enlightenment were still able to formulate their social criticism and protest by comparing ideologies; in the current process of dovetailing knowledge and power, a distinct trend toward the (ab)use of information as a tool for gaining economic and political power is fast gaining ground - ideologies are becoming minor ingredients in the technological power play.

Thus, for example, a single multimedia corporation can market simultaneously feminist movies, textbooks for a fascist military dictatorship in Latin America, and Marxist professional journals for sociologists. Indeed, the programming costs for the Indian SITE experiment are a mere nine percent of the total budget.

The other side of the coin, the trend toward an "informationalization" of power, becomes especially clear when one considers the political chances of realizing possible counter movements. Since the process of transformation toward the "post-industrial" information society takes place *sub rosa*, there is hardly any directly felt concern as a basis for protest and revolt; a socially relevant citizens' initiative against the computerization of the individual is not likely to take shape. And how, after all, is one to resist effectively the global process of "informationalization", when its protagonists such as the US delegation at the World Administrative Radio Conference of 1979 in Geneva, for example, can carry out the consolidation of the future computer society only with the aid of computers, when a large part of the data stored on computers consists of data on computer technology?

Besides, as long as almost every socially interest group - political parties, societies, nations - is as yet convinced that the main objective is to use the given information technology only in their own best interests - be that progressive or conservative, the cause of capitalism or socialism, the interests of the Third World - as long as these conditions obtain, then, the previously described knowledge/power-spiral, the "informationalization", will certainly not undergo any qualitative changes. To be sure, the final report of the McBride Commission to the UNESCO still holds to that idealistic notion; its central message reads as follows:

> The survey contained in this report has recorded a dramatic expansion of communications resources and possibilities. It is an expansion that promises great opportunities, but also raises anxieties and uncertainties. Everything will depend on the use made of the new resources - that is, on crucial decisions, and on the question of who will make the decisions. Communication can be an instrument of power, a revolutionary weapon, a commercial product, or a means of education; it can serve the ends of either liberation or of oppression.[14]

5. Conclusion

Before summing up and returning to the initial question as to the interrelationships between communications, the mass media and peace, it bears stating that I have only cursorily touched on some aspects of this entire complex in the attached Chart (see Chart 11.1). Only brief mention can be made here, for example, of a number of empirical studies conducted in the United States which came to the conclusion that the use of mass media, too, is subject to structural violence. According to these studies, the recent enormous increase in informational programming appears to have the effect of providing those already in the know with still more knowledge, while those who have been kept in the dark before are sinking into ever deeper ignorance. This scissors like movement of the "increasing knowledge gap" seems to reinforce the existing class structure now in the area of information an communication.

Many questions remain unanswered. Is it impossible for example, to provide an answer to the important question whether representations of violence have increased during the 50-year history of the mass media, because empirical time series analyses are practically non-existent. Or another problem: When Joseph Goebbels pronounced his propagandistic credo "We certainly do not want [...] our SA boys marching across the stage or through the movies. They are supposed to march through the streets"[15] - he actually announced policies that assigned to the seemingly apolitical, purely entertaining movies of the fascist ear the function of compensating for the very real every day violence and the later military violence as well. This simultaneous discrepancy between real and mediated violence during that particular time in history - could there be parallels to this phenomenon in other times and cultures? For example, what exactly is the function of the current onslaught of horror and violence in US films since about 1975, that is to say since the end of the Vietnam War?

No matter how carefully differentiated an answer to such questions would have to be, the initially offered interpretation (which took into consideration Max Horkheimer and Theodor W. Adorno's *Dialectics of Enlightenment*) appears to be universally applicable at this point in time. If mass-media reception as well as production are both the expression and the engine motor of structural violence; if communications technology can be understood, historically, only as an integral part of the emerging military industrial complex; if indeed, the "law of universal violence" obtains, then the mass media can be considered to fulfill their originally hoped for function as "peace-bringers" under rare and exceptional circumstances.

The representation of violence in the mass media, then, is part and parcel of the universal violence of the media themselves.

Communications produced by the mass media have always been an economical as well as an ideological commodity. The well-documented media trend toward the commercialization of production as well as content makes commodities out of the recipients, too; economics is fast becoming the primary concern. Thus, for example, more than 60 percent of the available space in the Latin American publications mentioned above is taken up by advertising and the military trade journals mentioned earlier receive 80 percent of their total income from advertising, which makes them precursors of the many scientific technical trade journals in the USA which are financed completely (100 percent) by advertising. In such journals, an expert author has to pay according to the "page-charge" principle to have a scholarly article printed.

The more advanced the communications technology, so it seems, the higher the degree to which mass media are commercialized. This primacy of economic considerations will continue to strengthen the system of structural violence, because it cannot comprehend the mass media and their content as a social resource for the common good. Only when they open up to a process to democratization on all levels - to the so-called New International Information Order (NIIO) - will the mass media fulfill their function as contributors to a peaceful society. Until such a time, every analysis of "communications and peace" must of necessity turn into an analysis of "communications and the prevention of peace".

Notes and References

1. Gerbner, George and Gross, Larry P.: "Living with television: the Violence profile", in: *Journal of Communication*, 1976, pp. 173-99; Gerbner, George et al.: "TV violence profile no. 8: the high lights", in: *Journal of Communication*, 1977, pp. 1330.

2. Cf. e.g. Glass, Daniel: *Die Dritte Welt in der Presse der Bundesrepublik Deutschland*. Eine ideologiekritische Fallstudie. Frankfurt: Haag & Herchen 1979.

3. Weihe, Karsten: "Rüstungswerbung in der Bundesrepublik", in: *Militärpolitik Dokumentation*, No. 9-10/1978.

4. Weihe, Karsten; Brzoska, Michael; Lock, Peter and Wulf, Herbert: *Advertising and Public Relations in the Arms Industries*: Their Role in the Mass Media, Paris: UNESCO 1980 (Doc. No. 50 of the International Commission for the Study of Communication Problems).

5. Becker, Peter von: *Straftäter und Tatverdächtige in den Massenmedien*. Die Frage der Rechtmäßigkeit identifizierender Kriminalberichte. Eine Untersuchung zur beispielhaften Konkretisierung von Medienverantwortung im demokratisch-sozialen Rechtsstaat, Baden-Baden: Nomos 1979; Schneider, Hans Joachim: *Das Geschäft mit dem Verbrechen*. Massenmedien und Kriminalität, Munich: Kindler 1980.

6. Kunczik, Michael: "Gewaltdarstellungen im Fernsehen. Besteht Anlaß zum Umdenken?", in: *Media Perspektiven*, No. 12/1980.

7. Senghaas, Dieter: "Kompositionsprobleme der Friedensforschung", in: *Kritische Friedensforschung*, ed. by Dieter Senghaas, Frankfurt: Suhrkamp 1972, pp. 313-361.

8. Naschold, Frieder: "Kommunikationstheorien", in: *Gesellschaftliche Kommunikation und Information*. Vol. 1, ed. by Aufermann, Jörg; Bohrmann, Hans and Sülzer, Rolf, Frankfurt: Fischer Athenäum 1973, p. 48.

9. Lerg, Winfried B.: *Rundfunkpolitik in der Weimarer Republik*, Munich: dtv 1980 (= Rundfunk in Deutschland. Vol.1), p. 34.

10. Lerg, Winfried B.: *Die Entstehung des Rundfunks in Deutschland*. Herkunft und Entwicklung eines publizistischen Mittels, Frankfurt: Knecht 1965, p. 43.

11. For more details see Landis, Fred: *Psychological warfare and media operations in Chile 1970-73*, Urbana, Ill. 1975 (unpubl. Thesis); Freed, Donald and Landis, Fred: *Death in Washington*. The Murder of Orlando Letelier, West Port: Hill 1980.

12. Schiller, Herbert I.: "Genesis of the Free Flow of Information Principles", in: *Communication and class struggle*, ed. by Armand Mattelart and Seth Siegelaub, New York: International General 1979.

13. Reyes Matta, Fernando: "The Information Bedazzlement of Latin America", in: *Development Dialogue*, No. 2/1976, pp. 29-42.

14. *Many Voices, One World*. Report of the International Commission for the Study of Communication Problems, Paris: UNESCO 1980, p. 259.

15. Goebbels, Joseph: "Rede in den Tennishallen am 19.5.1933", in: *Nationalsozialistische Filmpolitik*, ed. by Gerd Albrecht, Stuttgart 1969, p. 442.

12

From Prejudice to Dependency: Conflicts on the Way to a New International Information Order

1. Images and Distortions: The Third World as Reflected in the European Media

In his explosive short story "The Writer's Grain", young Zimbabwian author Dambudzor Marechera describes an African writer's cultural identity conflict. Ironically, the narrator/author has to use books to ward off the cat which has intruded into his study:

> I picked up a handful of paperbacks, a complete Shakespeare, a complete Oscar Wilde, the variorum edition of Yeats's plays, a concise Oxford Dictionary, and Thomas Hardy's Collected Poems and stood in the centre of the room my eyes glued to the cat's . Bloody cats used to white racist aunts. Shakespeare dazed it. Wilde was wide of the mark. Yeats stunned it. [...] I picked up a volume of the Encyclopaedia Britannica and bashed the shit to death.[1]

There is a similar passage in the novel "Season of Migration to the North" by Sudanese author Tayeb Salih, written ten years before Marechera's story. In it, an Arab economics professor, a Marxist, who has had an enormously successful career in Great Britain, regains his sense of identity when he returns to his native Sudanese village. He sees the last and most logical act of his liberation as the burning of his voluminous library:

> The books I could see in the light of the lamp that they were arranged in categories. Books on economics, history and literature, zoology, geography, mathematics, astronomy, the Encyclopaedia Britannica, Gibbon, physics, mathematics, astronomy, Macaulay, Toynbee, the complete works of Bernard Shaw, Keynes, Tawney Smith, Robinson, the Economics of Imperfect Competition, Hobson's "Imperialism", Robinson's "An Essay on Marxian Economics" [...], Alice in Wonderland, Richards, The Koran in English, The Bible in English, Gilbert Murray, Plato [...]. Not a single Arabic book. A graveyard. A mausoleum. An insane idea. A prison.[2]

These are not two isolated passages in the immense literature of Africa, Asia or Latin America. The *Encyclopaedia Britannica* plays an important role in both stories. It is this particular book which contains the totality of European culture in a condensed form and which has the reputation of being particularly objective and unprejudiced. Yet it must be admitted that an analysis of the volumes of this reference work would show that it has, for example, distorted the history and social position of Afro-Americans in the USA.[3] Literary attitudes are important in relation to the New International Information Order, insofar as at the beginning of the 20th century, it was authors from the Third World who were striving to develop concepts of national culture based on the African and Asian personality. This movement, which should be seen as the spearhead of anti-colonialism, played a similar role to that of the liberal German authors in the Paulskirche Parliament in 1848, who were also important elements in the search for German national and cultural identity.

The "Congress of Oppressed Nations" held in Brussels in 1927 was the first officially organized meeting of Third World intellectuals. Among those present at the meeting were W.E.B. DuBois, Ho Chi Minh, Felix Houphouet-Boigny, Aimé Césaire, Jomo Kenyatta, Kwame Nkrumah, Jawaharlal Nehru and Krishna Menon. The Bandung Conference of 1951, and many Third World authors, such as Afro American Richard Wright, took part in the deliberations, must be seen as the most important point of intersection between the culturally oriented nationalist movements of the 1920s and the institutionalized inception of the Non-Aligned Movement which took place in Cairo in 1961. The final communique of the Bandung Conference had this to say on the subject of cultural cooperation:

> The Asian-African Conference took note of the fact that the existence of colonialism in many parts of Asia and Africa, in whatever form it may be, not only prevents cultural cooperation but also suppresses the national cultures of the peoples. Some colonial powers have denied their dependent peoples basic rights in the sphere of education and culture which hampers the development of their personality and also prevents cultural intercourse with other Asian and African People. In particular, the Conference condemned racialism as a means of cultural suppression [...].[4]

At present in the Third World, literature and the mass media have much in common. Societies with a relatively new written culture are not familiar with a highly differentiated categorization of work as regards those who produce texts. The broadcast editor is, at the same time, a novelist, a poet and a journalist. Literary language has, sociologically, a much greater validity as an indicator of the prevailing political mood than journalism. Because of this, the above extracts from Marechera and Salih more accurately describe the increased identity crisis induced by the Western media in the Third World than do any of the Non-Aligned Movement resolutions. It is no coincidence that Third World authors have become involved in the struggle for the creation of a New International Information Order. Salih has become UNESCO's regional commissioner for information in the Arab World, while the Indonesian novelist Mochtar Lubis and Colombian Nobel prize winner Gabriel Garcia Marquez were members of the so-called McBride Commission, whose report "Toward a New and More Just and Efficient World Information and Communication Order" as it was subtiteld, was published by UNESCO in 1980.

If there is one statement that empirical social research can make with great certainty, it is that the Euro/US representation of the Third World, particularly that propagated by the media, is distorted and that it is highly probable that this has led to a disturbance of cultural identity. An example of the conclusions which such research arrives at is the comparative analysis of Third World reporting in three West German daily newspapers together with the weekly *Metall* published by I.G. Metall, the metal workers union. This was undertaken by the Swiss political scientist Daniel Glass and showed that:

> In its totality Third World reporting is oriented towards mobilizing feelings of superiority, of competition, and fear rather than the promotion of solidarity or understanding.[5]

No wonder that the characters which Marechera and Salih use to speak for the Third World direct their rage against the written word which emanates from the Northern centers of power and not just against the mass media themselves. Even if since the 16th century, ethnocentricity and a Euro-centric stance need to be seen as the major conceptual features of reports on what is today called the Third World, these general perspectives, however, have developed a host of different ways which hypothetically can a divided into four Euro-centric phases.

In the *first phase* of the early voyages of the "discovery" one finds extraordinarily detailed, "objective", observations and predominantly descriptive passages concerning the Third World in broadsheets, in travel reports and cosmographies as well as in almanacs and chronicles. Defamatory invectives leveled against "pagans" and "cannibals" are seldom found. At the center of these early forerunners of the mass media is an image of striving, sensual awareness and experience of such striking intensity that the reader could not but be convinced of its credibility. The notion of the noble savage which so often dominated these writings could be seen as leading to the hypothesis that in the initial stages of mercantile capitalism it was still so uncontrolled, unorganized, contradictory and helpless that it was forced into a conditional partnership in its relationship with the Third World. This was the only way Europeans could compensate for their ignorance of the language, customs, habits, religious beliefs, mineral resources and trading practices.

As Walter Rodney pointed out in his history of pre-colonial Upper Guinea[6], it was in no way unusual at this point in history for Portuguese traders, the "Lancador", to have to submit themselves to African laws in order to achieve their goals. The image of the "noble savage", be it in Christopher Columbus' diary, in Michel de Montaigne's essay "On Cannibals" or in the widely circulated stories of the marriage of the Indian "Princess" Pocahontas to tobacco planter John Rolfe in Virginia always dominated European perceptions while colonialism was still in its infancy. This particular image was appropriate as long as contact between Europeans and the peoples of the Third World was confined to isolated incidents and there was no systematic political or economic relationship between the Third World and the colonial powers.

During the *second phase*, that of European industrialization and imperialism, the Third World was discriminated against in books and newspapers in a most blatant manner. Open racism was the dominant tendency in these mass media. After the first phase of Third World penetration was completed (genocide, destruction of indigenous political structures, foreign domination, the exploitation of resources and natives), the European and US mass media assumed the role of openly legitimizing colonialism. The image of the "noble savage" no longer had a function in promoting the concept of loyalty to the "home country" as opposed to the systematic suppression and exploitation of the Third World which could be sustained only by a pliable media environment. The half-hearted anti-colonialism of the communist workers movement, the social democrats and churches was totally integrated into these mass media.

The dominant feature of the *third phase*, which can be dated from the 1950s to the present day, is the promotion of a kind of partnership ideology. This is the most prevalent image of the Third World purveyed by the mass media and now by television as well. The most overt forms of racism and discrimination have given way to an image of the great "Family of Man". This latter image, however, also has an ideological function according to which whatever is of advantage to the metropoles is also advantageous for the periphery. Within the economic domain, this image of partnership is a new form of penetration within the North-South conflict in which open discrimination would be dysfunctional.

The image of the Third World in today's mass media is less homogeneous and consistent when compared to the preceding phases, however. In the specialist media one finds adequate reporting and sometimes even expertise from the Third World feeding back into the Euro-American dominated media. Franz Fanon's book "The Wretched of the Earth", published by Maspéro of Paris in 1961, has become the anti-colonial manifesto par excellence. It points out that the sharpest critiques of the metropolises come, at least in part, from the metropolises themselves. The traditional image of the "noble savage" has, to some degree, recently resurfaced in the European alternative movement and overt media-related racism which has survived many historical epochs is by no means dead.

More recent developments may possibly result in a *fourth and future phase*. The total incapability of Western secret services and the monopoly of the four big Western international news agencies (AP, UPI, Reuters and AFP) in identifying in any way at all the scale of the pre-revolutionary movement in Iran, let alone its consequences, can be seen as a sign that present international information systems reflect to an ever decreasing degree the interests of the metropolises. As a direct consequence of the Iran debacle, internationally renowned politicians, such as Edward Heath and Robert McNamara, together with prominent industrialists, founded their own new agency, IRIS (International Reporting Information Service).[7]

However, IRIS only survived for a few years. It employed highly-paid correspondents in practically every country in the world who were mostly natives of the countries in which they worked. These correspondents were chosen for their specialized knowledge of economics and politics and it was their brief to provide clients with better, more objective and more up-to-date information on Third World affairs. A capitalist penetration of the Third World and particularly the refinement of the interaction between its state classes and transnational capital is only possible through such advances and by freeing Third World reporting from ideological restraints. For these reasons it can be expected that the philosophy developed by IRIS will be successful in the long term.

In the fourth and new media technologically oriented phase, cable TV, satellites, databases serve to ensure that the quality of Third World reporting is advancing as follows. The function of mass media/ICT reflects the division within Western industrialized countries where those who have it acquire ever-increasing quantities of knowledge and those left without sink into an ever-increasing pit of ignorance (the "increasing knowledge gap" hypothesis). The electronic entertainment media offer those trapped in ignorance accepted ideologies in a quantitatively enlarged form (cable and satellite TV), while those in possession of knowledge are able to receive information of the highest exactitude and quality from highly specialized print media and databases. Western databases provide a high level of relatively ideologically free information on the Third World which is available in no other quarter.

The empirical exactitude of the four-phase model suggested here needs to be firmed up on a number of levels. After all, the penetration of individual regions of the Third World by the different colonial powers has been of differing intensities and speeds and has thus produced varying concepts and media images. Well-informed time series content analysis is another desirable here. An analysis of how German newspapers have, over a period of four centuries, reported on world events has, for the first time, recently been undertaken. According to its preprint, reporting on Third World events has become less popular and has given way to coverage of domestic events.[8] No matter how rigorously one undertakes the study of Third World images, it must be stated that perceptions relating to the Third World are not uniform, even if they have always been distorted in a Eurocentric manner. Furthermore, there is another argument which states that such distortion in perception is pathological.

Perception can no longer distinguish between reality and image, but develops its own dynamic and creates its own images. Only when one is able to characterize a society as a pathological totality does this notion of pathological perception takes on a measure of adequacy. However, to define the capitalist system in its entirety as pathological would be a purely mechanistic exercise and would leave us explaining the distortion in Third World reporting as only a pure reflection of capitalism. This ignores the rupture in the entire system. The latter can given present prevailing trends unleash the potential for more discriminating forms of reporting. Current media reporting on the Third World is distorted also because the various interest groups within capitalism can no longer be said to be balanced and pluralistically represented.

2. The Political History of the New International Information Order

The debate concerning a New International Information Order has created a link between the discussions on the distortion of the Third World in the European media and the attempt to conduct a structural analysis of the mass media's localization, ownership, diffusion and reach, as well as access and control of the mass media. These analyses understand media content as a result of specific conditions of production. The demand for a New International Information Order has, since the beginning of the 1970s, been both the aim and content of a political movement within the Third World. It was first aimed at the traditional mass media, particularly publishing and the news agencies. Yet since the beginning of the 1980s it has concerned itself also with ICT.

It has developed from the unstructured anti-colonial resentment of the 1920s and 1930s into a systematic concept which has taken shape over the last decade. It was and still is the non-aligned countries that evolved this concept and promoted it as hosts of international forums and conferences. Without the power of leverage over the news agencies, media corporations or a highly developed press the only recourse which these countries have to promote their demands and points of view are international conferences and organizations.

A decisive step in this direction occurred at the Conference of the Heads of State of the non-aligned countries which took place during September 1973 in Algiers. In its final communiqué, the conference called for a "reorganization of the existing communication channels, which are the legacy of the colonial past and which have hampered free, direct, and fast communication between them". A symposium of the non-aligned countries mass media which took place in Tunis in 1976 precisely and analytically corroborated these demands, a process which has continued in other conferences. It is no accident that the non-aligned nations used "emancipation" as a slogan for the conference.

In the Third World the concepts of freedom and liberation struggle are very close to that of emancipation. In 1976, these countries again took a practical step towards the creation of a New Information Order when they decided to set up a news agency pool. The political declaration of the fifth conference of the Heads of State of the Non-Aligned Countries in Colombo in August of that year was both an agenda and a signal.

The accusation that a New Information Order would open the door to state censorship within the Third World was raised by Western interests particularly at the 19th General Assembly of UNESCO in Nairobi in 1976. It was directed, above all, against Article XII of the General Secretariat's draft Media Declaration which said that "states are responsible for the activities in the international sphere of mass media under their jurisdiction". Dissent over Article XII was the main reason why a consensus could not be reached. The General Secretariat was charged with establishing an International Commission for the study of Communication Problems (the McBride Commission as it came to be known) and evolving a new blueprint for the 20th General Assembly. This paper, which was delivered to the 20th General Assembly in Paris, voiced the Third World's and the Non-Aligned states' critique at a variety of levels.

- Article I demanded that the imbalance concealed within the concept of the "free flow of information" be replaced by a "free reciprocal and balanced flow of accurate, complete and objective information".
- Article II suggested a "participation of the public in the elaboration of information" as a suitable model to encourage the involvement of affected recipients.
- Article IV spoke of a "new equilibrium and greater reciprocity in the flow of information" necessary to "correct the quantitative and qualitative inequality in the flow of information to and from developing countries".
- In conclusion, Article XI declared that it was the duty of the State to ensure that this declaration was carried out.

If one compares their proposals with the media declaration which was passed by acclamation at the UNESCO General Assembly on November 28, 1978, it is clear that very little of the flesh of the New Information Order proposal remained. The real struggle for the decolonialization of information was reduced, in Paragraph 16 of the preamble, to "an awareness of the aspirations of the developing countries for the establishment of a new, more just and more effective world information and communication order". There is no mention of the existence of global inequality. The Third World's call for a New Information Order was reduced to the call for a "greater reciprocity in the flow of information" in Article VI and Article X respectively. The comparative verbal forms, which were included in the final media declaration as a result of western pressure, are an attempt to hinder the recognition of the neo-colonial dependency structures inherent in the domain of international information.

The most important element of the media declaration must be seen as the formulation of the concept of the "free exchange and the wider and better dissemination of information" in Article X, Paragraph 2. The old "free flow" formulation was, for the first time, relativised within the framework of an international agreement of include the qualified acknowledgement of the Third World's demands. The McBride Report, which contained the first acknowledgement of the existence of imbalance, deficits, and dependency, was approved at the 1980 UNESCO General Conference.[9] It overcame the debate, in deadlock until then, on "press freedom" versus "state censorship" by developing a structural analysis of global dependencies within international media politics. The report's greatest achievement was that within the concept of the international democratization of the media it introduced key concepts such as dismantling concentration, the multilateral flow of information, receiver participation, as well as the awareness of social priorities.

3. Resistance to the New International Information Order

Initially the activities of the Non-Aligned Movement were directed against the press and news agencies. Yet, towards the end of the 1970s and initially quite independently of the above concerns, a controversy arose within the United Nations and particularly within the Committee of the

Peaceful Use of Outer Space (COPUOS) surrounding the introduction and use of satellites. The UN, in a declaration on the use of satellites passed by the General Assembly in 1972, ruled that one state can only transmit directly into another's territory with the agreement of the latter state.

This resolution was passed with only one dissenting vote, namely that of the United States. The entire procedure was repeated in December 1982 when, at the 37th General Assembly of the United Nations, 107 countries voted for the principle of "prior consent" of the receiving country, 13 states abstained, among them France, Canada and Greece, while 13 negative votes were recorded, among them the United States, West Germany, most of the EU countries, as well as Japan and Israel. In contrast to 1972, the 1982 debate was a highly politicized event. It was at this point in time that the Non-Aligned Movement fully incorporated the latest generation of ICT into the concept of a new Information Order.

In matters relating to high tech, which is an area vital to Western economies, voting patterns followed the "Group of 10" versus the rest of the world pattern. Yet, in areas relating to the "old mass media," the leading industrial countries have introduced the concept of an "integration strategy". An interesting concept of this kind relating to the Third World was developed by George Kroloff and Scott Cohen for the US Senate's Foreign Affairs Committee in 1978. In their analysis of the implications of a New International Information Order, they concluded that the creation of such a process would "affect the action of the US Government". As a means of deflecting possible danger, the authors suggested that the US should try to undermine the united position of the African states at the next international communications conferences. It was suggested that this was possible, given the fact that they were already split on the question of the Middle East, and this strategy could be accomplished by enticing individual African countries with the promise of media projects.[10]

At the 1978 UNESCO General Conference, the US delegation termed the Third World countries proposals for a New Information Order a "dangerous communist inspired rattlesnake" infiltrating into their midst "which must be replaced by a harmless "slow-worm"[11]. This conference saw the beginning of the implementation of their integration strategy. US ambassador John E. Reinhardt, offered the developing countries a package of "positive cooperation and a more effective programme of action".

This programme of action "included American assistance from both the public and private sectors and in particular to suitably identified centres of professional education and training in broadcasting and journalism in the developing world". It also included "a major effort to apply the benefits of advanced communications technology - specifically communications satellites - to economic and social needs in the rural areas of developing countries"[12]. This strategy, based as it was on a triangle of money, technology and journalist training for the Third World, was encapsulated in a special resolution of this conference. This resolution, co-sponsored by the United States, Australia, France, Tunisia, Sri Lanka and Venezuela, and which dealt with "policies, infrastructures, and training in the field of communication" stated that a situation must be created which will "lead to the provision in developing countries of the technological instruments and other means for promoting a free flow and a wider and better balance exchange of information of all kinds"[13].

Here again one should notice the use of the comparative form. One month after the UNESCO General Conference, the US tabled almost the same resolution at the Special Political Committee of the General Assembly of the UN, which was also structured in comparative terms and included the same triangle of money, technology and journalist training.

The Carter administration, even if it never made any actual concessions, paid lip service at the diplomatic and verbal level to the idea of compromise with the Third World. The same cannot be said of the Reagan administration, which has reverted to an overt policy of strongly opposing all demands for change and has blocked all attempts to begin the construction of a New International Information Order. The sole US and Israeli refusal to accept a UNESCO media resolution at the 1981 UN General Assembly is an example of the new Reagan administration policy. The vehemence of the US administration's opposition was further demonstrated in their submissions to the House of Representatives Foreign Affairs Committee[14] and the activity of the US delegation at the meeting of "The International Programme for the Development of Communication" (IPDC) at Acapulco during 1982. The impact of these actions was that the US, together with Japan and West Germany, suspended all direct financing of this special UNESCO programme.

At the ideological level, the new administration not only increased its support for the promotion of the principle of the "free flow of information" but it has also campaigned for the right of industrialized countries to free and unhindered access to the Third World telecommunication infrastructures. It is obvious that market access to spin-off technologies as they are known is an inherent facet of the evolution of ICT. It can also be said that such a promotion of the "free flow" doctrine is in the interest of these technologies themselves. According to the generally accepted interpretation of the law, information input is regulated by the international legal principle of the "free flow of information", while information processing and output is regulated by the current legal basis of state sovereignty within national law. It bears considering here that because of the increasing interaction between information technologies and computer communication it is no longer possible to clearly distinguish between input and output. It is, therefore, also necessary on a political and level for the metropoles to achieve unhindered access to the periphery's information infrastructure.

This is evidently the thrust behind the following excerpt from a report published by the US State Deptartment in August 1981. It recommends "to enlarge acceptance of the principle of the free flow of information and ideas, including acceptance of the applicability of this principle to newly emerging communications and information technologies"[15]. The United States' resistance to a New Information Order reached its tentative highpoint in President Reagan's announcement of the United States withdrawal from UNESCO. The US statement of December 28, 1983, on its intention to pull out of UNESCO said that:

> We view the fact that UNESCO [...] has attacked the basic principles of free market enterprise and the free flow of information, as well as the fact that it was guilty of mismanagement in a most negative manner [...]. It further states that it continues to work for the so called New World Information and Communication Order, which is a danger to the freedom of the press and to the principle of a free exchange of information.[16]

An interesting aspect of the US withdrawal is not so much the arguments used to justify this decision but the date which was chosen to implement it. During 1983 a widely publicized campaign against UNESCO was carried out in the United States, ranging from defamatory articles on its General Director M'Bow[17] to the suggestion from the conservative "Heritage Foundation", an organization close to the Reagan administration, that the New International Information Order was in reality the most important component in UNESCO's plan to turn the entire world into a socialist state.[18]

A suggestion that the UNESCO's Communications Department be replaced with personnel sympathetic to the US position, which appeared in a report submitted to Congress, was positively received.[19] There was little mention of the New International Information Order in UNESCO's 1984-89 Medium-Term Plan. The US delegation attending the UNESCO

General Conference in November 1983, which was headed by the president of the Mobil Oil Corporation, expressed its satisfaction at the "reasonable tone of the conference discussions". To put it another way: between 1982 and 1984 the USA was able to redirect the debate within UNESCO to ensure it conformed to her own foreign policy. Among the many negative responses which the US resignation aroused was the resolution proposed by Cuba and Saudi Arabia at the Conference of the Information Ministers of the Non-Aligned countries in Jakarta at the beginning of 1984 which called for a continuation of UNESCO's previous policies.

4. The Position of West Germany

It is impossible to give a detailed resumé of the West German position here. Generally speaking, however, two trends can be observed. The first is the fact that the Federal Government has kept a low profile over the last decade in the debate on the problems associated with the New Information Order; in fact this means that West Germany has no consistent policy in this area. Secondly, German diplomats have mostly taken a very hawkish stance in relation to information policy in the last few years. The fact that West Germany has adopted the hardline US position on the Law of the Sea Convention is also testimony to this second trends. There are no grounds for seeing these tendencies as being in opposition to each other. While the low-profile strategy gives its verbal support of the US hardline position it avoids further conflicts in a fragile Atlantic Alliance.

When confronted with Third World demands for a New Information Order, most West German politicians reply with offers of more media-oriented development projects. Yet very few of these promises have been carried out. Few objections could be lodged against Third World media projects initiated by industrialized countries because only the concrete qualities of a project can give an impression of its value within the domain of development policy. The fact that similar forms of argumentation are used by both Bonn and Washington is indeed peculiar.

More peculiar still is the fact that the media project policy replaces a debate on unbalanced information flows which the West German general public was not aware of in the first place. If one bears in mind fact that for every one thousand minutes of TV content transmitted from the US to the Third World there is only one minute of Third World material transmitted in the United States, then it is clear that individual media project can do very little to alter infrastructural dependencies on an international level. Those who refer only to Third World media projects when confronted with the debate on a New Information Order do not want to contemplate the question as to why there is nearly no exposure to Third World TV in West Germany given the fact that it exports between 5,000 and 6,000 hours of television programming per year to developing countries.[20]

Bonn's strategies related to media projects prevent any critical insight into the media activities of the political foundations, the public broadcasting systems or German private industry in the Third World. Given that it supports technology transfer and the financing of journalist training it has propagated the illusion that the press and the news agencies constitute the most important component of the world wide flow of information.

This is true on neither a quantitative nor a qualitative level. The press, it is estimated, accounts for only ten percent of the global flow of information, while the 40 largest communication concerns have a turnover which is between ten and 160 times larger than the intake of news agencies such as UPI, AP or Reuters. On a qualitative level, it is also clear that the international flow of information particularly in the area of satellite communications or transborder computer-based data exchange is subject to domination to a much greater degree than the press.

The various German governments have made exceedingly few offical statements on this subject and this, in turn, leads to the danger of over-interpreting the little that exists. It is also possible to discern a change of attitude in relation to this field which coincides with the change in West German government following the 1982 elections. In 1978, Foreign Minister Hans Dietrich Genscher, in a speech to the UNESCO General Assembly in Paris, warned that the world was in danger of being divided into those who possessed and those who consumed information. He also stressed that a more balanced flow of information between North and South was necessary. The German Social Democratic Party (SPD) went even further in its critique. Amongst those who spoke out at that time was Peter Glotz, the General Secretary of the SPD, who stated in an article entitled "Free Flow of Commercials" that:

> According to the letter and the spirit of the UNESCO agreements and the Helsinki Final Act, the principle is not to guarantee a free flow of advertising but a free flow of information and opinion contributing towards reciprocal familiarization of people and their cultures.[21]

Even then Chancellor Helmut Schmidt expressed doubts about the sacrosanct principle of the "free flow of information" when he criticized Radio-Télé-Luxembourg's plans to beam a satellite transmitting German language commercial programming into West German territory.[22]

Hans Dietrich Genscher's position remained unchanged in the post-1982 CDU/FDP government. Yet differentiated positions which insist that the difficult technical political and international legal problems associated with transborder data flow from computer to computer can and must be solved did not surface while that government was in office. Chancellor Helmut Kohl, in his speech in September 1983, negated Genscher's 1978 statement when he said that "the Federal Government recognizes, without reservation, the principle of transborder free flow of information".[23]

5. Freedom and/or Social Justice

Mass media and ICT-related dependence or domination theories devised by political scientists are a recent phenomena. It has taken mass communications a number of years to arrive at level equal to that of the social sciences where, for example, it is in a position to question the validity of the modernization theories. In West Germany, a breakthrough in this area occurred in 1981 when George Michael Luyken published his essay on communication and development research.[24]

This change of paradigm was not made by German communications scholars. Given their academic tradition, namely roots in journalism, Germans working in this field found it much more difficult than their foreign colleagues to divorce themselves from their tradition in what are descriptive historiography, the humanities and socio-psychology. It were particularly the analyses of Herbert I. Schiller (USA), Kaarle Nordenstreng (Finland), Armand Mattelart (France) and Cees J. Hamelink (Holland) that seriously tackled the dual character of information as a purveyor of ideology and as a commodity. These thinkers were among the first to elaborate a valid critique of the modernization theories and to demonstrate the imbalance and bias within the information flows and the access to media and information technology as a form of structural dependence in the North/South conflict. These works had a decisive influence on the political and theoretical concepts behind the McBride Report. The following can be said to be their principal theoretical and empirical observations:

- International information structures are both a product of and a factor in global economic structures.
- The penetration of the Third World by the media and ICTs has taken place in conjunction with the evolution of integrated international media systems.
- The transnational electronic and mixed media concerns are the main actors in the international information structures.
- The more modern the particular media or ICT are, the more the Third World becomes dependent on the metropoles.
- Only in very few instances does western media and information technology fulfill the needs of the people of the Third World.
- Information flows in a one-sided, hierarchical and vertical fashion from North to South.
- Direct metropole-to-metropole communication is the norm in the North. Yet the exchange of information between related peripheries can only take place indirectly through the agency of the relevant metropoles. This situation becomes even more pertinent when the peripheries wish to communicate with each other if they belong to differing information sub-systems.

The discussion on the "free flow of information," as we have seen, has played and continues to play an important role in the now institutionalized conflict around the concept of a New Information Order. Juan Somavia, the Director of the Latin American Institute for Transnational Studies (ILET), has stated: "Free flow in the cultural and information spheres is the key instrument in the structure of transnational domination in the area of communications."[25] Does that mean that the transborder flow of information should in future be consolidated, regulated and controlled by the state? Or that freedom of expression which is guaranteed in Article 5 of the West German Constitution be abolished? The answer is no, for the following six reasons:

1. Thomas Siebold demonstrated in his essay[26] that during the emergence of the European national states the interaction between the press and the state apparatus was, of necessity, different than it is today. Most of the people of the Third World are now at the initial stage of building nations out of old colonial structures, and their mass media have a qualitatively different role to play in this process of nation-building than their American or European counterparts. In both these continents this process has been largely accomplished,

whereas, the Third World situation necessitates that the mass media be allotted the task of the development of national consciousness and not the satisfaction of individual information related desires.

2. The manifold obstructions to press freedom in the United States and West Europe are overlooked in our obsession with the dualistic juxtaposition of "freedom" and "state censorship". This, however, occurs by other means, namely through cartels and monopolies, the political illiteracy inherent in our throw-away consumer society, the barriers to free media access which are caused by the lack of purchasing power, as well as educational and social stratification.

3. The protagonists of the "free flow" model use the concept of freedom as their justification. Yet this can be understood only as a component of an individualistically oriented concept of humanity. This model does not contain any socio-cultural or collective component. It fails to appreciate that freedom must be understood in real rather than in abstract or absolute terms. In the Third World, the concept of freedom only has validity within a larger conceptual framework, such as social justice, cultural identity or national defense. If the societies of the Third World are defined as societies controlled by outside forces which lack even the capacity to provide their own basic material requirements, then the insistence on the concept of individual freedom on moral and political levels without the implementation of conditions which would give rise to such freedom can only be regarded with skepticism.

4. Historically speaking, information has increasingly developed into a commercial commodity. Its availability or non-availability has increasingly come to be equated with the availability or the non-availability of political economic power. For this reason, it has become necessary, on an international level, to create a set of rules to govern this commodity flow. Goods such as raw materials and manufactured products are more or less covered by international agreements. The call for a New International Information Order is an attempt to improve on the long out-moded rules which govern the role of immaterial commodities, such as information within the domain of international trade.

5. In an interdependent international environment, where transnational corporations exercise an ever stronger influence than on an national level it is possible that the Third World's demands for national control of the mass media can restrict the activities of these corporations. As long as the choice is only between two evils (an indigenous state-controlled press or an alienated press controlled from the metropole by multinational corporations), then the nations of the Third World, regardless of their political orientation, must choose the first and lesser evil. Only in this way is an internally attained democratic and participatory media system foreseeable on a long-term basis. This is so because possibilities for political action against the transnational mixed media concerns are, by their very nature, extremely limited.

6. As the history of the struggle to achieve a national culture and that of the Non-Aligned Movement demonstrates, the demand for a New International Information Order is, in itself, a political movement which has developed in the Third World. The socialist countries have sided with the Third World against Western interests in many cases. Yet this should not obscure the fact that their underlying interests only partially coincide and particularly, in the area of high technology at some future date, may substantially differ. The difference between the socialist nations of Eastern Europe and the Third World lies in the nature of colonialism. While in the socialist countries media policies are often a component of repressive internal policies, the same can be said of Third World countries only on a descriptive level. When seen on a historical/analytical level the countries of the Third World do not have an internalized system of domination.

The above points are encapsulated in a speech by Urho Kekkonen, the former Finnish President, in which he said that:

> The publication of the Declaration of Human Rights after the Second World War [...] coincided with the elevation of free trade and enterprise ("laissez faire") to the point where they became the highest values of commerce and ideology, without considering what effect this would have. In this way the freedom of the strong triumphed while the weak, despite their so-called freedom, went under. [...] Could it be that the prophets who preach the gospel of unhindered information are not at all interested in the equality of nations but rather align themselves with the powerful and the rich?[27]

The following principles should be stubbornly promoted in the interest of the Third World: on a political level the "free flow of information" doctrine must again be called into question because it cements the prevailing structure of metropole/periphery relationships. On a technological level, it is necessary to amend the International Telecommunication Unions current "first come, first served" doctrine which applies to the distribution of radio frequencies. Ernst-Otto Czempiel was quite correct when he compared this principle to the notion of squatting.[28]

For a long time, radio frequencies were claimed and legally registered by those who were technically able to use them. This principle favors the most technically advanced countries. Finally, at the international level the Third World must be supported to promote the concept of "prior consent," whereby a country's prior agreement is attained before it is subjected to satellite remote sensing or foreign satellite broadcasting. Satellite remote sensing and direct broadcasting satellites should not only be governed by the unrestricted principle of the "free flow of information", as the leading authorities on international law in the FRG have maintained.

Suitable points of reference for developing a more differentiated international legal principle governing this field are the Broadcasting Treaty of the League of Nations (1936), the aspects of the 1961 Space Treaty which concentrate on protecting our common heritage and which also included a clause forbidding the monopolization of the advantages to be gained from space exploration, resolution 428A passed by the International Telecommunication Union in 1977 which stipulates that satellite spillover is permissible only with the prior consultation of the affected countries, the UN's Satellite Resolution from December 1982 and the general obligation to consultation which exists within International Law.

6. How Does this Concern Us?

1. Our relations with the Third World urgently need to be improved not just on a moral or a political level but above all for the following two reasons. First of all, the effects of the shortness of the German colonial period and the international isolation of the Third Reich can still be felt in West Germany's immense provincialism when compared to France or England. Clients of West Germany's media are cut off from [illegible] Third World's [illegible], religious, social and political [illegible]

act as a stimulus to our creativity. Secondly, given that a restructuring of the Atlantic Alliance is becoming necessary, it would be of advantage to West Germany to develop a qualitatively better relationship to the Third World. Raising the standard of reporting is essential if this goal is to be accomplished. The changes which are taking place in the Third World today will have a stronger effect on our future than any of us suspects.

2. The more intensively the new media are developed, the more likely it will become that external influences will not be tolerated in West Germany. All of the new media (cable TV, videotext, satellite TV, databases) must be seen as introducing new transmission processes and storage or distribution capacity. They have no new content. Given that West Germany's market for scientific or artistic know-how is limited and has only marginal development potential, then it is reasonable to assume that it must be fed with foreign software, which is the case in many Third World countries today.

Even though practically every member of the EU is extensively developing its TV transmission capacity through the use of satellites and cable TV(Dietrich Ratzke estimates that in addition to the five German programs, an additional 60 European satellite programmes will be available by the end of the 1980s/beginning of the 1990s[29]). European software in its entirety is currently able to fulfill the needs of only three extra channels.[30] The result of such a situation would be the widespread Americanization of the various European systems, as only the US has enough programmes to supply the entire European market.

3. A recent study[31] on the dependence of German databases on their US counterparts has shown that the transborder exchange of specialist computer-to-computer information is anything but balanced. The position of West Germany in relation to the US in the individual media can be compared to that of the Third World vis-à-vis the mass media in relation to the industrialized countries. This situation is exemplified by the fact that the US company Chemical Abstracts controls more or less all of the available data on chemicals in West Germany and that the US NTIS database possesses more data on West German energy, air and space research than any databank in West Germany. It is essential, if West Germany is to maintain its sovereignty in the technological domain, that a system of regulating foreign access to West German databases is introduced.

4. It is no longer possible to adhere to the old definition of the "free flow of information". Ongoing support for this concept will have a high price: according to current practice, which the United States seek to maintain for their own reasons, electronic financial transactions are classified as belonging to this category. In 1976 alone, the Citicorp Bank made US$ 46 million profit by electronically transferring money from European accounts and temporally "parking" it in Nassau, thereby avoiding tax which would otherwise have been due.

It would be absurd to continue to legitimize these forms of transborder data exchange by equating them with the freedom of expression which is guaranteed in Article 5 of the German constitution. Transborder data exchange of this kind is a specific form of international trade which, in the interests of German industry and the labor market, needs to be fully legally regulated. When one starts to examine the "free flow" concept, there is no reason why other possibilities which cause problems to the economies and cultures of Third World countries should not also be considered.

5. Research is another area which concerns us here and through which West Germany could contribute to the problems which have been dealt with in this essay. At present, those who are involved in national or regional studies or in the daily media habits of people in Third World societies should outnumber those who work at the macro-level. Current concentration on the political and economic function of state agencies, multi-national corporations and international authorities is reflected in much of the writing emanating from the field of communications research. This is necessary as a first step in order to come to terms with the problems associated with nation-building in the Third World. This can form the basis for developing a micro-sociological model to examine the concrete situation of the people of the Third World.

An analysis of the relationship between the macro and micro levels is urgently required. Such research is, at the methodological level, possible only when Third World scientists have an equal say in development projects. How does a Muslim woman react to pornographic films from Singapore? What influence does the BBC exert on the social structure of a village in Northern Nigeria? Such knowledge would, perhaps, give us a better idea of how we, who are or who may become, victims of the "old" information order, can replace it, than we can gain from the current process of global analysis.

It is clear that an attempt to create a New International Information Order through the democratization of national mass media and ICTs must now begin. So much is clear from the McBride Report. Despite the fact that the debate on the media has become stalled, the process of democratization in West Germany must still be defined as follows:

1. The retention and extension of the public broadcasting system.
2. The halting of tendencies toward privatization, concentration and commercialization.
3. The preeminence of social rather than technological considerations during the introduction of ICTs.
4. The development of the concept of data protection to encompass a law which would guarantee the citizen's right to inspect all government records. This has already come about in the United States and Sweden.
5. The inception of a media trade union and the strengthening of the laws pertaining to workers councils, in order to ensure that the introduction of ICT in businesses is carried out in consultation with the work force.
6. The promotion of alternative media.
7. The promotion of an increased critical awareness of the media in our educational process.

The implementation of the changes cited above would certainly be a precondition for the achievement of any qualitative change in the current relationship between West Germany and the Third World in the field of media and information.

Notes and References

1. Marechera, Dambudzo: "The Writer's Grain", in: Marechera, Dambudzo: *The House of Hunger*, London: Heinemann 1978, p. 100.
2. Salih, Tayeb: *Season of Migration to the North*, London: Heinemann 1969, p. 136.
3. Cf. Sloan, Irving: *The Treatment of Black Americans in Current Encyclopedias*, Washington: American Federation of Teachers (AFL-CIO) 1970.

4. Quoted in Tran Van Dinh: "Non-Alignment and cultural imperialism", in: *The Nonaligned Movement in World Politics*, ed. by A.W. Singham, Westport 1977, p. 74.

5. Glass, Daniel: *Die Dritte Welt in der Presse der Bundesrepublik Deutschland*. Eine Ideologiekritische Fallstudie, Frankfurt 1979, p. 323.

6. Cf. Rodney, Walter A.: *History of the Upper Guinea Coast 1545-1800*, Oxford 1970.

7. Cf. Lloyd, Andrew: "The Flagrant IRIS," in: *Transnational Data Report* (Amsterdam), Vol. V, No. 1/1982, p. 5; Ordelman, Tom: "Nachrichtendienst für die Reichen. 'Iris' ist objektiv", in: *Die Tageszeitung*, March 2, 1982. The fact that IRIS stopped functioning in 1983 because of lack of funds as well as internal difficulties changes little in relation to the significance of the objective conditions which an agency such as IRIS evolved. See also Samarajiwa, Rohan: "The Failure of IRIS and the Future of the Customized Business Information Market", in: *Transnational Data Report*, Vol. VII, No. 3/1984, pp.171-74.

8. Cf. Wilke, Jürgen: "Wie das Bild der Welt seinen Zusammenhang verlor. Der Wandel der Nachrichtenauswahl in vier Jahrhunderten", in: *Forschung. Mitteilungen der DFG*, No. 1/1984, pp. 27-29.

9. Cf. *Many Voices - One World*. Communication and Society Today and Tomorrow. Towards a new more just and more efficient world information and communication order ed. by Sean MacBride, Paris: UNESCO Press 1980.

10. Cf. Kroloff, George and Cohen, Scott: *The New World Information Order*. A Report to the Committee on Foreign Relations United States Senate, Washington 1978 (mimeo).

11. Quote from a letter written by the Chairman of the US-UNESCO Delegation, William Attwood, to the *New York Times*, Dec. 4, 1978.

12. Quoted in Nordenstreng, Kaarle: "Struggle around a New International Information Order", in: *Journal of Communication*, Spring 1979.

13. UNESCO: *Records of the General Conference*. Twentieth Session. Vol. I: Resolutions, Paris 1979, p. 105.

14. Cf. the Review of *US Participation in UNESCO*. Hearings and Markup before the Sub-committees on International Operations and on Human Rights and International Organizations of the Committee on Foreign Affairs, House of Representatives, Ninety-seventh Congress, First Session on H. Res. 142, March 10, July 9 and 16, 1981, Washington: U.S. Government Printing Office 1982; see in particular the submission by Elliott Abrams, p. 71.

15. Office of the Under Secretary of State for Security Assistance, Science and Technology: *International Aspects of Communication and Information*, August 4, 1981 (mimeo), p. 23.

16. Quoted in *UNESCO-Dienst*, No. 1/1984, p. 1 [retranslation into English].
17. See for example Bethell, Tom: "The Lost Civilization of UNESCO", in: *Policy Research*, Spring 1983, pp. 19-47.
18. Gulick, Thomas: "The IPDC. UNESCO versus Free Press", in: *The Heritage Foundation Backgrounder*, March 10, 1983.
19. *Reports to the Congress Requested in Sections 108 and 109 of public law 97-241*, February 24, 1983 (mimeo).
20. For more and detailed information see Gebrewold, Kiflemariam: *Fernseh-Export der Bundesrepublik Deutschland*, Bochum 1983.
21. Glotz, Peter: „Free flow of commercials?", in: *Socialist Affairs*, No. 2/1979. p. 75.
22. Quoted in Becker, Jörg: "Der weltweite Medienkommerz", in: *Ein anderer Rundfunk - eine andere Republik*, ed. by Michael Wolf Thomas, Bonn 1980, p. 61.
23. Quoted in *Bulletin* (Bonn), No. 100, September 30, 1983, p. 922.
24. Cf. Luyken, Georg-Michael: "25 Jahre Communication and Development-Forschung in den USA. Wissenschaft oder Ideologie?", in: *Rundfunk und Fernsehen*, No. 1/1980, pp. 110-22.
25. Somavia, Juan: "The Transnational power structure and International Information," in: *Development Dialogue*, No. 2/1976, p. 26.
26. Cf. Siebold, Thomas: "Zur Geschichte und Struktur der Welt-Nachrichtenordnung", in: *Medienmacht im Nord-Süd-Konflikt*, ed. by Jörg Becker and Reiner Steinweg, Frankfurt: Suhrkamp 1984, pp. 45-92.
27. Quoted in Nordenstreng, Kaarle and Varis, Tapio: *Television Traffic - A One-way street?*, Paris: UNESCO-Press 1974, p. 44.
28. Czempiel, Ernst-Otto: *Internationale Politik*. Ein Konfliktmodell, Paderborn 1981, p. 176.
29. Cf. Ratzke, Dietrich: *Handbuch der Neuen Medien*, Stuttgart 1982, p. 150.
30. According to an estimate by the English market research company CIT Research. See the article: "Kabelfernsehen in Europa kommt nur mühsam voran", in: *Süddeutsche Zeitung*, April 4, 1984.
31. Cf. Schulte-Hillen, Jürgen and Wietersheim, Beatrix von: *IuD-Online Datenbanknutzung in der Bundesrepublik Deutschland*, Munich 1984.

13
Information and Communication Technologies (ICT) and International Politics

1. Introduction

The current change in international relations has been essentially accelerated by the following two stimuli: It is on the one hand the increasing tendency towards the internationalization of capital, and on the other the enormous momentum of technological innovation, not just in its rapidity, but above all in its quality. Both tendencies show themselves in a clearcut manner in the field of mass media and information and communication technologies. They are part of the electronic industry, a sector of industry which currently has the highest growth rate. Technological innovation and the internationalization of capital cannot be discussed separately, especially in the field of ICT and the mass media. Whoever in the Federal Republic of Germany talks about fiberoptic cable systems, must be informed about the export interests of the glassfiber industry to the Third World; or, whoever ponders upon TV satellite projects for India cannot forget about the satellite plans of Radio-Télé-Luxembourg.

An analysis of these trends must take the following two premises into account: 1. the uniquely new quality of the current change in information technologies, 2. the values embodied in this technology. The novelty of this change in ICT does not lie in our discovery of a diversity of new services, such as videotext, cable television, satellite transmissions or electronic mail. Nor does it lie so much in the rapidity with which the new IT changes the personal and structural reality of our society. This novel quality can rather be emphasized by the two terms "Telematics" and/or "Compunications". For the first time in the history of technology two formerly separate lines of development converge. This can be seen on the hand one by the technical development of the media towards telecommunications and on the other hand, under the influence of the microchip, the development of the adding machine towards the minicomputer. This "marriage" of ICT and telecommunications is the qualitative novelty in current technological changes.

There is an in-built tendency in this new system not to differentiate between scientific-technical and mass communication, between individually controllable and passively received communication, between print and electronic media, between acoustic and optical signal-transmission, between information-storage, -processing and -transmission. The totality of this new system implies the obsolescence of two further features of earlier ICT systems: the separation of space and time. With a gap of just seconds this all-encompassing network makes possible the universal dissemination of all possible information processes developed until now anywhere on the globe. The future satellites - especially the technology of Direct Broadcast by Satellite (DBS) - are the last necessary link in the construction of this global network.

The future information systems are thus global, independent of time, linked together in one single network and most probably intelligence producing (this description of qualities poses "only" problems of definition). From this it must be clear that the problem of political power cannot be discussed only in traditional terms, as the continuation of known dependency mechanisms. Also the form of political power which accompanies this ICT is of a new qualitaty. This new network of ICT is in economic terms not only explainable in the "old" sense by the double character of "information" as a commodity, which not only has an intrinsic but also an exchange value, or by the visible and subliminal commercialization of communication increases worldwide, but mainly in the sense that all individual and social living conditions in the capitalist centers (capital, labour, everyday life) can be seen more and more as dependent variables arising out of our immersion in ICT.

This process of informatisation of society only superficially has so called positive or negative social effects. It is only a symptom of subsequently "humanizing" the "inhumanity" of a workplace by a computer terminal, or, to see optimistically in the two-way potential of regional cable-television systems the realization of participatory and grassroots democracy. Social change is inherent in the informatisation of society. Technology - ICT included - is not neutral, thus form and content correspond to each other, informatisation itself (e.g. formalization, mediatization, quantification and finalization of human communication) is the essential expression of social change. To speak only of the social effects of gleaning information would mean to neglect the inherent characteristics of future society. The value system of technology, my second premise, is very often ignored. The myth of the neutrality of technology is the more ominous and dangerous, because it poses even more basic problems than the novelty of changes in ICT, and because a sluggishness on the part of scientists and followers of all political leanings has resulted in the assumption that one can differentiate between positive and negative consequences. The most recent example of this "philosophy" can be found in the report of the Club of Rome on "Microelectronics and Society". The following is an example from Alexander King :

> [Microelectronics] can be a blessing for mankind, because it can contribute to improving living conditions and abolishing poverty. But in the event that it is falsely used it can lead to the disintegration of society.[1]

In this "philosophy" of balancing negative and positive, the technocratic socialist as well as the capitalist share the same perspective. One sees the solution to all problems in the control of technological development by the workers, while the other places his faith in the so called market mechanisms which in the long run propel technology to a breakthrough in the interest of mankind. Although different in their political motivations, both positions resemble each other in that both are based only on consequences and uses of this technology and not on its inherent structure. In this context one can quote from "Die Antiquiertheit des Menschen" (The Antiquatedness of Mankind) by Austrian philosopher Günther Anders which was published in 1954. In his chapter "Kein Mittel ist nur Mittel" Anders attacks the maxim beloved by all sides, namely that what is important with regard to technology is how we use it. The validity of this maxim is more than doubtful:

> The freedom of controlling technology which it presupposes, as well as the belief that there are aspects of our world which are nothing more than 'means' to be continually linked to the achievement of

'good ends' is pure illusion. Means themselves are facts and these form us. We cannot escape the fact of their forming us, no matter to which end we put them, even though we might downgrade them to 'means' on the level of language. Our existence, which is permeated with technology does not split into single, signposted 'means' while others are marked 'ends'. This division is legitimate only in regard to single acts and isolated mechanical procedures in industry, whereas when referring to the 'whole', in politics or in philosophy, it is not.[2]

An awareness of the value system of technology need not imply a full-scale rejection of it. It should rather entail a keener view of the necessity of rational planning processes, as otherwise we cannot identify with any precision what kind of social change and what quality of changes ICT is to be desired.

2. ICT and the Third World

Considering the two premises of the novel quality of change in and the value system of ICT, one has to examine in detail how this change has structurally affected the countries of the Third World until now. This shall be accomplished by using the following five categories laid down by Roy Preiswerk[3] as critical for the development of the Third World:

- foreign penetration,
- the relationship between intrinsic and exchange values,
- the regulation of need,
- the concentration of resources,
- identity.

Penetration/Dissociation from Foreign Penetration

If one discusses penetration taking satellite technology as an example, one has to be conscious that the economic aspects of satellite technology cannot be reduced to the more commercial possibilities of the satellite itself. This space segment in fact only constitutes a relatively unimportant part of a complicated and long technological chain. Thus, for example the aeronautics concern Dornier in its feasibility study of a South American Satellite System for the German Federal Ministry of Development and Technology has computed that the space segment constitutes less than a third of the total investment costs.[4]

Thus, first and foremost satellites systems make economic penetration of the Third World possible by way of the so called follow-up business: earth stations, antennae, signal and amplification transmission systems terrestrial cable networks, equipment (TV, telephone, telex, etc.), car, parts, buildings, fuel for diesel engines. The follow up business in fact constitutes the main commercial possibility. The implementation of a pure information network certainly compels the adoption of the accompanying software, such as film, curricula, computer language, since these can be produced more cheaply in the metropoles than in the peripheral countries, due to the lack of know how and/or capital. For the same reasons the education and training of engineers, programmers, teachers and social scientists is carried out in the industrialized nations The above stated study by Dornier acknowledges this relationship; sometimes by way of implication, sometimes very openly:

> A number of companies [in South America] are engaged in the production of television sets, mainly assembling parts delivered to them. [...] However, one should not ignore the fact that part of the technical hardware still has to be imported [...] As a conclusion a [satellite-]test program seems [...] useful, [because it] would strengthen the influence of German and/or European technology in South America.[5]

In the Dornier-study for an African satellite it is put in more blunt terms:

> The penetration and the consolidation of markets [in the field of telecommunication] is extraordinarily important for the future of the industry and the export oriented nations. [...] Seen against this background participation in a regional African communication satellite system is [...] naturally of interest. Being associated with the satellite system - which obviously profits from a certain sex appeal [sic!] - creates penetration possibilities into other fields bringing advantages for specific ranges of products.[6]

Whereas the above described mechanisms apply in the first place to news satellite systems, other similar mechanisms howver apply to weather and remote sensing satellites. These satellite systems can only come up to expectations if they are fed an enormous amount of further information in addition to their original LANDSAT data. As there are relatively little statistical data in the Third World, which also lack a time-series basis, statistical methods are often not valid, and as available data do not keep pace with the everchanging demands of planning - for all these reasons taken together particularly remote sensing satellites in the Third World require the construction of complicated computing systems.

They contribute in an essential way to the fact that the Third World has become an ever more important market for the leading computer manufacturers of the industrialized nations - General Electric (USA), Fairchild (USA), Advanced Micro Devices (USA), Signetics (USA), Motorola (USA), Siemens (Germany), Thomson CSF (France) and Philips (Netherlands) - so that between 1972 and 1975 alone the export of computers to African countries increased by 44 percent, to Latin America by 38 percent and to Asia by 14 percent.

Because the transfer of technology in these fields neither strengthens the domestic market for mass-produced consumer goods, nor contributes to restructuring of an export oriented local agriculture, ICT significantly fosters a reliance on the global structures of capitalism. This tends to undermine any national economic and political stance promulgated by the respective countries of the Third World. The preceding analysis of transfer of technology fits into the various forms of service transfer between North and South; which for a long time and to an increasing degree has resulted in the Third World posting a negative trade balance for services. Through this mechanism those countries of the Third World deficient in raw materials become ever more dependant on the industrialized countries; their balance of payment problems becomes ever more acute, their ability to service their debt becomes ever smaller. A study by the Swiss PROGNOS company in 1979 comes to the following conclusion in this context:

> Within the framework of [UNCTAD-estimates] we assume that expenditure for the transfer of technology will outpace industrial production in the developing countries by 250 percent. [...] We can predict with certainty that as developing countries become increasingly industrialized, their expenditure for the commercial transfer of technology will rise proportionately and their respective dependence on the industralized nations will also grow.[7]

It is self-evident that economic dependencies have political consequences, which can be fully demonstrated by the two following examples. The Indonesian national news satellite system PALAPA can with one push of a button be switched off by the American Department of Defense. A similar situation applied to the Iranian INTELSAT-link during the Iranian-American Crisis 1979-81. An US-American government study provided for the termination of this link as one of several degrees of escalation in such a crisis. This would have rendered defunct the Iranian telephone and television system, the electronic fund transfer and flight reservations and would have at the same time reduced the international reach of the Iranian telecommunication system by 70 percent.[8]

Intrinsic Value/Exchange Value

Only when foreign penetration is discussed analytically and not in its concrete forms, can it be separated from the question of the interrelationship of intrinsic and exchange value. The worldwide capitalization of information implies everywhere the victory of exchange over intrinsic value: Satellites and computer technology have hardly anything to do with their utilization potential within the national economics of the Third World, but rather with the transference value which the products of this technology gain in the form of money for foreign capital.

At this point one can make the generalization that satellite technology is historically the last offensive on the part of the industrialzed nations towards the developing countries. After the institutionalization of violence on a human level (slave trade, braindrain), on a material level (raw materials, energy resources) and on a commercial level (markets, import-substitution) there follows now, as a result of this technology, a process of depriving the Third World of knowledge about itself. This can be made clear by the following example. Currently maps of the scale of 1:50,000 exist only for approximately 30 percent of the global surface, and such exact cartographic data are for the most part only of the industrial countries. For a great part of the Third World no maps exist and those that do are not suitable for planning purposes.

The current surveying of the Third World by remote sensing satellites has to be seen as an essential precondition and basis for the penetration of that which up until now has remained, either in full or in part, outside the exchange system. As a result of this new satellite technology those projects which necessitate a high degree of functional planning including division of labor, specialization or professionalization and the necessary capitalization (which runs parallel to these processes) be it a population census, industrialization projects, planning of dams, opening up of raw material resources or the exploitation of forests become, not only more prevalent but also assume a different qualitative nature.

Remote sensing satellites in general have to be seen as by far the most effective part of a new and very aggressive intellectual penetration of the Third World by the industrialized nations, which cannot afford any longer to base their offensive on prejudgment, ignorance, false or misinformation. The satellites are the modern linguistics, anthropologists and missionaries who always have had the most detailed knowledge about microstructures in the Third World. Bearing in mind the observations of the Indian educationalist A.K. Jallaluddin it is important to consider that not only are the excessive interests of Western scientists in the study of such sensitive problems as religious and cast conflicts, ethnic, linguistic and group conflicts in developing countries are examples of this intellectual penetration[9], but that this is also true to an increasing degree for the satellites. The former collect "soft data", while satellites collect "hard facts" on a small, limited, regional and communal level. And thus, it is no co-incidence that the UN Committee for the Peaceful Use of Outer Space (COPUOS) when discussing the question of prior consent on the part of the countries subject at satellite photography concentrated among other issues on the degree of potential size reduction of the photographs.

How little intrinsic value photography of the remote sensing satellites has for the economies of the Third World can be demonstrated using the example of the satellite storm warning system in Bangladesh. It is only superficially true that in 1979 the lives of thousands of people were saved because of the early detection of a cyclone over the Bay of Bengal. Bangladesh is one of the 25 poorest countries on earth: 500 people inhabit one km^2, the income per capita of the population, of which 90 percent are peasants, is US$ 80 per year, 10 percent of the population possess 40 percent of the total land. It is estimated that 80 percent of the population lives below subsistence level, which means their income does not provide for the bare necessities, such as food, shelter, clothing, education and health care.

When one takes into account that only in approximately 100 urban and semi-urban areas of Bangladesh there is adequate shelter, tap water, health- and community services, then it is bordering on cynicism to emphasize the advantages of saving lives through the early storm warning. To put it differently, for the mass of Bangladeshis the intrinsic value of this early warning satellite is of an extremely ambivalent nature; given the already subhuman standard of living, their bare physical survival led to a greater intensity of human misery.

Basic Needs/Induced Needs

[Satellite technology] "will be increasingly necessary in adapting human needs to the limited possibilities of our globe."[10] This conclusion arrived at by one of the many scientists involved in the LANDSAT programme should be considered less as a Freudian slip than as an unwitting but correct perspective in the relationship between man and high-level technology. It lies in the nature and internal dynamics of such technologies that - in keeping with their economic realization principle - they must create new needs, to which the user only later adapts, after a period of appropriate conditioning. To orient satellite technology towards the needs of humanity, thus, demanding the reversal of the technocratic principle, would be the first step in the direction of a need oriented development strategy. However, its necessary precondition would be the active and participatory involvement of those affected by this technology and thus a strengthening of the intrinsic value and a reduction of extraneous influences, which is definitely not the case either in the Third World or in regard to the consumers in the industrialized nations.

Satellite technology strengthens, what Joseph Ki-Zerbo from Upper-Volta described as muteness in relation to the activities of the monopolized news agencies. When one, without the possibility of its rejection, is overwhelmed by foreign information, not being able to present one's own images and information, then one is mute. This means that one must assume a passive role serving the basic needs of others. "The capacity for communication is one of the essential characteristics of mankind. A mute country has no sovereignty."[11]

Concentration/Distribution of Resources

In the domestic as well as the foreign political sector the question of how available resources are distributed has to be regarded as essential to the evaluation of the degree of democratic potential in a specific sector; this is true for the production sector of the respective resources as well as for the regulations governing their use. It may well be that one of the current most dominant myths is that the future forms of telecommunication and ICT make possible social decentralization processes that they provide for mass participation, if not in the production of the technology, then at least in its decentralized utilization. This has to be opposed first of all in general terms. The increased automation of all sectors of life has resulted in an ever increasing complexity and intertwining of effects which favor centralization of power, decisions and control in the economy as well as in private and public institutions. This historical tendency is especially true for the ICT sector.

The involvement in the production of the new resource that is ICT depends on immensely high capital outlays which in the case of satellite technology or overall fiberoptic cabling goes into billions, thus limiting it from the beginning to international corporations and/or state bureaucracies. Participation of socially competing groups, such as the production sector, the middle class, single-interest groups or agriculture, which is deemed necessary even by liberal democratic standards is thus already initially excluded from this rapidly expanding industry. The politically and economically pre-existing advantage of the transnational corporations and state bureaucracies increases manifold. "Whoever previously possessed the capacity for knowledge, control and decision making ('power'), can multiply it now automatically and (through telecommunication) can disseminate it to any chosen place."[12]

This extraordinary concentration of power is even more strongly apparent in the relationship between the industrialized and the developing countries, as will be demonstrated by two short examples. When INTELSAT tried to convince the African states at the end of the 1960s and beginning of the '70s to link up with this international satellite system, they promised that this would lead to a greater connection between the remote areas and the centers as well as to a strengthening of inter-African exchange. Dornier, an aerospace corporation, stated in 1980:

> These stations, however, have contributed little to the improvement of the inter-African telecommunication system, because they mainly replaced the old HF-connections to the former mother countries."[13]

In other words: satellite technology has only made more effective the already existing centralization of power in the native bureaucratic class and the foreign metropoles which cooperate with it. A further empirical example can be drawn from the study comparing Algeria and El Salvador undertaken by Harvard University. Here the effects of satellite and ICT on two culturally and politically extremely different peripheral societies were examined. The implementation and use of this technology has in both countries led to an increased centralization of decision-making processes.[14]

Even when the apologists of this new ICT concede that it triggers centralization, the concentration of power and control of information within the production sector, they still mostly point to its decentralized use. There emerges the image of the user whose involvement in this technology is directed by his individual needs and the image of the Third World, which, through decentralized access to the databanks of the industrial countries by means of satellite transmission, can draw every information relevant to its own needs.

This is also a myth. Although decentralized access to the large information systems is possible, it is still dependent on the filter-, selection-, decision- and control-mechanisms which emanate from one control center. It is not the decentralized access possibilities to the overall-system which are the decisive features of the system, the reverse is true: It is the center which insures its access possibility to the periphery.

Thus, the utilization of this technology only seems to be decentralized. However, there is a further mechanism in regard to use and reception which can give prominence in power and information as well as in the access to knowledge. This is the capacity to transform the available data into decision-making knowledge and the possibility to gain prominence from this knowledge which only few participants are capable of realizing. Within the Third World only three groups profit from this knowledge and its consequent possibilities:

1. transnational corporations which deliver the technical products,
2. international banks which finance the import and installation of these technologies and
3. the new bureaucratic class in Third World centers.

As one can already observe an increasing knowledge gap due to the increasing availability of mass media information - those already educated make better use of the enlarged supply, whereas, those kept ignorant fall further behind in their standard of information - so likewise with ICT an increasing data gap has developed. The gap between those with and those deprived of information widens; the centralization tendencies in the metropole-periphery-model grow.

Identity: Conservation/Loss

Satellite technology is in a way the pinnacle of ICT, the technological spearhead in the socio-psychological penetration of Third World cultures. This manifests itself in various respects. As a part of a vast chain of technology, this part of the electronics industry contributes to the development of social differentiation, and that means internal alienation. Extreme forms of division of labor, specialization, professionalization, education and training will be the accompanying effects of this technological drive. At the same time, the self-colonialization process is promoted by importing or manufacturing on an import-substitution bais of goods for production or consumption by this technological chain. I believe, however, those two mechanisms which can be called the weakening and the homogenization of Third World cultures are more important in this regard.

The era of colonialism and imperialism can in some ways be characterized by the aggrandizement of the metropoles with cultural articles, i.e., European museums were stuffed with cult objects, artworks and profane items, likewise the remote sensing satellites pilfer non-material goods from the Third World, namely knowledge and information of itself. These are stocks of knowledge which constitute the state of the Third World itself, but for which it cannot or will not have any systematic access possibilities. The systematic knowledge about the Third World thus, becomes even more thorough and intensive outside of it. The manifold possibilities for external control, created in this way, will reduce the cultures of the Third World into a functional variable in technological planning processes. The diversity of the human element enriching different cultures will be sucked dry.

Parallel to this drain of cultural identity the international news satellites, especially the projected DBS, contribute to a reversed mechanism which is the cultural penetration from without. Even at this time, through the "traditional" media, such as books, press, television and partly the radio, the Third World is exposed to an extreme and one-sided information flood from the industrialized nations The contents of the Western mass media have already promoted cultural disintegration and identity-conflicts within the Third World (even when there is little empirical knowledge on the concrete process of absorbing these messages). The global networking of all entertainment media and the related software such as is now possible by news satellites will expose the cultures of the Third World to even greater cultural pressure.

3. Possible Resistance Strategies

It would be an illusion to hope that the above described mechanisms of intensified linking of the peripheries to the metropoles by ICT could be changed on a short-term basis, because the structural laws of the internationalization of capital, the uncontrollable proliferation and the "cancerous" and uncontrollable dynamics of technological innovation oppose it. Whereas in the United States the Carter Administration showed at least on a diplomatic level and in negotiations some willingness to compromise with the Third World, without ever being able to grant any concessions, the new administration under Ronald Reagan returned to a clearcut and outspoken opposition to all demands for change, for the beginnings of the realization of a New International Information Order.

In spite of this new pressure there are various weaknesses and inconsistencies as well as political forces which can counteract the above described tendencies and which in different and changed historical circumstances can exert their influence.

1. On the part of the Third World the politics of the Non-Aligned Movement must be seen as the most potent force for resistance in this area. Since the beginning of the 1970s the theme of mass media and ICT have played an ever increasing role at their summit conferences. However, heterogeneous this movement seems, they are united in their demand for the decolonization of the mass media and ICT. As the linking of the peripheries to the metropoles will increase through projected satellite technology and not decrease, the common protective interest of the non-aligned countries will be homogenous enough to be effective as a political weapon.

   A few countries of the Third World have in the meantime managed relatively well to dissociate themselves from the world market in certain areas of ICT. Thus for example Algeria has prohibited transborder data flow from computer to computer, because it does not see any possibility of regulation and control. Also the Indian satellite technology program has managed to achieve relative autonomy. India, as one of the seven countries engaged in space development, can independently build its ground stations, 40 percent of its satellites and 70 percent of its rockets. This relative dissociation has, however, no internal political parallel, but national dissociation can be the first necessary step towards developing a strategy of resistance.

2. The countries of the Third World can build up further resistance potential through the application of the strategy of multi-laterali-zation in UN-bodies. This strategy has in the last few years been relatively successfully applied. On the political level the Third World must continue to actively resist the doctrine of the "free flow of information," because this principle legitimizes the current structure of metropole-periphery-relations. On the technological level the doctrine of "first comes, first served" held by the International Telecommunication Union in regard to the distribution of radio frequencies has to be abolished. This principle always serves the interests of the technologically most developed countries.

   On the level of international law the Third World must uphold its right of "prior consent," which means prior consent to remote sensing and satellite transmission of the affected country. Especially the aspect of international law concerning remote sensing by satellite or DBS in all events must not be subjected to the unlimited principle of the "free flow of information" as it is interpreted as international law in the Federal Republic of Germany.

   The following international treaty agreements deal more thoroughly with the foregoing issues: the International Radio Treaty, League of Nationals, 1936; the clause in the First International Space Treaty, UN 1961, which states that "the exploration and use of outer space should only be for the betterment of mankind." This implies the rejection of the advantage of any one party; Resolution 428A of the International Telecommunication Union, 1977, which says that spill-over by satellites is allowed only by the prior consent of the affected countries; the basic principles of international cooperation.

3. Finally, there are further political possibilities for resistance in the behavior of the EU countries. These countries have long since, out of a fear of American economic competition, realized that the un-hindered development of satellite and ICT drives them into a variety of dependencies on the USA. Possible agents of Western European resistance strategies are the national PTT's, the Council of Europe and some national governments which, like the French and the Swedish, though for different reasons, become ever more conscious of their foreign political dependencies.

4. The growing informatization of international relations will in addition intensify the structural conflict between transnational

corporations and nation states. Already now many state-controlled bodies in developed countries find themselves in the awkward situation that the quality of decision-making knowledge possessed by transnational corporations is by far superior to their own. This conflict could be intensified by another historical tendency, namely the growth of national consciousness in the Third World.

5. In the monetary sphere the increasing informatization of international relations is currently inhibited most by recession, budgetary imbalance and the impending collapse of the international credit system.

6. Technological and infrastructural conditions hinder total informatization now as before. One of the essential preconditions for penetration of the Third World by means of ICT is up until now in many cases only partially existent, that is a fully developed infrastructure. Without an electricity supply, a stable electrical current or a continually functioning telephone system, to name only a few of the everyday necessities missing in the Third World, it is only partially possible to implement ICT systems. In the peripheral countries it is most probably still impossible, due to their infrastructures, to gather valid individual and social data. But it is just this validity which is a necessary precondition for automatic data processing.

   Currently all programs fed with population data from the Third World are in danger of producing false analyses. The input of non-valid data multiplies many times the occurrence of inaccuracies in a complex computing process. Because of this deficient infrastructure the extremely unequal access to ICT within the Third World will probably in the long run develop into their subtlest means of defense. The centralization tendencies of the new technologies give perhaps enough time and space to the marginal populations to become conscious of and to organize their own indigenous means of defense.

7. Further difficulties result from specific characteristics of ICT systems which can be named a Weizenbaum-effect[15]. The input of non-valid data into computer programs poses a more profound problem than non-valid population data in the Third World. In the industrial countries as well forecasts are frequently computed on

the basis of non-valid data. Considering for example, that large research teams work on an exclusively theoretical level to deduce certain macro-economic relevant indices and, furthermore, that these various theoretical schools are in conflict with each other, then there is hardly any reliable criteria left to determine which data are to be used and which are not.

Weizenbaum predicts an additional development. Data processing systems have only existed for the last twenty years, so that the long-term effects of the accumulation of non-valid data have hardly made themselves felt. According to Weizenbaum it is only a question of time until the cumulation of "dirty data" produces such grave miscalculations that misplanning in business and bureaucracies will have reached such dimensions that they are obvious to everybody.

Notes and References

1. King, Alexander: „Mikroelektronik und globale Interdependenz", in: *Auf Gedeih und Verderb*. Mikroelektronik und Gesellschaft. Bericht an den Club of Rome, ed. by Günter Friedrichs and Adam Schaff, Vienna: Europaverlag 1982, p. 352.
2. Anders, Günther: *Die Antiquiertheit des Menschen*. Vol. 1: *Über die Seele im Zeitalter der Zweiten Industriellen Revolution*, 5th and rev. edition, Munich: Beck, 1980, p. 99.
3. Preiswerk, Roy: "Kulturelle Identität, Self-Reliance und Grundbedürfnisse", in: *Das Argument*, No. 120/1980, p. 176.
4. Rausch, Gerhard and Lohle, Hans: *Kommunikationssatelliten für Südamerika*, Bonn: Der Bundesminister für Forschung und Technologie 1979, p. 9.
5. Ibid., pp. 62 and 139.
6. Kriegl, Wolfgang and Laufenberg, Wilfried: *Kommunikationssatellitensystem für Afrika*, Bonn: Der Bundesminister für Forschung und Technologie, 1980, p. 64.
7. Bergmann, Christel and Grundmann, Helge E.: *Aussagen zur Interdependenz zwischen Industrie- und Entwicklungsländern*. Gutachten in Auftrag des Bundesministers für wirtschaftliche Zusammenarbeit, Basel: Prognos AG 1979 (mimeo), p. 13.
8. Cf. Schiller, Herbert I.: *Who Knows?* Information in the Age of the Fortune 500, Norwood, NJ: Ablex 1981, p. 110.
9. Interview with the author in April 1980 in New Delhi.
10. Mühlfeld R.: "Bilanz uber den Einsatz der Satellitenfernerkundung in den Bereichen Geologie/Lagerstättenkunde, Hydrologie, Bodenkunde/Landnutzung im Rahmen von Projekten der Bundesanstalt für Geowissenschaften und Rohstoffe", in: *International Archives of Photogrammetry*. Vol. XXIII. Part B8. Commission VII/1980, p. 652 [italics by the author].
11. Ki-Zerbo, Joseph: "Unterricht über die Dritte Welt und die Probleme ihrer Entwicklung", in: *Die Dritte Welt in Schule und Jugendarbeit*, ed. by Jörg Becker, Frankfurt: Haag & Herchen 1980, p. 20.
12. Steinmüller, Wilhelm: "Informationstechnologie-Folgen", in: *Nachrichten für Dokumentation*, No. 6/1981, p. 249.
13. Kriegl, Wolfgang and Laufenberg, Wilfried: *Kommunikationssatellitensystem für Afrika*, *op. cit.*, p. 22.

14. Cf. Clippinger, John H.: *Who Gains by Communications Development?* Studies of Information Technologies in Developing Countries, Cambridge, Mass.: Harvard University. Program on Information Technologies and Public Policy 1976 (= Working Paper 76-1) (mimeo).

15. Cf. his following works: Weizenbaum, Joseph: *Computer Power and Human Reason.* From Judgement to Calculation, San Francisco: Freeman 1976; Weizenbaum, Joseph: "Once More: The Computer Revolution", in: *The Computer Age: A Twenty-year View*, ed. by Michael L. Dertouzos and Joe Moses, Cambridge and London: MIT Press 1979, pp. 439-58.

14
Information and Communication Technologies (ICT) and International Law

1. Information and Communication Technologies and Economic Growth

For the last few years, mass media research and those members of the general public who are interested in such questions have focused on the so-called new media, information and communication technologies (ICTs) or multimedia. These terms cover such different specialized areas as new technical transmission processes (satellites and network technologies), new service sector facilities (videotext), new audio-visual storage media (VCRs and laser discs) or new text storage media (databanks). The debate on these ICTs is of great importance, yet much of what is being discussed ignores the real structural problems of social change which are discernable only on a superficial level in phenomena such as cable television or satellite broadcasting.

A number of descriptive-empirical indications of the above will serve to illustrate what has just been said. If the critical layman considers the term "satellite broadcasting" it, quite correctly, brings to mind the increasing preponderance of affirmative American entertainment films such as "Dallas" (Stolz 1983; Darnton 1984) or "Denver Clan" and he would define its ideological opposite as a realization of a transnationally practised media freedom.

Yet the data pertaining to the satellites of the international satellite organization INTELSAT show a totally different situation. Even though the transmission of television material has increased by approx. 25 percent between 1965 and 1982, it still accounts for no more than 5 percent of total transmission capacity which is, for the most part, comprised of telephone traffic and data transmissions (Hultén and Hultén 1984). Another example of this is the fact that phrases such as "databanks" or "transborder data flow" are immediately equated, according to one's ideological point of view, with "Information Society", "informed society" or "alienation through the increase in instrumental thinking".

As pertinent as one or the other aspect of such estimations may be, the empirical statistics pertaining to data transmissions in West Germany give a very different picture. 40 percent of all such transmissions can be attributed directly to the banking and brokerage sectors and another 30 percent of this traffic is concerned with the exchange of industrial planning and management data. This last example drastically demonstrates that the parallel and interdependent growth of the information and financial flows is a necessary prerequisite for the growth of the commodity flow which has all but become a symbiotic relationship between the financial services industry and the information sector (Hamelink 1983; Moffitt 1983).

The development of such a finance-information symbiosis is to a large degree dependent on two new technical innovations. In the telecommunications sector, the introduction of digital technology has enabled data and voice transmission, while in the data processing industry, ever increasing computer capacities for storage, processing and transmission at will have been created, meaning that information in its mature form can be utilized as an economic commodity and this becomes an optimal tool in the implementation of various international capital strategies. The combination of ICTs is creating a fusion and integration of production and reproduction, of nearness and distance, of the individual and society and heralds nothing less than a second Industrial Revolution.

While the first revolution socialized the concept of manual labor and submitted it to the wage principle, i.e., it industrialized work, the second revolution will submit mental work to economic principles, in short, it will mechanize and industrialize the mind. Just as the first revolution changed society, so the second revolution will cause enormous social change and conflict such as capital concentration, bankruptcy, changes in the division of labor, unemployment, poverty and changes in our value systems. While the first revolution brought about the movement towards the creation of working classes and their political conscious organization into parties and trade unions, its dialectical correlation, a new kind of strong and homogeneous counter movement is nowhere in sight.

To put it more strongly: the Trade Union Movement in western industrialized countries has lost so much political power, as well as, organizational and numerical strength that the second revolution could be seen as its unobserved kiss of death. This is aptly illustrated by the following example: The management of the *Frankfurter Allgemeine Zeitung* reacted to the printer's strike in West Germany during the spring of 1984 by printing editions of the paper that were electronically laid out and set by leading white collar personnel. In this way, the strike lost its purpose and collapsed, clearly demonstrating the anachronism of this form of labor agitation. Because the paper continued to be physically distributed, the only possible area was to hinder the distribution. When in the future, not only the production of newspaper products, but also their distribution directly into the individual citizens private home will be fully electronic, then the trade union's capability to act in solidarity will be even more reduced.

Two particular variables, speed and scale, clearly distinguish the formal aspects of the second revolution from the first. In particular, it is the ever shorter production cycle and speed of innovation which allow the economic dynamics to accelerate at an ever faster pace. In 1981, Siemens, for example, derived about 50 percent of its turnover from products which were developed over the previous five years. They expect that 50 percent of their 1986 turnover will be derived from products which were developed over the previous two or three years. It is possible to argue that in earlier historical epochs the long "trickle down effect" acted as a kind of state regulation which gave the lower classes access to new technologies.

This form of argumentation is becoming obsolete because the economic dynamic of the second revolution has accelerated to such a degree that the social and legal period of adjustment to new technology is continually being shortened. Besides scale and scope, there are other pronounced differences between the first and the second revolutions. Apart from the necessary volume of investment, the scope and nature of monopoly, the second revolution is much more than just the linear progression of its predecessor.

With its capability to integrate and combine which has been mentioned above, the second revolution is much more the completion of the first in a particularly varied and logical form. Indeed neo-conservative social scientists such as Daniel Bell (1975) have long stressed the importance of the two variables, "scale" and "speed", in the current societal transformation. However, they insufficiently analysed basic questions concerning domination tendencies or avoided them all together through the use of such irrelevant slogans as "post-industrial" or "information society" (Offe 1976; Mosco/Herman 1980). It must be stressed that only in its form is the future society an information society. In its essence, character and content, this society will be a capitalist society of a most dynamic kind. The second Industrial Revolution should be characterized in its form and content as a capitalist information society.

Some mass communications researchers tend to analyse individual media and then relate this analysis to general economic processes. Such methodology can easily lead to a false estimation of real processes. The interrelation between single and general events can be grasped guardedly only when at the same time conclusions for single events are drawn from general economic conditions. If the current social transformation which was alluded to above has very little to do with the new contemporary mass entertainment media, then such ideas appear all the more incorrect when one analyses the macro conditions of the current economic crisis.

Whether one agrees with the theory of "tendency of the profit rate to fall" it is clear that all ideological factions agree that the current world wide economic crisis is no passing conjuncture weakness. Since the beginning of the 1970s it has been possible to perceive such phenomena as obsolete production facilities, the inability to use industry to full capacity, stagnant and sinking demand for goods and services as well as stagnant or saturated markets, which are an expression of a fundamental structural crisis. ICTs fits easily into such a situation. Their integration potential offers exactly those technological innovations which are needed to create a new long wave of economic growth. In such periods of social transformation, two forces, the transnational corporations and the military, must be especially active if they are not to lose their privileged positions in the society.

It is precisely for this reason that one "Giant Merger" after another is taking place at the moment. In the electronic entertainment sector, only Phillips and Thomson-Brand can be classified as belonging to the international giants in Western Europe. On a global level the telecommunications giant AT&T is preparing to do battle with IBM, while two European concerns, Bertelsmann and Olivetti are trying to gain access to the internal US market through link ups with RCA and AT&T respectively. Finally, the imminent acquisition of RCA by General Electric will be the most expensive transaction ever undertaken outside the oil sector.

The military has an extremely close relationship with the mass media and their related technologies (Schiller 1976; Smythe 1986). Yet the intensity of its dominance over and access to technological innovation has not been consistent and has operated at various levels in different periods of history. It is exactly within this context that SDI should be seen. This initiative is interesting not just from a military perspective, but above all because of the enormous economic program which is linked to it, which, in its scope, can only be compared to the "New Deal" of the 1930s. This program is the vehicle through which the military will regain the enormous amount of terrain it lost with the introduction of ICT.

In the last thirty years, particularly in the area of microelectronics, the civil sector has produced such fundamental technologies as the transistor and the integrated circuit. Such advances, coming as they did from the civil sector, understandably enough has given the military much cause for alarm. The initial dynamics of this Second industrial revolution in the USA during the 1960s and 1970s was so strong that civilian ICT development was more discriminating, innovative and mature than its their military counterparts. This is precisely what the military wish to change through SDI. The increased use of the Cocom guidelines by the USA should be seen in a similar way. The US military (in its increasingly pivotal role as a competitive instrument against its Western allies) is trying to regain and extend its control of the timelag between possible spinoffs from American military research and these being transferred into the Western European civil technology sector. This interpretation interestingly enough, was put forward in a study commissioned by the West German Federal Ministry for Research and Technology (Hein 1984).

2. Changes in Political Structures

When "information" can be used as a commodity, it can also be subject to current market mechanisms. Yet this marketing of information can only take place when an aura of exclusivity is created around it through the interplay of political, technical and economic factors. One of the greatest obstacles to the creation of exclusive or marketable knowledge[1] is the domain of public knowledge with its own long history.

1. Marketable knowledge is only that which can be defined as instrumental knowledge. Human experience, the ability to experience on an aesthetic level, historical collective knowledge or spiritual knowledge are themselves not marketable and thus, remain potential sources of rejection and revolt.

One other observation should also be made. The cost of creating integrated ICT systems, i.e., coupling telecommunication transmission systems to computer-supported networks and terminals is so high that neither the state nor the private sector alone can provide the necessary finances. For this reason, mechanisms must be found which will entwine the private enduser in the process of financing these systems. In this way a capitalist information society touches the relationship between the public and private spheres on two levels.

a) In the conflict between the public and private sectors, it is in the interest of a market based private owner of information to minimize the importance of the entire public information sector. When one recalls that West German book publishers estimate that the official production of knowledge by the government, communities and organizations, etc. according to the number of book titles and editions published, has become almost as important as the private publishing sector itself, then the relevance and competitiveness of the public sector's production of knowledge becomes clear. What is even more important is that public knowledge in the form of books is statistical knowledge produced by a variety of official sources, which is increasingly coming under the exclusive control of private databases.

   The effect of databases on the commercialization of public knowledge in the USA, as described by Herbert I. Schiller (Schiller/Schiller 1982; Schiller 1986) is to a lesser degree and with a certain element of time lag, true for Western Europe as well. Both the European Commission and the Federal German Government have called for a greater level of privatization in the data bank sector. The increasing pressure on universities, colleges and schools, i.e., those institutions where public knowledge is produced, by the private sector must be seen in this context. If one considers the role of pedagogical installations, it becomes clear that knowledge has always been regarded as a collectively evolved and historically accumulated resource. Thus, it should be seen as the common inheritance of all mankind and by extension as something to be used for the collective benefit of the whole community (Luyken 1986).

b) In the conflict between the public and the private spheres the relationship between what is considered public and what is considered private has undergone a considerable change. Jürgen Habermas described a decline in the public domain as early as 1962. Yet at the same time he was unable to predict the now acute forms of socializations of the individual through the introduction of ICTs. The private domain which up until now has been barely affected, has been increasingly open to and controlled by outside interests. This has lead to the following seeming paradoxes. Electronic goods and services are being promoted in the open market in ever increasing volume and variety. Their use has become increasingly multifaceted and individualistic. Yet the entire reproductive sector of a society could in the future, be externally controlled, so that the individual's potential for autonomous and independent action could be drastically reduced.

This negative form of individual socialization is grounded not just in new pressures emanating from international capital to bind the private domain with stronger rationalization strategies and controls, but also in the fact that the development of private sector controlled telecommunications infrastructures are being increasingly funded by privately raised finances. The private individual who in any case, finances these new infrastructures through his taxes is now being additionally burdened. He is being forced to contribute to this process by such new financial levies as the public broadcasting services, so called "Kabelgroschen" (Cable TV fee) and through the fees derived from the new electronic selfservice, such as tele-shopping or telebanking etc.

It is these phenomena which clearly show that specific concentration on the mass media entertainment sector is too narrow. It is so because it ignores the fact that the promises made by the purveyors of these technologies are just a bait which when risen to will lead to an increased penetration of the individual domain and/or the periphery by the forces of capital, particularly from the service, trade, banking and insurance sectors. Finally, the mass media function, as well, as a support for investment in the entire ICT sector, in addition to operating as kind of ideological binder.

Both tendencies discussed above, the privatization of knowledge and the individual's reduced possibility for action must be seen as deeply and essentially undermining every accepted aspect of the capitalist information society. It will usher in unprecedented economic and technological growth dynamic. For this reason, it will also lead to the end and the destruction of the state social security and welfare system. The maturation of information as a productive force seems to be taking place in parallel to the realization of all of the individual's social and existential orientations. If the individual is seen in western industrial countries as a kind of financial reserve capacity which can be tapped in order to develop integrated ICT systems, then it can be said that, within the global context the Third World plays a somewhat similar role. Since 1965 it has been so financially tied to the INTELSAT satellite system that it co-financed the system's metropolitan interests. The same process is now taking place again in relation to the financing of the international ISDN network. The Third World's role in this area becomes clear when one compares the following statistics.

The Third World currently receives around US$ 35 billion in development aid from Western industrialized countries. Yet it pays approximately US$ 12.5 billion for various forms of know how transfers from North to South and its loss, in terms of the intellectual braindrain to the industrialized countries has been estimated by experts at another US$ 5 billion. In other words for every dollar of development aid which the Third World receives, it must pay back approximately 50 Cents to the west for information related goods alone. As has already been exemplified by the above comparison, the tendency towards the privatization of knowledge and its attendant reduction of the individual's and the room to act contains potentially explosive international and, therefore, legal consequences.

3. International Legal Problems

It can be said that a truly effective and binding international code of law has only existed since the Nuremberg trials and the creation of the United Nations. It was the longing for peace, social justice and freedom in the wake of World War II as well as the concept of the universal right to self-determination which gave rise to the process of de-colonization which shaped the development of modern international law. Pacifism and anti-colonialism historically were and are two of the most important and productive pillars of this new international legal system. It is only under the umbrella of super-national organization, such as the UN that this system of international law can function as a kind of supernational corrective to the long dominant system of bi-lateral international law.

The latter can often be an expression of inequality because the stronger partner can suppress the rule of law to the point where law itself appears to be a cloak for real inequity. Against this, the UN-inspired concept of multi-lateral international law brings the idea of global equality much nearer.[2] The UN-related system of international law comprises not only formal and content considerations such as pacifism and anti-colonialism but also guarantees freedom of civil rights, sovereignty, self-determination, territorial integrity and the equality of all nations.[3]

No one can be surprised by the fact that the second industrial revolution will call the entire international legal system into question when it happens. However, a general legal problem can be seen in the fact that is impossible to define what exactly constitutes information (IBI 1983). For similar reasons, it is impossible to arrive at a clear legal definition of what constitutes matter. When one considers that the current international telecommunications law governs or better said, does not govern, such different specialized areas as international electronic homework, electronic fund transfer, the international exchange of television films or international video conferences, then it is safe to assume that the scope for transgressing the old laws is very great.

Legal Definition

The existence of international corporations poses many unsolved international legal problems. As concrete and extremely effective instruments of transnational politics, the international corporations have been able to avoid their responsibilities within international law. There exists an ethical and not legally binding "Code of Conduct" on international corporations which is supposed to regulate foreign direct investment. Yet the delegates at the UN have, for a long time, not been able to ratify it. Furthermore, an international cartel law is nowhere in sight. If international corporations are able, through the internationally open ISDN network operating independently of space and time, to engage in economic relationships with individuals, groups and/or governments, is it then still possible to

2. In opposition to dominant theories in international law, multi-lateral law is of a higher quality than bilateral and international treaty law. Whoever insists on the primacy of international treaty law, and this is increasingly the case in Western industrial countries, can possibly be suspected of elevating the interests of individual states above that of international compromise.

3. This order, of course, implies no set of priorities. Legal values though first and foremost formal norms, have also an inherent content component present which can be generally derived from the content's specific form. Thus no legal discussion is free of political or content considerations.

distinguish in law between subject and object or to define what is the legal quality of such a transaction? What is the legal situation of an electronic homework process where a transnational corporation, which is legally registered in country A using a telecommunications network which transmits through countries B to F and an office worker in the tax-free zone of country G, electronically delivers material to its subsidiary in country H?

Sovereignty

It is difficult enough to talk of sovereignty in relationship to current transnational politics. There is enough evidence to suggest that the sovereignty has become just a reactive defense category. When integrated ICTs systems can be said to operat independently of place then the difference between internal and external, between national and international law disappears. When it becomes technically impossible to distinguish whether a computer is connected with a terminal in one's own or a foreign country, how is it possible to sustain the concept of sovereignty? Is it still possible, in the face of transnational technology to actively and positively conceptualize the idea of sovereignty?

Cultural Identity

Max Horkheimer and Theodor W. Adorno had, already in the 1940s, coined the term "culture industries" to expose, using critical ideological methodology, "enlightenment" as mass deception (Horkheimer/Adorno 1969; Mattelart/Piemme 1982). Yet now the commission and the judgements handed down by the European Court of Justice confirm these ideas in a most cynical way: If the exchange of international broadcasts is, according to the EU-treaty, to be equated with the free flow of service sector transmissions then this kind of liberalization when followed to its ultimate conclusion more that justifies the economic characterization of the culture industry. Yet at the same time such a legal concept means the dismissal of the every idea of regional or national cultural unity, of cultural identity through the mass media, of the possibility of unrestricted, creative and rebellious culture and art. How can one affirm a right to ones own culture in the face of the international rationality of ICTs without it being reduced, in the long term, to the level of folkloristic kitsch?

Freedom

The progression from transborder "free flow" to "free and balanced flow of information" is long and tenuous and it is anything but a generally accepted principle within international law (Schiller 1975; Nordenstreng 1984). The increasing integration, of all which is understood as information, makes this legal problem even more difficult. When one considers that air pollution, when present in large quantities, is contrary to international law then such questions become increasingly pertinent to the international flow of information.

Even the most biased observer of the current commercialization of the information sector would admit that something resembling "information pollution" exists. Should such "information pollution" be defined within the totally unregulated "free flow" category, regardless of whether people in the respective country wish to receive this form of "information pollution"? How are pollution and enlightenment to be distinguished from one another in the information sector? Is this division a question of dosage; too much being poisonous, too little having no effect and only the correct amount bringing a cure?

Civil Rights

If one accepts within the realm of international law, that individual and collective civil rights are on an equal standing with each other, then it has to be admitted that the individual must be allowed access to international communications. The collective concept, however, demands the realization of a protective mechanism against uncontrollable external influences. Besides this, what are the international legal consequences of the active implementation of civil rights laws in the area of communication?

If the protective component of the data protection laws are to be extended to include the right of the individual to control and have access to the information content of state institutions (freedom of information), then the law allowing information to be received should be expanded to include the active right to communicate. What are the international legal consequences of such concepts?

Equality

Technological competition gives rise to and results in economic inequality between nation states. This is particularly true for ICTs and has, in this sector, created a situation whereby economic inequality has led to inequality among sovereign states. In this manner, for example, the 1966 space treaty decreed that access to space was defined on the basis of equality and not by national interest. Yet the 1977 moon treaty, which contained similar stipulations was ratified by neither the United States or the USSR.

Does this mean that technologically advanced nations are more equal than other states? How can the basic desire for equality be protected and implemented within international law in the face of the enormous international rise of technology and its resulting dependencies? How can the concept of the "common heritage of mankind", which constitutes a basic tenet of international law, be of help in the development of new resources such as space, the deep sea, the Arctic, genetics, knowledge?

To pose such questions, does not mean to believe at a naïve level that the system of international law can solve the international problems of the second industrial revolution. Not to pose such questions, however, means to despair of ever attaining the dream of global social justice. If creative social science is assigned the task of anticipating the consequences of technology and its related research, that is to adequately predict future areas of technological conflict and find political solutions to these possible areas of dissension before the attitudes of antagonists harden, then the same is to be expected from the legal sciences. The rule of law is capable of providing humane guidelines today for tomorrow's potential conflicts.

References

Bell, Daniel: *Die nachindustrielle Gesellschaft*, Frankfurt: Campus 1975.

Darnton, John: "Private Catalan TV Station Ends Spain's Government Monopoly", in: *International Herald Tribune*, Jan. 1, 1984.

Hamelink, Cees: *Finance and Information*, Norwood, NJ: Ablex 1983.

Hein, Werner: *Beschränkung des internationalen Technologietransfers durch die USA*. Auswirkungen auf die Innovationsentscheidungen deutscher Unternehmen. Studie im Auftrag des Bundesministeriums für Forschung und Technologie, Bonn: BMFT 1984 (mimeo).

Horkheimer, Max and Adorno, Theodor W.: *Dialektik der Aufklärung*, Amsterdam: de Munter 1968.

Hultén, Olof and Hultén, Charly: *Television Transmissions via the Intelsat System 1969 and 1982*. Paper delivered at the XIVth Congress of the IAMCR, Prague, August 27 - September 1, 1984 (mimeo).

Intergovernmental Bureau for Informatics (IBI): *Meeting of Experts on Informatics Law*, Rome: IBI 1983 [= DR 10] (mimeo).

International Space Law, ed. by A.S. Piradov, Moscow: Progress 1976.

Mattelart, Armand and Piemme, Jean-Marie: "Cultural Industries: The origin of an idea", in: *Cultural Industries. A challenge for the future of culture*, Paris: UNESCO 1982, pp. 51-61.

Moffitt, Michael: *The World's Money*. International Banking from Bretton Woods to the Brink of Insolvency, New York: Simon & Schuster 1983.

Mosco, Vincent and Herman, Andrew: "Communication, Domination and Resistance", in: *Media, Culture and Society*, No. 2/1980, pp. 351-65.

Nordenstreng, Kaarle: *The Mass Media Declaration of UNESCO*, Norwood, NJ: Ablex 1984.

Offe, Carl: "Postindustrielle Gesellschaft. Ein Politisches Programm. Zu Daniel Bells Analysen", in: *Merkur*, No. 9/1976, pp. 878-99.

Schiller, Herbert I.: "Genesis of the Free Flow of Information Principle", in: *Instant Research on Peace and Violence*, No. 1/1975.

Schiller, Herbert I.: *Die Bewußtseins-Manager*. Medienindustrie der USA. Struktur und Einfluß, Munich: Hanser 1976.

Schiller, Herbert I.: "Information - A Shrinking Resource", in: *The Nation*, January 1, 1986, pp. 708-10.

Schiller, Anita and Schiller, Herbert I.: "The Privatization of Information. Who can own what America knows?", in: *The Nation*, March 17, 1982, pp. 461-63.

Smythe, Dallas: "On the Political Economy of C^{3}I", in: *Communication and Domination*, ed. by Jörg Becker, Göran Hedebro and Leena Paldan, Norwood, NJ: Ablex 1986, pp. 66-75.

Stolz, Joelle: "Algerien sieht 'Dallas'", in: *Palaver* (Munich), No. 1/1983, pp. 8385.

15

Transborder Data Flow (TDF) and International Relations

The First International Conference on international data flow (TDF or TBDF) was held in the Spanish coastal resort of Torremolinos in 1978. It was organized by the Inter-Governmental Bureau for Informatics (IBI), a Rome based special organization with a high degree of autonomy within the framework of UNESCO. The IBI, in its conference documents, stressed the necessity for worldwide cooperation in studying and solving those problems attributable to TDF and common to all countries. At that time already it was clear that the problem of achieving a balance between the principle of "the free flow of information" and the necessity to control this phenomenon, should be given the highest priority. Special consideration should be given to the political, economic, social, cultural and legal dimensions of the situation. It was also necessary to acknowledge the special position of Third World countries in such debates, given the unequal rate of technical advancement between the industrialized and the underdeveloped nations, which engenders specific problems and tensions. This conference, called SPIN I (Strategies and Policies for Informatics) was to lead to a second - SPIN II - scheduled to take place in Cuba in 1984. This follow up conference has not been convened till now. Instead an argument broke out between the IBI members Cuba and France concerning the proposed venue.

This resulted in France resigning from the organization altogether in 1984. While at present the IBI is endeavoring, particularly in the Arab World, to gain new members as a means of maintaining its international image, many politicians and scientists in West Germany are still unclear as to what exactly TDF, IBI, or for that matter, the entire debate is all about. IBI, this special UNESCO organization, is one in which the Latin American and Southern European Countries are particularly well represented, at governmental level. The USA, England, West Germany and the socialist countries have never been members, while the Asian states are also poorly represented. Even though the organization, led by the former Argentinian Director General F.A. Bernasconi, was successfully recruiting members in Black Africa till recently, nevertheless IBI still suffers from the disadvantage of being largely a Latin American Organization. This short summary on IBI leads to the first thesis on TDF.

Hypothesis 1

The international flow of data will in future be of strategic importance for all countries with a view to their ability to maneuver in international markets. The countries of Latin America recognized at an early date the problems associated with assessing the consequences of technology at an international level, and created their own political forum for anticipatory and far-sighted policies. The IBI was boycotted by the West, ignored by western academics, kept at a distance by the socialist Eastern Europe, with the result that within a short space of time the organization, which was the Third World's own initiative, has become politically irrelevant.

In the meantime, the debate on TDF has been transferred to other international groups with a result in shift in thematic emphasis and a return to the old pattern of western domination. The IBI narrowly defined TDF as "the movement across national borders of data and information for processing and storage in computer systems". This definition makes it difficult for the layman to fully comprehend the possibilities, scope, quality and consequences of TDF. Only if this definition is qualified by concrete examples is it possible to formulate a political estimation of the effects of TDF. Some examples of the implementation of TDF may help here:

- Housewives in Barbados work at terminals in their own homes carrying out office, accountancy and book keeping duties. They are connected directly, via satellite, with companies situated in the United States of America.
- When companies find the data protection laws in their own country too strict and an obstacle to investment, it is possible to transfer data

to a computer in a country with laxer or even no data protection laws, via international online connections.[1]

- The internal, inner-polish booking system for flight reservations is stored and calculated by a computer in Atlanta.
- The firebrigade in Malmö, Sweden, has terminals in its mobile fire fighting vehicles which report exact data on the fires to be extinguished. The smoke detectors in industrial plants are connected via satellite with a computer in Ohio which gives the terminals in the fire-brigade optimum suggestions for extinguishing the fire.
- Canadian studies have estimated that many thousands of work places are lost annually to the USA because of Canada's intensive TDF with its southern neighbor.
- The negative balance of trade in TDF between the EU and the USA is increasing annually.
- The Swedish furniture concern IKEA is at present constructing a worldwide, flexible information system to which approximately 80 branches will be connected. The daily computation of the sales data of all the branches allows the Swedish company headquarters to synchronize production, delivery and marketing of its products both at branch and global level in an optimum manner.
- Remote sensing satellites in combination with appropriate databases are able to provide interested industrial clients in the West with information on undiscovered minerals and resources in Third World countries without the latter's knowledge.
- The western banking multinationals electronically transfer approx. US$ 400 billion around the globe daily. Electronic taxevasion by banks on a large scale have become an everyday occurrence.

1. There was an interesting case of data protection law evasion in the West German province of Baden-Württemberg in 1987. After the Regional Data Commissioner, Dr. Ruth Leuze, in her 2nd Activities Report from 1981, had presented a very detailed and extensive documentation as to how the Mannheim based Zentralinstitut für Seelische Gesundheit (Central Institute for Psychic Health) offended against Baden-Württemberg's data protection law by storing and processing the personal data of psychically ill persons, this institute surprised the interested public in May 1987 with the announcement that in future it would carry out its research with data from the Danish Psychiatric Case Register. As the Danish Ethical Committee and the Danish Board of the Psychiatric Case Register approved this research work it can be assumed that the Danish data protection law is less strict than its Baden-Württemberg equivalent.

These examples, and we could cite many more besides, represent only the initial stage in the development of a global information network. They can be said to be only in the early stage of development because a compatible combination of the three systematic levels necessary for such a system is not yet possible. These three levels are:

1. telecommunication connections (sea cables or satellites),
2. computer-supported networks,
3. end user terminals.

The wild, competitive market of these terminals is another weak-point in such a global information network. Despite these limitations, however, the examples quoted demonstrate that TDF has become a factor in international transactions involving production, trade and advertising. It influences every branch of industrial, as well as the individual in his own home, touching on matters of economic, social, legal and cultural importance. The second theses will formulate a definition of TDF which is both in opposition to and a conscious political enlargement of IBI's narrow definition.

Hypothesis 2

TDF expresses a radical change in the international division of labor. As it operates independent of time and place and is highly flexible as an international information and control system, TDF breaks down the difference between internal and external, between one's own and foreign national sovereignty. The permeability of internal and external sectors causes traditional political and legal instruments of regulation to fail. On the whole, international politics becomes less controllable. Effective maneuverability, particularly for the Third World, will exist mainly on the market for enduser terminals.

As can be seen from the few scientific studies available the West German interest in TDF derives due to very different considerations, namely from the tradition of data protection for personal data. Hessen's trail-blazing role can be taken as exemplary - being the first region worldwide to implement a data protection law. The 1985 finding by the West German Constitutional Court concerning a planned census clearly demonstrates the conceptual basis of data protection. Data protection is concerned with ensuring the individual's right to control over information about him or herself, is concerned with the individual's legal and constitutional right to protection from undemocratic forms of control by state bodies. The relevant resolutions adopted by the council of Europe and other European organizations concerning TDF and human rights can be viewed in the light of this tradition. The concept of data protection naturally is of relevance for the Third World countries[2], but it does ignore certain important aspects of the TDF problem complex:

1. Only a small percentage of TDF can be defined as being both international and personal. About two thirds of all TDF relate to non-personal data and information exchange conducted by banks insurance companies and multinationals communicating with their overseas subsidiaries.
2. The basic concept of protecting the individual from an all-powerful state apparatus is not fully adequate for many Third World countries because of the presence of other traditions which necessitate the development of an additional concept of collective protection.
3. A legal discussion on TDF cannot do justice to the economic implications for the new forms of labor division on an international scale involved in the question. This conclusions lead to the my third hypothesis.

Hypothesis 3

If TDF is viewed within international politics from the legal perspective of data protection, then this could all too easily obscure the debate, because the infrastructural changes taking place within the global economy would not be discernable. The Non-Aligned Movement and the Group of 77 within the UN represent another intellectual tradition intensively involved with the TDF question. This can also be said of the student protests and critical scientific movements of the late 1960s and early 1970s in the western industrialized countries. The activities of these groups threw light on the importance of transnational concerns for the countries of the Third World. Attention quickly focused on the question of

2. According to confidential information available to me, the telephone system installed by the Swedish Firm Ericsson in Zambia a short time ago was conceived from the very beginning in such as way as to enable the Zambian Ministry for Information to have full control over who telephones with whom.

direct investment by transnational concerns in Third World countries. The UN's "Code of Conduct on Transnational Corporations" was intended to regulate such forms of investment. The intention remains, but the "Code of Conduct on Transnational Corporations" has become paralysed in a jungle of the UN red tape. Given that transnational corporations are the principle actors in TDF and that direct investment is conducted through this medium, the UN's Centre on Transnational Cooperations", based in New York (UNCTC), was destined to focus its attention, politically and scientifically, on TDF policy.

The fact that numerous empirical and national studies have been compiled on this TDF problem is to a large degree thanks to the ongoing work of West German scholar Karl Sauvant, who is attached to this center. Critical discussion of the role of transnational concerns in international relations and thus in TDF has been dampened due to numerous political factors, such as inertia in development, changes in the political landscape, the Third World debt, the depoliticization of scientists both in the USA and Europe, the increase in superficial discussion on alternatives such as "free market versus state planned economies", etc. My fourth hypothesis follows from this.

Hypothesis 4

TDF, in all its dimensions, can only be adequately understood if TNC's potential to stimulate and also to block its development is simultaneously analyzed. The cultural political climate in West Germany today, however, is such that practically no one institution is strong enough to conduct such an analysis without damaging itself.

In Canada, the Clyne Report commissioned by the federal government, warned as early as 1979 that the increase in TDF with the USA was undermining national sovereignty. This led to a new direction in the TDF debate, for West European countries were forced to recognize their own increasing dependency on the United Stated in the domain of TDF. This shift of emphasis pushed the North-South conflict within the TDF discussion into the background while on the other hand, bringing to light the tensions with the North Atlantic Alliance. While a high US government telecommunications official published an article entitled "The coming Information War" in the 15th January, 1978 edition of the *Washington Post,* directed against the EU, a number of data bank reports provided the interested West German public with some insight into the extent of the West Germany's dependence on the USA. There follow some details on this: certain US databases deny access to clients from the Germany; some US databases contain more West German research data than their equivalents in West Germany itself. The classification and re-classification of US data as security-relevant is on the increase and this hinders the free flow of high tech data from the USA to West Germany more and more.

These new forms of conflict have led to behind-the-scenes conflict between the US import and export sectors as well as between the State and Defense Departments regarding TDF. This has also spawned enormous (though never officially admitted) tension between the United States and CoCom (Coordinating Committee for East-West-Trade-Policy), and to further tensions with regard to the conditions for the transfer of technology within the framework of the SDI-project. If one temporarily ignores the specific historical-colonial nature of the relationship within the North-South conflict, which is admittedly difficult to justify from a theoretical point of view, then on the surface at least it would appear that West Germany on the question of TDF has similar problems with the USA as the Third World with the industrialized nations: loss of sovereignty and cultural identity, growing external control and vulnerability, rising negative balance of trade, growing economic financial and technical foreign penetration, passive-reactive role in the international division of labor, etc. These considerations lead on to my fifth hypothesis.

Hypothesis 5

West Germany faces a problem of credibility in relation to many aspects of high-tech policy, especially concerning TDF. One cannot force the countries of the Third World to accept a radical free flow position when in your own relationship to the United States you are forced to adopt other, more differentiated policies. From West Germany's point of view, a consistent TDF policy implies a critical confrontation with the partner with whom it is in conflict, the United States, which, in turn, raises the question of a Europeanization strategy. For fear of being branded "anti-American", a large section of the West German public is avoiding taking an offensive stand public on this issue. As TDF continues to develop into an economic and technological conflict between the Western countries themselves, it comes as no surprise that the most significant debates on this subject have been held for years now, under the auspices of the OECD, with West

Germany playing a particularly invisible and non-committal role. Free of political and moral obligations towards the Third World this body can develop TDF regulations tailored to meet the collective interests of the industrialized nations.

Only "Gaullist" France (regardless of which political party held power) seems interested in initiating debates on sovereignty, American domination, national self-determination, etc. It was also France which was responsible for the "OECD Guidelines on TDF" containing the phrase "to promote access to data and information related services" before being adopted in 1985. The principle of "right of access" propagated here, aimed of course at US-American databases and was originally an argument in the debate on the "right to communicate" initiated by the Third World and the Non-Aligned Movement.

This small addition to the OECD declaration which was interpreted in West Germany as a victory for the EU over the USA, should not obscure the fact that the real discussions on TDF will take place in the present Uruguay Round of GATT talks. For the Americans expect and are applying pressure to ensure that this round of talks is dominated by the issues of the deregulation of the service sectors, including banking, insurance, telecommunications, data processing, etc. This in principle, would lead to a worldwide liberalization of TDF. It would seem from the preparations for this GATT round of talks, going on at the moment, that the EU states have already agreed to this liberalization.[3] The possible resulting penetration of Western Europe by US capital will have enormous consequences for their industrial and labour policies. Of the Third World members of GATT, only Brazil and India seem to be fighting against such a liberalization in the services sector. The Indian Minister for Finance and Trade, Vishwanath Pratap Singh, said on this matter:

> Services include banking and insurance as well as undertakers and hairdressers. We have nothing against liberalization for the hairdressing sector, but our banks are not just finance institutions. They are also a part of our social policy.[4]

---

3. Neither from the press nor from scientific literature is it clear what position the socialist GATT members (Cuba, Czechoslovakia, Hungary, Poland, Romania, Yugoslavia) or the USSR which is aiming at membership will take on this matter.
4. Quoted from John, Elliott: "India sees focus on services as a diversion", in: *Financial Times*, September 20, 1985, p. 6.

The US government has already taken legal and political steps to counter Brazil's protectionist information law, passed in October 1984, and the West German post office's policies which are also regarded in Washington as being protectionist. Thus, it can also be assumed that Brazil's and India's resistance within GATT will be undermined by a policy of "Divide and Rule". By conceding small concessions in the global goods trading sector (e.g. textile products), the US can push through a liberalization of service sector products. This conflict within GATT is the basis for my sixth hypothesis.

Hypothesis 6

In general, external trade policy is most difficult for a government to regulate in one specific direction. Opportunism and pragmatism can and often even must (!) dominate this sector. Thus, there is no fundamental difference between the SPD, CDU or FDP policies relating to external trade. For all parties the argument that "exports secure our social progress" is the condition *sine qua non* of their actions. But as TDF could alter the new international division of labor to such an extent that West Germany could become marginalised, this argument could be turned on its head: "The export dependency of West Germany impedes social progress."

A recently completed empirical examination of the institutional legal and economic conditions for TDF in West Germany (Müller 1987) comes to the conclusion that TDF is of practically no significance at the moment in West Germany, and if at all then only for few economic sectors. Even though the number of leased line connections for data transfer increased from 1978 to 1985 by 200 to more than 1.400, and even though the number of data transfer installations increased in the same period from 65.000 to 286.000, nevertheless, foreign trade has remained at 1 percent.

However, such an argument, which is based essentially on the quantitative trade volume for TDF, could lead to hasty, relativist conclusions on the social relevance of TDF. Actually, the relevance of TDF has less to do with the quantity and more with the quality of these new, international services. On September 4, 1987 in the course of the first long-distance sale via satellite TV between France and Japan, not only was a French chateau sold for 3 million DM, but also three pairs of ladies stockings for 120 DM - this absurd example of TDF gives us an idea of what qualitatively new changes can be expected of international trade.

When the above mentioned examination of TDF concludes that the future significance of TDF is dependent basically on the future quality of the telecommunications infrastructure, the access conditions and the quantity of future information sources, then this is only partially true. What is more important for the relevance of TDF is how the quality of social relations will change, both on a national and international scale.

Only very late did the West German Trade Union Congress recognise the problem. A short time ago a study under the title "Information without Border Limits" was issued by members of the IG Metall, the West German Trade Union which traditionally has the best experience in international trade-union work[5] This study is less concerned with the quantitative aspect of TDF, but more with the qualitative changes in the international division of labor. With a certain amount of alarm the authors reach the conclusion, that TDF opens up whole new possibilities for the entrepreneurs (flexibility, rationalization, centralization of decision making, increasing dependency of supplying industries, etc.), and that at the same time a considerable shift in the balance of power is taking place which will affect trade conflicts to the disadvantage of the trade unions. A seventh general thesis follows on these considerations.

Hypothesis 7

The ongoing second industrial revolution, which is still only in its initial stages, has been more of less ignored by interest groups which traditionally favored the welfare state model, such as trade unions, Social Democrats and the Church. This second revolution was able to begin when technical development made possible the sweeping economization of the product "information". In accordance with their traditions, the above name interest groups have till now only concentrated their attention on the process of re-structuring the labor market, without noticing that the second industrial revolution will alter all social sectors, even the field of international relations. Only a political perspective which embraces all the individual aspects of this change can aid these groups in developing a survival strategy for the welfare state in the 1990s.

---

5. Cf. *Information ohne Grenzen*, ed. by Thomas Klebe and Siegfried Roth, Hamburg: VSA-Verlag 1987.

16

Telematics and Another Foreign Development

A single computer can just as well be used to secure political control over the mobility of black workers in South Africa as it can be to identify the most appropriate storage form for perishable and limited food supplies. However correct this observation may be, it trivializes a technically induced social change which takes place nationally and internationally at the present time. For this change is not characterized by a single computer, but by a complex of computer and network technologies, i.e., telematics. Whereas one can debate the tool-like character of a single computer this is no longer possible for the system perspective of informatization or computerization. The following example can illustrate this system perspective: When a country has built up a highway system, a conscious and selective use of this road system simply between milestone 211 and 212 is no longer practicable.

Something very similar is true for the concept Third World. However, correct it may be to point out the divergent historical and cultural development patterns of individual Third World countries and nations it is not very helpful - especially if one claims not to conduct an ethno-centric debate - because such a perspective exclusively based on individual countries is not able to recognize system and structural interrelations.

Even if, for example, Brazil's nationalistic protectionist policy as regards computerization supported due to the country's populist tradition by the left as well as the right, has produced annual growth rates of 30 percent on the domestic computer market since the isolation of 1979 and whose informatics law of October 1984 caused considerable annoyance in West German industry - and, even if Brazil's policy must be regarded as entirely different from the enforced buildup of informatics in Zaire it is necessary to insist on the following historical realization. In a narrow sense it is only really possible to speak of an international system with dependent and independent connections since 1945. Whereas nineteenth century European nation states went through self controlled developmental processes relatively easily, this has not been the case for Third World countries since 1945. The increasingly exogenous influence of the Third World economies force one to speak of the Third World as if it were one, albeit not homogeneous, systemic unit.

It is only when these two relations - telematics and Third World - have been related systematically, that it is possible to define the structural changes and that is what it is needed unless one wants to continue a policy of mollification. In this context, I wish to discuss two complexes:

1. What sort of impact does the transfer of telematics have on foreign aid policymaking?
2. What sort of foreign trade strategy serves the interest of West Germany with its strong export focus?

Our main interest will be centered on the second complex of question for the following reason: the best morality as regards foreign-aid-policy will remain idealistic, i.e., without consequences, as long as it cannot be tied to political and economic interests. (That, admittedly, the present West German policy on the Third World is against West Germany's own interests is only to be hinted at at this point.)

1. Telematics and Foreign Aid Policy

Before discussing aspects specific to technology, it must be pointed out that most foreign-aid-political indicators have worsened to the detriment of the Third World in the past few years. The annual foreign aid reports issued by very dissimilar organizations all agree on one thing, namely that the instruments of foreign aid policy have failed to date. They repeat this message year after year, while at the same time the gap between Third World and the industrialized nations increases.

These general statements can be fleshed out by means of one single annual report by an international organization. In its 1984 report, the OAS (Organization of American States) states that more than 30 percent of Latin America's population will live in absolute poverty in the year 2000 and that the number of unemployed will rise by another 11 million through 1990. The per capita income in Latin America's debt servicing devours at least 60 percent of foreign exchange earnings. And this mountain of debts is still increasing, according to the OAS report, especially because the Third World raw materials are becoming less and less important (decreasing markets in industrial nations, substitution by synthetic products, increase in recycling economic cycles).

Third World indebtedness - only the monetary top of the dependencies' iceberg - devours 5 to 10 percent of the GNP in many Third World countries, an enormous sum if it is compared to the much-toted 0.7 percent of their GNP which industrialised nations have promised in Third World aid but never coughed up. Put succinctly: there's hardly one Third World country which is sovereign in the economic, financial and exchange policies. Since after 30 years of realistic political and scientific experiences about developmental processes, structural changes in the Third World have made these countries even more dependent, it is naive to assume that these generally restrictive developments can be positively changed by the implementation of a specific set of technologies.

Theoretically and empirically the assumption that Third World development can be positively influenced by the deployment of computers, seems patently absurd. Only one question must be asked if Third World countries want to deploy telematics meaningfully: is it possible, and - if so how and to what extent - to remove the intrinsic systemic character of computerization and return to the various, non-connected parts of the system their tool-like character? Put differently: are there in the Third World relative areas of freedom and niches in which individual information and communication technologies can be deployed for positive, autonomous developmental processes? Numerous empirical and theoretical studies since the mid-1970s have claimed that the deployment of telematic technologies has indeed aggravated the situation in the Third World and they have provide ample proof. I now want to give a thumbnail sketch of the results of three select studies.

Firstly, in a survey about the consequences of TV on the slum population in Jakarta, Karamoy and Sablie (1975) came to the following conclusion: TV bears a grave responsibility for cultural uprooting, the generation gap and conflicts between social levels.

Secondly, a Harvard University Center for Information Policy Research Project (Clippinger 1976) compared the consequences of technological deployment (satellites, data processing nets, telecommunication systems and TV) on the sharing of social power in such politically divergent countries as Algeria and El Salvador. In both countries the deployment of telematics showed the same results. It increased the power gap between the class in power and poorer parts of the population. Such results are not only relevant for the mass media which are only a small part of telematics, but also for information and communication technologies which play an important role in production.

Thirdly, a brief glance at Kaplinsky's (1982) research on the use of Computer Aided Design (CAD) is revealing. Whereas, CAD systems are increasingly utilized in industrial nations the rationality behind it all is clear to detect: After a short initial phase productivity is tripled on the average by deployment of CAD system, while at the same time the number of workers can be reduced considerably.

After all the experiences gathered in industrial countries, CAD systems can only be successful if there are close synergetic relations between users and manufacturers. As the software of these systems must meet very divergent demands, the closest cooperation with the manufacturer is the key to consumer specific software development. These two elements suffice to make the deployment of CAD systems in Third World countries more than a little questionable. One the one hand, the necessary linkages to the manufacturers do not exist, on the other, they aggravate the already precarious unemployment situation.

The costs of hardware also are such high that only the wealthiest firms in the Third World can consider them. Whereas, the smallest CAD system with a micro computer costs US$ 25,000 per terminal, the costs per terminal increase to US$ 200,000 for CAD systems as part of a main-frame system. According to available statistics the following problem also arises: At present CAD systems which are being deployed in industrial branches in South-East Asia resulted in extraordinary growth rates in the seventies, but this advantage over industrial countries has been lost, when the comparative wage advantages disappeared as a result of automation. So this third example also shows that telematics tend to reinforce the North-South gap rather than making a worthwhile contribution towards developing autonomy.

Admittedly, the intense deployment of telematics can lead to enormous growth increases in Third World countries, as can be seen in the policies practiced in Hong Kong, Singapore, Taiwan and South Korea.

Such an industrialization policy as pursued by the four Tigers can quite obviously not be executed without considerable social, political and economic costs. The example of South Korea shows very clearly the costs of such a path of development: domestic political repression, enormous foreign debts, enormous limitation of foreign policy options, enormous economic concentration processes and far-reaching cultural conflicts. It is not without irony that it was the Korea Exchange Bank which, in one of its last Annual Reports, lamented over the absence of middle class industry and pointed to the increasing gap between the rich and the poor and considered the uneven development of Seoul compared with the rest of Korea extremely harmful.

Whereas, these briefly described developments are or should be well known, they do not indicate a frame of reference apart from the "economic niches" strategy referred to briefly. Theoretically and scientifically no novel or innovative idea can be derived from further study of the aggravated situation in the Third World (in spite of the cultural arrogance implied in such a statement). Perhaps if potential conflict situations within the western industrial nations and in competition with one another is described and analyzed, this could provide possibilities for a strategy of action as regards the Third World. Therefore, as two decades of increasingly more helpless debating on adequate development strategies for the Third World have produced absolutely no structural improvements to the actual situation (Die Armut der Nationen 1987; Schuldenkrise und Dritte Welt 1987), the questions raised in "Another development" (1977) must be asked a new and in a different manner.

In the same way as "Another Development" was devised as a great concept for an alternative development of the Third World, "Another Development" should, indeed must, be adapted for the industrialized nations using the same theories and arguments as in 1977, but directed towards the industrial nations themselves and not the Third World. It appears to me that "Another Development" for the Third World is only possible from a starting point of this kind. That is why in the course of the paper the foreign trade aspects of telematic transfer will be examined taking Germany as example. Questions will be posed above all about the internal consequences of this transfer, the assumed or real necessity and last but not least the long-term and autonomy interests of a nation such as Germany.

2. Telematics and Foreign Trade Politics

It is a truism that the West German economy has an export focus, and especially in the context of high technologies (microprocessing, ICT, biotechnology) a national discussion no longer makes any sense. The argument that West Germany must expand exports to survive is not proven by constant repetition. For increasing export surpluses have made West Germany more vulnerable politically and economically in its relations with foreign countries, e.g., exposed it to the ups and downs of the US dollar exchange rate and interest rates since 1979 without it being able to exert any influence.

Moreover, the West German economic fixation on exports has led to a neglect of the West German domestic market and to its uneven development. The neglect of the West German domestic trade market can be deduced from the following comparative figures, for example: In 1982 the per-capita consumption of microelectronics amounted to DM 42 in the US, DM 44 in Japan and DM 23 in Germany. We cannot, however, automatically conclude that this suggests the presence of aggressive, competitive foreign trade strategy, as would most traditional economists do. Even though the West German market is comparatively small, on the basis of such a deficit comparison the conclusion may be drawn that there are still substantial gaps in the West German market which have not yet been closed. An increased orientation of the West German industry towards its own national market would not only have the advantage of reducing political dependencies abroad.

Since, compared with the US and Japan the socially relevant forces, who insist on the social acceptability of telematics, are relatively well-developed in West Germany, and an increased focus on the national market would contribute to the production of socially accept able and socially adapted new ICTs. Such technologies, if tested for their social acceptability, would surely sell well on the world market. In the usual international "hit and run" procedure, such technologies could then present a consciously qualitatively different counterpart.

Under no circumstances can an international eco-political discussion on telematics be conducted which does not - however briefly - mention IBM as the most important international frame of reference. No national government and certainly no manufacturer of computers can worldwide afford to ignore IBM; actively, counteractively or pre-emptively all worldwide computer strategies are connected to IBM in some form or another. When the anti-trust proceeding by the European

Commission in Brussels against IBM were concluded, even the magazine *Wirtschaftswoche* - closely connected to the West German business world - spoke of IBM's worldwide "dictatorship", which made the other manufacturers "fear for their naked existence".

Since the gap between IBM's sales and that of other computer manufacturers increases, since IBM's sales are several times that of the most important computer manufacturers (Bull, Siemens, Olivetti, DEC, ICL, Nixdorf, Boroughs, NCR, Hewlett-Packard, Ericsson) combined, the most important European and US computer firms met in Paris at the beginning of December 1984 with the only purpose of developing common standards against IBM. Before turning our attention to Japan, it is important to be conscious of the United States' technological dominance: 97 percent of all computers are made by firms in the US; moreover, US firms in the field of integrated circuits worldwide control 50 percent of the world market compared with a Japanese share of 30 percent and a European one of 17 percent.

Keeping in mind the dominance of IBM and the US, the international eco-political discussion will be limited to a comparison with Japan, because Japan is being used as an argument to promote the unchecked development of telematics. This was done in a most pronounced form in the West German Government's Report on ICT of February 1984. Its analysis can be reduced to the statement that there exists a technological gap between Germany and the USA and Japan. The solution is surely a matter of the enforced expansion of telematics pushed jointly by the state and private enterprise as a component part of a growth economy trying to catch up with the world leaders. Analysis as well as solution are insufficient to the point of being false; in the long run such a strategy is detrimental to Germany as a whole. The following should be considered in detail.

3. Japan - Germany: a Comparison

The racist prejudice against the "yellow peril" from Japan is still not dead in West Germany. And as is well-known from research about prejudices, latent enemy images and prejudices can very quickly be reactivated during economic depressions. The motto "Turks go home" as well as the anxiety-ridden image and spectre of the technological giant Japan have had this social psychological function in Germany since the economic recession and the GNP growth rates of 2 percent per annum. Especially during the labor strikes in the spring of 1984, the image of Japan as the enemy was flogged to death. These socio-psychological mechanisms must be considered and postulated, before a sober analysis of foreign trade politics can be entered upon.

a) Japan's economy differs from that of Germany in many respects. On the basis of its per capita income Japan is at present as "poor" as Germany in the mid-1960s and the very same impressive Japanese growth rates of today were to be found in Germany at that time. Japan's successes in the world market are above all focused on mass production. This focus as well as the fact that West Germany's license balance far exceeds that of Japan's shows that Japan does not play such a leading role economically or technologically as is generally assumed. In spite of all its successes in the world market Japan's information industry is much more oriented towards a domestic than a foreign market: whereas, 13.5 percent of all goods produced in Japan are exported, the West German figure is 26.7 percent. The Japanese electronic concern Hitachi does not sell even a third of its products abroad.

Japan's success in the telematics field is limited to a very small number of products, especially in the field of entertainment electronics, especially on the radio, TV and recording markets. Japan has a slightly bigger world market share of communication, measurement and data technology products than Germany; as regards generators, transformers and electricity distribution plant, both countries have a similar share of the world market. In the fields of lighting engineering, household appliances, medical appliances or data technology West Germany has far higher export values than Japan.

In 1981 the world export share of medical devices was 21.5 percent for Germany and 7.5 percent for Japan; of data processing products the West German's share amounted to 12 percent and Japan's to 6.3 percent. In the field of micro-electronics Japan surpasses West Germany technically as in world exports. In spite of this above-mentioned dominance we must not forget that, for example, there are chip manufacturers in Germany who export their products to be embedded in Japanese watches, that other German firms produce millions of microprocessors to be built into American cars and alarm-clocks, that even hybrid integrated circuits are being exported to Taiwan, Hong Kong or even Japan. In conclusion it can be said that the product range of West Germany's export industry is many times bigger and more differentiated than Japan in the field of telematics. As a result and also due to Japan's main orientation towards a domestic market the global competition between Japan and Germany is much smaller than generally believed.

b) Although the names of Japan ICT corporations like Fujitsu, Nippon Electric or Hitachi often dazzle and frighten the general public, the Japanese information industry is much more oriented towards small holdings than in West Germany or the United States. Whereas in Japan, for example, 70 percent of all industrial products are produced by small and middle sized firms, it is only 40 percent in the United States. A comparison with West Germany reveals a similar pattern. Japanese firms with less than 1000 employees produce 75 percent of industrial turnover and employ 86 percent of industrial workers, the figures for Germany are 44 percent and 49 percent respectively. Similarly unfavorable is the West German Federal government's technology promotion of small and middle-sized firms. The Federal Ministry for Research and Technology in Bonn awarded 60 percent of its financial support to 10 large firms only between 1973 and 1982; about 25 percent of the total amount was awarded to the Siemens group.

While the research promotion by this ministry was accused of excessive bureaucracy, incompetence, corruption and parasitism by the *Manager Magazine*, the following structural mechanism of research promotion are far more serious. As a result of the continued awarding of major projects by the Ministry of Research, and especially by the Postal Ministry, to few firms, their innovation capacity has diminished. When investment decisions are regulated more or less by the state commissioning on a primogeniture basis, the competitive principle of free enterprise becomes meaningless, and the big concerns lose their ability and inner compulsion to participate in the international market. The relevance of small and middle-sized companies in Japan can offer two maxims for West Germany: Small and middle-sized companies in the field of telematics should be encouraged. Whereas, on the one hand, this is already partly being practiced though as a result of entirely utopian and nature communal initiative concepts "à la Silicon Valley", on the other, and this is the second point, a very stringent and consistent anti-monopoly and anti-trust policy does not exist.

At present the telecommunication expansion in West Germany has sharply triggered a new wave of concentration. The latter not only impacts negatively on the internal structures of West Germany, but also on the competitiveness of the West German ICT industry on the world market. Admittedly only multi-national concerns like Siemens have the capital, know-how, technological and marketing experience to be able to play a large role in the world market.

On the other hand, they are so much controlled by the law of magnitude and mass production that, partly, they have simply become incapable of participating in the world market. Thus, the anti-concentration recommendations in their fifth main experts' report by the Anti-Trust commission for the Federal Government are not only relevant for the federal republic's internal situation. The commission's report proposes that free-enterprise newspaper publishers should not have access to the new media. Furthermore, it considers it necessary that the anti-trust department should be given authority over the deployment of broadcasting frequencies (this last proposal is surely one of the must radical economic proposals imaginable). Such concepts should also be pursued with the interests of a successful foreign trade policy in mind.

The Siemens concern is a good example for the internal and external immobility of "colossi". At present this firm has floating capital assets of about 17 billion DM, and that is more than 40 percent of Siemens worldwide turnover which are invested in stocks and shares and bonds, especially in the US-American money market, and is therefore, not gainfully employed for production purposes. Think of all one could do with these 17 billion DM in differentiated and quality-oriented production of telematics by numerous small and middle-sized firms! The inflexibility of multi-national information concerns also bears demonstrably negative consequences in the field of foreign aid policy. Their size and the laws of mass production prevent them from developing an economic interest in the sometimes very specific problems of the Third World.

Say Burma was looking for a manufacturer of computers, which transcribed the Burmese alphabet for photocomposition, or made it compatible on the terminal with the Latin alphabet, no West German manufacturer would be interested in such a project within the framework of German foreign aid, since the Burmese language and alphabet are only used within Burma, and such a limited market does not interest a multi-national information concern in the least.

Or to use another example: some time ago the Sudanese government ordered Siemens to construct a complete system of signals, level-crossing barriers and controls to modernize its railway net.

The condition for this multi-million dollar business was that the system should be constructed in such a way that it would hardly have to rely on electronics but would, in the main be operated by mechanic and manual means. Given this condition Siemens showed not the least interest in this contract, and the Sudan transaction did not come about.

c) Using the presently so persuasive Japan argument people like to "overlook" the following facts: By spending 3.4 percent of its GNP on pollution controls Japan leads all other countries, and by spending 0.98 percent of its GNP on defense it commits far less than any NATO country. In other words: Japan's success in the telematics field is linked to its build up of a constructive, civilian infrastructure as a matter of priority compared with the priority of a destructive, militaristic infrastructure as in the United States. As far as West Germany is concerned the following conclusion ought to be drawn from this very inconvenient Japan argument: If her foreign trade position is to be boosted in the telematics field, then this would be best accomplished by reduction of military spending.

At present there is no indication in this respect in sight. The government report on ICT quoted above interestingly enough also uses the military-technical argument: the West German Ministry of Defence is planning the build up a very expensive as well as very vulnerable C^3I (communication, command, control and information) system, the rejuvenation of the West European Union and its Rome Declaration of October 1984 point to a United European military coordination in the telematics field, and finally the European space rocket Arianne and the satellites pertaining to it must not only be seen from a civilian but of course also from a military point of view.

d) Finally, Japan's telematics successes can only be adequately understood against the background of a consensus-oriented cellular society as compared to Western individualistic free-enterprise societies. The peculiarly Japanese mixture of Confucianism, Buddhism and Shintoism had already in the pre-Meiji period given rise to work ethic which although it is individualistic, achievement oriented and competitive, has always remained embedded in the commonwealth of clan, firm or the whole country. Expressed in western terms this means that the respective business management rationality is always within the framework of the national economic rationality. As far as West Germany is concerned two conclusions may be drawn.

First, the cultural roots of the Japanese work ethics can be as little transposed onto West Germany as can Japanese management methods. Not only can they not be transferred, there is no reason to do so. For the structures which lead in Japan to that which is called consensus society between management and employees, would in West Germany be a highly ideological harmony strategy between management and trade unions. Second, West Germany can learn, however, the following principle from Japan: that individual business management rationalities, which make sense for a single West German telematics firm but are in the short-term interest of the national economy only, should be replaced in favor of a national economic overall-rationality and a long-term policy.

We can conclude generally, that based on the various Japan arguments no enforced West German foreign trade policy in the field of telematics can be deduced. What can be deduced, however, and in the interest of securing future German export markets is that by reducing concentration, imposing stricter anti-monopoly and anti-trust laws, and providing more support for small and middle-sized firms, cutting military expenditure and paying greater attention to West Germany's economic interests instead of the interests of individual companies, the foreign trade situation of West German telematics would benefit structurally in the long term.

4. Conclusions

Three conclusions can be drawn on the basis of these considerations: for the Third World, for West Germany and last but not least, for the relationship between West Germany and the Third World.

1. If the *Third World* wants to reduce its economic, political and cultural dependencies on the western industrial nations it would be well advised to make very careful and selective use of telematics. The industrialization strategies of the "four Tigers" (Singapore, Taiwan, Hong

Kong and South Korea) cannot serve as an example, unless enormous social and political costs are accepted. On the contrary a successful development strategy should be based on the following two premises: first of all, and this has top priority, operational economic systems must be erected for the national agriculture which ensures the provisioning of the population and the income of the peasant producers; secondly, everything must be done to convert the production apparatus to mass production for mass consumption based on a fundamentally domestic technical basis.

Local efforts at industrialization must be granted priority before technology transfer induced from abroad; and this is the perspective from which the deployment of telematics should be regarded. Neither agricultural nor industrialization policies can be conducted without certain elements aiming at dissociation from the world market. Protectionism, negation, diversification of dependencies, isolation of domestic markets, erection of non-tariff barriers, restriction and control of international capital transfers, circumvention of copyright and patent licensing conditions, indigenous imitation of western technology products, expansion of regional and north-south economic relations, etc. These are the most important catchwords in a dissociative development strategy, as successfully practiced - sometimes more, sometimes less - under very different conditions and historical circumstances by the German Customs Union in the 19th century, by Japan at the beginning of this century, by Burma, the People's Republic of China, India, Cuba or post-revolutionary Iran.

The difficult momentum of this strategy of disengagement is not the choice of starting point for such a strategy - at present deteriorating results of a continued strategy of open markets can hardly be surpassed as far as the Third World is concerned. It is difficult to determine when to change such a strategy in favor of an integrative opening toward the world market. It remains to be seen whether the People's Republic of China has chosen the right moment for such an opening and when and if at a later point in time it barricades itself a new and just as sensibly against the west.

2. Contrary to popular-scientific opinion, it would be in *West Germany's* own interest to stay out of the suicidal technology race between the USA and Japan as far as possible. Apart from the reasons already mentioned the following chain of reasoning should be considered. In 1982 and 1983 US foreign trade with the Pacific countries was considerably bigger than with the EU. In 1982 it amounted to 165 billion dollars, trade with Western Europe amounted to only 115 billion dollars, and just the USA and Japan together produced almost 40 percent of the world's

GNP. The more world trade will be concentrated on the Pacific Rim, i.e., Japan, the ASEAN countries and the west coast of Canada and the USA in the next 30 years, the more the role of West Europe and West Germany will become different. Merely as just a secondary industrial nation West Germany would literally be racing to its death if it continued to back a strategy of ever greater growth in the telematics field.

This will become evident if the strategy does not change especially in the cost-intensive field of unemployment. At present there is a basis of structural unemployment of about 2 million people in Germany. On the basis of demographic changes - in no ways linked to technically induced unemployment - there will be further 1.2 million umemployed in West Germany in 1990. If to these 3.2 million umemployed there is added the number of unemployed due to informatization, economic dimensions are reached, which are intolerable for West-Germany. (At any rate, the Siemens study "Office 1990" is based on a rationalization potential of 2.5 million people.)* To catch up with the pacific basis as far as foreign trade is concerned would only be very cost intensive for West Germany.

First of all, foreign trade competition can only be neutralized domestically by increased rationalization, and secondly most of the technologies that could possibly be considered are in any case hardly labor-intensive. Consequently, the West German foreign trade policy should be to break out of this race which cannot be won, and develop a strategy of being second best instead of a worse and worse first. Canada, under the Trudeau administration, can be used as an example for such a strategy which on the one hand tried to establish a policy of protectionism versus the USA in the telematics field, while, on the other hand, it cultivated its other foreign relations according to the normal world trade pattern (Mansell 1984).

3. This leaves the relationship between *West Germany and the Third World.* If West Germany were to follow the route described above, this model would not guarantee a qualitatively new policy and one less detrimental to the Third World, but it would be a first step towards a foreign trade policy geared towards Germany's autonomous interests. Although West Germany's trade with the Third World and East Europe together is not quite 10 percent of its foreign trade, an increased West

---

* 14 years after first publishing this essay, it is clear that my calculations on the progress of rationalization and unemployment were not inaccurate. Today, there are 7.5 million unemployed people in Germany.

German orientation towards these markets would be advisable, although at the moment only tentatively capable of being put into effect. Whereas, East Europe does not have the hard currency for intensive trade relations, in the Third World countries an intensification of trade is inhibited by their present crypto-capitalistic dependent and one-sidedly distorted economic systems as well. These impediments can only be overcome, if incisive arms controls relieve Eastern Europe financially and finally enables these countries to enlarge the domestic market for mass-produced goods and if, on the other hand, the Third World by means of strategies of disengagement is to build up more absorbent markets than is the case at present.

Even more sensible would be qualitatively novel cooperation with the Third World from a united West European perspective. But this would only be possible if the European Parliament had larger powers than at present and only when elements of social acceptability in the exporting of telematics into the Third World are adopted. The way the European Commission's promotion policy is being carried out at present, a coherent and united West European cooperation only seems to take place between Siemens and Philips, Marconi and Thomson, Thomson-Brandt and Telefunken, Matra and Norsk Data. In spite of this reservedly critical comment there can be noted a novel consensus between the Third World and Western Europe which is primarily the result of an altered US foreign policy.

Between the US and Western Europe there is hardly any common ground in energy policy; whereas, the US only obtains 3 percent of its crude oil from the Gulf states, Western Europe obtains 28 percent. In defense policy, the concept of "Star Wars" (SDI) has estranged the West Europeans from the US, because it has suddenly deprived them of their protective shield. The Americans' return to a policy of military interventions has caused dissension with the West Europeans about the US policy in Central America. A profound dissent could occur in high-technology policy between the United States and Europe if the impediments which the United States has imposed on technology transfers to East Europe are intensified even more than at present and this should prove to have a more restrictive effect on West Europe itself than it has already now.

Finally, differences have appeared between the United States and West Europe in UN policies. Whereas, the United States is withdrawing from multi-lateral decision making bodies (IDA, UNESCO, flouting of the International Court of Justice, the refusal to sign the International Maritime Law Convention and plans to leave the UNCTAD), West Europe still regards these bodies as instruments for international cooperation, especially with the Third World.

References

Another Development: Approaches and strategies, ed. by Marc Nerfin, Uppsala: The Dag Hammarskjöld Foundation 1977.

Die Armut der Nationen. Handbuch zur Schuldenkrise von Argentinien bis Zaire, ed. by Elmar Altvater, Kurt Hübner, Jochen Lorentzen and Raul Rojas, Berlin: Rotbuch Verlag 1987.

Ayal, Eliezer B.: "Value Systems and Economic Development in Japan and Thailand", in: *Journal of Social Issues*, No. 19/1963, pp.35-51.

Browa, Hans and Wolff, Heimfried: *Das Forschungs- und Technologiesystem Japan.* 4 Vols., Cologne: Verlag TÜV Rheinland 1983.

Clippinger, John H.: *Who Gains by Communications Development?*, Cambridge, Mass.: Harvard University, Program on Information Resources Policy. Centre for Information Policy Research, 1976 (= Studies in Information Technologies in Developing Countries) (mimeo).

Kaplinsky, Raphael: *Computer Aided Design.* Electronics, Comparative Advantage and Development, London: Francis Pinter 1982.

Karamoy, Armir and Sablie, Achmad: "The Communication Aspect and Its Impact on the Youth of Poor Kampongs in the City of Jakarta", in: *Prisma. Indonesian Journal of Social and Economic Affairs.*Vol. 1, No. 1/1975.

Lecher, Wolfgang and Welsch, Johann: *Japan - Mythos und Wirklichkeit,* Cologne: Bund Verlag 1983.

Mansell, Robin E.: *Industrial Strategies and the Communication/Information Sector*, Burnaby, British Columbia: Simon Fraser University. Ph.D Thesis at the Department of Communication 1984 (mimeo).

Schuldenkrise und Dritte Welt. Stimmen aus der Peripherie, ed. by Dieter Boris et al., Cologne: Pahl-Rugenstein 1987.

Siemens AG: *Büro 1990*, Munich: Siemens 1977 (mimeo).

17

Euro-American Conflicts in the Sphere of Transborder Data Flow (TDF)

In 1978 and 1980, two extremely important analyses of the sector of international information policy appeared quite independently of each other. The earlier of the two came out in France, was several volumes long and prepared by a special presidential commission under the title "L'informatisation de la Société" by Simon Nora and Alain Minc; the 1980 report was presented by the UNESCO's MacBride Commission, as it was known, was entitled "Many Voices, One World". The two reports are the result of very differing historical, national and international approaches and motivation.

The Nora-Minc Report deals primarily with scientific and technical information from the media high-tech segment, and discusses how "telecommunications" and "ICT" dovetail - under the heading of "telematics". It refers to possible decentralized applications for telematics in a strongly centralized society as well as the impact this could have on the French computer industry. The Nora-Minc Report sees French sovereignty threatened by US dominance of the computer market (hardware and software). In order to minimize job losses and be in a position to create and expand an independent service society, the report recommends the development of a national French computer industry and collective European efforts.

French government policy has since accorded a high political, economic and financial priority to telematics: at present, annual expenditure is approx. US$ 700 million annually on fostering ICT, US$ 360 million on supporting the major French computer manufacturers, and US$ 235 million on the components industry. French government policy and the Nora-Minc Report represent the logical continuation of what Jean-Jacques Servan Schreiber had already written and called for in 1967 in his book "Le défi americain":

> [The European governments cannot afford] to leave the Americans holding the field in the world of computers. [...] A consequent European policy must consist of uniting all available forces [...] in a joint action by means of immediate support of the German, French and Dutch industry [...]. Only a market on such a scale would enable a computer industry to start to compete with the US companies by 1980. [...] No industrial sector will ever be able to be independent if we do not begin with computers. If there is a struggle for the future, it will be fought in the field of data processing.[1]

Contrary to the Nora-Minc Report, the McBride Report is chiefly concerned with the situation of the mass media in terms of the North-South conflict. The statements and recommendations included in this report on the subject of media high-tech and ICT are only of insubstantial nature. (These aspects were taken into consideration at a relatively late stage during the work of the Commission.) The McBride Report concentrates on the dependence of the Third World on the mass media of the industrial countries. It calls for radical rethinking as it lays greater emphasis on the social factors of communication than on purely technological considerations. It recommends the development of communication infrastructures in the Third World countries, as well as their regional and horizontal cooperation; the aim: to reduce their dependence on the industrial countries.

The isolated liberal perspective that hinges solely on the concept of freedom of the press without integrating this in a structural analysis of political dependencies is abandoned in the McBride Report in favor of a notion of comprehensive international democratization in the field of media policy. The main demands made of democratic insights of this kind are that the prevailing concentration be brought to an end, versatility and reciprocity be ensured in information flow, and the active involvement of those affected. In the McBride Report, only the realization of these demands will establish the necessary pre-requisite for the free flow of information.[2] In the context of the North-South conflict, the McBride Report includes, among other things, the following comments:

> Data at hand demonstrate that the industrial countries dominate more than 95 percent of the computer industry. Inequality in this sector will tend to increase given that every new step towards ever more advanced technology consolidates the advantages of a very small number of countries.[...] To be really free, the flow of information must be two-sided, it should not move in one direction only. [...] A situation of dependence still exists in many parts of the world. [...] This flow of information is neither free nor balanced. This substantiated criticism is the basis for the current endeavor to achieve a new world communication order.[3]

The McBride Report is the result of almost a decade's debate on the decolonialization of the media in the Third World. Individual Third World countries, the non-aligned movement, critical social scientists in Western industrial countries, the UNESCO, the UN's COPUOS and the ITU have played the key roles in this debate. The conflicts addressed by Servan Schreiber and in the Nora-Minc Report are aptly summarized in the article by J.M. Eager, Director of the Office of Telecommunications Policy, published in the *Washington Post* on January 15, 1978 and entitled "The Coming Information War". Here, the central players are the French government, engineering experts and lawyers, the OECD, the European Council, and the Commission of the European Community.

These two debates have hitherto been conducted primarily parallel to each other, without any analytical linkage of the two, and without the experts involved in the one or other sphere of the conflict adapting a broader, more comprehensive perspective. If an attempt is made to relate the two debates, it becomes apparent that the most varied patterns of argument and strategies correspond to something of an international role game between the Third World, the United States and Europe. In other words, the US/European conflict on questions of transborder data flow (TDF) repeats the conflict over mass media between the Third World and the industrial nations; only this time Europe plays the part of the Third World.

According to the definition drawn up by the Intergovernmental Bureau of Informatics, TDF means the "movement across national borders of data and information for processing and storage in computer systems". TDF occurs primarily in three sectors: broadcasting across borders, earth resource satellites, and computer-to-computer communications. It is the latter sector which is of particular importance in the US/European conflict. If we consider hardware and software separately as regards computer-to-computer communications, then the US/European situation on the hardware sector can be seen as follows. In the course of the 1970s, it was the export of computers and related equipment which contributed in particular to growth in the US foreign trade balance. At US$ 3.4 billion, computer exports by the United States in 1978 had tripled over the level of 1970. In 1979, 50 percent of these exports or a total of US$ 4.1 billion were destined for the European community alone, of which 72 percent concentrated on Great Britain, France and West Germany.

By contrast, the United States imports computers primarily from Canada, France and Japan, whereby the total comes to only US$ 700 million. In terms of a single country in Europe, Austria's dependence on foreign computer technology, for example, means that IBM dominates the Austrian market, where it accounts for 66 percent of the total, followed at a great distance by Univac with 9 percent, Honeywell Bull with 8 percent, and Siemens Data with 5 percent. The world market leader IBM dominates the overall European market with 55 percent, with a stake of 61 percent in West Germany, 55 percent in France 40 percent, in Great Britain and 36 percent in Japan.

West Europe is most definitely a computer growth market. If the increase registered on this market is measured in terms of online interactive searches per annum, the following growth rates are determined for the bibliographic databases in West Europe: 1972 +400 percent on a y-o-y basis, 1973 +50 percent, 1974 +200 percent, 1975 +40 percent, 1976 +155 percent 1977 +66 percent. Since the West European computer market is still young in comparison to that in the United States, the growth rates for alpha-numerical on-line interactive searches is not quite as strong: 1972 +35 percent on a y-o-y basis; 1973 +135 percent, 1974 +90 percent 1975 +63 percent, 1976 +35 percent. If the growth of the computer market in Western Europe is measured in terms of the number of terminals, the figure was 625,000 for 1979, as against estimates of 1,720,000 for 1983 and 3,960,000 for 1987.

As regards the time-lag between the two growth curves, comparisons between the computer market in the USA and West Europe arrive at differing forecasts as the size of the time differential and even as to whether the two developments curves run in opposite directions. But they say nothing as to the penetration of West European hosts by US databases. The USA continues to be the major world provider of databases, particularly in terms of volume. There are said to be over 55 million records (citations) in on-line bibliographic databases, over 80 percent of them provided by US-originated databases. Therefor, the meager data available on TDF covers only the tip of an iceberg, since it does not allow for the computer-to-computer-communications within a country and is based exclusively on US data.

Although no public figures are available on the software sector, that is to say for the intensity and quality of TDF between the United States and West Europe, it can and must be assumed that the predominant volume of data flows from the United States to Europe. We must also assume that the lion's share of this data flow involves an exchange of information between the headquarters of multinational corporations and their subsidiaries, and also that scarcely any personal data is transferred, but consists primarily of scientific and technical data, of private business networks than those of state or public authorities.

In summary, the US/European TDF can must be described as unbalanced, one-sided and non-reciprocal. The main actors are US multinationals, to whom, as in the debate over a new International Information Order (NIIO), we should relate the entire structure of the US military-industrial-communications complex in the United States. In the course of debates concerning a NIIO, the Third World had accused the industrial countries in general of information and media imperialism. This has met with a joint defensive front on the part of the United States and Europe. The industrial countries rejected the demand for decolonialization of the mass media in the Third World as raised by the Non-Aligned Movement conference in Algiers in 1973, for example. They have accused the latter demand of introducing political and ideological elements, as a communist conspiracy. In the TDF debate in relation to the United States, the language being used by the Third World is now being heard by the European side of the argument, with similar analytical considerations being raised in this sphere. A few examples here stand for many:

Simone Veil, President of the European Parliament:

> This phenomenon conceals obvious risks of a new imperialism [...]. We must together monitor what dangers may be presented by a society in which a system of communication of information, both sophisticated and highly standardized, becomes its vital axis.[4]

Hermann Kronz, Member of the European Commission in Luxembourg

> The flow of publicly available data between the United States and Europe at present runs only from West to East. It is absolutely essential that this one-way traffic soon develops into a two-way movement.[5]

A study prepared for the Austrian Federal Ministry for Science and Research comments on IBM's market policy in Austria:

> Thanks to the excessive sales prices charged in Austria, the initial investments of the parent company are already completely amortized within the 3rd or 4th year. This means, however, that in the form of excessive list prices Austria pays the sort of colonial surcharge [sic] otherwise only seriously expected of developing countries.[6]

Peter Canisius, West German Documentation Center:

> [We must first concentrate our forces], in order to be better able to meet an [...] international challenge from the other side of the Pond.[7]

The language used by the Europeans against the United States is somewhat more cautious than that of the Third World against the industrial countries. It is also inconsistent in its theoretical deductions and does not prevail in all West European countries, being heard more intensely in France and Scandinavia (for different reasons) than for example in West Germany. None the less, the reproaches being made by Europe against the United States are not limited generally accusing the United States of imperialism but also appeal to the principle of non-intervention in internal affairs and to the concept of sovereignty which plays a central role into argumentation in the Non-Aligned Movement case against the industrial countries. Here again a few quotations can serve as representative:

Louis Joint, Secretary-General of the French Commission for Data Processing and Liberties:

> Information has an economic value, and the ability to store and process certain types of data may well give one country a political and technological advantage over other countries. This, in turn, may lead to a loss of national sovereignty through supranational data flows.[8]

The study of "The Vulnerability of a Computerized society" prepared by the Swedish Defense Ministry includes the statement:

> Since Sweden depends on international data transmission circuits that pass through several countries, we are also dependent on the political situation in other countries. [...] The growing international data flow involves problems of security and vulnerability on a scale quite unlike those that existed under purely national conditions.[9]

The reference made to the concept of sovereignty is of special interest in light of the fact that prevailing doctrine in the West on international law (unlike the line taken on the same subject by proletarian internationalism or by the Non-Aligned Movement) has always subordinated this to individual human and civil rights, as was again made very clear in the UNESCO debate of the media declaration of 1978. The examples presented here in the form of the two concepts "information imperialism" and "national sovereignty" could easily be supplemented by aspects from all other conflict areas within the North-South debate and equally well applied to the "information war" between Europe and the United States, in particular, in relation to the following problems: rights of access, technology transfer, economic dependence, cultural domination, economic protection and "free" flow of information.

These European positions adopted against the United States can certainly be dismissed to a certain extent as verbal radicalism that has not been followed by deeds. As justifiable as this objection may be in part, it nonetheless overlooks that the language reflects a specific political culture in West Europe, one that traditionally taboos criticism of the United States, stigmatizes this as communist reaction, and generally represses any such inclination. This criticism of US dominance in the field of TDF has hitherto reflected a mistrust which can best be described as primarily populist in nature, scarcely systematic, and decidedly heterogeneous.

It feeds, on the one hand, on a nationalistic narrow-minded, conservative anti-Americanism, or a pessimistic cultural rejection of advancing technology as well as on general cultural ennui; on the other, it also draws on a social democratic/socialist critique of the growing power of multinational corporations and on the position of the smaller more neutral countries in Europe, such as Sweden and Austria. A serious threat to US dominance can only be expected to arise, however, if these still heterogeneous positions in West Europe and the power groups behind them join forces. This could happen if, as in Canada, TDF in West Europe had a far more unfavorable impact on the foreign trade balance, with an increasing loss of jobs being felt in Europe.

We can draw parallels to the attitude of the Third World towards the industrial countries in the mass media debate not only in the verbal reaction of Europe towards the United States but also in terms of the political action. Since it was always the strategic intention of the Non-Aligned Movement and the Third World in relation to the industrial countries to sanction their position on the mass media at the level of international law (something always attacked by the industrial countries as state intervention against the freedom of the press), they deliberately brought these debates before the forum of the UNESCO. The Third World had a yet greater interest in bringing its demands before the World Administrative Radio Conference held by the International Telecommunication Union (ITU) since ITU resolutions are of an immediately binding legal character.

By contrast, the industrial countries have regarded all UNESCO resolutions as nothing more than legally non-binding recommendations as if there were by no means such a thing as international common law or have tried (like the USA) to shift the mass media debate into less political UN institutions such as, the UNDP. The strategic approaches taken by the main parties involved in the "information war" between the United States and Europe has been very similar. In their national legislation on the data protection of natural persons (and in certain Scandinavian countries of legal entities, too), as well as in supranational legislation (for example, in the regulation of data protection of natural persons) the Council of Europe, the Europeans, with France at the forefront, have chosen the path of legal codification. In response, the USA are attempting to shift the debates out of the European Council (where it only has observer status) to the OECD, which is qualified to make recommendations only and is far more technologically oriented and less political than the European Council.

The development of independent national mass media systems in the Third World as reflected in the numerous government-sponsored national development plans for the mass media, corresponds to the expansion planned centrally in West Europe with massive government support, initiated and implemented on behalf of independent, national data networks for scientific and technical information and documentation. Thus, for example, the West German Information and Documentation Program of 1974 can clearly be attributed to national economic considerations and was motivated by the fear of foreign competition: "The inadequate utilization of existing information resources endangers national efficiency and the ability to compete, thus impeding scientific, economic and social progress." The Vith Research Report published by the West German Federal Government makes it apparent that state R&D costs on the information and documentation sector more than doubled from DM 49 million in 1975 to DM 102 million in 1980.

In the course of the mass media debate, individual countries in the Third World have developed a protectionist policy in relation to the industrial countries, endeavoring to shield their national sovereignty and cultural identity from outside influence. This has taken the shape of restrictions on entry permits for Western journalists, for example, on the complete ban on the imports of US entertainment films in post-revolutionary Iran or the legally backed shift of US soap operas on Haitian TV from prime-time to the late evening with low viewing rates. As demonstrated by a review published by the Office of the US Special Trade Representative for 1980, Japan and the European Community most certainly implement a protectionist policy in relation to the United States in the sector of standardization and fee policy for data processing and data services, although the European governments are eager to deny this fact.

As the most promising form of strategy against mass media penetration by the industrial countries, the Third World has chosen the path of regional and horizontal cooperation. Mention is made briefly here of the Press Agencies Pool of the Non-Aligned Movement, the OAU news agency, or the Latin American Working Council for National Information Systems (ASIN). These horizontal cooperations correspond in the US/European "information war" to the development of the European data network EURONET DIANE implemented 1979 and mainly financed by public funds from the EC member states. EURONET DIANE is intended not only to reduce the reliance of European users on US suppliers of information; with its public subsidies and thus cheaper access fees for European users, it also objectively represents opposition to the purely commercially run and expensive access fees charged by the US databases. Since US hosts are not permitted on EURONET DIANE, while US databases are, nonetheless, offered via EURONET DIANE, European users of EURONET may actually end up having cheaper access to US data than North American citizens. A mechanism of this kind could lead to considerable loss in revenue for Lockheed or Systems Development Corp. (SDC).

To summarize the position held by West Europe in international information policy, it is caught between the dominance of the United States and the ongoing confinement of the Third World to a dependent status; Graph 17.1 clearly demonstrates this seesaw position Europe has been forced to adopt. Since the dyad US/West Europe is structurally similar to the dyad West Europe/Third World, the overall triad US/West Europe/Third World will only remain stable in the interests of the overlapping multinationals for as long as West Europe maintains its balancing act. Departure from the narrow framework of international information policy and relation of this triad to more far-reaching political considerations would appear to suggest the following plausible assessment. The period following 1945 can be characterized less by a global loss of power for the US than by the growth of Western European power.

Graph 17.1:
The Nature of Transborder Data Flow

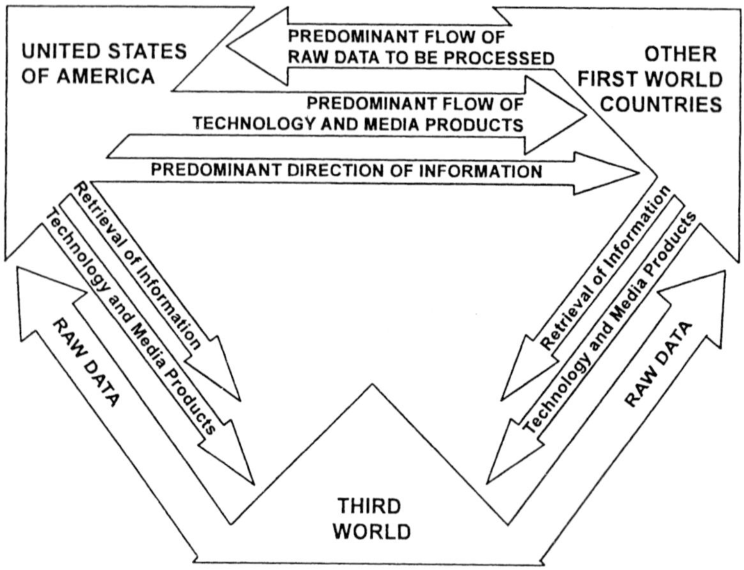

Source: Rein Turn (Chairman): Transborder Data Flows. Concerns in Privacy Protection and Free Flow of Information. Report of the AFIPS Panel on Transborder Data Flow. Vol. I, Washington: American Federation of Information Processing Societies 1979, p. 5.

Two peculiarities with reference to West Europe will work in the long term to loosen the symbiotic relationship within the North Atlantic Treaty System.

On the one hand, it is in West Europe's interests to at least minimize the nuclear armaments race, since an atomic war would have far more devastating effects for West Europe than for the USA. The present hesitation shown by West European politicians in implementing the NATO dual-track resolution, the refusal by certain NATO countries to permit neutron bombs to be stationed on their territory and increasing West European trade with East Europe despite the Afghanistan crisis could all be seen as indicators signaling independent West European interests in the sphere of security policy. Secondly, West Europe has been aware, at the latest since the Yom Kippur war, that it depends on the Mideast for oil. Since West Europe's dependence on outside oil is greater than that of the United States and since it relates to its relationship to the Third World, West Europe's interests in the energy sector are objectively different from those of the United States.

Whether West European policy in relation to the United States on the question of TDF (rejection of a dependency position, sovereign claims, agreements under international law as to the quantity and quality of TDF, development of national data networks, protectionism and regional cooperation within Western Europe) should turn out to be qualitatively new and part of a longterm process of gradually disengagement with the USA will depend to a large degree, on the one hand, on international trends in the security and energy sectors as outlined above. Secondly, the dyad US/West Europe will be very much affected by Europe's relationship with the Third World, in which differing positions from those of the United States are to be determined not only in the energy sector and on the El Salvador question. It is precisely in the services industry (and TDF is part of it) that a bitter struggle is already underway between the United States and West Europe for the markets of the Third World.

However, national control of TDF may emerge in the triad US/West Europe/Third World. It can already unequivocally be determined that competition between the transnational electronic oligopolies has already led to fiercer concentration both in the United States and in Europe. On the one hand, Siemens purchased a block of shares in Advanced Micro Devices Corp., reached an agreement on technology exchange with Intel Corp., acquired the companies Litronic and Microwave Semiconductor Corp., and bought shares in American Microsystems and Amdahl Corp. On the other, this European breakthrough into the US market prompted wide-scale stock purchases and support for the US semi-conductor producers by such powerful corporations as Exxon, Standard Oil and Honeywell. Against this background, the respective national control of TDF either by the USA or West Europe must be qualified considerably, since transnational ownership situation by the respective multinational corporations means that these have access to both US and West European data-base systems. This can be quite clearly illustrated by the following example:

The US Bibliographic Retrieval Service database, which, together with Lockheed and Systems Development Corporation (SDC) is to be connected to the three largest databases in the world, was recently bought up by Indian Head, Inc. Indian Head belongs to the German-Dutch industrial conglomerate Thyssen-Bornemisza which also acquired the US Predicasts corporation, which in turn holds a stake in Swiss host service

Datastar. The Thyssen-Bornemisza Group also owns the Information Handling Service in Denver and Scibt Verlag in West Germany. Access is planned to the data bases offered from the Thyssen-Bornemisza group via EURONET. As long as national governments do nothing to alter the flexibility, the trend toward concentration, and the cartel-like agreements made between multinational corporations clear limits will continue to be set to all forms of state policy aimed at the maintenance and expansion of an autonomous national economic, and that includes the case of TDF.

Notes and References

1. Servan Schreiber, Jean-Jacques: *Die amerikanische Herausforderung*, Hamburg: Hoffmann & Campe 1968, p. 173.
2. For a critical analysis of the McBride Report see *Communication in the Eighties*. A Reader of the McBride Report, ed. by Cees Hamelink, Rome: IDOC 1980.
3. *Many Voices, One World.* Communication and Society, Today and Tomorrow. Report of the International Commission for the Study of Communication Problems, Paris: UNESCO 1980, p.129.
4. Quoted from *Transnational Data Report*. Vol. III, No. 7/1980, p.12 [my emphasis, J.B.].
5. Kronz, Hermann: "Informationstechnologie im Europäischen Raum", in: *Gefährdet die Informationstechnologie unsere Freiheit?* Jahrestagung 1979 der Deutschen Vereinigung für Datenschutz, ed. by Thomas Bartel, Munich: Oldenbourg 1980, p. 30 [my emphasis, J.B.].
6. Schmolke, Michael and Signitzer, Benno: *Österreich im internationalen Mediensystem*. Beziehungen und Abhängigkeiten. Report for the Federal Ministry for Science and Research. First version, Salzburg 1980 (mimeo), p. 287 [my emphasis, J.B.].
7. Quoted from Kirchner, Walter: *DIMDI, Euronet and Infoline*. Radio RIAS Berlin manuscript of March 5, 1981, p. 15 [my emphasis, J.B.].
8. Quoted from Zycherman, Josef: "Data Protection Laws Must Not Become Non-Tariff Barriers", in: *Transnational Data Report*. Vol. II, No. 8/1980, p. 17 [my emphasis, J.B.].
9. Quoted from *Transnational Data Report*. Vol. I, No. 5/1978, p. 17 [my emphasis, J.B.].

18

Scientific Communication Between East and West

In many ways the term "East-West Communication" is ambiguous not to say confusing. Communicators in America might immediately think of the the East-West Centre in Honolulu, Hawaii, and the work of Daniel Learner may immediately spring to mind. This angle represents the strong pacific aspect of US foreign policy, still greatly underestimated in West Europe. "East meets West" - this has indeed become the key word used by the New Age Movement which (along with superficial borrowings from Rudyard Kipling, Hermann Hesse or Zen Buddhism), is busy searching for the "total redemption of the soul" in order not to have to deal with the collective loss of identity suffered under capitalism. Things do not get any easier if we approach the term "East-West communications" from the European perspective. Within Europe, the opposition characterized by the wording East-West functions at different levels.

First, we have to do with two different, antagonistic political and economic systems. Yet this systemic difference must be seen in light of the question of who holds sway over the means of production. In the capitalist countries these lie in the hands of private industry. In the communist countries, they are state organised. The current process of Perestroika in the communist economies does not mean that these countries are now favoring the principle of private economic control of the means of production; instead, it aims to substitute social responsibility for the principle of state organization. The process of non-state intervention and of de-bureaucratization is not a turn to capitalism, but more a return to the roots of the long since submerged communist traditions of the 1920s.

Second, the systemic difference in Europe becomes somewhat blurred if an historical or cultural argument is taken. What Europe as a whole represents cannot be adequately understood if grasped solely in terms of the political history of just the last 40 years. Such a perspective divides West Europe into four cultural regions: the Mediterranean region, the Northern countries, West Europe in the narrower sense, and Central Europe. Even communist Eastern Europe would then fall into two parts: East Europe and East Central Europe.

Third, at the level of international law Europe as a whole practically does not exist. In total, there are 12 European states with a capitalist economic order. The Council of Europe (CoE) is made up of 23 member states - and the number includes the Republic of San Marino, which recently joined. Moreover, the 35 member states of the Conference on Security and Cooperation in Europe (CSCE) include all the European countries, except Albania, plus Canada and the USA. Alongside the European countries, the Council for Mutual Economic Assistance (CMEA) includes the USSR, Poland, the German Democratic Republic, the CSSR, Hungary, Bulgaria and Romania, not to mention Cuba, Vietnam and Mongolia; yet neither factually nor legally has it attained the same level of cooperation between its member states. At the governmental level, the UN's Economic Commission for Europe (ECE) in Geneva is the only pan-European institution of any political relevance in which all European countries are represented. Its mandate, outlined in its Art. 1, is to "strengthen the economic relations of the European countries both among themselves and with other countries of the world": this would seem to secure it an active role in the face of the increasing economic significance of international communications. However, to date the ECE has not been particularly active in this field.

The current thrust of change in Europe is determined in part by the politically motivated reform policy in the communist countries and in part by the radicalization of the capitalist economics in connection with the enactment of the Single European Market in 1992. Even before it became a fact, the pressure exerted by the single European market was already affecting the countries that are not members of it. Thus, on June 25, 1988, the European Free Trade Association (Norway, Sweden, Finland, Austria and Switzerland) was in a process of disintegration, and in Hungary and the Yugoslavian Republic of Slovenia voices are to be heard calling for accession to the EU. Just how much the very different conceptions of Europe affect the future communications and information policy in the single European market was to be seen recently in the highly controversial debate on the notion of Europe in the Broadcasting Directive of the Council of Ministers of the European Commission of April 13, 1989. Against the votes of Belgium, Denmark and West Germany, the directive provides that in the future TV programmers in the EU must fill the "main portion of this broadcasting time" with films produced in Europe. Yet what "European" is meant here is as unclear as the term "national TV program", which is used in a prominent position in the green paper on setting up a common market for broadcasting, the paper which led up to the directive.

Whereas the green paper understands "national TV program" to mean both "private national" and "private international" programming (without, however, explaining the significant difference), in the directive "European" means a lot more than that. Under pressure from West Germany, the directive was made to apply firstly to all the members of the Council of Europe and secondly to the German Democratic Republic, due to the fact that in 1957 under the terms of the Treaty of Rome, West Germany had already ensured that no customs barriers would have to exist between the two German states. In other words, this broadcasting directive is directed against both the socialist states of Eastern Europe, and against the United States. This protective mechanism against the US TV and film industry is understandable if one considers that low cost, recycled US programming dominates West European screens. Currently, more that 70 percent of all non-documentary shows, films, serials and soaps are imported - and more than 50 percent of them originate in the USA. In 1988, the imports came with a price tag of some US$ 800 million.

In the debates surrounding the Broadcasting Directive, France tried in vain to have the phrase "main portion of their broadcasting time" replaced by a strict quota specifying "60 percent European productions". While at this point in time all the cultural and media associations in France are reproaching their government for having betrayed France's cultural interests in agreeing to this directive, the French Government is preparing the EUREKA TV project at the European level, a project which should result in a large subsidy program for Europe's audio-visual industry, similar to the general high-tech EUREKA project running in the European Community. France has also provided for the participation of some of the socialist countries of Eastern Europe in this EUREKA TV project.

In other words, "East-West communications" is a highly complex term. Yet for all its confusing aspects it still usefully mirrors the process of economic fermentation within the EU and of Perestroika within Eastern Europe. No discussion of the quantity and quality of scientific communication between East and West, and it is on this that I wish to concentrate here, can forego a brief discussion of the role of TV exchange between East and West as undertaken here. On a broad based and more far-reaching level than in the United States, the European Union (and here, in particular, West Germany) has developed plans for the implementation of ISDN in the late 1990s. By that time at the latest there will be a joint technical network for mass media transmission and scientific communication. And only then will it be meaningful to provide separate analyses of mass-media and scientific communication respectively.

1. Personal Communication Between Scientists in East and West

It is in keeping with the general technocratic and popular scientific understanding of the essence of the so-called information society that all too quickly information is equated with communication, communication with knowledge, and databases with knowledge storage. It is true that databases for technological-scientific information play an increasingly important role in scientific work, but above all technological communications are models of personal communication and run parallel to the latter. User interviews among scientists repeatedly demonstrate that the most important information source for the scholars' work is personal discussion with colleagues, and that research using databases often rates only 10th or 15th position on the information media scale; these results evidently also apply to the contact between scientists from European and CMEA countries.

Especially in the domain of scientific cooperation, which is made difficult by the systemic conflict, informal and so-called invisble colleagues manifestly play a very significant role. Contacts of this kind exist among scientists, engineers, medical scholars and especially among older scientists; and no doubt will continue to be. What unites scientists, engineers and doctors across systemic divides is the (inappropriate) notion that their work is apolitical. Older colleagues who know Europe from days before the Cold War are often united by the same or similar form of social recruitment as scientists. Scientists of this kind from the German Democratic Republic, the CSSR and Hungary were not "cut off" from West European science after 1945 although West European scientists "cut off themselves" voluntarily from trends in the CMEA countries. Statistical and sociometric studies of inter-change among scientists between East and West show these to be much more intensive than is officially conceded.

There are many and varying historical reasons why contacts are not as intensive with scientists in the USSR. And one must be careful when interpreting the overview (Table 18.1) on the participation of Soviet scientists in international meetings in the last 1970s. It is clear from this table that the USSR organized very few congresses including international participants, that the number of foreign participants at conferences in the USA is five times greater than the USSR, and that the number of conference travelers from the USSR was 36 times smaller that for the USA, etc. Yet it would be methodologically inadequate to interpret this and similar tables as conclusive evidence of the general worldwide isolation of Soviet science, as is often unfortunately claimed to be the case.

For many years now, in West Germany interchange with scientists from the CMEA countries has been growing less difficult and has been on the increase, irrespective of how tedious it may have been to achieve this goal. West German universities have signed cooperation contracts with about 100 universities in these countries. In quantitative terms, the following picture of academic exchange between West Germany and the CMEA countries emerges: numerically the most important partners are Poland and the USSR, followed by Hungary, the CSSR and Romania.

Table 18.1:
Participation in a Sample of International Scientific and Technological Meetings by Selected Countries in the Late 1970s

	USA	UK	West Germany	France	Japan	USSR
No. of international meetings in the country	137	67	48	47	27	5
No. of presentations by country's citizens at meetings in the country	4,026	988	436	517	538	113
No. of presentations by foreign citizens at meetings in the country	2,593	1,847	1,597	1,099	1,006	479
No. of presentations by country's citizens at foreign meetings	4,251	1,504	1,250	1,651	842	118

Source: A. Schubert, A.; Zsindely, S. and Braun, T: "Scientometric Analysis of Attendance at International Scientific Meetings", in: *Scientometrics,* No. 3/1983, p. 180.

In contrast to its population and the number of academic institutions, Bulgaria plays a relatively pronounced role. The East European participants are usually scientists and engineers, while those from West Germany tend to be scholars in the humanities.

All in all, the West is less interested in this type of academic exchange than the East; in fact, in West Germany, the available subsidies are not exhausted. This asymmetry is all the more unusual as there are approx. 400 million West Europeans as compared with 140 million East Europeans (including Yugoslavia but excluding the USSR). In the meantime, this same asymmetry applies to exchanges via general tourism between East and West Europe. In the 1970s, there was on average three West to every one East European tourist. This ratio has changed considerably. Due to the boom in exit visas from the GDR, Poland and Hungary, for the past two years, there has been a greater influx of East European tourists into the West than West European tourists going eastwards.

In summary, we can safely say that both the general mobility between East and West Europe and the specific mobility among scientists and engineers is much greater and more intensive than is usually assumed or acknowledged. It is this personal communication which provides the background for an adequate understanding of media communications, be it through the exchange of magazines and books or through databases.

2. Scientific-Technological Potential in the CMEA Countries

My critique of the common interpretation of Table 18.1 is intended to draw attention to a basic problem. Most Western scientists interpret the CMEA countries' scientific-technological system in terms of a deficit thesis, without being aware of the theoretical implications of such an approach. An example for this is the Report of the Committee for the Study of International Development in Computer Science and Technology to the National Academy of Sciences. In this report, there is constant reference to a gap between the USA and the USSR, to frustrated catchup strategies on the part of the CMEA countries, to the latter having fallen behind the world standard, etc.[1] Stating that such a deficit exists - often the case with regard to Third World countries, too - is problematic for four reasons.

First, by categorizing the CMEA countries as technologically "behind the times" one's own technological status seems secure. If we recollect the Sputnik shock of 1957 it is astonishing how quickly that event was collectively repressed in the USA, and just how little has been learned from such deficit-analyses. *Second*, deficit analyses cannot do justice to the often qualitatively totally different social organization forms in differnt countries, especially when they are made on the basis of country comparisons. How meaningful is the statement that the USA produces more mainframes than Norway? How significant is the fact that in France more PCs are used than in Romania? *Third*, deficit analyses are by their very nature technocratic. By creating a quantitative scale for the presence or absence of technological products, questions on the social conditions of the production of these goods and on social needs tend to get ignored. *Fourth*, deficit statements often blind commentators to the strengths held by the "deficit" side.

Allow me to mention in passing that the tracks of the Washington Underground were produced using a welding process based on a Soviet license and then move on to concentrate on some of the strengths of the scientific-technological system in the CMEA countries. I do this not just to turn the tables on the deficit theory or to ignore the weaknesses, but for the following reasons. *First*, references to the strengths of the CMEA countries can help to correct a false image. *Second*, by becoming aware of the strengths of the scientific-technological system in the CMEA countries we can create a platform for economic exchange which is in the interests of both parties. For if we are really interested in ongoing trade relations between East and West Europe that promote peace then this trade can only be meaningful for West Europe if it realizes that East Europe has more to offer than a market for cheap consumer goods, is more than just a supplier of raw materials for Western technology and know-how transfer.

The CMEA countries possess more than one third of the world's international knowledge potential and hold more than 20 percent of all patents for new technologies. In the CMEA countries there are 4,000 scientists to every one million inhabitants. In the West, the corresponding figure is only 1,800. The sanction and embargo policies imposed by the West on the CMEA countries since the beginning of the 1980s have boomeranged, mobilizing research and prompting great advances. In space research and technology, the USSR has a significant lead on the United States and in the fields of thermonuclear research, laser research or molecular genetics the USSR has attained a competitive edge. Similar statements can be made when comparing the USSR and the USA in the fields of biology, vacuum technology, ceramics, oceanography, high-pressure physics and ionosphere research. The relevant institute in Kiev has developed a processing electromagnetic casting system on which practically all aluminum foundries in the world depend. A number of Soviet institutes in the field of low temperatures and fusion research appear to be far more advanced than their US counterparts.[2]

Against this background, technology and knowledge transfer from east to West naturally exists, as illustrated in Tables 18.2 and 18.3, and not just from West to East as often assumed. To avoid misunderstandings, the following figures should be called to mind. In terms of total world trade, the percentage of East-West trade is only five percent (for the OECD states it is only four percent). For the CMEA countries East-West trade involves a significant 25 percent. The technology and knowledge transfer from East to West shown in Tables 18.2 and 18.3 is of only small economic volume; yet John W. Kiser, a US businessman specializing in patent and license imports from CMEA countries to the USA, speaks of "unexpected treasures" to be discovered in East Europe.[3] Thus, the important point in these tables is at the level of scientific quality and potential and not so much the economic relevance it has already had.

The great potential of Soviet science can be demonstrated with the aid of further examples. A short time ago, English researchers made an efficiency comparison between all major indexes, card files, computerized online files and the most important primary publications on the existing knowledge of the costs and economics of information transfer and means of mathematical modeling and optimizing these aspects of information processes. The results of this comparison are interesting for two reasons: 1. Printed media and bibliographies are much more efficient than online databases. 2. The Soviet magazine *Zhurnal Informatica* is more efficient than the corresponding DIALOG database in California. A final example[4] of the potential of Soviet science is chemical research and again refers to the medium of a database. At Chemical Abstracts Service (CAS) Columbus, Ohio, approx. 73 percent of the primary documents come from abroad, and with approx. 17 percent the USSR rates ahead of Japan, the FRG and the UK. To put it differently, after the USA, the USSR is the second most important supplier of primary documents to CAS.[5] In summary, it is safe to say that the scientific-technological potential of the CMEA countries, especially of the USSR, is generally underestimated. There are in fact 88 specific areas where the USSR is the world leader. Due to a long tradition in bibliography and documentation, the strength of many information centers in the CMEA countries is their ability to comprehensively and systematically process international specialist literature.

Table 18.2 :
Licenses Sold by CMEA Countries to Western Firms in the Early 1970s

CMEA Country	Description of the Technology	Western Licensee
Bulgaria	Automatic reeling and placing of spinning spools, electrolytic refining of copper	Carelli Indust. Tessili (I), Inspiration Consolidated Co. (US)
	Process for producing yogurt	Milifoma (FRG)
	Protection of graphite electrodes in steel production	British Steel Corp. (UK)
Czechoslovakia	Autom. textile-winding machines	Ensju (J)
	Production of electric ovens	Horn (FRG)
	Soft contact lenses	Bausch & Lomb (US)
	Skin protection varnish	Albus (Sp)
	Spindleless spinning machines	Nuova San Giorgio (I)
Hungary	Manufacture of equipment for condensing air	Mitsubishi Heavy Ind. (J)
	Manufacture of small rechargeable battery cells	William Old (UK)
	Method of water purification	Ebara Infilco (J)
	Rust-prevention process	Teccomex (Sp)
Poland	Manufacture of extract of the smokinghouse smoke	Hercules Powder (UK)
	Method of forging crankshafts	Sulzer (Swi)
USSR	Autom. loading of pulpwood	J.M. Voith (A)
	Casting of aluminum ingots	Kaiser Aluminum Chemical Corp. (US)
	Construction of blast furnaces	ANDCO (Can)
	Improved method of steelmaking	Ashmore, Benson, Pease & Co. (UK)
	Manufacture of a new type of metal-cutting machine	Demag (FRG)
	Manufacture of a pulsed waterflow gauge used in mining	Joy Manufacturing Co. (US)
	Manufacture of specialized mining machines	Sociedad Metallurgica Duro Felgurea (Sp)
	Production of double-walled plastic tubes by extrusion	Anger Plastik Verarbeitungsmaschinen Ges. (A)

Source: Wilczynski, J.: *Technology in Comecon.* Acceleration of Technological Progress through Economic Planning and the Market, London & Basingstoke 1974, p. 309.

Table 18.3.:
Licenses Sold by CMEA Countries to US Firms in the Early 1980s

	Technology	**Buyer**	**Seller**
Medical & Biomedical	Surgical stapling guns	U.S. Surgical 3M	USSR
	Soft contact lens	National Patent Development	CSSR
	Anticancer drugs	Bristol-Myers	USSR
	Cardiovascular drug	Squibb	GDR
	Psychotropic drug	American Home Products	USSR
	Method for producing calcium pantothenate	Diamond Shamrock	GDR
	Vitride chemical reducing agent	National Patent Development	CSSR
	Cardiovascular drug	DuPont	GDR
Energy	*In situ* coal gasification	Texas Utilises Services	USSR
	Heller-Forgo dry cooling	Babcock & Wilcox	Hungary
	Method for marking armored drilling hoses	Gates Rubber	Hungary
	OSO dewatering screen for coal	National Standard	Poland
Metallurgy	Electromagnetic casting of aluminum	Kaiser Aluminum Chemical, Reaynolds Aluminum, Alcoa	USSR
	Roller dies	Harrisburg Steel	Hungary
	Electromagnetic casting of copper	Olin	USSR
	Method for titanium nitriding of tool steels	Multiarc Vacuum Systems	USSR
	Magnet. impact bonding	Maxwell Laboratories	USSR
	Flash butt welding	J.R. McDermatt	USSR
	Evaporative stave cooling of blast furnaces	Andco	USSR
Misc.	Flock hemmer *Hefti*	Joy Manufacturing	USSR
	Pneumatic trenching tool *Hole Hog*	Allied Steel & Tractor	USSR
	Hydrocyclone *Trinclean*	Bird Manufacturing	CSSR
	Sprayprinting of carpets	Deering Milliken	GDR
	Inertial core crusher for extra hard rocks	Rexnord USSR	USSR

Source: Kiser III, John W.: "Tapping Eastern Bloc Technology. U.S. companies may find unexpected treasures behind the Iron Curtain", in: *Harvard Business Review*, 3/4, 1982, p. 88.

3. Databases in the CMEA Countries

Akademset, the USSR Academy of Sciences' network linking its institutes via a packet switched network, was planned in the 1970s. This network is intended to link regional centers throughout the USSR, which in turn are to be linked to local area networks. In the meantime, there are important local networks in Leningrad and Novosibirsk. There are two special areas which are prepared most intensively in the USSR for use in online databases: bibliographic reference materials and economic/statistical applications. The most important databases are in the Institute of Scientific Information in the Social Sciences (INION) and in the All Union Institute of Scientific and Technical Information (VINITI). The Moscow All Union Scientific Research Institute of Automated Applications Systems (VNIIPAS) is responsible for the technical coordination for foreign contacts.

A system has been established within the CMEA countries for scientific and technical information. The first online connection between the USSR and a CMEA country opened in 1980 with the Center for Scientific and Technical Information (CINTI) in Bulgaria. The Bulgarian institute, the National Technical Information Center and Library (OMIKK) in Hungary and the Center for Scientific and Technical Information (UVTEI) in the CSSR are the most important partners of the USSR in the other CMEA countries. The databases in the CMEA countries differ from those in West Europe or the United States in many ways:

1. Transmission is rather slow, analog not digital. There are only a few interactive terminals and only a few specialists who can use the databases effectively. The common interpretation of these facts is based on a theory of "technical obsolescence" and all too quickly reaches general conclusions on the inability of the socialist system to be innovative. This strikes me as a far too hasty interpretation. Social systems which do not know the pressure of permanent capitalist competitiveness and are less involved in the world economy can in fact afford to be slower in their technical development than, for example, West European countries. Slowness need not necessarily be equated with an inability to be innovative.

2. Normally access to databases in the CMEA countries is restricted to members of institutions (economic, scientific and research). The common conclusion drawn from this fact is that access to databases is generally restricted. Here, too, general statements about the system

are made too hastily. Such restrictions would correspond to a social system where the whole information policy is censored by state and party. Accordingly, reference is then made to the positive situation in the West where access to databases is public and free. This argument overlooks that the increasing commercialization of databases in the West in no way places them in the public domain, but rather restricts access to a selective group of only those users who are considered lucrative by an information market. Needless to say, any discussions on the term "public access" need to be more differentiated, as the wish to exercise social responsibility in information policy is not necessarily something that can only be achieved by state control. The model of public broadcasting in England or in West Germany represents another good example of a way to achieve social responsibility in information policy. This model corresponds neither to state and party censorship, nor to the private information market.

Given that there are such decisive differences between information policies in the East and in the West, and given that databases in the different economies play such different roles, it is interesting to observe whether cooperation between databases in East and West is taking place and just how this is achieved.

4. Database Activities Between East and West

There are not only database links between the CMEA countries, but also database communications between East and West European countries. This in itself deserves mention and indeed emphasis, as widespread general assumptions are that "this" is impossible and probably even prohibited.

According to my research work the first database links were established in 1981. Given the internal division of labor in the socialist countries, the state databases in Bulgaria and the USSR are the most important actors as regards database links with the West. In neutral Austria, it is Radio Austria AG which plays the central role as an interface for the data traffic between East and West and in this respect Austria maintains its unbroken historical tradition, for it was also the interfacing country for all telegraph traffic between Czarist Russia and West Europe. While the annual business reports of Radio Austria AG refer with pride to this

Table 18.4:
Database Utilization by Czechoslovak Users 1981 - 1987

Database Centre	Number of databases	Available from	Number of sessions	Total duration of sessions (h)
MCVTI	6	1982	141	116
INION	3	1983	2299	915
VINITI	46	1983	493	271
CINTI	11	1985	85	36
IAEA	3	1981	2054	3060
DATASTAR	80	1981	9983	1218
FIZ-INKA	49	1983	1973	369
QUESTEL	52	1982	357	65
CISI-WHARTON	36	1983	134	34
SDC	54	1983	1005	149
INFOLINE	40	1983	515	95
DIALOG	252	1986	3170	333
MIC-KIBIC	8	1986	106	17

Source: Puzman, Josef: "The Cross-border STI Flows Supported by Telecommunication Services", in: *Europe speaks to Europe.* International information flows between Eastern and Western Europe, with a preface by Willy Brandt, ed. by Jörg Becker and Tamas Szecskö, Oxford: Pergamon Press 1989, p. 248

mediating role in transmitting data traffic between East and West, the Finnish authorities are very careful about information on the role of their computer node. The direction of database communications between East and West European is one-way. Almost exclusively the information flows involve database researches by Eastern clients in Western databases. Only in the International Institute for Applied Systems Analysis in Laxenburg, Austria, and in the Technical Research Center in Espoo, Finland, does two-way information flow function on the basis of pilot projects which enable scientists from Finland and/or Austria to do research in Soviet or other East European databases. The opening of Soviet databases up to foreign users, as announced by the Moscow Institute for Automated Systems in 1983, must be seen with some skepticism, however.

As far as I can see, in this connection the term "foreign" refers only to CMEA countries and not to Western countries. Tables 18.4 and 18.5 provide an overview of database links between the CSSR and foreign countries, and/or between West Germany and East Europe. They also enable us to make further statements on the most important actors in

Table 18.5:
West German Databanks with Online Clients in East Europe 1984

Name	Countries
CISI-Wharton, Frankfurt	Czechoslovakia, USSR
Data-Star, Bern	Czechoslovakia, Hungary, USSR
DIMIDI, Cologne	Hungary, Yugoslavia
FIZ Energie, Physik und Mathematik, Karlsruhhe	Bulgaria, Czechoslovakia, Hungary, USSR
FIZ Technik, Frankfurt	Czechoslovakia, Hungary, USSR, Yugoslavia
FIZ Werkstoffe, West-Berlin	Eastern Europe
IZ Raum und Bau, Stuttgart	Bulgaria, Czechoslovakia
I.P. Sharp, Frankfurt	Hungary, USSR
UBA, West-Berlin	Czechoslovakia, Hungary, USSR
ZADI, Ratingen	Hungary

Source: Becker, Jörg: *Datenbanken im Ost-West Konflikt*, Schmitten: Protestant Academy of Arnoldshain 1985, p. 85.

such transactions with information as a commodity and their respective interests. In general, these interests hinge on scientific-technical information from the fields of medicine, chemistry, technology, physics, etc., but also from the fields of economics and specialist data, in particular such as is necessary for a strongly-based estimation of foreign trade interests. Based on the number of research hours, the multilateral database of the International Atomic Energy Organization (IAEO) in Vienna, Austria, takes first place in the USSR, followed by the DATA STAR host in Switzerland and databases with general technological data such as INKA in Karlsruhe, West Germany, or DIALOG in California, USA. The Hungarian clients of the database PERGAMON INFOLINE in England - to mention just one more example - are basically interested in information on petroleum; PERGAMON INFOLINE supplies the USSR with the latest research data from the field of metallurgy.

The volume of such database activity between East and West Europe is not particularly large. I would estimate it at approximately one percent of the total turnover of any one individual Western database. In the case of some databases the portion of sales generated with East European clients can, however, be significantly higher. This applies, for example, to the Radio Austria AG and DATA STAR, which benefit essentially from

Graph 18.1:
Pergamon Infoline Password Holders in Eastern Europe 1983 - 1988

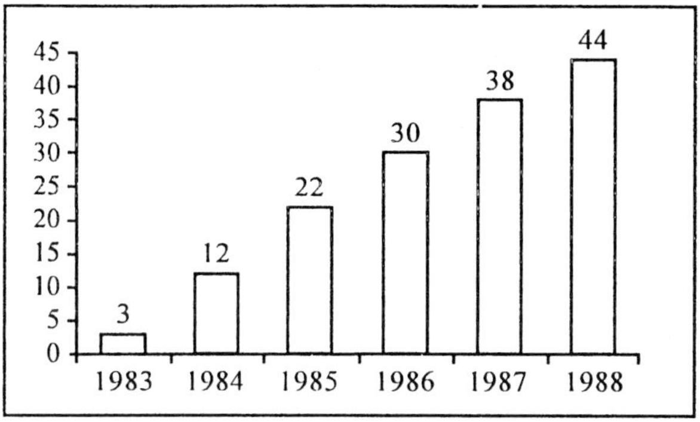

Source: Spender, David: "Eastern Europe and the United Kingdom: Forging online links", in: *Europe speaks to Europe*. International information flows between Eastern and Western Europe, with a preface by Willy Brandt, ed. by Jörg Becker and Tamas Szecskö, Oxford: Pergamon Press 1989, p. 299

interfacing transactions, or CISI-WHARTON, recently taken over by Reuters, which concentrates on economic time series and has been running its own computer node in Moscow for some time now. According to information available to me there have never been any invoicing difficulties for Western databases with their East European clients. On the contrary, although they contribute only little to general turnover, East European clients are highly reputed for their willingness to settle their accounts. The growth rate for East European clients is often considerably high, as seen in the PERGAMON INFOLINE example in Graph 18.1; however, this can vary quite substantially from one database to the next.

5. Conflicts and Problems

Primarily for economic reasons and only secondarily for cultural reasons, the quantity and quality of database cooperation between East and West Europe must be judged differently to that between, for example, the United States and East Europe. This applies in particular to West Germany. As far as high-tech transfer to the CMEA countries is concerned, the largest supplier was and still is West Germany, accounting for a share of 33 percent of total exports of all OECD states. It is followed interestingly enough by Japan with 11 percent, and then France and Italy with ten and eight percent respectively. In comparison the CMEA countries have never been of any such relevance for US exports.

In West Europe, total database use accounts for a mere two percent of all communications and represents the smallest share of data transmission's multifaceted potential. Yet these database retrieval service represent nearly 40 percent of all international data transmissions. The economic and political significance of online data services cannot be determined solely by quantitative calculations. It must also be measured in relation to qualitative importance; databases in the international information flow are increasingly becomingly factors in accessing, upgrading and marketing information, a "resource" for economic development. The impossibility in quantifying the extent of West-East data flow from West Germany should not result in its importance being dismissed. It is the general assumption that the extent of this traffic is so small as to be hardly measurable. One factor to be considered is that the flow of data is from West to East and to a large degree takes place by dialing in through public phone networks. Therefore, such traffic is immeasurable and escapes evaluation. The flow of data from West to East, as my research has discovered, is of far larger dimensions than experts and officials speculate.

My information gives rise to several conclusions:

1. Data flow between Western Europe and the CMEA countries is a relatively new phenomenon which has probably existed for no more than seven years. Empirical data confirm that a) the more commercial and international a host is, the more intensive its online contact with East Europe; and b) the stronger the database's or host's links with government agencies the fewer its contacts with East Europe.

2. The development of West-East data and telephone traffic reflects a pattern of highly differentiated behavior which contradicts the prevailing negative image of both the CMEA countries as hierarchically structured and a "Moscow-controlled Eastern bloc". Czechoslovakia, Bulgaria and Hungary have a dynamic relationship with West Europe in this domain.

3. From a technological perspective the data flow between East and West is to an increasing degree uncontrollable. In Hungary, there are

about 1,000,000 PCs which can be linked up relatively easily with international data networks. In spring 1988, ARD, West Germany's public TV channel 1, interviewed Polish hackers who had penetrated a Dutch computer system. What is impossible owing to technical incompatibility between some networks can be achieved through other networks, personal travel or concealment through transit countries. Austria is an active transit point, while Finland has a more passive role. The mobility of individuals and institutions plays a special role here. Ironically, such actions are not only fully legal within the framework of Basket III of the Final Acts of the Helsinki Accord but are in fact encouraged by the Accord. At the end of the 1970s, approx. 350 East European corporations were registered in the OECD countries. These companies are largely engaged in banking and service sector industries and it should thus come as no surprise that they might be active in data communications to their home offices. The open ISDN networks of the 1990s will mean that controlling all data flows, not just those from West to East, will become more difficult.

4. Despite the restrictions imposed by the US on database users from East Europe, experts consulted were of the opinion that there must be a large flow of data from US databases such as DIALOG, ORBIT, CAS and NTIS, into East Europe.

5. A number of politicians and scientists have, in recent years, suggested that West Europe should completely sever its database links with the CMEA countries. Such suggestions usually involve the claim that otherwise West Europe would be in danger of being taken out of US databases. This strategy is not in the interests of West Europe. It would be contrary to international law, would not be in West Europe's economic interests, would foster militarization of databases otherwise accessible to the public and would only help to strengthen and expand the existing US domination in the database sector in West Europe.

6. In the conflict between national security and export interests permeating this sector, it is questionable whether the security argument is the most important even for the USA. Thus, for example, in its 1987 study (see Table 18.6) the Committee on Science, Engineering and Public Policy calculated that if restrictions in foreign database traffic were tightened further, this could lead to the USA losing US$ 9 billion in contracts annually with at least 200,000 people losing

their jobs each year and the overall effect on US GNP would be an annual reduction of US$ 17 billion. Moreover, another study from circles close to the US export industry showed that with intensified restrictions on transborder data flow the level of knowledge of many US engineers would drop even lower than is the case at present.

6. Future Prospects

Communication relations between the Third World and the industrialized nations show that an increase in such relations does not automatically lead to a) a rise in internal wealth or b) a strengthening of the respective national state. On the contrary, whether the weaker partner's scope for activity is widened or narrowed depends on the conditions of such relations. This also applies, in principle, to relations between East and West Europe. However, compared with the Third World countries, the CMEA countries have a number of advantages as regards the possible intensification of their communications: their databases and technology, economic and political structures are very much stronger and more stable than that of most Third World countries. For example, however much the Polish government may be interested in increasing its technological links with the West, Poland is still aware that any such increased database cooperation involves possible dependence.

Up till now glasnost and perestroika are political concepts internal to the societies of most of the CMEA countries. As regards the mass media, libraries, archives and databases, there is a lively and controversial debate in the USSR at the moment on a special law regulating access to information. What is particularly remarkable about this debate is the emergence of new definitions of the public sphere. Thus, Vladimir A. Rubanov writes in the magazine *Communist*:

> The state is especially strong and effective when it permits publicity and openness in matters of information. Exaggerated secrecy is the condition and character of its dangerous deformation, its digression from the methods and aims of socialist development."[7]

However, what is still open to debate is how such ideas on the public sphere are to be regulated in external relations. Some answers may come

Table 18.6:
Components of Economic Impact on the United States of National Security Controls 1985

Component	Loss (US$ billion)
Lost West-West export sales	5.9
Lost West-East export sales	1.4
Administrative cost to firms	0.5
Reduced R&D spending	0.5
Value of licenses denied	0.5
Lost profits in foreign affiliate sales	0.5
TOTAL	9.3

Source: *Balancing the National Interest.* U.S. National Security Export Controls and Global Economic Competition, ed. by Lew Allen, Jr. (Chairman), Washington, DC: National Academy Press 1987, p. 121.

from the joint database conference organized by Britain's Learned Information Ltd. and the Soviet hosts VNIIPAS and VINITI scheduled for October 1989. Further answers to the question as to what these external relation will look like may also become clear when it is established which of the three largest Western hosts negotiating with VINITI on joint ventures is successful and under which conditions. At the international level, the future of database relations between East and West will be evident from the results of the current round of GATT negotiations. The pending liberalization of trade and services will increase, among other things, the enhanced or value-added of telecommunication services, i.e., transborder database cooperation. Of particular interest is the fact that the USA refuses to allow the USSR to join GATT as it desires, while, on the other hand, the CSSR, Hungary, Romania, Yugoslavia and Cuba are GATT members.

Finally, we must not forget Southeast Asia when talking about the worldwide dynamics of competition between the United States and the EU countries for the East European market. As yet Japan has not been particularly active in setting up databases, however, the Japanese government devised an international action plan worked out in 1985. If it is considered further that the South Korean information industry is at the moment working on extensive plans to industrialize Siberia, or that South Korean information companies have already established joint ventures with Hungary, then the Southeast Asian component in East Europe may still hold many a surprise.

Notes and References

1. *Global trends in computer technology and their impact on export control*, ed. by Seymour Goodman, Washington, DC: National Academy Press 1988.

2. Cf. Galuszka, Peter; Marbach, William D. and Brady, Rose: "What will they do when they get the right stuff? Soviet scientists use old equipment, have few computers - but make some big discoveries", in: *Business Week*, November 7, 1988, pp. 72-74; for the special case of low temperature chemistry see Klotzbücher, Werner E.: "Low Temperature Chemistry", in: *The Status of Soviet Civil Sciences*. Proceedings of the Symposium on Soviet Scientific Research. NATO Headquarters, Brussels, ed. by Craig Sinclair, Dordrecht: Martinus Nijhoff Publishers 1987, pp. 211-224.

3. Cf. Kiser III, John W.: "Trapping Eastern Block Technology. U.S. Companies may find unexpected treasure behind the Iron Curtain", in: *Harvard Business Review*, March-April/1982, pp. 85-93.

4. Davison, P. S.; McDonagh, M.; Meldrum, J. D. P. and Moss, A.: *International Bibliographic Review on Costs and Modelling in Information Retrieval*, Wetherby, West Yorkshire: British Library Research and Development Department 1988.

5. Baker, Dale B.: "Chemical Abstracts Service's Secondary Chemical Information Services", in: *Journal of Chemical Information and Computer Science*, 1985, p. 188.

6. National Academy of Engineering and Office of International Affairs of the National Research Council: *Strengthening US Engineering through International Cooperation*, Washington, DC: National Academy of Engineering 1987.

7. Rubanov, Vladimir A.: "Ot 'kul'ta sekretnosti' k informacionnoj kul'ture [From secrecy cult to information culture]", in: *Communist*, No. 13/1988, p. 29.

19
Dissimilar European Information Policy

1. The Non-simultaneous Nature of Simultaneous

Hampaté Bâ, the great historian and philosopher from West Africa, once stated: "In Africa every old man who dies is a burned library."[1] This sentence contains, in compressed form, many important pieces of information. If writing is unfamiliar to a given culture, then the individual develops a huge capacity for memorizing, in a comprehensive and precise manner, a great variety of information units.

An old man, who is two or possibly three times older than his associates, as is usual in conventional societies with short life expectancies, embodies the collective memory, his natural death is actually equivalent to the burning of the Alexandria library in 47 B.C. since large amounts of information and knowledge are irrevocably lost. For those who survive him, his death (probably violent and deliberately caused by people of an outside culture) becomes a kind of cultural identity crisis and can have the impact of cultural genocide.

Today, almost everybody knows or at least guesses that a close connection obtains between the quality of information processing and the level of technology, but the fact that both concepts should also be considered in a cultural context seems much more surprising to a German intellectual than it would to a French one. So when François Mitterand claims that the world's TV broadcasting stations depend on just two image banks, it is not surprising that his words echo those of Hampaté Bâ:

> The dissemination of information processed and largely controlled by a small number of dominant countries could cause the rest to lose their memory and sovereignty, thus jeopardizing their freedom of thought and decision. [...] All cultures and languages will be threatened with uniformity. [2]

In international information relationships, we can distinguish between dominating countries - those exporting more information than they import - and peripheral countries - mainly the developing nations and Central and East European countries. Within each national society there is a subdivision into the information rich and the information poor that corresponds to the above international differentiation.

Social scientists have long since known that when the flow of information increases in a given society, social mobility among those strata who possess this additional information is faster than by those with lower status. If social mobility in a society is weak, such different processes of information appropriation result in an increase rather than a decrease in the information gap between these social segments. In other words, the information gap between the political, economic and scientific elite, on the one hand, and social strata of a lower status, on the other, is constantly growing. This becomes evident if we consider, e.g., the information supply for foreigners in the countries of West Europe to which they have emigrated. The gulf between information rich and information poor in the Western industrial countries has widened since the 1970s.

First, generally over-saturated markets, especially in the consumer goods sector, and growing international competition result in an ever faster and sharper reduction of innovation cycles. This has also happened with ICT products and services. In the early 1980s, computing reached the "man in the street" in the form of PCs. The industry has now launched into many more complex applications of information processing, so called expert systems, computer-integrated manufacturing (CIM), just-in-time production, and multimedia systems.

Second, the penetration of ICT in Western industrial societies has changed the ratio of information to entertainment in the electronic mass media to a quite remarkable extent. The introduction of TV in the 1940s and 1950s was legitimated, first and foremost, with democracy theoretical arguments and those relating to education policy, and the share of cultural and informative programs in total TV programming was much higher than at present. Now there is much empirical evidence supporting Neil Postman's polemic on the deadly nature of entertainment offered by TV.

Those who contribute to the increase in the quantity of TV programs through cable, satellite or pay TV stimulate the growing provision of entertainment and the concomitant declining supply of information. Infotainment is a very suitable, though cynical, concept for new marketing strategies in the TV industry. If we view the TV sector and the highly specialized electronic media from the standpoint of polarization between the information poor and information rich, then this sheds greater light on certain consequences of ICT's permeation of society.

Small countries and members of lower social status increasingly become passive recipients of entertainment supplied through the mass media. In contrast, a small number of dominating countries (the USA, Japan and the core EU member states) and nation states, become active producers and users of electronic information. "Infringement for many and information of few" could well have been the title of this chapter.

Following the radical political changes of 1989 in Central and Eastern Europe, and the referendums in Denmark and France on the Maastricht Treaty, the notion of a two-speed Europe has become a commonplace. The idea is erroneous in many respects. First, if we consider the economic, technological and social differences among Albania, Andalucia, Apulia, Bohemia, Hungary, Baden-Württemberg, and the Rhein-Main region or Greater London, then it becomes clear that at least three or four speeds are involved. Second, the concept of speed conveys no interest in the quality of the vehicle and the quality of the final destination is indicated only very vaguely. Third, there is actually only one speed at which the development of Europe progresses - and this speed is indicated by the market dynamics of the dominating centers. The "non-simultaneous nature of the simultaneous" is an integral component of this single speed.* It bears considering in some detail this non-simultaneity of the simultaneous in the context of the technologically highly developed West, on the one hand and technologically less developed Central and East Europe on the other, with regard to databases and telecommunications in the latter.

* The concept of "non-simutaneousness of the simultaneous" was created in the 1960s and '70s by Latin American adherents of the dependency theory (Sunkel, Furtado, Cardoso, Córdova, Dos Santos) while developing the notion of structural heterogeneity and was then suddenly "discovered" by their European translators (first of all Dieter Senghaas) as a "new" theorem. Probably, owing to the narrowly economic approach of these dependence theoreticians, they did not notice that the concept of "non-simultaneousness of the simultaneous" as an aesthetic theorem of modernity was formulated 1926 by the art historian Wilhelm Pinder (1878-1947). See Pinder, Wilhelm: *Das Problem der Generation*, Munich: Bruckmann 1961, pp. 33-57.

2. Databanks and Telecommunications in Central and East Europe

The all-pervasive emergence of the information society presupposes the existence of certain technologies and only becomes possible once they have been mastered. In this context, databases acquire a prominent social function as electric storage systems. They demonstrate the following potential advantages with regard to consumer values: a comprehensive supply of information from all fields of knowledge, timeliness, fast and transborder availability, selective and individually combined access, and the possibility of differentiating all the information obtained by further kinds of data processing.

Electronic storage systems can be applied optimally only when they rest upon a well-equipped telecommunications infrastructure. What does the market for databases and telecommunications in the former CMEA countries look like? In what direction will the market change in the face of non-simultaneous development under the dictates of the simultaneous?

In the former CMEA countries, databases played an important role in the development of librarianship, information and documentation activities. The All-Russian Institute for Scientific and Technical Information (VINITI) in Moscow, which produces 1.3 million scientific abstracts a year, was probably the world's largest abstracts service. In the long-term plans of the former CMEA countries absolute priority was assigned to the development of the electronic exchange of special information. This was clearly formulated in the complex agenda for scientific and technological advancement of the CMEA countries introduced in 1985. The agenda was scheduled to run through 2000 and assigned priority among other things to placing the respective countries' economies on a firm electronic footing. An important means for achieving this goal was the online use of databases on the basis of an extremely broad distribution of PCs.

There are now about 1,700 databases in the former CMEA states. Of these, 15 percent are online and 85 percent off-line. In the Community of Independent States (CIS), 121 databases are offered through ten databank hosts. The online market in other countries include 15 hosts in Hungary offering 104 databases, seven hosts in the Czech Republic and Slovakia with 30 databases, and there are five databanks in Bulgaria which can be accesssed over two hosts. All databanks are focused on bibliographic information. Subdivided by specialist field, the natural sciences and technology account for slightly over 50 per cent of the total. An especially high proportion of the total is accounted for by mechanical engineering, earth sciences, mining and metallurgy. Chemistry is also well covered. Yet there are few databanks covering economic information, though it is precisely this section that has grown fastest since the dramatic upheaval of 1989.

The use of Western databanks from East Europe was always greater than appeared to be the case and can be traced back to the early 1980s. Besides, today there are also "alternative" relationships between databanks in the West and East European countries. The best known example of such relationships is that between the Freiburg Öko-Institute in Germany, the Robin Wood Movement for Environmental Protection, and an institute in Moscow. Taking the example of two databanks with similar subject profiles (metallurgy) from Moscow and New York, Russian databanks can be quite competitive in comparison with their Western partners. According to the number of languages processed (this concerns especially Japanese special publications, inadequately covered in the West), some Russian databanks even appear to provide a higher level of services.

A very noteworthy fact is that one of the 1988 US Government Reports on worldwide trends in computer technology, prepared under contract by the National Research Council, stated that "the Soviet are probably about even with the West in the area of information retrieval systems".[3] This positive evaluation should certainly not preclude a sober look at the weak features of the databank sector. These include insufficient computer power, lack of software, shortage of qualified programmers, inadequate user knowledge, no marketing, weak dissemination structures and above all very poor telecommunications facilities.

The situation as regards telecommunications in the former CMEA countries was much worse that in the field of databanks. One anecdote from the Soviet history of telecommunications may show simultaneously its strong and weak points. Against the background of a technically very poorly developed telephone system, Soviet researchers designed electrical switching networks to optimizing telephone exchanges in the 1950s. While these networks were never applied in the USSR, American specialists spent US$ 200,000 on investigating the same problem. They succeeded in solving it five years later than their Soviet colleagues as they were absolutely ignorant of the Soviet specialist literature on the topic.[4]

Today, the discrepancy between research in communications technology in the former USSR and the mass application of its results may be as large as before. The research lab at Gosteleradio in Moscow has, nevertheless, developed its own HDTV standard, and the research project on an ISDN (Integrated Services Digital Network) at the Institute of

Information Transmission where experimentation is conducted at the laboratory for automatic control devices run by the Russian Academy of Sciences Moscow stands up well to any international comparison. In contrast to such individual outstanding technological performances the general technical level achieved in telecommunications in the former CMEA countries was rather low. The following trends can be discerned as regards the general situation in telecommunications.

1. Such indicators as the number of phone numbers per 100 inhabitants suggest that the technical level of the former CMEA countries is comparable with that of Turkey or Argentina, though this indicator varies over a rather broad range from sixteen for Bulgaria to five for Poland and two for Cuba.
2. The share of private phone numbers was between 60 and 74 percent in different countries.
3. The waiting lists for private telephone numbers included millions of people in all the former CMEA countries, resulting in delays of several decades.
4. The switchboard facilities were exclusively analogue.
5. A very large share of switchboards was over 40 years old. Maintenance and repair costs were correspondingly high.
6. A large share of international phone calls had to be switched manually in the cases where it was possible to establish a connection at all.
7. The level of telex services was much better than that of telephone services.
8. Data networks are still in their infancy.

There are extremely complex reasons for this low technological level for telecommunications in the former CMEA countries. The following factors bear mentioning here, without the sequence indicating any ranking: war damage; the agricultural base of most CMEA economies after 1945; restrictions on the export of technology introduced by West European states and the US; erroneous theoretical and practical evaluations of the functions of information in the production process; a lack of economic stimuli for the transport of faster, more reliable and greater information flows of every kind. The consensus is, however, that the new market economies in Central and East European require a radical, fast modernization of their telecommunication infrastructures. How will the databank and telecommunication sectors develop in the former CMEA countries? On the premise that a) the opening up of the world market and

b) privatization constitute the two single most important parameters for answering this question, the following trends seem highly probable:

1. Similar to the brain drain for engineers and scholars from the developing to the industrially developed countries, the best qualified professionals from the Central and East European scientific and technological communities will move to the rich West. Thus the respective countries will lose vast knowledge resources. Their technological level will fall.

2. Prior to 1989, there was a pronounced imbalance in all the information flows between the former CMEA countries Western Europe countries. For example the Intervision countries screened ten times more TV programming from the Eurovision countries than the latter did from East Europe, and about 65 percent of imported TV programs in a former CMEA country originated form the non-socialist states. By contrast, only three percent of West European TV materials were of East European origin. Though, since 1989, the information flows between East and West have become dense, the old imbalance seems to persist. While the former CMEA countries import a growing flow of information from West Europe, the latter show little interest in importing such.

   For instance, in Hungary 120,000 copies of the biography of the Austrian Empress Elizabeth by Brigitte Hamann sold (an inconceivable large number for a country of 10 million inhabitants), while in Austria only 1.5 books p.a. are translated on average from Southeast European countries - Serbia, Macedonia, Croatia and Slovenia. Compared to the situation before 1989, information flows from West to East have decreased in such cases where, against the background of presently privatized structures, they can be bought only for hard currency. For example, the acquisition of Western literature by the former Lenin Library in Moscow is close to collapse. Indeed, Jaroslav Kubik from Czechoslovakia reports as follows on the field of specialist information provision:

   > The input flow of foreign information sources has decreased substantially, especially since the 1970s. We can suppose that at present Czechoslovakia receives nearly one-third to four-fifths of information sources compared to the total size of acquisitions in 1990.[5]

3. The fragmentation of formerly large national markets (USSR, Yugoslavia, Czechoslovakia) into many small national markets, the previously one-sided focus of all Central and East European countries on the West, and their possibly growing inability to cooperate mutually serve to substantially reduce the indispensable economies of scale in establishing information telecommunications.

4. A mixture of high and unexpected demand for telecommunications with a) competitive Western partners and b) technologies that are partly mutual substitutes will be detrimental to the integrity of the technical network. This may torpedo the objectives pursued, such as greater reliability, security and timeliness.

5. The economic basis of a telecommunication market consists, precisely when it is relatively small, in substantial economies of scale and economies of scope. Both economic parameters can only be achieved through the private mass telephony market. (It bears remembering here that the Deutsche Bundespost-Telekom, which in overall supplies about 500 products and services, turns a profit only with two of its services provided: telephones and telex.) The revenue from mass retail business makes technological innovations and value-added services possible. When like Lithuania, phone charges for private end users were raised by 300 percent in the course of a single year (1991), the resulting new sources of income, on the one hand, sourced urgently needed capital for modernization (for example, for the link in place since February 1992 to the Scandinavian mobile radio system via the Norsat B satellite) but, on the other hand, this has undermined the economic basis of the entire telecommunications system in Lithuania.

6. Owing to the lack of internal capital, it will only be possible to modernize the telecommunications sector in the former CMEA countries with the assistance of Western capital. As comparable modernization strategies in countries of the Third World show this leads most often to an increase in external debt and results primarily in an improvement of external telecommunications connections instead of the uniform development of the internal telecommunications market.

7. The race by Western telephone companies to secure East European markets should not conceal the fact that the pace of change is

evidently rather slow. For example, although Siemens AG seems to be very active on the Central and East European markets, sales from all activities of this enterprise in those regions (50 percent of it booked for medical equipment) amounts to less than one percent of the group's total turnover. In other words, Western telecommunication enterprises compete in these regions only for the local cherries. In so doing, they stimulate a socially non-uniform development for telecommunications.

8. With Central and East Europe now open to the world market - in the field of ICT and databanks as well - those industrial and service enterprises are taking the foreground that are, by their nature, nothing more than the extended arm of Western enterprises. Before 1989, there were four large and flourishing electronics enterprises in Hungary; two of them are now on the verge of collapse and the others (Telefongyar and Müszertechnika) have become the extended tools of Siemens and Ericsson.

9. The non-simultaneous nature of the simultaneous - the starting point of my discussion - entails one Europe running at a single speed. The engine driving trends is the competitive technological triad USA-Japan-EU. Even if the Central and East European countries are allowed to join the European train, they will only make up the rear wagons. This will undermine the spread of ICT in their societies - both internally and in comparison to West Europe - by the sharper contrast between the information-haves and the information have-nots.

3. Dysfunctionalities in the Spread of the Information Society in Europe

The political strategy of creating an information society, as formulated for the first time in 1978 by the French Government in the Nora-Minc report[6] and repeated 12 years later by the central committee of the CPSU in connection with perestroika in the former Soviet Union[7], probably entails at least two serious mistakes. First, informatisation has nothing to do with knowledge accumulation. Second, creating an information society in order to successfully realize the desired modernization process can only advance if technological reforms are culturally anchored.

First, how fatal the identification of information with knowledge is, can be shown taking the example of the statistical information systems of the former CMEA countries. If we take a glance at the comprehensive study by Markus Güttler we can conclude, for example, that the statistical information system in the former German Democratic Republic (GDR) was very efficient and remarkably well organized, that technical software solutions were found that enabled fast processing and sourcing of a great volume of comprehensive data.

> The government statistics on which the GDR relied made use of an information system which were unparalleled in the West in terms of processing speed and capacity.[8]

Güttler singles out two reasons why this system still could not function. First, the information could not take into account a special quality of the information, namely its being subjective, purposive and context-dependent. This may be clear to anyone knowing that the mathematical concept of information should not be confused with social communication processes. Güttler's second reason may seem quite surprising and stun the laymen. According to his computations, monthly reports produced within the statistical system of the former GDR included about 45 million items of decision-relevant information - or the processing time of about 2,604 man-days at 24 working hours a day or to the monthly capacity of 5,760 bits per decision-maker at 0.2 bits per second. In other words:

> The quantity of required relevant items of information for planning and management, received on the basis of the statistical information system, was so high that it was not possible to evaluate it centrally and apply it accordingly.[9]

It could be said (if somewhat crudely and thus exaggeratedly, and by extension wrongly) that the former GDR choked on the bulk of its information. This view may seem surprising only if information is equated with knowledge, and if we do not admit that information scarcity should never lead to unwillingness in decision-taking and inertia and also realize that an abundance of information does not result automatically in minimized uncertainty. It seems extremely bold and irresponsible if computer scientists nowadays infer the knowledge concept form the mathematical information concept and further define knowledge as "the stock of all statements on the represented world accepted by him are actually true"[10]. In contrast it should be insisted that knowledge is based not only on items of knowledge as such but on experience, reason, habits and practice.

At present in the United States annual printing output includes 40,000 books, 17,000 newspapers and 12,000 journal titles; there are 27,000 lending outlets for videocassettes, 400 million radio and 350 million TV sets and 41 million photographs taken daily. Consequently, though the dominating countries, like the United States, are without doubt rich in information, it is an absolutely different question as to whether they are rich in knowledge. On the contrary, people from small and dominated countries could turn out be rich in knowledge since their knowledge has long since been saturated with the experience of scarcity, poverty, pain, dependence and oppression. This knowledge is deep, lasting and ineradicable. If this distinction between information and knowledge is accepted then it follows that it is unreasonable for any country to enlarge its information systems quantitatively; the objective should instead be to improve them qualitatively.

My *second* argument runs that strategies for extending the information society cannot function without concomitant cultural anchoring. To put it more precisely: owing to a multiplicity of factors. such an extension at present also means internationalization, and this process will always be accompanied by the world-wide homogenization of cultures, as was stated at the outset when quoting François Mitterand. It is precisely this process of externally introduced international informatization that is contributing to the internal cultural erosion within the former CMEA countries.

The collapse of theaters, the publishing, music, film culture, circus, libraries and media spheres, that is to say of the official culture, and the simultaneous inrush of Dallas, the cheapest pornography and bad trivial literature into the Central and East European countries has reached an intimidating scale. And I would like to mention as the tip of this iceberg of cultural erosion the fact that 100,000 freshly printed books from the stores of the former GDR's publishing houses (incl. works by Heinrich Mann, Arnold Zweig, Ernesto Cardenal, Richard von Weizsäcker) were destroyed in incinerators in Saxony: another example is the smuggling of icons from the former USSR to the West at a total loss of some US$ 13 million, which ranks such smuggling among the most profitable areas of international business after the arms and drug trades. Vaclav Havel states:

> The return of liberty in a society with completely decayed moral scales has led - probably inevitably - to an explosion of all the bad human qualities imaginable. And even if this was probably inevitable and hence was to be expected, the extent of it was by far greater than could have been imagined before-hand by any of us.[11]

Despite this process of cultural erosion, culture represents precisely the factor that will hamper any externally controlled informatization of Central and East Europe. Culture cannot be spread from above; indeed, it always comes from below. By its nature, culture is usually local and regional. It is also not limited to what is defined as culture by bureaucrats. It is instead the world in which people actually live; it embodies the collective knowledge accumulated over generations, reflects the properties and specifications of one group in comparison to another, manifests itself in language and dialect, the feelings of belonging to a native identity. It is precisely in this sense, however, that culture does not lend itself to instrumentalization, privatization or commercialization.

With this relationship in mind and in order to maintain the balance between homogenization as technological rationality and the diversity of cultures, the EU's Treaty of Rome deliberately excluded any clauses on the EU's jurisdiction in the sphere of culture. The EU Commission has, nevertheless, long since been active in the field of cultural policy. This contradicts, first, German constitutional law and second severely violates even the legal foundations that have long since applied in the field of cultural policy since said Treaty was signed back in 1957.* Probably on the basis more of suspicion than firm knowledge of such circumstances, widespread distrust has arisen in West Europe towards the Maastricht Treaty. There is a justified fear behind this distrust connected with the wish to preserve local or regional cultural identities.

If we bear in mind the civil wars in the Caucusus or former Yugoslavia it is hard to believe that precisely from suffering, scarcity and

---

* There are two reasons for this infringement of law. 1. According to German constitutional law, cultural policy falls exclusively within the competence of German federal provinces. 2. Mass media policy, as an section of cultural policy, is regulated by Art. 5 of the German Constitution. This Art. 5 is part of the human rights catalogue innate to the German Constitution. As long as there are no democratically legitimated human and constitutional rights at the European level (and the European Convention for the Protection of Human Rights and Civil Liberties of 1950 fails to provide precisely this constitutional legitimation), the interference of the EU Commission in German mass media regulations represents a violation of the German Constitution.

untrammeled outside control something like a cultural identity may one day arise that is internally peaceful and non-aggressive. Still, a look at Jamaica, as an example for all developing countries, shows that this is possible. Rex Nettleford, the Nestor of Jamaican social science, emphasized the following when speaking to the 21st Assembly of the Caribbean Broadcasting Union in June 1990:

> Our Caribbean heritage constitutes the suffering under enslavement, indentureship and colonialism. It also constitutes survival and what exists beyond that survival which is why we are all here. A knowledge of that process is vital as well as a grasp of its implications for what is happening and what is likely to happen in the future. That knowledge lies deeply embedded in the collective wisdom of our ordinary people. [...]
>
> This is indeed a cause for much despair but I take my cue and declare, instead, for hope, thanks to the Calypsonians and the reggae composers as well as to all those who have invoked the authenticity of a Caribbean reality either for the purpose of independence, or for creating works of art, or for just simply surviving. More than that I invoke that hope-in-despair which is also part of the heritage keeping us in dialectical embrace not only with the travails of the contemporary world and the doubts of an uncertain future, but also with the knowledge that despite the uprooting, the suffering and the pain, we have survived.[12]

Notes and References

1. Cf. Calvet, Louis-Jean: *Die Sprachenfresser*. Ein Versuch über Linguistik und Kolonialismus, Berlin: Arsenal 1978, p. 107.
2. Mitterand, François: *Technology employment and growth*. Report to the summit of the industrialized countries, Chateaux Versailles, June 5, 1982.
3. Committee to Study International Developments in Computer Science and Technology: *Global Trends in Computer Technology and their Impact on Export Control*, Washington: National Academy Press 1988, p.171.
4. Cf. Locke, William N.: "Translation by Machine", in: *Scientific American*. Vol. 194, No. 1/1956, p. 29.
5. Kubik, Jaroslav: "The way to Europe Lies through Information: Current Problems in the Development of Information Activity in Czecho-Slovakia", in: *International Forum on Information and Documentation*, (Moscow, USSR). Vol. 16, No.3 /1991, p. 28.
6. Cf. Nora, Simon and Minc, Alain: *L'informatisation de la société*, Paris: La Documentation Française 1978.
7. Cf. "On the Development of the Concept of Informatization of the Soviet Society. Resolution of the Political Bureau of the CPSU Central Committee and a note of the CC Departments", in: *Izvestiya of the CPSU Central Committee*, 1989, pp. 55.
8. Cf. Güttler, Markus: "Das Informationssystem der staatlichen Statistik in der DDR. Computergestützte Entscheidungsunterstützung für die Planung und Leitung von Volkswirtschaft und Gesellschaft", in: *Informatik Forum* (Vienna, Austria). Vol. 6, No. 3/1992, p. 118.
9. Ibid.
10. Reimer, Ulrich: *Einführung in die Wissensrepäsentation*. Netzartige und Schema-basierte Repräsentationsformate, Stuttgart: Teubner 1991, p. 6.
11. Cf. Liehm, Antonin: "Osteuropa: Aufstieg in die Freiheit", in: *UNESCO-Kurier*, No. 7-8/1992, p. 44.
12. Nettleford, Rex: "Preserving the Caribbean Heritage", in: *Combroad*, September 1990, p. 31 and 34.

20

The "Latin Americanization" of the Public Sphere in East Europe

1. Censorship, Pathology and the Dual Society in East Europe Before 1989

The following brief item of news must be one of the most macabre and depressing newspaper reports of the year 1990. In an interview with the London *Times* Mihau Barbulescu, a representative of the State Meteorological Office in Romania, admitted that for years Nicolai Ceaucescu had the Romanian weather forecasts falsified so as to deceive a population plagued by bitter cold into believing that the weather was actually warmer. The meteorologists were instructed never to allow the official temperatures to fall below minus 15° Celsius. This newspaper disclosure tallies with other reports according to which since the late 1930s Soviet cartographers had been instructed to falsify Soviet maps and city plans, deliberately distorting the location of towns, streets, city quarters and rivers so as to make orientation more or less impossible.

But it is not necessary to go as far back as the 1930s to find examples of just how widespread and intense the rigorous censorship of the media, opinions and information by the Communist Party and the state leadership in the former Council for Mutual Economic Assistance (CMEA) countries had become. In early 1990, Horst Mempel, an editor with the former television network in the German Democratic Republic (GDR), gave the following examples of everyday censorship - and thus consequently of self-censorship in that particular audio-visual mass medium.

Example 1: Rural single family houses became victims of censorship because in view of the general supply crisis in the GDR the wealth of the farmers had to be kept out of the limelight.

Example 2: In an interview a farmer claimed that losses could be avoided in the prevailing circumstances. Cutting the words "prevailing circumstances" from the interview was justified on the ground that they seemed to refer to a "catastrophe".

Example 3: In another interview a blind person mentioned that not everyone was able to come to terms with his fate and that many had failed. The censor's justification for cutting this statement: "In the socialist system no one except an enemy of that system fails."[1]

Example 4: The very names of Western companies were taboo. Thus, if a Western machine bearing a company or brand name appeared in a scene then the name was simply blotted out (Baum 1990).

Research work on the extent and the different features of such censorship mechanisms is, however, only in its infancy. However, it can already be proved beyond a doubt that censorship was carried out and coordinated very consciously and assiduously by the highest committees of state and party. For example, the *Gesamtdeutsches Institut* (founded in 1969 in Bonn as an institution of the Cold War) issued documentation on how the Communist Party monitored the press in the GDR (Holzweissig 1991). This report reads like a horror story and contains a list of tabooed themes on which the GDR press was not permitted to report. This list is dated November 12, 1968 and was compiled by the Ministerial Council of the GDR. Among the themes were the "Nord" nuclear power plant, the Carl Zeiss company in Jena, and the status of electronic data processing.

---

1. This cynicism towards the blind is oppressively close to the tenor of the following "joke" which was current in Germany's Nazi period: "No one is to go hungry or freeze; anyone who does so will be sent to a concentration camp." What fascism and socialism à la GDR have in common is that what is not permitted by the system is also not possible. However, and this is even more oppressive, Adorno and Horkheimer refer to this "joke" for the Nazi period not in their analysis of anti-Semitism or fascism, but in their essay on the culture industry: "The joke from Hitler's Germany might shine forth as a maxim from above all the portals of the culture industry" (Adorno/Horkheimer 1979, 149). Where the formal freedom of the individual is guaranteed, as in the culture industry of capitalism, where the mass media purportedly satisfy all the needs of their recipients, and the off-switch has to function as the best argument for that very formal freedom of the individual then social monitoring does not take the form a threat of dispatch to a concentration camp or state censorship, but of conformist behavior. In other words: "In capitalism, too, no one fails who is not its enemy."

Ironically, however, where taboos prescribed from above impede an adequate perception of reality, empiricism and empirical science become weapons of criticism (Splichal 1987). Thus, we have the paradox that it was possible for empirical science in East Europe to formulate a critical theory of society, whereas in West Europe it seldom managed to shed its affirmative character. Wherever a state and party leadership focused on suppressing freedom of opinion, what occurs is a spiral of repression which becomes more and more autonomous. On the one hand, the political elite would like to know everything about that society, and on the other hand information which might even potentially threaten the system has to be suppressed. To illustrate the mechanisms involved in this, reference will be made to the former GDR's statistical information system and to the designation of the contents of certain dissertations in the GDR as unsuitable for the public and the problems involved in keeping them secret. What will also become clear is the element of the absurd inherent in these mechanisms and the aspiration to totality and perfection which they signify.

On the basis of a comprehensive study by Güttler (1992) it can be asserted that the statistical information system in the former GDR was highly efficient and remarkably well organized, and that it developed software solutions which guaranteed the swift processing and assessment of quite considerable volumes of data. As regards the capacity and the speed of processing, Güttler writes: "The GDR's State Office of Statistics had at its disposal an information system quite without parallel in West Europe" (Güttler 1992, 118). Nevertheless, Güttler sets out two reasons why this system was still unable to function: first, it failed to take into account certain features peculiar to information, namely that it is always relative to a subject, focused on a goal, and context-dependent.

While this first reason may seem plausible (as it should to anyone who realizes that a mathematical understanding of the term information is not be to confused with information on social and communication processes) Güttler's second reason is somewhat striking and remarkable, this time for the lay-person as well. He has established that the monthly reports drawn up by the GDR's statistical system contained the results of approximately 2,604 man-days, a man-day being 24 working hours, or a monthly capacity of 5,760 bits per decision-maker at 0.2 bits per second. In other words:

> "The volume of information gathered on the basis of the statistical information system and deemed relevant and necessary for planning and administration was far too large for anyone to be able to evaluate it centrally and apply it appropriately" (Güttler 1992, 118).

That not only the collection of as much information as possible can produce strange results, but also its opposite, namely the suppression of information, is illustrated by a study undertaken by Bleek and Mertens (1994) on dissertations in the GDR which were designated to be kept secret. Among other things, this thoroughly-researched study comes to the conclusion that the bureaucratic effort involved in carrying out the appropriate classification of the dissertations was so cumbersome that in the end no consistent criterion could be discerned as to why the decision went one way in one case and the other in another. Thus, the political decision not to make certain dissertations available to the public actually resulted in arbitrariness, uncertainty and confusion - not to say absurdity, ludicrousness and empty phrases.

These two examples, an information collection mania of totalitarian proportions and a perfect system of information suppression, highlight certain pathological elements inherent in the aim of achieving a society with total censorship. Where censorship sets its sights on the totality, it is almost destined to degenerate into something quite unlike what it was intended to be. Wanting to know everything can block the capacity for decision-making.

To summarize in a somewhat curt and pointed (and thus in its brevity) false phrase: the former GDR suffocated under its own enormous blanket of information. Moreover, the very act of wanting to suppress all knowledge can create clandestine knowledge, generated in secret, concealed in niches. In this context of censorship mechanisms, Jürgen Kuczynski's biographical treatise "Dialog mit meinem Urenkel" (Dialogue with my great-grandson) contains a remarkable passage. Kuczynski, who was born in 1904, was an active anti-fascist and communist, and a GDR historian of international repute. In his book, which was only released for printing in the GDR after some very wearisome difficulties, he writes:

> The press is neglecting a great part of its educative task by failing completely to exercise sufficient criticism. [...] By contrast, how clear an impression of our times is to be gained from our novels. Indeed, is it not strange that if later historians want to discover something about our struggles in the printed matter of our era, one will have to advise them to read our novels, not our academic literature, and not our press? (Kuczynski 1986, 39).

Klaus Selbig, formerly the official in the GDR Ministry of Culture responsible for printing permits, explained the political function of the novels mentioned by Kuczynski in an interview (Franke 1991):

> What they represent is warning literature, in which heroes are attributed modes of behavior and opinions which were not really typical of developments in socialism but which were used nevertheless in such a way as to possibly prevent or halt certain developments in socialism from the very outset. As kind of warning, therefore, that things ought not be allowed to take such a course.

The observations and insights offered by Kuczynski and Selbig are of practical and theoretical relevance. They point to the fact that in East Europe before 1989 there was not only state-managed censorship of the media but also a controversial debate that was conducted simultaneously - above all in the realm of literature. The existence of these controversies only becomes clear when we turn our attention away from the local, power-sustaining media such as television, radio and the press, in other words when we eschew academic political analysis and instead examine the everyday reception of foreign mass media from a sociological point of view. While the reception of West German TV played a prominent part in everyday life in the former GDR, in the other East European countries it was the reception of West European and US radio stations via short wave. This reception of foreign mass media had a dual function in East Europe.

On the one hand, it contributed to the emancipation of the East European peoples from the unbearably repressive state and party structures (Manaev 1991); on the other, foreign mass media were also repressive and affirmative in the sense that they made their own active contribution towards cutting off the people in East Europe from any other political or life world alternative other than Western capitalism and Eastern bloc communist state and party supremacy.

This juxtaposition and opposition of official and private worlds in East Europe has been characterized by Günter Gaus, the first West German ambassador to East Germany, as the "niche society" (Gaus 1981, 27), that is to say a society in which the people find self-realization in the private sphere, in a retreat from the realm of politics, a society where the black labor market, mutual assistance (for example, in building holiday homes), and a little trade with some hard currency constitute a lifeworld in which the authoritarian party secretary from the world of work in the morning becomes the considerate neighbor in the garden next door in the late afternoon. The problem, for example, of how to organize roof tiles for their respective garden huts in an economy marked by scarcity (and thus a problem relevant to both the supervisor and the subordinate), served to bind them just as much as their different degrees of integration into the Communist Party hierarchy served to separate them.

These contradictions were typical of the reality of everyday life in socialism. A public speech at a conference was immediately relativized later in a private discussion; official phrases by the party and state leadership were always followed by a private political joke in which the political elite came off very badly. The designation "dual society", introduced by Wagner in his study of Poland (Wagner 1981), would seem even more appropriate and more pointed that "niche society", as by its very choice of terms it makes clear that the official and the private worlds not only represent an opposition but also a juxtaposition in one and the same person who potentially existed in both worlds.

Prior to 1989, East Europe enjoyed a decidedly lively public share in the private realm, in the shadow of official censorship. Only when one takes this phenomenon into account it is possible to grasp how the incredible dynamic of social change could finally develop such momentum. An underground press and pamphlets, jokes and literature, Western music fashions and TV; these were all instruments and expressions of a publicly concealed form of communication. Although we know today that the Polish trade union "Solidarnosc" was subsidized to the tune of several million dollars by the CIA via the Vatican, this cannot detract from the fact that within Poland's dual society there were autochthonic social forces which had massive grass roots support among religious believers, farmers, workers and intellectuals, and which created their own channels of communications. The vision these various channels imparted of an as yet only vaguely defined counter-world finally won the day - a latent public sphere became manifest.

There are certain similarities between the communication and media aspects of the process of change in East Europe and the Islamic Revolution in Iran in 1979. Although unnoticed by public opinion in the West, there had always been autochthonic social forces at work in Iran with their own channels of communication - even during the worst period under Reza Shah Pahlavi. In the case of Iran, an organized and fully-functioning communications network made up of approximately 90,000 so-called minbars or pulpits in the mosques (Fathi 1979). Just as observers in the West were not able to anticipate the changes in Iran because they were blinded by a distorted view of the decay of traditional societies (Samarajiva 1987), so too many Western analysts were unable to recognize the dual societies in East Europe because they had involuntarily become victims of their outward projection of their own anti-Communist image.

By 1988 and 1989, more or less soberly thinking analysts could and should have already been able to discern in the changes in the former USSR a process heading in the direction of a transformation of the system, and not just political cosmetics. Those who considered the 1988 Soviet media policy nothing more than a typical communist diversionary tactic (Daniloff 1988; Liminski 1988) or interpreted this policy merely as a brilliant public relations strategy on the part of Gorbachev (Naylor 1989) in fact proved to be "Cold-War-mongers."

2. The Public Sphere and Social Fragmentation in Western Capitalism

In their own eyes, the mass media in Western democracies constitute the so-called fourth estate. By means of the media, a plurality of opinion is articulated publicly, and this in turn acts as a democratic corrective to the formulation of political demands and objectives as proceed in parliament, government and the economy. However, given that such ideals have long since degenerated into political soap-box oratory, critical scholarly research can neither theoretically nor empirically ignore what Jürgen Habermas wrote about the term "public sphere" in 1962.

According to his analysis at the time, the public sphere in capitalist society has long since become an instrument of power in the hands of political interest groups which have no democratic legitimacy. However, Habermas' political analysis of the public sphere ought perhaps to be expanded to include a decisive economic element which Canadian economist Dallas Smythe defined theoretically in 1977, taking up and elaborating on the staple theory[2] put forward by his compatriot Harold Innis (1950): If in the process of the realization of profit, advertising (communicated

2. Neither Harold Innis nor Dallas Smythe could have known that Karl Bücher (1847-1930), an expert on constitutional law, economist and communications researcher in Leipzig, had argued in a very similar vein in the economic theory of the newspaper which he developed - especially given the fact that communication studies in Germany have not even considered Bücher's works (1981).

through the mass media) was regarded for a long time as an important but secondary support which could thus be offered as a kind of "free lunch" by the editors responsible for media content, then today the relationship between editorial content and advertising is exactly the opposite.

It is the editorial contents of TV programming and the press which have become the "free lunch" inside totally commercialized media structures. In this altered process, which has been brought about by economic forces, the media contents no longer "affect" their recipients. The main concern now is to buy over specific groups of recipients for the respective editorial "free lunch"; advertising now impresses its mark on the editorial surroundings.

These somewhat complicated sounding theoretical considerations have long since been internalized by every media manager in the capitalist West, who by necessity are business-minded. Newspaper owners have known for some time now that in their overall calculations income from advertising has now greatly outstripped subscriptions or news-stand sales. TV managers are more than familiar with the growing economic relevance of ad revenues in the face of sharply rising production costs.

Advertising lies at the very heart of capitalism and is in fact contrary to what the term public relations would seem to suggest, namely, the concept of public sphere. Historically, advertising emerged in the 19th century (the US-American advertising agency J.W. Thompson was founded in 1864) when it had became necessary for the very first time to industrialize consumer needs in the face of over-production and market saturation. As a producer of ideology, advertising provides the essential cheap substitutes for the political loyalty of large sections of the population whose faith in traditional institutions (church, political party, parliament) has long since been shattered. In the end, the pseudo-rationality and mendacity of the entire advertising branch become paradigms of the fragile and unevenly distributed progress of Western capitalism.

What political science politely calls "corporatism" is defined much more vividly in the vernacular by terms such as "graft", "cronies" and "cliques" - all point to the close symbiotic network of relationships between party representatives and representatives of business. It is this very corporatism between political parties and the economy which has robbed the state of its democratic innocence in dealing with the public sphere. One point to be considered here is that the state has always been, and still is, the largest producer of information and knowledge (schools, universities, R&D, patents and norms, statistics).

In West Germany, experts estimate that financially speaking, state-funded publishing activities are as significant as those of the entire private book industry. Under Thatcherism in England, the advertising budget of state institutions and so-called charities, of all things, exceeded that of private business and industry. In West Germany in 1990, the advertising budget of the Deutsche Bundespost came to 219 million deutschmarks, meaning that the Deutsche Bundespost ranked fifth on the list of the advertising industry's largest clients - following on from the major washing powder and detergent manufacturers. In West Germany, too, the public broadcasting media's independence of the state, an independence which is guaranteed in the constitution, has become a mere fiction. In the name of so-called balanced opinions, the aspiration of public broadcasting to be a forum for debate in the public sphere has given way to a king of lowest common denominator dictated jointly by the Christian and Social Democratic parties.

Where an overall public sphere is no longer able to function in society as a whole, that public sphere becomes a residual category, persisting in different social groupings (gays, senior citizens, managers, yuppies, ecologists, etc.). In other words, we see social fragmentation in which "anything goes." Where the technical restriction of frequencies and channels no longer plays much of a role, growth in the number and type of electronic media who buy their specific recipient groups in a fragmented society proceeds in leaps and bounds. Such trends are best observed in the radio broadcasting sector in California's San Francisco Bay, where 22 medium-wave and 46 short-wave radio stations broadcast their respective programs to around seven million inhabitants: KYS devotes itself exclusively to oldies, NWSS to country music, KJAZ to jazz, KKHI to classical music, KOED exclusively to news, while CHR addresses itself exclusively in Spanish to the Chiansos, etc.

Currently the relationship between the mass media and social reality is suffering a radical break. So complete is the break that the new kinds of illustrate magazines, such as *Weekly World News* (USA), *The Plain Truth* (Australia) or *Die Neue Spezial* (Netherlands and West Germany) are deliberately dispensing with true stories and instead printing everything their readers send them in the form of articles and photographs. In these magazines Elvis Presley is still alive, John F. Kennedy is being glimpsed in the White House, and the Loch Ness monster is likely to crop up in a front-page photograph. Tired of the fictional crime of television, the relationship between the mass media and social reality in the United States is also experiencing changes in that US TV stations are opting more and more to show, for example, real criminal pursuits. Live video camera shots from police helicopters are indeed more exciting than fictional police chases.

After all, when the "zapping" televiewer increasingly zaps away the advertising, advertising has to become an integral part of the fictional plot, in the shape, for example, of product placements. Where mass media and political parties are merely advertising themselves (in constant pursuit of the illusion that the real world is identical with the goods they offer) the increase in death motifs in US ad campaigns may not be all that wide off the mark. Neither are the Benetton advertisements by photographer Oliviero. If reality cannot communicate itself to the public any more via the mass media then it will do so via Benetton advertising, be it in the image of a man dying of AIDS in the arms of his father or a poster showing a priest and a nun kissing (Arthur 1992; Becker 1992; Leggewie 1992; Seidl, 1992).

3. The Latin Americanization of the Mass Media and Public Sphere in East Europe After 1989

In his article "J'accuse", which appeared in 1949, the sensitive and thoroughly conservative German aesthete Thomas Mann gave vent to his fury about the communist witch-hunts in the United States and West Germany, appalled as he was by the double standards and mendacity of the press at the time. Mann commented on the economic reconstruction in West Germany as follows:

> [It has] emerged [...] that at the time of the 'currency reform' a few middle-class businessmen made a private profit of approximately 40 million deutschmarks by holding back goods. This is called the renewed flowering of the creative personality in the economy; it is called private initiative; and under these headings a barbaric clique of speculators, immune to the needs of the people, has turned the goods which they held back from the consumers into millions of deutschmarks of new wealth. (Mann 1991, 1441)

There could be no better description of the economic structures in East Europe in the wake of the dramatic changes since 1989. On the one hand, there are the short-term cash strategists who originate in the mafia and via the black market penetrate right into the realm of government. On the other, there are the pure market economists who are only conspicuous at international conferences by their naivety. In this economic chaos, a large portion of the population is heading at an even greater speed down the slippery slope to material destitution.

Thus, two thirds of the citizens in the CIS countries have to spend more than half of their income on food. They have no savings and live from hand to mouth. Only less than a quarter of all the CIS citizens has a flat which they do not have to share (Narsikulow 1992). Close behind material impoverishment follows spiritual impoverishment: 60 percent of the population agreed with the statement that the prevailing attitude is one of every man for himself. Science in the former USSR is being invaded by superstition, obscurantism and spiritism, penetrating even as far as the once renowned magazine "Social Sciences and the Modern Era", published by the former Soviet Academy of Sciences (Kapitza 1991). Corresponding to these phenomena, we are seeing a great increase in the number of programs on Russian TV about faith healers and people with so called supernatural powers (Vartanov 1991).

This profound spiritual crisis into which most of the people in East Europe have been catapulted is also to be discerned not least in the most intimate sector of human communications, namely in the realm of sexual relations. What is blossoming is not some kind of life-asserting, joyful open and pleasurable sexuality but exploitative prostitution, telephone sex services and pornography, especially in Hungary, the Czech and Slovak Republics, and in large cities in the CIS.

With dramatically declining industrial production, falls in turnover in the retail sector, rising prices for consumer goods and a contracting real income for the majority of the population, with growing unemployment, an almost total decline in internal trade in the former CMEA countries, high rates of inflation and high debts owed to Western countries, with underdeveloped infrastructures in the communication, transport and bank sectors, and finally, with an almost total absence of legal systems, it is no exaggeration to claim that in view of these structural features, the East European countries find themselves in the deepest economic and political depression since the 1930s. It is thus a complete mystery how it is possible to argue, as did Dimitry Chereshkin and Mikhail Tsalenko (1989), that a strategy aimed at the total informatization of society could eliminate the effects of economic and social chaos in the former USSR.

At most, this argument might possibly make sense against the background of the blind faith in technology which has always been a feature of the history of the Soviet Union, for it was always the respectively latest technology which was expected to lead the country out of its backwardness: in the 1920s such hopes were placed in the program of electrification, in the 1930s it was the then propagated "great revolution of nature", this was followed by research in space travel and nuclear energy, and finally by the great hopes attached to the rerouting of the Siberian rivers.

In the face of this enormous crisis in East Europe the two parameters which have become decisive in the assessment of future developments are *privatization* and *opening up to the world market*. It is precisely these two parameters which are in the process of bringing about fundamental changes in the sectors of culture, the mass media and communications in East Europe.[3] These changes take the following forms:

Changing Social Structures

In the former CMEA countries cultural policy was always an asset which was constantly flaunted. If one disregards certain ideological functions which this cultural policy also fulfilled, then in many areas the cultural sphere in the former CMEA countries had in fact plus points compared to West European countries. Thus, for example, a comparison of the distribution of cinema seats per 1,000 inhabitants showed the following: Bulgaria had 79 seats, Hungary 52.2 and Yugoslavia 18.9 compared to 13 in the Federal Republic of Germany, 11 in the Netherlands and nine in Great Britain. In the meantime, this highly subsidized state cultural policy

3. "Soviet mass communications between openess and reconstruction" is the title of a study by Lerg et al. (1991) in which the main focus of interest is concentrated on the "role of the Soviet broadcasting media in the current process of change" (page 8). A quantitative content analysis was used to examine television and radio programmes during certain weeks in 1989, and the contents of the the magazines *Ogonjok* and *Literaturnja Gasjeta*. This study comes to the conclusion that the media supported perestroika strongly at first, but then became ambivalent, and by the time of the conclusion of the examination refrained from a clear evaluation (see page 217). What is arlarming about this study is not so much the boredeom of its results or the inappropriateness of the method given the professeed aim of the examination, or even the fact that this academic research project was financed by the West German Federal Ministry of Defence. The alarming thing is the defence ministry's concept of rationality, its assumption that it is possible to conduct politically relevant planning on the basis of such naïve studies.

in the former CMEA countries has totally collapsed, throwing thousands of unemployed, broken and bitter writers, journalists, directors, sculptors, musicians, actors, dancers, and museum and library employees onto the scrap-heap of history. A make-up artist at the Moscow Film Studio "Mosfilm" commented resignedly on her present situation:

> In former times we had cosmetics, better wages, and greater work discipline and, above all, we had the motivation to work. Today everything seems hopeless. Now we know that we are a developing country. All that is left is shame, suffering and heads to roll. (Lemper 1992)

Table 20.1:
Selective Quantitative Data on the Brain Drain from Central and East Europe to the Richer Industrial Countries

Country	Quantitative Data
Hungary	At present 4,200 Hungarian engineers and scientists (5 %) work abroad.
Romania	In 1990, 150,000 Romanians emigrated, four percent of them being intellectuals.
Poland	Between 1981 and 1988, 760,000 Poles stayed abroad for more than 2 years. Of these 77,000 (10 %) had university degrees, 19,000 (2.5 %) were engineers, and 5,700 (0.7 %) were medical physicians.
USSR	Between 1987 and 1989, 376,000 Soviet citizens went abroad. Of these, 19 % had a higher education and 25 % were skilled workers. In 1989, 70,000 scientists and engineers left the USSR. In 1990, 184,000 Soviet Jews went to Israel. Of these 39 % were scientists and people with a higher education (mostly engineers and architects). In 1989, the Academy of Sciences in Moscow alone lost 250 scientists. In recent years, the Lebedev Institute of Physics, Academy of Sciences, Moscow, has lost about 20 % of its staff, who have gone to research institutes in West Europe and the United States.

Source: Angell, O. and Kouzimov, V.A. (1991): *Report of the Working Party on "Brain Drain Issues in Europe"*, Paris: UNESCO Regional Office for Science and Technology for Europe; Rhode, Barbara (1991): *East-West Migration/Brain Drain*, Brussels: EU-Commission, Cost-Committee (mimeo); reports from current news sources.

The publishing sector in the former USSR is facing total collapse. The database sector in Poland has almost ceased to exist. And "Barrandov", the state film studio in the Czech Republic, has had to release 2,100 employees. In view of these structural changes, a quotation by a Czech artist printed in the *International Herald Tribune* rings a particularly bitter note. "The German mark has replaced the state censor as the bête noire" (Lobrano 1992). At the same time as the employment market for artists, intellectuals and scientists in East Europe is collapsing, there is a constantly growing brain drain to be detected running from East to West. Despite the difficulties on West European labor markets, many people in East Europe still believe that the West represents the only possibility of survival.

This brain drain is taking place more among scientist and engineers than among artists, especially as the latter group is more dependent for its professional advancement on being rooted in its own mother tongue than, for example, engineers of scientists (Wright 1991; Rhode 1991). Indeed, 15 percent of all Hungarian scientists, that is to say approximately 4,200 people, are working abroad. 39 percent of all migrants from the former USSR to Israel in 1990 were academics, and of these, 64 percent were engineers and architects. This brain drain for the East European countries will have disastrous consequences. The very people who are emigrating are the ones whose energy, activity and expertise are so urgently required on order to transform and renew those societies.

Privatization

When East European scientists and politicians speak about models for the social organization of the mass media today, privatization appears on the scene like some *deus ex machina*. The public broadcasting system, as exists for example in West Germany, is suddenly unknown. There is neither any desire on their part to even perceive that the French News Agency AFP, for example, is state-run nor do they show the least interest in the fact that there is a growing number of small so-called independent broadcasters in the United States.

The adjective "public" is all too quickly rashly and crudely equated with Stalinist, statist, collectivist. In the light of this prejudice, forms of privatization are developing in the mass media in such countries, the brutality and penetrative power of which would be hard to find in any West European country. A few examples: For some time now, the logo of the

Italian Olivetti corporation appeared on state TV in Russia every evening on the clock which is to be seen shortly before the beginning of the main news program. In an exclusive contract, a French ad agency handles the entire structure of advertising on the two state TV networks in the Czecho-slovak Republic, producing the commercials and assuming responsibility for negotiations both with the consumer goods industry and with other advertising agencies. In Hungary, there are (still incomplete) plans to rent out TV frequencies to foreign groups, an organizational model which has not been seriously debated in any other country in the world today.

In telephone communications from western to eastern Germany private satellite consortia can also use satellites for the transmission of speech although in the new West German Postal Structure Act of 1989 that very sector of voice transmission was reserved for the state telecommunications monopoly and not earmarked for privatization, the argument being that the state bore a social responsibility in this domain. And, finally, in the former USSR there are official discussions in progress on the privatization of the so-called space segment of satellite communications (carrier rockets, launching systems, etc.) which good well beyond anything the Federal Communications Commission in the USA, for example, has thus far permitted in the form of deregulation in this sector.

The privatization of formerly public communications systems hits the lower social strata of the population and people in rural areas particularly hard. For example, in the former USSR there was a cable radio set with one to two radio channels installed as a fixture in practically every flat. This radio service used to be free of charge, but of late a fee has to be paid for it. The same applies to local telephone calls: these used to be free of charge but are now subject to payment (or will soon be). Such charges mainly affect those people who can only live from hand to mouth. Without their radio and telephone, thousands of pensioners living alone and below subsistence level are now cut off from public communications.

Media communications in village and small towns in East Europe have also changed radically since 1989. Until that date, there was a publicly subsidized so-called "house of culture" in almost every community, available for dances, theatre plays and guest orchestral performances. In smaller villages there was even a cinema. Today, many of these installations have been discontinued, and privately managed pubs and discos simply cannot survive in villages as the purchasing power of the local population is not strong enough to support them (Reich 1992).

Not only do the scale and shape of privatization in the field of the mass media in Eastern Europe go far beyond what has been practiced to date in Western capitalism. There is also every reason to suspect that for Western media capital East Europe has become an experimental laboratory for privatization strategies which are still being hampered by state social obligations in the West and which it might be possible to eliminate via the lever of East Europe.

Foreign Influence

Before broadcasting in West and East Germany was restructured, some voices were to be heard in West Germany warning that it was necessary to avert the media colonization of East Germany. One of those voices was that of Hartwig Kelm, then Chairman of ARD, Germany's public TV channel 1 (ARD press release, Feb. 14, 1990). Eight months later Kurt Biedenkopf, a CDU politician from the State of North Rhine Westphalia and at the time candidate for the Premier of the new Federal State of Saxony, made a similar statement (*Welt am Sonntag,* Oct. 14, 1990, p. 26). Today, such statements are can no longer to be heard form official quarters, and the very people who had once warned against media colonization are actively involved in promoting their own particularist interests in the former GDR. More shamelessly than ever before in the history of West Germany, the broadcasting structures which existed in the former GDR were sacrificed to the interests of the two large West German political parties (Frenkel 1990; Frenkel 1991; Frank 1992).

While it is still a moot question how exactly foreign Western influence will manifest itself in radio and in particular TV broadcasting in the individual east European countries, the printed press in many of those countries is already securely in the hands of Western media capital. This applies especially to Poland and Hungary, but also, and for all the specific differences, to the former GDR. In the case of the five new federal states in east Germany, an analysis of press concentration there (Schneider 1992a; Schneider 1992b) shows that this concentration is higher at the moment than in the days of the former GDR, and that the former SED party newspapers which still dominate the market in the new federal states are today owned by the largest West German newspaper publishing houses.

In the case of Hungary, research work undertaken by Zoltán Jakab and Mihály Galik (1991) demonstrates that the Hungarian press is also securely in the hands of West German (in minor sectors, Austrian) publishers. The same applies to the Hungarian telecommunications industry A few years ago, studies by the World Bank found that this industry was ready for the global market. However, a recent study (Apáthy/Lamberger/Rácz/Szanyi 1991) banishes such forecast to be complete illusion. Of a total of four Hungarian companies active in the telecommunications industry, two are facing bankruptcy while the other two have become merely extended work-benches for the Siemens and Ericsson companies.

For many economists in East Europe, privatization and openness to the global market are the two single most important elements in any successful attempt to modernize their countries and catch up with the West. Drawing on a variety of statistics, they point out that the situation in their countries is similar to that in West Europe so and so many years ago and that they will have brought their country up to the West European standard in so and so many years. Yet the various forms of brain drain, privatization and foreign influence prevailing speak against such analogies and predictions. In fact, the developments could be more readily compared with what could be termed "Latin Americanization".

This phenomenon can be best illustrated with reference to the structure of Russia's foreign trade. Before the October revolution Russia's industrial output had experienced enormous growth, yet the extraction of Russian oil was wholly in foreign hands, mining 90 percent, chemical industry 50 percent and the textile industry 30 percent. In this context, it is significant that the structure of foreign trade between Czarist Russia (and the later Soviet Union), and the West has scarcely changed. At a steady rate of approx. 45 percent of all-Russian/Soviet imports in the mechanical engineering sector, the basic pattern of the East exchanging raw materials for technology from the West has remained constant over the past 70 years (Gotthelf 1979).

This means that even the communist state in the former USSR (and also some other East European countries) could essentially be understood as peripherally capitalist and not just as a qualitatively different political and economic system. Ever since the opposition between the systems disappeared in 1989, what has remained is just the periphery, comparable to Latin America. In fond memory of its former power and glory days, therefore, and without shying away from racist comparisons, some former USSR generals who had been sent into early retirement recently compared Russia in its present desolation to the "Upper Volta + atomic weapons".

In recent history, and measured in terms of growth in industrial output and active participation in global trade (but excl. growth in social justice), only the "four small tigers" of Southeast Asia, namely Singapore, Taiwan, Hong Kong and South Korea, have been successful in modernizing and catching up economically. They, too, started out with a system involving peripheral capitalism. The declining importance of raw materials worldwide is one of several reasons why the former USSR will not succeed in its attempt to catch up with capitalism.

The European Energy charter signed on December 17, 1991 is bound to make an very important contribution towards further entrenching Russia's traditional role as a dependent energy supplier. The ongoing prospecting for natural resources in Siberia by foreign investors is comparable in its early capitalist manifestations to the US Gold Rush in the 19th century.

A second reason why the strategy of catching up with capitalism is destined not to succeed has to do with East Europe's enormous foreign debt, which between 1981 and 1989 increased by 25 percent. Before 1917, Russia actually had very positive terms of trade owing to its immense grain exports, but in 1989 the foreign debt the former USSR owed the West was approx. 40 billion US dollars, that of Hungary was almost 20 billion, and that of Poland approx. 40 billion. Many indicators suggest that, like the developing countries, East Europe will be unable to free itself of the mechanisms of the debt-trap.

4. The Public Sphere and Peripheral Capitalism in East Europe after 1989

To conclude summarily that censorship of the media, of information and of the freedom of expression by a party and state bureaucracy has now been replaced by media capital censorship would be only partially correct. And yet in a theoretical treatment of the issue of what might constitute the public sphere in Eastern Europe after 1989, such a conclusion would still be more apt and more in keeping with a tradition of critical thought than all the abstract talk about media freedom. Elizabeth Fox, a North American specialist on mass communication in Latin America, have offered a catchy definition for media imperialism:

> Media imperialism has taken hold when an advertisement is shown on television for Colgate toothpaste and the viewer does not even have the money to buy a toothbrush.

In other words, as long as the overwhelming process of material deprivation among large sections of the Eastern European population continues, that is to say as long as no concrete implementation of that abstract freedom of the media is possible that very freedom remains ideological to the highest degree, i.e., it reinforces power. In order to be able to adequately determine what communication in the public sphere could be in East Europe after 1989, not only must the gradual capitalist structure of the mass media be take into account, but also the question of what kind of social structures give this capitalist public sphere its specific form. In this context, the following points deserve particular attention:

1. The above-mentioned process of material deprivation among large sections of the population will exclude them from access to the mass media, silencing their voices and keeping it silenced. In contrast to this, in the metropoles and a few high-tech islands (tax-free zones, teleports) there will at the same time be the most modern of links to Western ICT. In view of our experience to date with such zones (for example, in the Caribbean), the trickle-down-effect this has on the economy of the county in question is bound to be negligible.

2. With the exception of the former GDR, whose economic and political elite has been almost completely replaced by West German managers, in most of the East European countries the old nomenclature has more or less been left intact. For the mass media this means a novel and strange mix of private-sector economy and its constraints on the one hand, and a work force which is accustomed to acting within bureaucratic, authoritarian structures, on the other. In Russia, this situation means that about 92,000 civil servants are pre-occupied with the task of privatizing state companies.

   This paradoxical state of affairs can either be a complete failure or lead to strange new and authoritarian forms of public spheres. In contrast to the West European bourgeoisie, who in the course of the past 200 years was able to fight for and gain private property and the means to protect this in their own interests (through a combination of freedom of expression and of the press) there will be no bourgeois class in the strict sense in East Europe, even in the near future, that is in a position to establish its status on the basis of personal property. What is likely to emerge in these countries is a new old type of state class whose understanding of the public sphere will necessarily be authoritarian and undemocratic.

Some examples from the Russian Federation may illustrate this trend: At the end of 1991, there was the case in which state prosecutors from Moscow sold video films of the interrogation protocols of the August putschists; up to this very day, high ranking military personnel improve their salary by selling valuable German books from the spoils of the Second World War, some employees at the Moscow *Business World* magazine think nothing of raising their salaries by means of friendly articles on companies which show their gratitude to the tune of 2,000 rubles per article.

3. The public sphere as traditionally understood by Western democracies involves a conscious, dispassionate, and on-going debate with history. One important pre-requisite for this is sufficient time. And in the former CMEA states there is just not enough time. The haste with which streets and cities were renamed or the sudden longing for the return of monarchs living in exile point towards a tendency to unleash history from the realm of the present. Where the difficulties of coming to terms with the recent past are concealed by taboos, what takes hold is repression and certainly not a public sphere. If a country does not come to terms with its past history then in the long term no future is possible.

4. The transformation from the bankrupt communism to the peripheral capitalism in East Europe is destined to proceed with brute force. Accordingly, there will be brutal forms of apparently public spheres. The sheer physical brutality of this new understanding of the public sphere emerges in the following example (Weskott 1994). It was in Summer 1991 when about 100,000 brand new books from former GDR publishing houses were found on rubbish heaps in Saxony, among them works by Heinrich Mann, Leo Tolstoy, Stefan Heym and Ernesto Cardenal. The former GDR state-run monopolistic book distribution company had thrown away these books because they had proved unsellable in the face of competition for the new Western products. After the public burning of books by German fascists in 1933, this act of destruction, especially of an author like Heinrich Mann, has proved to be a more than embarrassing event.

5. Many East European countries and most of the states of the former Soviet Union have only a small domestic market. Given the capital-intensive nature of mass media and information and communication

technologies, in small economies there is always then a neglect of so-called local content and an intensification of the foreign influence on capital, technology and content. In addition, where old centralized media structures are forced to give way to decentralized structures in the process of democratization, the abruptness of the change often leads to chaotic internal fragmentation and not decentralization.

6. It is inherent to the inner logic of peripheral capitalism that it is not controlled by the respective national capital but by foreign, multi-national and metropolitan capital. These capital forces are stronger than all national capitals. Furthermore, and logically in East Europe, such forces have a different interest in the media than the respective national capital may have (should anything worthy of that name emerge). This impacts on East Europe in two ways: First, economically, this process blocks the establishment of an indigenous media industry, and second, culturally this process will lead to the indigenous population perceiving the public sphere as indebted to foreign capital and thus strange and threatening.

   Foreign influence on the media before 1989 certainly involved a quantum of political emancipation. But After 1989 that foreign influence has merely been accelerating cultural heterogeneity in the East European countries. "Convinced Westerners" stand in stubborn opposition to autochtonic groups. These processes have already been observed and thoroughly researched in the course of the so-called cultural clash between the Third World and the industrial countries of the North.

   For two reasons such processes may potentially be more a source of dangerous conflict in East Europe than they are in the countries of the Third World. *First*: the privatization of the mass media in East Europe is more drastic in its contours than even in Latin America. *Second*: since the advent of colonialism (for the past 500 years), the Third World has become acquainted with all the various types of cultural clash. Thus, the developing countries have had 500 years to create manifest and latent forms of resistance to such outside influences, whereas, the time pressures exerted on East Europe are so enormous as to make it almost impossible to avoid them.

7. If a dual society, with its typical form of clandestine public sphere, turns into a public society, then what was once concealed and forbidden suddenly loses its sting. What is also lost is that clandestine

public sphere's vision of a better life. Where private and intimate communication no longer prefers the dream of a better world (however vague that dream may be), where the once longed-for better life proves (at least in its infancy and for most people) to be worse, then what was once public in private communication quickly turns into narrow, bourgeois conformism. The once lively communication becomes trivial.

Whereas, for example, in Poland at the time of the rule of the old state and party, there was once a very strong sense of a "We", of community among the people who were thoroughly fed up with "the powers that were", this "We" feeling has since given way to an "I" feeling, with each person pursuing individual interests to his/her own advantage and if necessary to the detriment of others.

Advertising plays a central role in the extremely complex process of re-structuring the public sphere. Furthermore, it should not be forgotten that Hungary and Yugoslavia, countries which for many years conducted the experiment of a socialist market economy, were already quite familiar with advertising in the same economic function as it has in Western capitalism (Hanson 1974). Advertising form West Europe reaches many East European countries via commercial TV stations. Advertising for Western consumer goods was so intense and common in former Czechoslovakia, for example, that a comparative survey there (Kirschhofer-Bozenhardt 1990) of the products of the Coca Cola, Pepsi Cola, Sony, Kodak and Michelin companies revealed that they were better known and had a greater appeal there than in the former GDR, even though East Germany was far more exposed to foreign media than any other East European country.

A survey of the CIS countries shows that Western advertising is well-known there essentially via cinema, radio and daily newspapers. Almost half of those interviewed found Western advertising interesting, well-made and necessary. The following social groups frequently ranked as full-fledged *pressure groups* in favor of Western advertising (VCIOM/SINUS 1990): young men in Moscow and St. Petersburg with an academic background and high salaries, i.e., sociologically, the classic group which normally constitutes the motor of social change, both for the good and the bad.

Initial (and still inadequate) data on Russian advertising agencies show that these are more likely to be active in the service-sector market (banks, stock exchanges, large companies) than in the consumer goods market. Behind the 200-300 ! stock exchanges in Moscow are often old state trading firms given a new guise, and their intensive advertising campaigns are already causing bad feeling among the general population. According to the newspaper *Moscow News*, stock-exchange advertising ought to be restricted because it is causing growing irritation among the population (Wesselow 1992, 12). Advertising, in particular of the kind imported from Western capitalism, is destined to become one of the core elements in the intensification of cultural heterogeneity in East Europe.

In his conclusion to a study on mass culture in the USSR, published in 1991, Yassen Zassoursky writes: “I believe it is possible to find measures that allow the market to operate wisely” (Zassoursky 1991, 18). Unfortunately, both, historical experience and analytical insight speak against this conviction. The demise of that deplorable East European form of communism throws up an urgent question about the “enemy in ourselves” and forces us to finally give some thought to the failures of the market.

In the 12th century Nestor Chronicle there is a description of Russia’s beginnings. In the year 862, the Eastern Slavic peoples called on the Norsemen to help them reconstruct and outwardly stabilize their empire, which had fallen into disarray. The plea they made at the time to the Norsemen was more or less as follows: “Our land is large and rich in nutrition, but it has no order. Come, rule and reign over us” (quoted from Grasshoff et al. 1975, 36). A 19th century philosopher, today considered unimportant, once said that history is enacted twice over, once as tragedy, once as farce. “Come, rule and reign over us”, this plea is going out yet again from Russia, this time in the direction of Western capitalism.

What comes after the farce?

References

Adorno, Theodor W. and Horkheimer, Max: *Dialectic of Enlightenment,* London: NLB 1979.

Angell, O. and Kouzminov, V. A.: *Report of the Working Party on "Brain Drain Issues in Europe",* Paris: UNESCO Regional Office for Science and Technology for Europe 1991.

Apáthy, Ervin; Lamberger, Galina; Rácz, Margit and Szanyi, Miklós: *The Change of Regime and the Hungarian Telecommuniation Industry.* An Empirical Study, Budapest: Institute for World Economics of the Hungarian Academy of Sciences 1991.

Arthur, C.: "Agony in advertising: Appraising recent media images of suffering and death", in: *Media Development,* No. 4/1992, pp. 19-23.

Baum, K.-H.: "Soll der Klassenfeind doch pfeifen, der Fürst hat gelächelt. Zehn Zensoren für eine einzige Sendung: Wie die SED-Führung Fernsehjournalisten entmutigte", in: *Frankfurter Rundschau,* January 24, 1990, p. 3.

Becker, C.: "Rosarote Zungen. Der italienische Konzern Benetton trägt die Skandalfahne der 'Image'-Werbung", in: *Die Tageszeitung,* March 21, 1992, pp. 22-23.

Bleek, W. and Mertens, L.: *DDR-Dissertationen.* Promotionspraxis und Geheimhaltung von Doktorarbeiten im SED-Staat, Opladen: Westdeutscher Verlag 1994.

Bücher, Karl: *Auswahl der publizistikwissenschaftlichen Schriften,* Bochum: Brockmeyer 1981.

Chereshkin, K. and Tsalenko, M.: *Information Processing 89,* ed. by G.X. Ritter, Amsterdam 1989, pp. 1083-87.

Daniloff, N.: *Media Developments in the Soviet Union,* Washington: The World Press Freedom Committee 1988.

Fathi, A.: "The Role of the Islamic Pulpit", in: *Journal of Communication,* No.3/ 1979, pp. 102-106.

Frank, G.: "Rundfunk in den neuen Bundesländern. Vom Partei- zum Parteienrundfunk", in: *Kritische Justiz,* No. 4/1992, pp. 463-72.

Franke, K.: "Ein Zensor, der ganz gut reinpasste. Gespräch mit Klaus Selbig, in der DDR zuständig für Druckgenehmigungen", in: *Süddeutsche Zeitung,* July 3, 1991.

Frenkel, R.: "ARD und ZDF über alles. Die Neuordnung des deutschen Hörfunks und Fernsehens: Gewinner im Westen, Verlierer im Osten", in: *Die Zeit,* November 2, 1990, p. 3.

Frenkel, R.: "Rundfunkkolonie Ost. Ein Jahr nach der Einigung: Hörfunk und Fernsehen folgen dem schlechten westdeutschen Beispiel", in: *Die Zeit,* October 3, 1991, p. 65.

Gaus, G.: *Texte zur deutschen Frage,* Darmstadt: Luchterhand 1981.

Gotthelf, M.: *Außenhandelsentwicklung und Außenhandelsstrategie der Sowjetunion,* Frankfurt: Haag und Herchen 1979.

Grasshoff, H.; Müller, K. and Sturm, G.: *O Bojan, du Nachtigall der alten Zeit.* Sieben Jahrhunderte altrussischer Literatur. 3rd edition, Berlin 1975.

Güttler, M.: "Das Informationssystem der staatlichen Statistik der DDR. Computergestützte Entscheidungsunterstützung für die Planung und Leitung der Volkswirtschaft und Gesellschaft", in: *Informatik Forum* (Vienna, Austria), No. 3/1992, pp. 108-23.

Hanson, P.: *Advertising and Socialism,* London 1974.

Holzweissig, G.: *DDR-Presse unter Parteikontrolle,* Bonn: Gesamtdeutsches Institut 1991.

Innis, Harold: *Empire and communications,* Oxford: Oxford University Press 1950.

Jakab, Zoltan and Galik, J.: *Survival Efficiency and Independence.* The Presence of Foreign Capital in the Hungarian Media Market, Düsseldorf: The European Institute for the Media 1991.

Kapitza, S.: "Wissenschaftsfeindlichkeit in der Sowjetunion", in: *Spektrum der* Wissenschaft, October 1991, pp. 130-136.

Kirschhofer-Bozenhardt, A.v.: "Ost Marketing: Deutsch hat wieder Saison", in: *Viertel-Jahreshefte für Media und Werbewirkung,* No. 3/1990, pp. 2-9.

Kuczynski, Jürgen: *Dialog mit meinem Urenkel.* 6th edition, Berlin: Aufbau 1986.

Lemper, Ute: "Human dignity trampled by perestroika", in: *The European,* May 10, 1992, p. 31.

Leggewie, Claus: "Europa in den 'United Colors of Benetton'", in: *Kunstforum International,* No.118/1992, pp. 147-57.

Lerg, W.; Ravenstein, M. and Schiller-Lerg, S.: *Sowjetische Publizistik zwischen Öffnung und Umgestaltung.* Die Medien im Zeichen von Glasnost und Perestroika, Münster: Lit-Verlag 1991.

Liminski, J.: "Desinformation. Ein Relikt Kalten Krieges?", in: *Aus Politik und Zeitgeschichte,* No. 52-53/1998, pp. 34-46.

Lobrano, A.: "Czech Artists Mull Free Market's Cost", in: *International Herald Tribune,* April 25-26, 1992, p.7 and 10.

Manaev, O.: "The Influence of Western Radio on the Democratization of Soviet Youth", in: *Journal of Communication,* Spring 1991, pp. 72-91.

Mann, Thomas: "J'accuse. Wider die Selbstgerechtigkeit der besseren Welt", in: *Blätter für deutsche und internationale Politik,* No. 12/1991, pp. 1435-45.

Narsikulow, R.: "Die Mehrheit ist arm, die Bedürfnisstruktur noch einheitlich", in: *Moskau News,* No. 4/1992, p. 12.

Naylor, T. H.: "Von den Russen lernen", in: *Viertel-Jahreshefte für Media und Werbewirkung*, No. 3/1989, pp. 34-36.

Reich, A.: "'Dann kam der Westler mit dem Spielsalon'. Mit den Kulturhäusern verlieren die kleinen Gemeinden im Osten auch ein Stück Lebensqualität", in: *Die Welt*, April 3, 1992, p.19.

Rhode, Barbara: *East-West Migration/Brain Drain,* Bruxelles: EU-Commission, COST-Committee 1991, (mimeo).

Samarajiva, Rohan: "The murky beginnings of the communication and development field: Voice of America and 'The Passing of Traditional Society'", in: *Rethinking Development Communication*, ed. by Neville Jayaweera and Sarath Amunugama, Singapore: The Asian Mass Communication Research and Information Centre 1987, p. 319.

Schneider, Beate (a): "Pressemarkt Ost II: Nur die Konzentration macht Fortschritte", in: *Pressemarkt Ost.* Nationale und internationale Perspektiven, ed. by W. Mahle, Munich: Ölschläger 1992, pp. 35-45.

Schneider, Beate (b): "Die ostdeutsche Tagespresse - eine (traurige) Bilanz", in: *Media Perspektiven*, No. 7/1992, pp. 428-41.

Seidl, C.: "Kein Platz für tote Italiener. Über die neue Ethik und Ästhetik der Reklame", in: *Der Spiegel*, No. 11/1992, pp. 296-98.

Splichal, Slavko: "Public Opinion and the controversies in communication science", in: *Media, Culture and Society* 1992, pp. 237-61.

Smythe, Dallas: "Communications: Blindspot of Western Marxism", in: *Canadian Journal of Political and Social Theory*, No. 3/1977, pp. 1-28.

Vartanov, A.: "Television as Spectacle and Myth", in: *Journal of Communication,* Spring 1991, pp. 162-71.

VCIOM (Moscow) and SINUS (Munich): *USSR intern.* Basisdaten 1990. Auszüge aus einer Verbraucherbefragung. Analyse für die Verlage *Das Beste* und *Änne Burda*, Munich 1990 (mimeo).

Wagner, H.: *Die Doppelgesellschaft: Systemwandel in Polen,* Berlin 1981.

Weskott, M.: *Eine Kultur verlässt den Raum.* Gehören Bücher auf den Müll?, Katlenburg: Edition Anton Berg 1994.

Wesselow, S.: "Das Werbegeschäft in Russland", in: *Moskau News*, May 1992, pp. 12-13.

Wright, R.: "Why Soviet science collapsed. The experiment that failed", in: *The New Republic*, October 26, 1991, pp. 20-25.

Zassoursky, Yassen N.: "Mass Culture and Market Culture", in: *Journal of Communication,* Spring 1991, pp. 13-18.

21
Contradictions in the Informatization of Politics and Society

1. Informatization and Social Change

The expression and concept of "informatization", used for the first time in the Nora-Minc Report[1], suggests an active, forward moving force, implies that Western industrial societies are undergoing a structural change in which "information" as a commodity assumes an increasingly greater social importance. This increased significance is, so the argument goes, to be seen from a number of indicators: for example, in the rising share of GNP sourced by the service sector, in the increase of white-collar workers, or the growing turnover of the electronic and media-related industries. If, for example, we add together the combined annual turnover of the media and electronic industries in West Germany - in other words, if we combine the "software" and hardware sectors - then the joint figure for these two branches of industry is over DM 100 billion, which makes them the second largest industrial sector after the chemicals industry, with a total payroll of approximately one million persons.

Needless to say, the concept of "informatization" also blurs things over, as it does not name the social conditions, interrelationships and principals which promote the "information" in question. Although the quite manifest political terms of reference of the Nora-Minc Report differs reassuringly from the technocratic perspective of its West German counterpart, the Telecommunications Report (published in 1976), in general it offers no clear analysis of related structural development. Quite obviously, "informatization" designates a qualitative change in late capitalist industrial societies, a change in which the contradiction between productive forces and the means of production converges in an unprecedented manner. Finally, it is a transformation in which Francis Bacon's dictum of 1598, "Knowledge is power" has undergone a change from the realm of ideology to that of reality, and today power and knowledge can no longer be separated. The informatization of power and the rise of information as a means to power are interrelated and coexist parallel to each other. The novel quality of social change through informatization can be shown quite tangibly using the following example:

> The firebrigade system in Malmö's industrial zone (Sweden) complied a register of all factories in the vicinity, listing what is produced and what fire-fighting materials need to be used. The data gathered was then transmitted to a computer in Cleveland, Ohio (USA), because the fire brigade in question did not own a computer and the costs of using a Swedish computer center would have been higher than that in the USA. When a fire breaks out in one of the factories, the smoke detectors send out the alarm for the firebrigade; at the same time, the relevant information is transferred by phone to a satellite station in England which in turn passes the information on to a satellite in geostationary orbit. From here, the signal goes directly to the computer in Cleveland which downloads the necessary data and sends them back to the fire brigade in Malmö by the same process direct to terminals in the fire-brigade vehicles such that the firefighters receive data on buildings, access fire fighting materials, etc.

At an abstract level, the novel quality of social change through informatization is as follows: The interrelationship between computer telematics and telecommunications would suggest that there is now one comprehensive and singular information network. This network is advanced to a stage where it recognizes no distinction between professional and mass communication, between print and electronic media, between acoustic and optic signal transmission, or between information storage, processing and transmission. The totality of this new system contributes to the nullification of two further characteristics of earlier information technologies: The non-simultaneous nature of time and space.

Only differing in terms of the few seconds required for transmission, the theory thus suggests that this all encompassing network enables us to possess all conceivable information processes at one and the same time and in all corners of the globe. The future information systems will be global, independent of time, technically connected together in one single network and probably intelligence-producing, if only in the sense of instrumental reason.

Moreover, the technology on which the process of informatization is based is a convergence technology, in other words a technology which has repercussions for the productive forces, means of production and for all areas of life. A further characteristic is the rapidity factor, the speed at which a discovery within a single area of ICT is put to multiple use.

Take, for example, the German invention of the telephone by Philipp Reis in 1861 and its almost mass global use a hundred years later, and compare it to the invention of videotex and how it had spread only a few years later. Put differently, the period of time which a social system needs to adapt relatively without conflict to technical innovations has been drastically pruned. It is these mentioned characteristics that separate the process of informatization and the corresponding information technologies of today from the single technologies for the past. Historical comparisons with (for example) the invention of the railway or the bulb and the fashionable retrospection of "Maschinenstürmerei" or of the Luddites in the early 19th century are thus false and serve additional distracting functions.

Arguments critical of technology may at present use similarly pessimistic modes of languages as before, yet their political function need not be as retrogressive as at that time. Even when the objective conditions of informatization are of a novel quality, these once pessimistic arguments may serve a progressive function today.

An important element of the present social change through informatization becomes evident if we examine words such as satellite and telecommunications and through these the conquest of space by mankind. The universe, space which is extremely distant from us, is submitted to the principle of commoditization by ICTs. A parallel to this would be the development of genetic engineering which touches on something extremely close to us - there, the principle of commoditization is applied to begin to bring our biological reproduction under social control. The emphasis on biologization and informatization implies a qualitative change. To put it more abstractly: when the commodity principle conquers distance and closeness, late capitalist industrial society enters a new phase.

Two differing scholarly schools of thought have emerged in the last fifteen years in response to the theoretical discourse on the informatization within western industrial societies.

The work of the post-industrialists (Marc Uri Porat, Daniel Bell, Herman Kahn, Karl Steinbuch, Alvin Toffler) focuses on the influence of ICT on economies, on strategies for maximizing profit and productivity, and on the changes in the industrial sector. According to Daniel Bell the microelectronic "revolution" (transistors and microchips) has heralded a new relationship to production in the 20th century. Products will no longer be manufactured from a material basis of coal and oil as in the 19th century, but on the basis of information production. Accordingly, the blue collar factory worker gives way to the service sector worker.

These scientists, technicians, information producers/disseminators, and members of all the service sectors are the guardians of a new social order, whose knowledge and whose potential to systematically deal with the emerging new order (game theory, systems analysis, "sentient" computers) will break the formerly predominant power of profit-oriented finance and industrial capital. There are indeed also pessimistic prognoses from among the post-industrialists: Sarcastically French philosopher Jacques Ellul can only imagine future society not as an universal concentration camp, because, thanks to technology, it will not be so ugly, because everything will have an order, and human emotions will no longer be recognizable among all the glittering chrome.[2]

By contrast, the work of the dominance theorists (in the US, for example, Herbert I. Schiller and in West Germany Ulrich Briefs) concentrates first of all on the ineluctable reference to the power-related character of ICT followed by analyses of the maintenance and strengthening of inequality, dependence and repression through these very technologies in the interest of capital and the political elite. Under different social circumstances, ICT could be used as an emancipative and liberational force.

At the political level, it is no injustice to the German conservative CDU/CSU parties to locate them on the side of the post-industrialists as the following quotation from Christian Schwarz-Schlling, at the time German Federal Minister for Post and Telecommunications, demonstrates:

> The new information and communications technologies, for which the post is responsible, function as a catalyst for the entire economy."[3]

In contrast, the left SPD is surely to be found on the side of the dominance theoreticians. Former Chancellor Helmut Schmidt, for example, stated at the media seminar of the SPD in 1979:

> There is [...] a danger that the new media will basically change democratic society by overexposure and by eliding difference. There is a danger that a great deal of political influence and power will end up in unregulated hands.[4]

These two statements make it evident that the CDU/CSU have a very clear understanding of informatization as the politics of structure, while the SPD still often mistakenly perceive informatization as a sector issue in media politics. That said, both positions have a number of theoretical weaknesses in common. By using contradictory catch-phrases like "Risk and Opportunity" (the title of the SPD seminar on the media), "For Better or for Worse" (the title of the study on microelectronics commissioned by the Club of Rome) or "Curse or Blessing" (cover story in *Der Spiegel* magazine, 5/1982 on the Report of the Club of Rome) both schools of thought show a utilitarian pluralistic approach, which assumes that one or the other goal can be reached with neutral technology. But this approach fails to grasp that the relationship of power of the means of production can be found in the productive forces which by definition include ICT. Herbert Marcuse has formulated these ideas in the following manner:

> The incessant dynamic of technical progress has become permeated with political content, and the Logos of techniques has been made into the Logos of continued servitude. The liberating forces of technology - the instrumentalization of things - turns into a fetter of liberation; the instrumentalization of Man. [...] The world tends to become the stuff of total administration which absorbs even the administrator.[5]

One-dimensional thought is inherent in both directions: the lateral outlook of the post-industrialists prevents one from grasping that the momentum innate in the dialectical dynamic of the process of informatization is directed against itself. The lateral thought of the dominance theorists who all too often can only think in terms of increasing repression is all too easily caught up in a chain of self-fulfilling prophecies which leaves no room for alternatives. He reminds one fatally of the following aphorism from Theodor W. Adorno:

> The glorification of the great underdogs implies a glorification of the great system which brings them forth in the first place.[6]

Although informatization is bringing about incisive change (as we have already explained) as new areas are touched by commodatization, nevertheless the dynamic of this change is self-contradictory. On the one hand, the post-industrialists must consider the question why their success has not evolved as quickly as they supposed it would and what they intend to do to avoid becoming a victim of their own strategies. Conversely the dominance theorists must ask themselves whether more intensive involvement with the contradictions inherent in the process of informatization will not lead them to different conclusions. There is, according to US communications scientist Vincent Mosco. "Some trouble in paradise"[7].

2. Trouble in the Informatization Paradise

The all-encompassing process of informatization must not only anticipate imminent contradictions, not just with explicit political opposition (parts of the labor movement or with the non-aligned nations), but indeed also with purely technical problems of which we shall only list a few here. In the realm of satellite communication orbiting sections of the launch rockets and obsolescent satellites seriously threaten unhindered development; there is in practice only a finite number of radio frequencies which have thus far be used effectively by means of multiband technologies; the limitation of satellite positions in geostationary orbit cannot be used effectively because of the unsolved problem of satellite platforms.

In the realm of computer communications there is, for example, the problem of heat emission resulting from ever quicker computing times and ever greater density in highly integrated computers which up until new were technologically not possible. Not to mention the phenomenon of the so-called nuclear electromagnetic pulses which, after the ignition of an atom bomb at a great height, would disable all electrical circuitry - a phenomenon, by the way, which poses severe problems to the military in industrialized countries. After all, the entire information and early warning systems run by electricity would be knocked out. Even if the technical problems can be solved, a number of inherent contradictions arise with the informatization of politics and society.

Internationalism vs. National Sovereignty

The debates on the "free flow of information" in the early 1970s resulted from the Third World's situation as a passive recipient of unhindered media (and information), over-exposure that was generated by the industrial nations. From an a-historical, formalistic and short-term economic perspective the Western industrial countries rejected these issues, reducing them to a question of either freedom or state censorship. That may have been too sudden for some Western countries and not in their own interest. As informatization is certainly a very quick, effective and relatively cheap form of internationalization, (and it only makes sense technically as well as economically if it increasingly unravels on an international scale), the problem of state sovereignty over national media/electronic and information industries becomes ever more acute for many of the industrialized nation states in the West. We may be emphasizing the anachronistic sovereignty of the post-War era, but sovereignty for many Western states faced with international informatization as well as economic pressure from the USA has become the problem of the day.

Sovereignty has become a problem in the realm of transborder data flow, in the exodus of advertising accounts to foreign firms and over-exposure to foreign TV programs. All these phenomena have caused an acute, structural conflict between Canada and the USA, and Canada's protectionist interests have in part already been legalized. In the realm of military remote sensing satellites the USA have violated Australia's sovereignty and rudely interfered in the internal affairs of the country through the CIA's Rhyolit satellite program. The same seems true for Greenland which is under Danish sovereignty. There, the USA have deployed satellite receiving stations whose functions are not known to the Danish government. Ironically, the problems of sovereignty arising from crossborder satellite communications should have repercussions on Germany, too. In 1972, in the UNESCO West Germany voted against the basic declaration on the use of satellites, because, influenced by Art. 9 of this declaration, it feared state censorship of satellite communications by Third World countries. In 1979, in an essay on media politics, Helmut Schmidt drew attention to the possible political and economic consequences of the Luxembourg satellite on the advertising industry in Germany.

The present debates on protectionism on the rival electronic industries in the USA, Japan and West Europe are political results of international informatization, whereby the weaker participants seek to maintain their position vis-à-vis the USA. This protectionism is no "scourge of the times", as some newspapers see it, but rather a necessary response on the part of national economies which in this historical situation in the interest of their own survival can no longer tolerate outside control for any reason. (In a different situation the "Deutsche Zollverein" - German Customs Union - pursued similar goals, albeit it under the influence of metropolitan Prussia.) And for these very reasons most Western industrial countries could for the time being prevent the motion that the United States unexpectedly tabled at the last GATT Conference. The USA did not succeed in imposing its concept that, in future, the service sector should be subjected to GATT regulations, and that the "free flow of information" should be legally sanctioned for the international informatization process.

First Hypothesis:
The more global informatization increases, the less the doctrine of the "free flow of information" corresponds to the national economic interests of most Western industrial countries.

National vs. International Capital

As the debate in the USA on the relationship between national security and scientific and technical transfers of information shows, the Reagan Administration is trying to regulate export-oriented information transfer through its "Executive Order on National Security Information" from 1982. We can view this within the strategic framework of the East-West conflict; it can also additionally be seen as the attempt by a national government to use a displaced ideology (in this instance, anti-communism) to oppose the interests of enlightened international capital in the hope that it can actively remain in control. It is by no means coincidence that a leading international corporation in the field of semi-conductor technology accused the Reagan Administration of a violation of the doctrine of the free flow of information on the basis of an analysis of export regulations for technical scientific data. This investigation on the part of a leading manager at Texas Instruments ended with the following passage:

> Contrary to official claims, the US cannot be defined as a totally free and open society, as certain information controls do exist.[8]

As statements by the German Federal Confederation of Industry (BDI) concerning a boycott of exports to Iran or in relation to technological transfers to the socialist states (especially in relation to the gas pipeline project) demonstrate, the big industrial players concern themselves very little with political ideology. Analyses of economic boycotts show that these industries still effectively ignore boycotts instituted by national governments. Numerous takeovers, mergers, cooperation agreements and bankruptcies within the information and electronic industries over the last few years illustrate that branches of these industries are witnessing a process of concentration at a breath-taking speed. The resulting transnational conglomerates can hardly be controlled by national governments. They are also a danger to the middle classes, to the crafts and small industries. Exactly, this awareness motivated Lothar Späth, then Premier of Baden-Württemberg, the home of German SMEs, when on November 29, 1979 he addressed the West German Parliament as follows:

> It is already evident that in the field of advertising the inflow of funds into the so-called "print-media" is being drastically changed in favor of electronic processes by the use of foreign satellite transmissions. It is feared especially by the periodicals that a large part of their advertising intake will be threatened by the inter-regional and international nature of the advertising business. At the same time, this implies that mid-sized and large publishers must accordingly re-focus their business interests. [...] Thus, there is the real danger that our situation will come to resemble the American or Italian experience and many periodicals or papers will be left without any economic basis.[9]

Second Hypothesis:
A process of global informatization serves the needs, above all else, of international capital. It harms SMEs and tends to bite the hand that feeds it.

Specific Contradictions Between Sectors of Capital

In the developing global informatization network there are still a number of areas in which the functional possibilities of the entire system do not yet harmonize: There are a great variety of varying technologies for information storage and transmission that all carry out exactly the same functions. Microchips, computers or the bubble chip can store a much higher concentration of information that traditional print media. Videodiscs and video films are replacing color film.

As these differing technologies are being introduced simultaneously on the market by competing industrial concerns it is not yet certain which of them and its related capital backers will win out. The TED videodisc, developed by AEG-Telefunken, after having been shelved since the early 1970s could not, on its introduction in 1975, compete with the burgeoning video boom. This coincides with a complete misinterpretation of the market potential for the videodisc by the Prognos-Institute in 1972. This experiment has possibly contributed to the catastrophic situation of AEG-Telefunken today. Another instance of this is that many corporations invested heavily in so-called floppy discs using „bubble"-chip technology, only to realize in 1981 that this technology could not be mass-produced and thus is not cheap enough for the consumer.

Third Hypothesis:
The information market can only in part be subjected to controls. It is hard to discern what exact shape this market will take. When fully developed, the market will eliminate some sectors of industry.

Distorting of Information vs. Marketing Interests

In 1979 the Western secret services and the major Western news agencies (AP, UPI, Reuters, AFP) had absolutely no grasp of the revolutionary situation in Iran and no adequate understanding of its results. This confirms in a very striking manner the decades-old dictum of the empirical social sciences: the industrial countries perceive the Third World in a distorted and Eurocentric fashion. As a result of the Iran debacle, some internationally respected politicians such as Edward Heath and Robert McNamara, together with big industrialists, have established their own information service, IRIS (International Reporting Information System) to be quicker, better and more objectively informed about the Third World.

Fourth Hypothesis:
Distorted news reporting on the Third World in industrial countries corresponds less and less with the interests of productive capital. With the increasing importance of the Third World as a market for this capital, more detailed and exact information on local market conditions is needed in order to avoid unwise investments. In the long run, industrial countries need public support in their endeavor to formulate a better understanding of the Third World.

Stability vs. Volatility

A study on vulnerability in society, commissioned by the Swedish Defense Ministry (1978), show that highly computerized societies can, in certain circumstances, be more vulnerable than lesser computerized counterparts. The stability of a society can be shaken by an interruption of foreign trade owing to a scarcity of computer spare parts. Criminal acts involving large computer systems can paralyze wide areas of the service sector. Illegal databases often operate side by side with their legal counterparts. They are mainly used for industrial espionage or for gathering of personal data.

Computer crimes in the USA cause damage of some US$ 100 million p.a.. So banks, insurance and industrial corporations must reckon with increasing losses. It is through the millions of US homes which have installed PCs that computer fans and skilled programmers have access to outside databases. This is dangerous for big international banks which transfer more than US$ 400 billion a day, they fear penetration of their transmission systems by outside computers. Despite repeated attempts using secret codes or theft-proof hardware, the insurance companies recently refuse to cover banks against losses arising from the interception of their transmission systems by third party hacking. In this view highly specialized programmers hold a key position in computerized societies. Their decision to construct programs with self-destructing mechanisms or periodic reprogramming settings cannot be controlled, so the old problem of who controls the controller reappears in an intensified form.

It is hardly surprising that the military in particular are worried by these possibilities: Three times in a few months in 1980 the US central strategic command fell victim to computer errors, informing them of supposed Soviet nuclear strikes. It is a moot point whether the ADA computer language, developed as a result of these experiences, is actually able to distinguish between a real and an imagined nuclear attack. At the heart of this matter is the fact that the ADA computer language can only be tested through simulations and not in reality. Even in peace time the collective decision-making process of the NATO-NICS system does not function smoothly. This suspicion is certainly fueled when the commander-in-chief of NATO's Central European Forces expresses his displeasure with the interaction between programmers and military officials.

Fifth Hypothesis:
Highly computerized societies are extremely susceptible to disruption and volatility.

Production vs. Consumption

In both national and international contexts, informatization is creating a contradiction between production and consumer potential. As an important attribute of the international service industries the global process of informatization increasingly contributes to the national balance of payment problems of Third World countries which at present may be in the region of US$ 500 billion. This process of informatization will considerably increase the trade imbalance given the swift penetration of the related markets by the service industries. In this context, a 1979 Prognos-study came to the following conclusion:

> According to UNCTAD estimates outlays for technological transfer have grown 2½ times as quickly as has industrial output in the developing countries. It can be predicted with confidence that as the rate of industrialization in developing countries increases, so will technological transfer. This in turn will increase their dependence on the industrial countries.[10]

Taking this situation into consideration, we must ask how the Third World will be able to maintain its purchasing power in order to pay for the consumer products of informatization from Western industrial countries. One consequence of this situation could be that metropolitan capital may completely withdraw its investments from the 25 lowest developing countries (LDCs) since these markets are no longer of interest to them and instead leaves them to their "fate". Similar contradictions between production and consumer potential can also be seen within Western industrial societies. Informatization as a catalyst for automation, robotization and rationalization is, on the one hand, a crucial factor causing structural unemployment, while, on the other hand, it produces a multitude of consumer products for which the purchasing power of the unemployed is no longer sufficient. Thus, the recent lack of demand for cable TV in England must be seen not so much as a problem of acceptance as superficial analyses suggest, but instead as a problem of depleted purchasing power.

Sixth Hypothesis:
The global informatization may destroy its own markets.

The Individual vs. Society

The worldwide introduction of approximately 50 million home computers by 1985 will make the division between the "private" and "public" spheres even more redundant than it is today. Home computers will not only have a considerable impact on family social structures, but will give rise to a much more fundamental problem. Up until now the so-called private sector has provided, among other things, recreational possibilities through which the individual has recharged his/her batteries in order to return revitalized to the work process. This psychologically important safety valve may be impeded if the work place is introduced to the living room.

If one considers that the terminal as workplace is the most visible point of contact with telecommunications and computerization for the end user, than we must reckon with the consequences of diminished possibilities for physical recreation. A variety of surveys conducted in terminal workplaces gave rise to the following findings: it has been statistically shown that such workstations can results in eye trouble, headaches, dizziness and curvature of the spine; those who are constantly exposed to artificial light at the place of work can suffer from stress hormone concentrations and such light can damage embryos in pregnant women.

Seventh Hypothesis:
As the quality of the individual's opportunities for psychological and physical recreation decreases, so motivation and physical fitness which are necessary to actively participate in the production process will drastically sink. Thus, the quality of the production process could be vitally impaired.

Flexible Reserve Work Force vs. Dangerous Conflict Potential

Juan Rada, in his study of the impact of microelectronics on the Third World[11], explains how, through automation, many areas of production will lose the comparative advantage which they now enjoy as a result of indigenous cheap labor. Thus, industries will be withdrawn from underdeveloped countries and re-established in the industrial countries. Automated production has become even cheaper than the use of low-paid workers in South-East Asia and in the off-shore-industries of the Caribbean. Within Western industrial countries working women may have to face very similar problems. As workers in terminal workstations in industrial countries or as female workers on assembly lines producing parts for electronic products in Third World countries, women are especially effected by informatization.

A Canadian survey on the connection between microelectronics and the professional situation of women in industrial countries comes to the following conclusion: Even though the amount of jobs on offer to women who are qualified for office work has increased, the automation of the office has led to the loss of an increasing work places. It is reckoned that by 1990 there will be more than one million professionally qualified secretaries and office personnel unemployed.[12] Traditionally immigrants (legal and illegal), low-paid workers within the Third World, and women in the Western industrialized countries have been used as a reserve work force to fill the gaps created by market fluctuations, to act as a buffer against the demands of the trade unions or as sweat-shops. So long as these related social conflicts were not so large, these groups can be used as a pacifier of potential resistance, emanating from their own ranks.

Eighth Hypothesis:
Through automation it has become possible to withdraw reserve work-forces from the production process and, under certain circumstances, this can produce such potential flashpoints that a society may no longer be in a position to control the ensuing conflicts.

3. Closing Remark

The informatization of society on the national and international level has not brought about what most post-industrialists hoped would be delivered and what must dominance theorists feared, at least not as quickly and not without enormous contradictions and conflicts.

Notes and References

1. Nora, Simon and Minc, Alain: *L' informatisation de la société*, Paris: La Documentation Française, 1978.
2. Ellul, Jacques: *The Technological Society*, New York: Vintage 1964, p. 427.
3. Quoted from: "Der Mann, der die Republik verkabeln will", in: *Impulse*, No. 12/1982, p. 16
4. Schmidt, Helmut: "Grundsatzreferat", in: *Dokumente*. Medienpolitische Fachtagung "Medien von Morgen. Risiko und Chance für eine humane Gesellschaft", November 22-3, 1979 in Bonn, ed. by the Vorstand der SPD, Bonn: 1980, p. 102.
5. Marcuse, Herbert: *One Dimensional Man - The Ideology of Industrial Society*, London: Routledge and Kegan Paul 1964, pages 130 and 137. Even in 1941 in the face of fascism Herbert Marcuse had espoused the utilitarian approach in his essay "Some Implications of Modern Technology" (in: *Studies in Philosophy and Social Science*. Vol. 9). An excellent critique of the utilitarian approach is to be found in Winner, Langdon: *Autonomous Technology*. Technics-out-of-Control as a Theme in Political Thought, Cambridge and London: MIT Press 1977.
6. Adorno, Theodor W.: *Minima Moralia*, Frankfurt: Suhrkamp 1962, p. 25.
7. Mosco, Vincent: *Pushbutton Fantasies*. Critical Perspectives on Videotex and Information Technology, Norwood, NJ: Ablex 1982, p. 154.
8. Bach, Gabriel G.F.: "US Export Control of Technical Data. Cross-border data flow control?", in: *Telecommunications*, July 1982, pp. 45-46. [Interestingly enough this analysis was published only in the US-American, but not in the "global edition" of this magazine.]
9. Quoted from: Becker, Jörg: "Der weltweite Medienkommerz", in: *Ein anderer Rundfunk - eine andere Republik oder die Enteignung des Bürgers*, ed. by Michael Wolf Thomas, Bonn and Berlin: Dietz Nachf. 1980, p. 60.
10. Bergmann, Christel and Grundmann, Helge E.: *Aussagen zur Interdependenz zwischen Industrie- und Entwicklungsländern*. Gutachten im Auftrag des Bundesministeriums für wirtschaftliche Zusammenarbeit, Basel: Prognos AG 1979 (mimeo), p. 33.
11. Cf. Rada, Juan: *The impact of Microelectronics*, Geneva: International Labour Office, 1980; see also Wad, Atul: "Microelectronics. Implications and strategies for the Third world", in: *Third World Quarterly*, No. 4/1982, pp. 677-97.
12. Menzies, Heather: *Women and the Chip*. Case studies of the effects of informatics on employment in Canada, Montreal: The Institute for Research on Public Policy 1981. p. 33.

Sources of First Publication

1. Paper presented at the conference of the International Association for Mass Communication Research (IAMCR) on "Mass Media and Man's View of Society" in Leicester, Great Britain, August 30 to September 4, 1976.

2. Paper presented at the UNESCO Symposium on "The Media and Disarmament" in Nairobi, Kenya, April 18 to 22, 1983. [This paper was read in the author's absence due to illness.]

3. Paper presented at the conference of the National Book Trust in India on „Publishing for Rural Areas in Developing Countries" in New Delhi, India, March 1 to 4, 1980.

4. Paper presented at the XIVth conference of the International Association for Mass Communication Research (IAMCR) on "Social Communication and Global Problems" in Prague, Czechoslovakia, August 27 to September 1, 1984.

5. Paper presented at the conference of the German Association for Informatics on "Computers Against Poverty - Poverty Through Computers? Perspectives for a Basic Needs Oriented Approach", Berlin, West Germany, October 2 to 4, 1987.

6. Paper presented at the XIth World Congress of Sociology of the International Sociology Association in New Delhi, India, August 18 to 24, 1986.

7. Paper presented at the XIXth conference of the International Association for Mass Communication Research (IAMCR) on "Communication in the New Millenium: Communication Technology for Humanity" in Seoul, South Korea, July 3 to 8, 1994.

8. First published under the title "Social and Economic Aspects of Video Cassette Recorders in Third World Countries", in: *Media and Development* (London, Great Britain), No. 1/1985, pp. 11-13.

9. First published in German under the title: "Kultur und Entwicklung - Gedanken nach dem Golfkrieg", in: *Zeitschrift für Kulturaustausch* (Stuttgart, West Germany), No. 4/1992, pp. 525-536.

10. Paper presented at the 3rd Annual BIMA International Conference and the 7th Annual AUSACE International Conference at the Lebanese American University, Beirut, Lebanon, October 31 to November 3, 2002.

11. Habilitation lecture held before the Faculty Council of the Social Sciences and Philosophy Faculty of the University of Marburg on January 28, 1981. First published under the title: "Communication and Peace. The Empirical and Theoretical Relation Between Two Categories in Social Sciences", in: *Journal of Peace Research* (Oslo/Norway), No. 3/1982, pp. 227-240.

12. First published in German under the title: "Vom Vorurteil zur Abhängigkeit. Konflikte auf dem Weg zu einer Neuen Internationalen Informationsordnung", in: *Medienmacht im Nord-Süd-Konflikt.* Die Neue Internationale Informationsordnung ed. by Becker, Jörg and Steinweg, Reiner, Frankfurt: Suhrkamp 1984, pp. 16 - 44.

13. Paper presented at the IXth Annual Conference of the Society for International Education, Training and Research in San Gimignano, Italy, May 10 to 15, 1983.

14. Paper presented at the seminar "Evolution Technique et Economique dans le Secteur des Medias et Necessité d'un Nouvel Ordre Internationale Democratique de l'Information" of the International Association of Democratic Lawyers, Brussels, Belgium, March 1 to 2, 1986.

15. Paper presented at the international seminar of experts on "New Communication Technology and International Law", organized by the Institute of International Studies of Karl Marx-University Leipzig, in Dresden, German Democratic Republic, September 15 to 16, 1987.

16. Paper presented at the XVIth conference of the International Association for Mass Communication Research (IAMCR) on "Mass Communication and Cultural Identity" in Barcelona, Spain, July 24 to 29, 1988.

17. Paper presented at the Fourth International Conference on Culture and Communication by Temple University in Philadelphia, Pennsylvania, USA, April 9 to 11, 1981 and at the Workshop of the Section on International Communication of the International Association of Mass Communication Research (IAMCR) on a ferryboat between Stockholm, Sweden, and Helsinki, Finland, August 26 to 29, 1981.

18. Invited Lecture for the International Lecture Series on the Social Implications of ICTs, sponsored by the Batelle Endowment for Technology and Human Affairs at Ohio State University, Department of Communication, Columbus, Ohio, USA, May 22, 1989.

19. First published in German under the title "Informationen für alle oder Wissen für eine Elite", in: *Informationspolitik als Kulturpolitik*, ed. by Schnelling, Heiner; Segbert, Monika and Stroetmann, Karl A., Berlin: Deutsches Bibliotheksinstitut 1993, pp. 123-146.

20. First published in Spanish under the title „La relación entre público censurado y público comercializado en el cambio de sistema en Europa Oriental", in: *Comunicación Social 1992/Tendencias*, ed. by the Fundación para el Desarrollo de la Función Social de las Comunicaciones, Madrid: FUNDESCO 1992, pp. 136 - 150.

21. Paper presented at the annual convention of the Association for Education in Journalism and Mass Communication (AEJMC) in Corvallis, Oregon, USA, August 6 to 9, 1983.

INDEX